THE
ANCIENT
CHURCH
AS FAMILY

THE
ANCIENT
CHURCH
AS FAMILY

Joseph H. Hellerman

FORTRESS PRESS
MINNEAPOLIS

THE ANCIENT CHURCH AS FAMILY

Old and New Testament citations are from the NRSV and Apocrypha citations are from the RSV, unless otherwise noted.

Cover art: Breaking of the Bread. Early Christian fresco. Catacomb of Priscilla, Rome Italy. Copyright Scala/Art Resource, New York. Used by permission. Background image by Photodisc, copyright 2001.
Cover design: Marti Naughton
Book design: Zan Ceeley

Library of Congress Cataloging-in-Publication Data

Hellerman, Joseph H.
        The ancient church as family / Joseph H. Hellerman.
            p. cm.
        Includes bibliographical references and index.
        ISBN 0-8006-3248-6 (alk. Paper)
        1. Church history—Primitive and early church, ca. 30–600. 2. Kinship—Religious aspects—Christianity—History of doctrines—Early church, ca. 30–600. I. Title.

        BR165 .H44 2001
        270.1—dc21   2001023781

Manufactured in the U.S.A.   AF 1-3248
05   04   03   02   01   1   2   3   4   5   6   7   8   9   10

DEDICATED TO
"THE MAMA"
HELEN ELIZABETH HELLERMAN
1915–1991

*Who saw me through hell,
so I could find my way to heaven*

Contents

3. Origins of the Surrogate Kin Group Idea

List of Figures

Preface

THREE ENVIRONMENTS, WHICH HAVE ALTERNATELY CONSUMED AND DEFINED my life for the past three decades, generated and nourished the activity that finds its consummation in this monograph: the academy, the church, and my home. I owe a tremendous debt of gratitude to persons in all three arenas for inspiring and underwriting the research that went into *The Ancient Church as Family*.

My academic pilgrimage led me from Biola University to UCLA, and back to Biola again, where I now teach New Testament. I will always recall with great warmth the professors at Talbot School of Theology who provided me with my formal introduction to biblical studies. The rigorous foundation laid in the areas of biblical languages and exegetical method prepared me well for both ministry and further education, and I am grateful for my seminary training. I am now delighted to call a number of my former professors colleagues, and special thanks go to Dr. Michael Wilkins, my dean at Talbot, for strongly encouraging me to submit the manuscript for this book to Fortress during a postdoctoral period of self-searching and self-doubt.

The primary academic inspiration for the book came, however, from my doctor-father at UCLA, S. Scott Bartchy. Dr. Bartchy spent hours and hours with me poring over the pages of the dissertation, which has become this book. I valued Dr. Bartchy's encouragement at every point in the writing process, I treasure his friendship, and I remain particularly indebted to him for the trajectory he has given me for my own academic pursuits. Dr. Bartchy's scholarly passion—utilizing resources from the social sciences (especially cultural anthropology) for the study of early Christianity—has become my own.

I liken my experience along these lines to Dorothy's, in the MGM classic *The Wizard of Oz*, when she first gazed upon the land of Oz. You may recall the point in the film at which the scene suddenly changes from black and white to color. My transition into the world of the social sciences was more gradual than Dorothy's leap to Oz, but now, thanks to Dr. Bartchy and his colleagues in the Context Group, I truly believe I am reading these familiar early Christian texts in living color for the first time. And, unlike Dorothy, to (perhaps painfully) press the analogy, I have no desire to go back to Kansas. I am convinced that the future of our discipline lies, to a great degree, with the careful application of insights from the social sciences to early Christian history. *The Ancient Church as Family* is my first book-length attempt to demonstrate the usefulness of such methodology.

Though somewhat technical in nature, the book is, in the final analysis, about the church as a loving, supportive family. For many readers, the contrast between community as it was experienced in the early house churches and what passes for Christianity in the West today will be regrettably obvious. In this regard, I must count myself quite fortunate, for I have been blessed with almost unspeakably wonderful church experiences since my conversion to Christianity in 1975. My dream to pursue a terminal degree became a reality in 1989, when the loving leaders of Community Baptist Church, in Manhattan Beach, California, encouraged me to reduce my hours to part-time and to seek financial support from persons in our congregation for expenses associated with my doctoral program. One hundred or so individuals and families responded over a five-year period, and many of them filled up our backyard to celebrate my graduation from UCLA one sunny afternoon nearly a decade later.

My past five years in the pastorate have been spent at Oceanside Christian Fellowship (OCF), in El Segundo, California, where I have had the joy of seeing a number of the principles outlined in this book become a reality in the lives of members of a local church community. On a personal level, the OCF church family proved itself to be an eminently safe place, emotionally and spiritually, for me to put the results of several years of research into publishable form. The prayers and encouragement of my fellow elders in the church were especially meaningful in this regard. My brothers on the board—Denny, Dan, Duke, Ed, Tom, and Stan—faithfully prayed me over writing hurdles, past deadlines, and through times during which I could hardly get myself to turn on the computer. Kudos, also, to two of the brightest persons I know, OCF staffers Margy Emmons and Michelle Cutrona, for their careful proofing of the manuscript.

Undoubtedly the greatest source of support and encouragement came from my wonderful wife of twenty years, Joann, and from my two adolescent daughters,

Rebekah and Rachel. In a culture that seems to offer nearly insurmountable challenges to healthy, long-term family relationships, I find myself blessed with a wife
who loves me, understands me, and animates my spirit, mind, and body in every
way. May God give me the grace to continue to do the same for her. The delight of
finishing this project, as great as it is, pales in comparison with the prospective
delight of spending the rest of my life with you, Joann.

My commitment to be there for my children has inevitably and appropriately
delayed the completion of this project, and for that I have no regrets. Teachable
moments at home and opportunities to provide fatherly encouragement at school
events, once lost, can never be recaptured. The library, on the other hand, will still be
there when the kids are gone. Rebekah and Rachel, I trust you are learning well, from
our example and from your experiences at Oceanside Christian Fellowship, that our
natural family only thrives and grows according to God's design when we are deeply
embedded in our surrogate family of faith. May you each grow up to share your
mother's passion for the Lord, and may you emulate her commitment to the family
of God. You are our daughters for a season . . . our sisters in Christ forever.

I

Christianity in Its Social Environment

INTRODUCTION

FERGUS MILLAR RECENTLY PREFACED HIS IMPORTANT MONOGRAPH on the Roman Near East with the categorical assertion, "The spread of Christianity must indeed be taken as the single most important development which occurred in the period from the reign of Augustus to the death of Constantine."[1] The marked expansion of the Jesus movement during the pre-Constantinian period ranks among the more perplexing problems confronting specialists in ancient history.[2] How could a small Judean sect, arising in a province located at the easternmost fringes of the Roman Empire, expand its ranks steadily for more than two centuries in the face of often sporadic and local, sometimes consistently legislated, opposition? Robin Lane Fox, who persuasively contends that we have overestimated the numerical growth of early Christianity, nevertheless concludes his survey of the evidence with a striking observation: "Christians spread and increased: no other cult in the Empire grew at anything like the same speed, and even as a minority, the Christians' success raises serious questions about the blind spots in pagan cult and society."[3] The issue is not *whether* the early Christians grew in number and influence. Rather, the challenge is to explain the marked growth of the early Christian movement.[4]

Explaining the Expansion
of Early Christianity

Ideological Explanations

E. R. Dodds provides us with a helpful survey of various explanations for the striking success of the early Christian movement.[5] Scholars have traditionally sought solutions in the spheres of imperial politics and ideology. The transition during the Hellenistic period from *polis* to *kosmos*—from the relatively isolated Greek city-states in the West (and temple-states in the East) into what were to become the Greek and Roman Empires—was truly a world-changing development. Subject peoples were faced with tremendous challenges along with great opportunities. Among the former was the daunting task of choosing from among a plethora of religious options. Although Roman authorities took an initially conservative stance toward the westward expansion of Near Eastern religions, the official position was ultimately one of tolerance. The success and stability of an ever-expanding empire depended upon maintaining the religious cults of the various conquered peoples.

So much for public policy. For the individual, this proliferation of religious options proved more frightening than encouraging. For how could one guarantee that all these gods, goddesses, and other supernatural forces would act in one's favor? The early Christians countered with an appealing alternative to religious toleration:

> There were too many cults, too many mysteries, too many philosophies of life to choose from: you could pile one religious insurance on another, yet not feel safe. Christianity made a clean sweep. It lifted the burden of freedom from the shoulders of the individual: one choice, one irrevocable choice, and the road to salvation was clear.[6]

Recent studies of magic and the demonic among peoples of Greco-Roman antiquity reinforce Dodd's contention that the ancient peoples did not feel "safe" in the face of so many gods and goddesses.[7] The publication of Hans Dieter Betz's English translation of the Greek magical papyri has generated a variety of monographs from historians of early Christianity.[8] Common to most is the assumption that the unseen world of malevolent supernatural beings posed a pervasive conscious threat to the people of antiquity—thus the proliferation of magic, and the alternative appeal of the Jesus movement. The victory won by God through the death and resurrection of Jesus of Nazareth guaranteed for his followers "the demise of the devil," as one writer entitles her recent interpretation of Luke-Acts.[9]

To the fear of the supernatural in this life Dodds adds the fear of death and perplexity about the afterlife as concerns addressed by the belief system of early Christianity. Preoccupation with life after death, reflected in writers from Plato (*Resp.* 330d) to Seneca (*Ep. Mor.* 4, 24), is graphically evidenced by the popularity of mystery cults during the Hellenistic era. To be sure, we can no longer maintain that the promise of a blessed afterlife is central to all the mysteries. Nevertheless, such hope certainly plays an important role in the Eleusinian cult, the Dionysiac mysteries, and, most likely, in the worship of Isis.[10] As Plutarch asserts, many people "think that some sort of initiations and purifications will help: once purified, they believe, they will go on playing and dancing in Hades in places full of brightness, pure air and light" (*Non posse* 1105b). In such an environment, the Christian message understandably found great appeal: "Christianity held out to the disinherited the conditional promise of a better inheritance in another world."[11]

Sociological Explanations

Ideological explanations of the rapid multiplication of Christ-confessing communities ultimately fail to satisfy. Sociologists have confronted us with the truth that ideology is inextricably woven into the social fabric of a people. To arrive at a truly comprehensive explanation for the expansion of Christianity, we must somehow move beyond ideology and enter into the social world of the early Christians in order to understand their relations with one another and with their pagan neighbors. Already some three decades ago, Dodds identified as the most important cause of the growth of the Jesus movement not ideology but rather the social solidarity evident in many of the early Christian groups.[12] Fox also perceives a "powerful ideal of community" at work among local congregations, adding that "Paul's letters had abounded in the language of a 'family' and a 'brotherhood.'"[13] And Gerhard Lohfink has provided a wonderful historical survey of tangible expressions of Christian communal activity down to circa 400 C.E.[14]

The realization that the expansion of early Christianity owed much to the social cohesiveness of the local churches has driven researchers to attempt to define more precisely the nature of these communities in light of the social environment in which they were situated. What did the early churches look like to outsiders? When they reflected upon their social identity, what kind of a group did Christians perceive themselves to be? How did this conceptual social model affect actual relationships among group members? The balance of the chapter will situate early Christian congregations in the social world of the early Roman Empire.

Various Social Models in Greco-Roman Antiquity

The early Roman Empire witnessed a proliferation of clubs, cult associations, trade groups, and social groupings of all kinds. These groups, now typically referred to as voluntary associations, were generally small—thirty to forty members constituted an average-sized group—and local in nature. The associations came together for a variety of purposes. Some groups consisted of persons who worked the same trades. Other groups gathered together to worship a specific god or goddess. Also to be included under the broad rubric of voluntary associations are the empire's synagogues and philosophical schools. Association activities typically included participation in communal meals and the election of members to magistracies or other positions of honor in the group.

Students of Roman social history offer several explanations for the spread of voluntary associations. The dislocation and corresponding alienation caused by steady urbanization during the first two centuries of the common era likely encouraged the formation of these alternative models of social organization. This explanation views the voluntary associations as compensatory in nature, offering avenues of relational support and opportunities for the acquisition of honor that were unavailable to group members in the society at large. They provided "fictive families for those uprooted from clan or family and fictive polities for those excluded from political power."[15] Expressions such as "fictive family" and "surrogate kinship group" will surface repeatedly throughout the book. For our purposes, a "surrogate family" may be defined as a social group whose members are related to one another neither by birth nor by marriage, but who nevertheless (a) employ kinship terminology to describe group relationships and (b) expect family-like behavior to characterize interactions among group members. The urban location of the associations argues in favor of such an explanation, as does the common tendency of transient populations to look to familiar organizations for social and relational stability in their new surroundings. It is also the case, however, that even in the absence of social alienation and dislocation, people often seek out relationships with others like themselves for purely social reasons. As Stephen G. Wilson recently observed, "We should never underestimate the basic and instinctive desire of most people to socialize with those with whom they share things in common—devotion to a deity, a trade or skill, a similar background, or even just a love of eating and drinking in good company."[16]

Whatever generated the rise of the associations, it is important for our purposes to note that second-century Roman officials, and others who wrote as opponents of the Jesus movement, sometimes identified local churches with such organizations (Pliny, *Ep.* 10.96; Origen, *C. Cels.* 1.1; Tertullian, *Apol.* 38.1-3).[17] Accordingly, modern scholars have sought at times to understand the earliest churches as patterned along these lines. In the words of one writer, the associations "offered an initial reference point that placed churches comfortably within the parameters of Greco-Roman society—especially when the Jesus movement consciously and deliberately wished to appeal to gentiles."[18] There are certainly some striking similarities between the associations and the early Christ-confessing communities in the Roman East.

Abraham Malherbe, for example, highlights the importance of trades and crafts in early Christianity, suggesting a possible connection with craft organizations.[19] Other scholars, following the second-century physician Galen, offer the empire's philosophical and rhetorical schools as social groups best approximating the earliest churches.[20] Yet another candidate for the social model that influenced the Jesus movement is the Judean synagogue.[21] The latter suggestion would seem the most obvious, since Christianity began as a Judean sect, and a number of similarities do exist.[22] Finally, scholars have sought the origins of early church communal practice among the various cult groups and mystery religions so common to the Hellenistic era.[23]

Such comparisons at times seek to identify early churches with voluntary associations on the basis of shared terminology. Efforts to develop a model of associations based solely on terminology have been frustrated by the "rather bewildering array of terms used in both Greek and Latin to designate these organizations, coupled with a striking lack of consistency on the part of ancient authors in the use of the terms."[24] A more promising comparative approach instead examines the social characteristics of these groups in order to discern differences and similarities.

Figure 1.1 compares by way of summary five important types of voluntary associations with the early church (*ekklesia*). The comparison takes into consideration ten social functions and characteristics (listed across the top of the chart). A brief definition immediately follows each function and characteristic.[25]

In the discussion that follows, I have divided these characteristics into three broad categories. We will proceed across the chart from left to right—from characteristics shared by nearly all the groups surveyed to those social attributes that increasingly served to set Christ-confessing communities apart from alternative contemporary models of social organization.

Characteristics Common to All the Groups

Voluntary in Nature. The first characteristic on the chart is self-explanatory. Participation in each of the six groups reflected above was voluntary or elective in the sense that the individual typically made a personal choice to associate with the

Fig. 1.1. Characteristics of Voluntary Associations

COMMON TO ALL → COMMON TO SOME → DEFINING FOR *EKKLESIA*

	Voluntary in Nature	Religious Orientation	Common Meals	Trans-local in Nature	Socially Inclusive	Structurally Egalitarian	Focus on Study	Opposed Dominant Culture	Exclusive Allegiance	Familial Emphasis
Christian *Ekklesia*	✓	✓✓	✓✓	✓✓	✓✓	✓✓*	✓	✓✓	✓✓	✓✓
Professional Association	✓✓	✓✓	✓✓							✓*
Domestic Association	✓*	✓	✓		✓*				✓*	✓*
Cult Association	✓	✓✓	✓							✓*
Philosophical School	✓✓	✓*	✓*	✓*			✓✓	✓*	✓*	✓*
Jewish Synagogue	✓*	✓✓	✓*	✓	✓		✓	✓*	✓✓	✓*

✓✓ very strong emphasis
✓ clearly present
* present with qualification

group. Even here, however, qualifications are in order. The freedom to personally choose one's social options was much more limited in the group-emphasizing culture of Mediterranean antiquity than is the case in such highly individualistic societies as ours today. This was especially true where family was involved, since kinship in antiquity encompassed areas like religion and economics in ways not characteristic of contemporary Western society. Participation in a specific domestic cult or synagogue, for example, may have been more or less obligatory. Nevertheless, the associations are to be distinguished, as being voluntary in nature, from such institutions as the family, the city, or the state, in which membership is automatically acquired by birth. In this way, trade groups, cult and domestic associations, philosophical schools, and churches and synagogues may be viewed together.[26]

Religious Orientation. Religious orientation, noted for almost every group on the chart, should be understood as a product of ancient society in general rather than as an attribute unique to voluntary associations. It is now widely recognized that religion in the Mediterranean world did not exist as a self-standing institution. Religion was embedded, instead, in the defining institutions of state and family. Unlike the place of religion in the West today, religion in antiquity was not simply an isolated component of human experience—it was woven into the very fabric of daily life. As a result, nearly every voluntary association had a religious component.[27]

The degree of religious orientation varied, however, from group to group. For churches, mystery cults, and synagogues, religious devotion was foundational. Among the other associations, cult was less central, though present nonetheless. Thus, one trade group entitled itself "the association of the Beirut Poseidoniast wholesale merchants, shippers and receivers."[28] A woodcutters' association appropriately paid homage to the deity Silvanus, the Roman god of uncultivated land, or to the Great Mother.[29] The regular meetings of trade associations like these typically included prayers and cult offerings as a prelude to the main social practices of eating and drinking together. Religion was therefore ancillary and not constitutive.

Ascertaining the religious orientation of the schools is more problematic. The philosophical outlook of antiquity included at its heart the conviction that any useful philosophy should train the student well in the "bedrock social values of piety toward the gods (*eusebeia, pietas*) and justice (*ta dikaia, dikaiosyne, iustitia*) or philanthropy toward humanity."[30] Religion, in a general sense, was thus understood to comprise ← an important aspect of the philosophical enterprise. This potential for religious orientation was mitigated, however, by a critique of traditional religion that characterized nearly all forms of philosophical inquiry. These conflicting tendencies, combined with the paucity of our source material, render any observations concerning the cult practices of Hellenistic philosophical schools highly tentative and provisional in nature. Some groups, such as the Stoics and the school of Epictetus, seem to have met together only for study and reflection. The Epicureans apparently experienced more in the way of cult and community.[31]

Common Meals. A final feature characterizing nearly all associations in Greco-Roman antiquity was communal eating and drinking. This is hardly surprising. Associations assemble for fellowship, and a most obvious expression of fellowship in every culture is a shared meal. Mediterranean people, however, attached to table fellowship a higher symbolic value than is the case in the modern Western world. Plutarch refers to the "friend-making character of the table" (*Quaest. conv.* 614 A–B).[32] Specifically, for the associations, mealtime exhibited a solidarity-making function, which served to delineate group boundaries by affirming as members those who shared the common table.

As in the case of religion, however, the importance of the meal in association life varied. Common meals surely served as the chief reason for the existence of some groups. Trade associations are probably illustrative. For other groups, in which different activities took on a more central role, table fellowship still found regular expression, albeit in service of more important ends. The philosophical schools are representative, where entertainment at the symposium (an extended period of leisurely drinking that followed the main meal) might center around the reasoned discussion of some topic pertinent to the meal occasion (Plato, *Symp.* 176e; Athenaeus, *Learned Banquet* 5.185a; Plutarch, *Quaest. conv.* 7.7).[33] Yet other groups provide more limited evidence of table fellowship. For example, judging from the degree of emphasis in our sources, members of Judean synagogues were much more concerned with Torah reading and prayer than with sharing in a common meal.[34]

Perhaps most familiar are the eating practices of the early Christians and of the members of the mystery cults. Each viewed table fellowship as a defining aspect of the group's respective gatherings. Among the early Christians, the common meal both reinforced kinship imagery, which portrayed community members as siblings in a fictive family, and established boundaries distinguishing community members from outsiders (Acts 2:46; 20:7; 1 Cor 11:18-20, 33; Gal 2:12; Pliny, *Ep.* 10.96.7). A strong sacramental aspect was also present (Mark 14:24; John 6:54; 1 Cor 10:16; 11:24). For Mithraism—the mystery cult for which we have the most information concerning social structure and shared activities—the common meal constituted (in addition to initiation to the cult) one of two key activities reflecting the ongoing life of the association. Like early Christian meals, Mithraic table fellowship was social in nature but also strongly sacramental. The meal shared by devotees replicated an episode in the cult's myth in which Mithras and Sol celebrate a banquet on the hide of a slaughtered bull.[35]

Characteristics Common to Some of the Groups

We move now to practices or social characteristics of the early Christian communities less commonly reflected among other voluntary social groups in Mediterranean antiquity. Here we are dealing with (a) traits that the early churches share with only a few contemporary models—the focus on study, for example, common to both the churches and the schools—or (b) attributes that, although attested elsewhere, find more consistent expression in early Christianity than among the voluntary associations.

Trans-local. As the chart indicates, only churches, synagogues, and the philosophical schools exhibited more than a local presence in the ancient world. No organizational structure united any of the various trade groups, for example, into an empirewide movement. The same was true, of course, of household associations, which were restricted by design to a single household. Among the religious associations, some informal ties can be traced. Troupes of performers, for example, moved from one Dionysiac center to another offering their skills in the service of the cult. Local expressions of the same cult, however, remained autonomous and differed from one another to a significant degree.[36] The philosophical schools exhibited a degree of universal presence in that members of a given school throughout the empire would be trained in similar traditions. It is not clear, however, that these philosophical commonalities engendered much in the way of intercity communication among the members of a specific school.

Synagogues, on the other hand, possessed a unifying geographical point of reference in Jerusalem. Diaspora Judeans sent money to underwrite the expenses of the sacrificial cult for generations, until the destruction of the Temple at Jerusalem in 70 C.E. The First Judean Revolt, followed a half-century later by the Bar-Kokhba Revolt (135 C.E.), temporarily ended any influence that Judean leadership in Judaea may have exercised in the Diaspora, and there is some debate about when relations resumed between Judeans in Palestine and Diaspora synagogues.[37] It is clear from their writings, however, that Judeans in the empire consistently conceived of themselves in trans-local terms well after the loss of their central cult site in 70 C.E. So, too, did their pagan contemporaries, who generalized about the Judeans in ways in which they did not speak, for example, about members of a local trade association. Non-Judean writers view Judeans in universal terms, referring consistently to Judeans' observance of the Sabbath, their abstention from pork, and their practice of circumcision—that is, to the Judeans' common social behavior. To these unifying elements we may add their Scriptures (whether in Hebrew, Aramaic, or Greek), which Judeans throughout the empire taught and studied in their synagogues, and which they passed on from generation to generation as their common tradition (*paradosis*).

The Jesus movement exercised an even more pronounced trans-local presence. The earliest followers of Christ consistently conceived of their movement in universal terms. Nowhere is this more clearly illustrated, during the first generation of the church's existence, than in the collection Paul of Tarsus gathered for the impoverished believers in Judaea. Paul expected each of his Gentile congregations to express its solidarity with the church in Jerusalem by contributing to an offering designed to alleviate economic hardship (2 Corinthians 8–9). A half-century later, we find a leader in the church at Rome challenging the behavior of the Corinthian church in a letter that assumes common values and a common brotherhood (*1 Clem.*; see also the Ignatian correspondence). During the middle of the third century, Cyprian of Carthage repeatedly communicates with leaders of other Christian communities around the Mediterranean, discussing issues both practical and theological. It is precisely this literary corpus of intercity communication between congregational leaders that renders the trans-local nature of early Christianity distinct from both pagan associations and the Judean synagogue.

Socially Inclusive. There is substantial consensus among scholars that members of the earliest churches came from a broad cross section of Mediterranean society.[38] Paul's Corinthian congregation has been the object of the most specific attention in this regard. In an important passage written to the community, Paul reminds his readers, "Consider your own call, brothers and sisters: not many of you were wise by human standards, not many were powerful, not many were of noble birth" (1 Cor 1:26). Passages like this were formerly cited to emphasize the low-status character of the early Christian movement. Paul does, however, allow for the presence of a few high-status persons in the above citation (see "not many"), and these individuals have recently been given names through the prosopographic work of Gerd Theissen. As a result, we now know that a small minority of local elites populated the church in Corinth. This, in turn, parallels the small minority of upper-status persons reflected in ancient urban society at large.[39] Although the evidence is seldom as extensive, the same appears to be the case for Christian communities located elsewhere in the pre-Constantinian empire.[40]

Moreover, the broad social makeup that characterized the urban *ekklesia* was not incidental—it was a foundational aspect of the early Christian movement. We find in our earliest documents social convictions that intentionally relativize the defining lines that existed in the dominant culture with respect to both class and gender: "There is no longer Jew or Greek, there is no longer slave or free, there is no longer male and female; for all of you are one in Christ Jesus" (Gal 3:28). Such a view of the people of God inevitably demanded a socially inclusive approach to the admission of new members. As Tatian would write a century later:

Not only do the rich among us pursue our philosophy, but the poor enjoy instruction gratuitously; for the things which come from God surpass the requital of worldly gifts. Thus we admit all who desire to hear, even old women and striplings; and, in short, persons of every age are treated by us with respect. . . . As for those we wish to learn our philosophy, we do not test them by their looks, nor do we judge of those who come to us by their outward appearance. (Tatian, *Ad. Gk.* 32)

It is fair to assert that the same was not the case for other Mediterranean social groups. Indeed, the multidimensional status of the Christian churches in the early Roman Empire continues to be cited as a characteristic that distinguishes local expressions of the earliest churches from the voluntary associations.[41]

We may at the outset dismiss for purposes of comparison groups whose members were exclusively male, such as the Mithras cult; most philosophical schools (the Epicureans are the exception); and certain trade guilds. Indeed, we may eliminate the schools on other grounds, since philosophy in the Greco-Roman world was generally reserved for elites who had the leisure time necessary for such pursuits, along with their slave-tutors who supported such endeavors. Synagogues were markedly more inclusive. Both genders found a place in the synagogue, of course, as did persons from various strata in the social hierarchy, to the degree that Judeans were represented in the different levels of society to begin with. For the rest of the associations, it is normally the case that membership remained confined to the lower classes: slaves, freedpersons, and the urban poor.

At the other end of the social scale were groups for the upper class, such as the Iobacchoi and the official Roman sacerdotal colleges and sacred sodalities. The isolation of elites and non-elites in separate voluntary associations only served to reinforce the highly stratified social order. We do, however, find a few examples of associations reflecting a broader membership base. In a household cult, membership could run from slaves at the bottom to the senatorial class at the top.[42] Typically, however, Christ-confessing communities distinguished themselves from cults and other voluntary associations in the ancient Mediterranean world by their more heterogeneous social makeup.

Structurally Egalitarian. The internal social organization of the associations generally mirrored the strongly hierarchical flavor of the broader society, especially where leadership positions and other honors were concerned.[43] Formal titles of a variety of magistracies and other positions are attested, for example, in inscriptions describing members of household associations.[44] The same is true of cult groups, in which we again find numerous honorific titles and even, in the case of Mithras, a highly defined set of stages delineating the initiate's progress in the cult.[45] Positions of honor in the synagogues were also assigned on the basis of status, wealth, and the ability to act as a patron.[46] For the Roman associations in particular, the city or the army was often the preferred pattern for internal organization. The Romans utilized what was known as a *cursus honorum*—a graded series of honorific offices—to mark the progress of an individual as he ascended the ranks of the social hierarchy in Rome. This "course of honors," however, was open only to the smallest minority of persons in Roman society. John Kloppenborg insightfully suggests that local associations afforded each member of their communities the opportunity to participate in a *cursus honorum* to which he or she could never aspire outside of the association.[47] Associations were thus, according to Andrew Clark, "expressly organized in such a way as to reflect and reinforce the dominant social order."[48]

Yet this emphasis on the social hierarchy of the associations must be qualified by mention of some contrasting evidence for egalitarianism in the groups. For example, in addition to the stratified series of seven successive stages of progression in Mithraism, all members of the cult viewed one another as "brothers," "handshakers," and "initiates." Thus, it is reasonable, with Roger Beck, to assume "a tension of hierarchy and egalitarianism" in the Mithraic cell.[49] The same mixture of status consciousness and communal solidarity likely characterized other associations as well.

Local churches were more egalitarian during the first several decades of the movement than they were in the ensuing years. Paul's letters, for example, lack the generous variety of titles and positions of honor that characterized the voluntary associations. By the third century, however, local churches had developed as many different positions of leadership as we find reflected among the associations. Correspondingly, plurality leadership, attested throughout early Christianity during the first century, gave way to a monepiscopate (one-man oversight), and the role of women was increasingly circumscribed.[50] Nevertheless, sibling terminology remained ubiquitous in the literature, as church leaders continued to address the lowliest members of their communities in fraternal terms and, often, to treat them accordingly. Christians of the second and third centuries, therefore, likely experienced the same "tension of hierarchy and egalitarianism" (to adopt Beck's phrase) that characterized other voluntary social groups in the empire. This, however, contrasts with the earliest period, when the social organization of the *ekklesia* was more egalitarian, and hierarchy was intentionally deemphasized: "But you are not to be called rabbi, for you have one teacher, and you are all students. And call no one your father on earth, for you have one Father—the one in heaven. Nor are you to be called instructors, for you have one instructor, the Messiah. The greatest among you will be your servant" (Matt 23:8-12).

Focus on Study. Study was, of course, central to the pursuit of Hellenistic philosophy. The schools sought to work out a comprehensive way of living for members who passed on the traditions of their founders from generation to generation. Like the philosophical schools, but decidedly unlike trade and cult associations, the Christian *ekklesia* and the synagogue also emphasized study as an important aspect of group life. More specifically, both traditions, to varying degrees, intentionally sought to be identified as schools of philosophy in order to secure credibility in the eyes of their contemporaries. And it is patently clear that some outsiders viewed the churches and synagogues in philosophical terms.[51]

In the case of Judaism, outsiders apparently made the connection before Judeans themselves did. Beginning in the fourth century B.C.E., Aristotle, Theophrastus, Megasthenes, Hecataeus of Abdera, and Strabo each associate Judaism with philosophy.[52] This is not surprising. Like adherents to the philosophical schools, Judeans emphasized moral instruction, exhibited a disciplined lifestyle, and possessed a body of tradition handed down from a revered founder. By the Roman period, the parallels were even more apparent to pagan observers. Cultic aspects of Judaism, which had already been geographically limited to the Temple at Jerusalem, ceased completely with the Temple's destruction in 70 C.E. Elsewhere in the empire, even prior to 70 C.E., Greco-Roman observers would have recognized little activity among the Judeans that they typically associated with religion—for example, public sacrifice and worship. Diaspora synagogues instead emphasized the study and discussion of sacred texts, along with moral exhortation. In this regard, synagogues looked more like philosophical schools than religious associations.[53]

The parallels hardly went unnoticed by insiders. Among Judean writers, Philo and Josephus are most commonly associated with efforts to consciously portray Judaism to the Greco-Roman world as an alternative philosophy. Such developments, however, were already under way by the mid-second century B.C.E. in the works of Aristobulus of Alexandria. Aristobulus believed that the most esteemed Greek philosophers—Pythagoras, Socrates, and Plato—owed many of their insights to the earlier teachings of Moses. The Judaism of Aristobulus's day, therefore, constitutes a philosophical school on par with any in the surrounding culture:

> For it is agreed by all the philosophers that it is necessary to hold holy opinions concerning God, a point our philosophical school makes particularly well. And the whole constitution of our law is arranged with reference to piety and justice and temperance and the rest of the things that are truly good. (Eusebius, *Praep. Evang.* 13.12.8)[54]

Josephus would pick up this theme and elaborate on it later. Not only does Josephus introduce Second Temple Judean sects as "schools" that "philosophize" (see *J. W.* 2.119, 166), but he also characterizes at least two dozen major Old Testament figures, including Abraham, Moses, and Solomon, as philosophers in his paraphrase of the Bible.

Philo of Alexandria also portrays Judaism in philosophical terms for his readers. He describes Sabbath Torah study as follows:

> The Judeans every seventh day occupy themselves with the philosophy of their fathers [*patrion philosophian*], dedicating that time to the acquiring of knowledge and the study of the truths of nature. For what are our places of prayer [i.e., synagogues] . . . but schools [*didaskaleia*] of prudence and courage and temperance and justice [the cardinal virtues]? (*Mos.* 2.216)[55]

In similar fashion, some observers viewed the early followers of Christ as a race of philosophers, and Christian writers occasionally made a concerted effort to portray themselves as such. The earliest extensive evidence of both insiders and outsiders viewing the *ekklesia* as a philosophical school begins to surface during the mid-second century.[56] Among Christians, Justin Martyr and Athenagoras prove especially noteworthy in this regard. Earlier scholarship identified this philosophical portrayal of the Jesus movement as a marked departure from first-century and early-second-century perspectives.[57] Scholarly consensus has since shifted on the issue, and it is now considered reasonably certain that some followers of Christ were interpreting the movement in philosophical terms as early as the first century of the common era.

The evidence Steve Mason amasses reasonably supports his contention that the authors of Hebrews, Luke-Acts, and the Pastorals, in particular, draw intentional parallels to Hellenistic philosophical values. It is much less clear that earlier Pauline literature reflects the same tendencies, as Mason himself acknowledges. What is clear, however, is that early in Paul's ministry his opponents in Macedonia had leveled charges against him that are routinely associated in ancient literature with less-than-scrupulous wandering philosophers (1 Thess 2:3-12). As early as 50 C.E., therefore, Paul is already being viewed as a Hellenistic philosopher by outsiders, even though Paul himself did not portray his movement in these terms.[58]

Social Attributes Increasingly Defining for Early Christianity

Opposed Dominant Culture. Synagogues, churches, and schools shared another social trait not found among the other voluntary groups: the potential to forcefully challenge, rather than reinforce, the central values of Greco-Roman society. None of the groups surveyed consistently sought to overthrow or directly alter the existing political system.[59] In contrast to the conservative nature of trade and cult groups, however, synagogues, churches, and philosophical schools championed social convictions and behavioral priorities that flew in the face of the values of the surrounding culture.

I will begin with the philosophical schools, since their opposition to cultural norms was strongly tempered by the socioeconomic status of the very persons who championed their traditions. In their purest form, the values of the schools differed quite markedly from those of the dominant culture. As a result, "the potential for at least intellectual subversion was always present."[60] After all, the esteemed Socrates had been tried and condemned as an enemy of the state, and biting criticism of the social pretense so characteristic of status-conscious Mediterranean society had always found a place at the heart of the philosophical enterprise. Some four centuries after Socrates' demise, while the early Roman emperors were establishing themselves in power, philosophy was often connected with vestigial republican opposition to the imperial program. Nero exiled or killed several philosophers, among them Seneca, because they allegedly opposed the emperor's autocratic ways (Dio Cassius, *Hist.* 62.24.1; 62.26.1). Vespasian and Domitian later had their own run-ins with philosophers, expelling, exiling, and (in the case of Domitian) executing several prominent citizens "on the charge of philosophizing" (Dio Cassius, *Hist.* 67.13.23). The narrator of these events, Dio Cassius, refers disapprovingly to the abusive employment of philosophy "to insult those in power, to stir up the multitudes, to overthrow the established order of things" (*Hist.* 65.12.2). Philosophers, in the words of one of Dio's characters, "look down on everybody" (*Hist.* 65.13.1).

Philosophy's opposition to the dominant culture was decisively mitigated, however, by another social reality. Philosophical reflection was typically an elite concern in the ancient world, and it was the upper stratum of society that had the most to gain from preserving, not challenging, the status quo. Nowhere is the elite provenance of philosophical inquiry more self-evident than in the ubiquitous presence of a certain moral theme that worked its way into the writings of almost all the philosophers: the inability of wealth to guarantee true happiness. Seneca actually thought it necessary to apologize for the amount of effort he expended addressing monetary issues. He explains, "We talk much about despising money, and we give advice on this subject in the lengthiest of speeches, that mankind may believe true riches to exist in the mind and not in one's bank account" (*Ep. Mor.* 108.11).[61] Seneca's contemporary Persius claimed that (Stoic) philosophy taught the pupil "what limit to set on money . . . what is the use of hard cash, how much you ought to spend on your country and on those near and dear to you" (Persius 3.66, cited by Mason, *Philosophiai*, 34). Seneca, of course, assumes his readers possess a bank account; Persius assumes that students of Stoicism have surplus hard cash to distribute to others. Both assumptions are appropriate only for the privileged few in Greco-Roman antiquity. Philosophy, therefore, was generally the purview of elites who possessed the financial resources and leisure time necessary for such intellectual pursuits.

It was precisely the privileged few, however, who could least afford to have philosophy challenge or undermine the social order. As a result, the schools were viewed ambivalently by those in power. On the one hand, philosophy had positioned itself as "the natural crown of education."[62] All persons of breeding—Roman senators, equestrians, and the local decurion class—completed their studies with philosophy. On the other hand, philosophy always carried with it the potential to subvert the social order. The emperor Nero, for example, murdered his own philosopher-tutor. Mason aptly summarizes the status of philosophy during the Roman period: "As a cheerleader for the accepted mores, philosophy was welcome enough among the educated class; but when its call for whole-hearted commitment sounded like fanaticism, or when its social criticism was too sharp, its proponents found themselves vulnerable."[63]

The synagogue also found itself at odds with the dominant culture. Purity laws, Sabbath observance, and a disciplined moral lifestyle set the Judeans of the empire apart from their pagan contemporaries. Judean separation was tangibly reflected in separate living areas in certain cities of the empire, the Alexandrian Judean quarter being the most notable in this regard. In spite of cultural differences, relative peace obtained between Gentiles and Judeans for more than a century after Alexander the Great's conquests in the East. In the middle of the second century B.C.E., however, severe antipathy arose between Judeans and their Syrian Greek overlords as a result of an attempt at forced hellenization on the part of the Seleucid king Antiochus IV. The Judeans forcefully resisted Antiochus and his successors, and they ultimately gained both their independence and (for many of their number) a permanent suspicion of Gentile power and intentions. Mutual animosity between Greeks and Judeans began to manifest itself rather consistently in the form of atrocities committed by both sides in Greek cities throughout the eastern Mediterranean world. The synagogue became the local flash point for a number of these disturbances. The Roman imperial period, in particular, saw the empire intervene with legislation designed to quell local synagogue-related unrest in Asia and Alexandria, while Judeans in Palestine simultaneously chafed under Roman hegemony with a resentment that would vent itself in outright rebellion in 66 C.E.

The Judeans thus existed in a rather tenuous relationship with broader Greco-Roman society. To be sure, their religious convictions and social practices marked them as peculiar to pagan observers. The Roman historian Tacitus makes his opinions about the Judeans patently clear:

⟨handwritten:) religion + ethnicity intertwined⟩

They regard the rest of mankind with all the hatred of enemies. They sit apart at meals, they sleep apart, and though, as a nation, they are singularly prone to lust, they abstain from intercourse with foreign women; among themselves nothing is unlawful. . . . Those who come over to their religion adopt the practice [of circumcision], and have this lesson first instilled in them, to despise all gods, to disown their country, and set at nought parents, children, and brethren. (*Hist.* 5.4-5)[64]

This hostile description of the Judeans is tempered in Tacitus, however, by another statement that serves, almost singularly, to explain the toleration and support consistently extended to the Judeans by the Roman imperial government. Persons in the Mediterranean world highly esteemed values, religious traditions, and philosophical beliefs that could boast an ancient pedigree. Among the Romans, who were particularly conservative in this regard, the antiquity of the Judean people and their Torah awarded Judeans a credibility that served strongly to mitigate potentially alienating social and religious practices: "[Judean] worship," as Tacitus informs us, "is upheld by its antiquity" (*Hist.* 5.5).

Tacitus's observation needs to be unpacked somewhat for modern readers. Not only did the Judeans need to establish convincingly the antiquity of their beliefs and practices—the ancient pedigree, that is, of "Judean worship"—in order to guarantee some semblance of toleration on the part of Rome, but—since religion and ethnicity were so intertwined in the ancient world—the Judeans also had to demonstrate the antiquity of their *nation* (*ethnos*). Finally, every *ethnos* in the ancient world was also associated with some locale, so the Judeans needed a homeland in order to authenticate their pedigree, as well. We are not surprised, then, to discover that Tacitus includes, along (a) with his comment about the antiquity of Judean religious practices, (b) an extended discussion of the origin of the Judeans as a *people* and (c) a description of Judea and its surroundings, the *land* of the Judeans (*Hist.* 5.2-3, 6-8).[65] The antiquity of this inseparable triad—religion, ethnicity, and region—afforded the synagogue a sense of toleration, if not respect, in the Roman world, despite Judean social peculiarities.

The Jesus movement also found itself at odds with prevailing cultural values. We saw, above, how Paul of Tarsus relativized contemporary class and gender distinctions in his communities. Indeed, the whole Christian enterprise based itself on a founding narrative that utterly inverted the world order: the story of a crucified—and subsequently honored—cult figure. Paul readily acknowledges that the crucifixion of Christ is "foolishness to Gentiles." No matter, for in Paul's eyes, "God's foolishness is wiser than human wisdom, and God's weakness is stronger than human strength" (1 Cor 1:23, 25). Paul proceeds to contextualize this truth in the lives of his readers by summarily dismissing three indispensable marks of social status of the Roman world: education, power, and pedigree of birth (1 Cor 1:26-29).

Similar sentiments find their way into a number of documents. Paul's letter to the community at Philippi is particularly noteworthy for its graphic presentation of Christian convictions concerning the inversion of prevailing social realities. Jesus, the cult hero, willingly descends what can only be called a ladder of shame—from equality with the deity to the utter degradation of a Roman cross (Phil 2:5-8).

In a cultural context that highly valued the acquisition and preservation of honor, along with the exploitation of power, the activity of Jesus, as Paul portrays it above, would have appeared utterly foolish. In God's social economy, however, it is only the willing sacrifice of his position of public honor—and the corresponding use of his power for the benefit of others—that guarantees Jesus' ultimate vindication and exaltation at the hand of God. As our text in Philippians continues, "*Therefore* God also highly exalted him and gave him the name that is above every name, so that at the name of Jesus every knee should bend, in heaven and on earth and under the earth, and every tongue should confess that Jesus Christ is Lord, to the glory of God the Father" (2:9-11; emphasis added). The causal connection ("Therefore") in Paul's mind between Jesus' humiliation and exaltation must not be missed. The world-inverting result, as Paul assures the few Christian residents of the Roman military colony of Philippi, is that Jesus, not Caesar, is "Lord [*kyrios*], to the glory of God the Father." It is difficult to imagine a more pointed challenge to the prevailing social order. We may assume that Paul had already begun to resocialize his Philippian converts along these lines during his ministry among them a decade or so earlier. We are not surprised, then, when Paul's opponents in Thessalonica, the next city in which he preaches, exclaim: "These people who have been turning the world upside down have come here also" (Acts 17:6).

The incompatibility of Greco-Roman and Christian values was exacerbated by another social reality. The Jesus movement lacked the very qualities that gave Judean state religion a social foothold in the Roman world. In contrast to the Judeans, the Christians lacked an ethnic and geographic identity. This meant that Christ-confessors had no shared blood upon which to build conventional kinship solidarity, nor could they point to a homeland somewhere in the empire. And, certainly most troubling, Christianity was apparently a recent phenomenon. Recognizing the liability of novelty in the Roman world, and capitalizing on the movement's origins as a Judean sect, a number of writers passionately argued that Jesus of Nazareth and the communities established by his followers constituted the true fulfillment of the Old Testament promises to Israel. Christianity was, therefore, as old as Judaism.

Other convictions, however, undermined the integrity of such arguments in the eyes of detractors. Most obviously, an increasing percentage of Christians dispensed with Judean purity laws, as the Gentile mission became central to the pro-liferation of local churches. Here, then, was a group that claimed to be the fulfill-ment of Judaism and appropriated Israel's Scriptures as their own, but that failed to adhere to the commandments found in those very writings. Instead, Gentile Chris-tianity defined its relationship to Judaism in spiritual, rather than ethnic-regional, terms: "For a person is not a Jew who is one outwardly, nor is true circumcision something external and physical. Rather, a person is a Jew who is one inwardly, and real circumcision is a matter of the heart—it is spiritual and not literal" (Rom 2:28-29). As Paul elsewhere summarizes, "There is neither Jew nor Greek" in the Christian church (Gal 3:28). What this meant, finally, was that God, "in Christ," had broken down the wall of enmity between Jew and Gentile "that he might create in himself one *new* humanity in place of the two" (Eph 2:16; emphasis added). Another writer was even more forthright. Compared to the rest of humanity, encompassed under the rubrics "Judean" and "Greek," the followers of Christ constitute a *"new race"* (*Ep. to Diognetus* 1.1)—all this in a social context that "glorified . . . the value of ancestral custom, and had a *horror* of innovation."[66]

One of the more perceptive second-century opponents of the Jesus movement, Celsus, found himself greatly troubled by the implications of the Christian world-view. He accurately perceived that Christian convictions and social organization inherently threatened the very fabric of both city-state (*polis*) and nation (*ethnos*). Robert Wilken explains why. His important overview of Celsus's critique of Chris-tianity ends with this observation:

> [T]his exchange between Celsus and the Christians. It is not simply a debate between paganism and Christianity, but a debate about a new concept of religion. Celsus sensed that Christians had severed the traditional bond between religion and a "nation" or people. The ancients took for granted that religion was indissolubly linked to a particular city or people. Indeed, there was no term for *religion* in the sense we now use it to refer to the beliefs and practices of a specific group of people or of a volun-tary association divorced from ethnic or national identity. . . . The idea of an associa-tion of people bound together by a religious allegiance with its own traditions and beliefs, its own history, and its own way of life *independent of a particular city or nation* was foreign to the ancients. Religion belonged to a *people*, and it was bestowed on an indi-vidual by the people or nation from which one came or in which one lived.[67]

As Celsus clearly recognized, Christians prided themselves on their claim to be sub-jects in a kingdom—and citizens of a *polis*—that had no ethnic or geographical boundaries (see Phil 3:20; Heb 13:14; 1 Pet 2:11; John 17:16). And they challenged their converts to change their loyalties accordingly. As a later Christian would assert, "We should be aliens from this world, just as Christ did not belong to this world."[68]

Such notions set the early churches sharply at odds with the dominant culture of Mediterranean antiquity.

Exclusive Allegiance. "The exclusivity of Christian truth claims" has recently been cited as the "most pronounced contrast" between the churches and other voluntary associations.[69] Greco-Roman cult groups and professional associations did not demand exclusive allegiance of their members. For practical reasons, such as geography and time availability, most persons probably limited their involvement to a single group. Nothing in principle, however, would have hindered a person's participation in more than one association.[70] Membership in domestic groups was exclusive, but only because the boundaries of the household defined those of the association.

A stronger argument can be made for the exclusive nature of the philosophical schools. According to one line of reasoning, the whole-life demands of the schools—encompassing matters of work, eating habits, friendship, finances, and sex—meant that philosophy required "conversion" of its members in a way not characteristic of cult and trade groups.[71] These observations must be qualified, however, by the fact that persons in antiquity often moved from one philosophical school to another. Note the example of Justin Martyr, whose pilgrimage led him from one philosophical option to another until he finally settled on Christianity (*Dial. Tryph.* 2; see also Lucian, *Men.* 4). Most revealing is the case of Tacitus's father-in-law, Agricola. Tacitus describes Agricola's early training as follows:

> I remember how he would often tell us that in his early youth he was tempted to drink deeper of philosophy than was allowable for a Roman and a future senator, but that his mother, in her wisdom, damped the fire of his passion. One can well understand that his lofty, aspiring nature was attracted strongly, if not too wisely, by the fairness and splendour of fame in its higher and nobler aspects. In time, age and discretion cooled his ardour; and he always remembered the hardest lesson that philosophy teaches—a sense of proportion. (*Agr.* 4)

Notice the author's ambivalent attitude toward the philosophical enterprise. Although Tacitus acknowledges the noble nature of philosophy, too much philosophy is inappropriate "for a Roman and a future senator." Indeed, Agricola's life, as Tacitus proceeds to describe it, fails to exhibit exclusive allegiance to any voluntary association. Agricola directed his loyalties to the dominant culture and to his career as a Roman senator and military leader. His situation probably typifies the experience of many of philosophy's elite practitioners.

It was otherwise for the church and synagogue. Each demanded, in different ways, exclusive allegiance to God and his people. The monotheistic worship of the God of Israel had always excluded involvement with the cults of other gods and goddesses on the part of faithful Judeans. Among the Christians, such "either/or" convictions were more narrowly associated with Jesus, as God's representative. They find expression throughout the Gospel traditions (Matt 10:34-37; 12:30).

Later Christian leaders sometimes included among the demands associated with conversion the giving up of one's means of livelihood, particularly when a person's vocation had strong cultic associations or immoral overtones—for example, acting in the Greco-Roman theater. To be sure, persons reacted with varying degrees of loyalty to such stringent demands, and evidence suggests that at least some Judean and Christian converts continued to maintain ties with pagan associations.[72] Defining rites of passage, however, sharply delineated the boundaries of both church and synagogue. Christians baptized new converts. For Judean males, circumcision served as the key rite of conversion. Judaism and the Jesus movement were distinctive in this regard.

The association of Christian baptism with cleansing, on the one hand, and the death-burial-resurrection complex, on the other, reveals the decidedly transformational nature of the rite. By means of baptismal immersion, the initiate visibly transfers allegiance from the "unclean" world to a community of persons variously described as "washed," "sanctified," and "justified" (1 Cor 6:11). Baptism, moreover, identifies the convert with the experiences of Jesus through a symbolic reenactment of, and participation in, his death and resurrection.[73] Represented in each of these motifs is the major shift that a convert to Christianity experienced—from the social structure one shared by birth to one's new commitment to the local Christian *ekklesia*. Wayne Meeks, therefore, appropriately describes conversion to Christianity as "extraordinary, thoroughgoing resocialization."[74]

Familial Emphasis. We come now to the final and most significant social characteristic of early Christianity, one that will occupy the balance of this book: the metaphor of the church as a surrogate kinship group. It is now commonly recognized that Christians viewed their communities according to a family model. Kinship language occurs throughout early Christian literature. Moreover, a number of the behavioral ideals prevailing among the early Christians—and often realized in day-to-day community life—appear strikingly consonant with the Mediterranean kinship norms these believers had known in their natural families.

Scott Bartchy, for example, has shown that Luke's description in the Book of Acts of the communal life of the early followers of Jesus in Jerusalem is eminently plausible historically when read in the context of kin group values and practices. Bartchy argues, contrary to Hans Conzelmann, that Luke's depiction of the sharing of goods among the early Jerusalem Christians is neither idealized nor fictional. Rather, Luke presents the group's understanding of itself as an alternative kin group practicing fundamental Mediterranean kin group norms, including the "obligation to be certain that the needs of everyone in the group are met."[75]

Recently, Wayne McCready compared the Jesus movement's family orientation with contemporary social options. McCready enumerates several traits that serve to differentiate early churches from other voluntary groups in the ancient world. Included among them is "the degree of intimacy among fellow members." He properly situates this intimacy in a kinship context, and his summary in this regard will serve as a fitting introduction to the discussion that follows: "The amount of language emphasizing close personal ties, brotherly and sisterly love, greetings with a holy kiss, concern for the well-being of community members, and so on—not only reinforced a sense of community, but it underscored the internal cohesion that distinguished the assemblies of early Christians."[76] The familial orientation of the movement found expression at the levels of both language and behavior. Family language, so common in Christian writings, was more than mere formality. Mediterranean family values were also expected to define interpersonal relationships among the early Christians. In both arenas—terminology and behavior—the churches departed significantly from contemporary social alternatives in its familial emphasis.

Language provides an illuminating point of departure, as we begin to compare the kinship orientation of the Christ-confessing communities to other groups in the empire. Social theorists have shown us that language, like ritual, serves to reaffirm the social order, particularly in societies or groups that reflect a high level of solidarity.[77] In chapter 4, we will see this truth graphically illustrated in the letters of Paul, in which the density of kinship terminology consistently corresponds to the urgency with which Paul seeks to encourage behavior characteristic of a Mediterranean family—to reaffirm the social order. Terminology, then, can be quite informative. And Christian writers utilize kinship vocabulary to a degree wholly unparalleled among contemporary social organizations. John Kloppenborg, for example, identifies the ubiquitous presence of kinship vocabulary as "the most striking innovation" on the part of the Jesus movement vis-à-vis the collegia.[78] This, in turn, suggests that the early churches were attempting to create and affirm a social order markedly different from that which obtained among other groups in the empire.

Scholars have long noted the relative absence of kinship terms—so common in Paul's writings—in sources portraying trade groups.[79] Among Greek associations in particular, kinship terminology (especially *adelphos*—"brother"—as a designation for members) was a rarity.[80] Sibling terminology was more common with Roman groups, but only among social equals. Kloppenborg cites as an example the Roman *fratres*

Arvales. He then proceeds to offer the important qualification that "membership in this elite priestly collegium naturally was not open to non-elite persons."[81] The application of fraternal terminology to slaves is almost wholly unattested even in Roman associations.[82] By contrast, we find Paul suggesting that the slave Onesimus should be considered a "beloved brother" in an important early Christian document (Philemon).

Finally, those kinship terms that do occasionally appear in collegial texts and inscriptions must be interpreted in their proper context. We must do more than simply identify common terms. We must ascertain the connotations of these terms for the respective groups that used them. For example, we cannot argue from the simple fact that the term *adelphos* is used to describe initiates at Eleusis that "the cult association is primarily a family."[83] Such reasoning fails to take into consideration the literary and social context in which kinship language, where it occurs at all, typically appears in the associations. Several of the instances that Arthur Darby Nock cites to buttress the above claim represent honorific titles for patrons of the group ("father" and "mother") and do not imply family structure at all.[84] Moreover, we know that initiates at Eleusis failed to maintain the kind of ongoing social network that the presence of sibling terminology might imply.

In contrast to the associations, family language appears throughout early Christian literature, over a broad geographical range, for at least the first two centuries of the nascent movement's existence. The following chapters will explore in some depth the significance of kinship words and images in Christian writings. Only some brief comments are in order here, comments that pertain particularly to our comparison of the early churches with other voluntary groups. As we saw above, trade groups or cult associations simply did not demand of their members an exclusive allegiance to group solidarity that supplanted loyalty to all other groups. Christian communities, on the other hand, demanded precisely this kind of loyalty from their converts, for this was at the very heart of what it meant to be a surrogate Mediterranean family.

Here the categories on our chart inevitably blur, for we must now allow for a close connection between the family metaphor and Christian exclusivity. Specifically, the radically exclusive allegiance that the early church demanded of her converts finds a powerful linguistic symbol in the family metaphor. The reasons are fairly obvious. On the one hand, "in the whole Mediterranean world, the centrally located institution maintaining societal existence is kinship and its set of interlocking rules." Kinship thus serves to focus personal loyalty and "holds supreme sway over individual life."[85] Moreover, common sense requires that one can conceive of belonging to but a single family. This was particularly so in antiquity, where shared blood was the defining family attribute. Therefore, for the early

Christians to self-consciously define the church as a surrogate kinship group was to implicitly demand of community members a loyalty that excluded every competing social entity in the surrounding culture—including a convert's natural family.

This conflict of loyalties between natural and church families surfaces quite often in the literature. Again and again, the denial of loyalty to one's natural family serves as the paradigmatic expression of commitment to the new faith—to the family of Jesus. We will return to this theme in detail in later chapters. Here are but three New Testament examples:

> As [Jesus] went a little farther, he saw James son of Zebedee and his brother John, who were in their boat mending the nets. Immediately he called them; and they left their father Zebedee in the boat with the hired men, and followed him. (Mark 1:19-20)

> Another of his disciples said to him, "Lord, first let me go and bury my father." But Jesus said to him, "Follow me, and let the dead bury their own dead." (Matt 8:21-22)

> I mean, brothers and sisters, the appointed time has grown short; from now on, let even those who have wives be as though they had none. (1 Cor 7:29)

The surrogate family orientation of the early churches is lacking among the Greco-Roman voluntary associations. In addition to differences in terminology, such as those cited above, the associations also failed to demand of their members the kind of either/or loyalty reflected in the above New Testament text-segments. The mystery cults provide a final and illuminating point of comparison. Walter Burkert presents a threefold typology of the major forms of social organization reflected among the mysteries. Of the three alternatives Burkert discusses, only the last—the *thiasos*—even approximates community as experienced among the early Christians. To be sure, a mutual attachment can be observed that manifests itself in common activities, even including assistance with lawsuits and burial. As we will see in the following chapter, such solidarity could be interpreted according to a kinship model. What is lacking, however, is precisely the kind of either/or loyalty central to genuine patrilineal kin group values.[86]

Burkert cuts to the heart of the matter when he observes that the members of the cult group continued to live as "autonomous, detached individuals with private interests, occupations and property."[87] They remained "independent, especially at the economic level, fully integrated into the complex structures of family and *polis*."[88] As Wayne A. Meeks asserts even more categorically, "Being or becoming religious in the Greco-Roman world did not entail either moral transformation or sectarian resocialization."[89] Contrast the "extraordinarily thoroughgoing resocialization"[90] reflected in the Gospel of Matthew:

While he was still speaking to the crowds, his mother and his brothers were standing outside, wanting to speak to him. Someone told him, "Look, your mother and your brothers are standing outside, wanting to speak to you." But to the one who had told him this, Jesus replied, "Who is my mother, and who are my brothers?" And pointing to his disciples, he said, "Here are my mother and my brothers! For whoever does the will of my Father in heaven is my brother and sister and mother." (Matt 12:46-50)

Jesus of Nazareth publicly dissociates himself from his natural family, professes loyalty to a new surrogate family, and apparently expects his followers to do the same. It is this resocialization—at the kinship level—that marks early Christianity as distinct among the voluntary associations of Greco-Roman antiquity. The social solidarity characteristic of the family model, in turn, goes a long way to explain both the intimacy and sense of community so often cited as unique to early Christianity, and the attractiveness of the early Christian movement to displaced and alienated urbanites in the Greco-Roman world.

THE ANCIENT CHURCH AS FAMILY: A ROAD MAP FOR THE FOLLOWING CHAPTERS

The centrality of the family matrix for early Christian social organization calls for a careful examination of the nature of family in Mediterranean antiquity and the appropriation of the surrogate family model on the part of the early Christians. This leads to the subject matter of this book. I will demonstrate in the following pages that the ancient Mediterranean family provided the dominant social model for many of the early Christian congregations. Specifically, local churches understood themselves to constitute surrogate patrilineal kinship groups, and local leaders expected their members to behave in a manner consonant with such a model of interpersonal relationships.

It will be helpful to conclude with a conceptual road map for what is to follow. The balance of my study will build on the current chapter as follows:

Chapter 2. The family model appropriated by the Jesus movement differed greatly from the nuclear family system typical of modern Western society. Before exploring the surrogate family orientation of the early Christians, it will be necessary to examine the structure of the patrilineal kinship model of family organization characteristic of Mediterranean antiquity. A nuanced understanding of ancient family values and relational priorities will greatly aid our examination of the early Christian communities.

Chapter 3. Here the genesis of early Christianity's kinship model will be explored. Evidence will be presented for the surrogate family idea in the Hebrew Scriptures and in later Second Temple literature. Much of the chapter will examine the establishment of the family model among the first followers of Jesus.

Chapter 4. This portion of the book is devoted exclusively to Paul of Tarsus and his use of the kinship construct. I will establish the centrality of the family metaphor for Paul as well as the presence of a strong continuity in this regard between Jesus and Paul.

Chapter 5. The fifth chapter will survey the surrogate family theme as it appears in second-century Christian writings. Authors include Clement of Rome, Ignatius of Antioch, Justin Martyr, and Clement of Alexandria. Second-century writers exhibit both continuity and innovation in their employment of the metaphor.

Chapter 6. A single city of the Greco-Roman world, Carthage, North Africa, will serve as the focus of this chapter. The writings of Tertullian and Cyprian, as well as the *Passion of Perpetua,* graphically reveal the importance of the kinship metaphor well into the third century for Christians in North Africa.

Chapter 7. The conclusion in this chapter will argue strongly for the integrity of the early Christian family model. It is presently quite fashionable in academic circles to interpret religious images and metaphors in purely negative terms—symbols employed by those in power to keep community members in submission to their leaders' authority. I maintain that this is decidedly not the case among the early Christians. For a high-status Christian leader like Cyprian to repeatedly refer to the indigent members of his community as his "brothers" was to level the social playing field in a way that afforded Christianity a much deserved credibility in the world of Greco-Roman antiquity. As one vociferous detractor of Christianity exclaimed in apparent frustration: "Why do we not observe that it is their [the Christians'] benevolence to strangers, their care for the graves of the dead and the pretended holiness of their lives that have done the most to increase atheism? . . . When . . . the impious Galilaeans support not only their own poor, but ours as well, all men see that our people lack aid from us" (Julian the Apostate, *Arsar.*).[91]

2

Mediterranean Family Systems:
Structure and Relationships

Introduction

Constructing a model for the early church as family demands as its point of departure a culturally sensitive appreciation of the important values and characteristics of ancient Mediterranean kinship systems. The universality of family—consisting of highly valued relationships with those to whom we are related by birth or marriage—ironically hinders, rather than enhances, our ability to appreciate some of the most important values obtaining in kinship constructs that differ from our own.[1] It will prove helpful first to distinguish between what anthropologists call descent group kinship structure, which is characteristic of Mediterranean antiquity and many other societies throughout world history, and our more familiar American kindred system of family relationships. I will focus on a particular expression of the descent group model, namely, the patrilineal kinship group (PKG), since the PKG is the type of family reflected in ancient Mediterranean society.[2] I will then outline in some detail the structural characteristics and relational values common to the PKG. This information, in turn, will serve as our model for investigating the early church as a surrogate family based on faith, in the ensuing chapters.

Kinship Then and Now: How Family Is Defined

Introductions to the study of kinship targeted at U.S. readers consistently emphasize the fundamental differences obtaining between our American kindred family system and the descent group model common to many other cultures, including the world of Mediterranean antiquity.[3] To be sure, kinship structure and family relationships are not wholly static constructs. American family systems, in particular, are presently undergoing change at an almost unprecedented rate.[4] Nevertheless, a brief comparison of our kindred system (as traditionally envisioned) with the descent group form of family organization will serve well to highlight salient aspects of ancient family systems, which will then be elaborated upon later in this chapter.

The basic structural difference between kindred and descent groups lies in the manner in which family membership is reckoned by persons of the respective societies—that is, who is considered part of the family. Descent groups determine family membership on the basis of shared blood via a common ancestor. A kindred system, in contrast, is constructed on the basis of relationships between group members and a single living individual. The diagrams that follow highlight the key differences between the two family systems. Figure 2.1 represents the kinship model most familiar to Western readers—our American kindred group system.

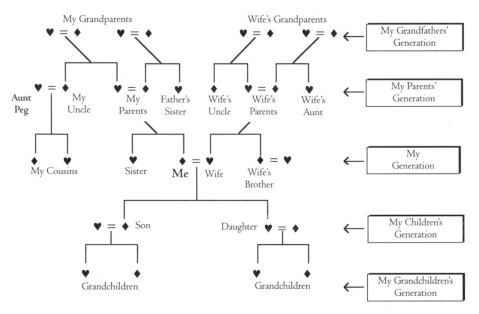

KEY:

    ♦   represents a male
    ♥   represents a female
    =   represents a marriage
    | vertical lines coming down from "equals sign" (=) connect parents and offspring
    —   horizontal lines connect siblings

Figure 2.1. American Family System

We will assume the diagram represents my family. Locate **Me** on the diagram. As a typical American, I regard as members of my family those who are related to me within an arbitrary limit of time (a few generations up or down) and extent (cousins usually included; second cousins excluded). Persons related to me both by ancestry and through marriage are considered to be part of my extended family.

Note that I share no common ancestor with a number of the people in my family. For example, locate the second line down from the top on the chart (My Parents' Generation). Now go all the way to the left. You will find listed there my aunt on my mother's side. I have named her **Aunt Peg**. While I consider her to be a part of my family, **Aunt Peg** and I share no common ancestor and are not, therefore, consanguine (sharing the same blood). Notice, as well, that my wife and I are not blood relatives. She has her set of ancestors (above her on the right side of the chart) and I have mine (above left). Yet the marriage relationship is traditionally extolled as the epitome of "family" in kindred group societies like our own. We will discover that this is not the case for descent group cultures like those of Mediterranean antiquity.

The point of all this is to demonstrate that we in the United States define family in terms of a constellation of relationships to a single living individual, in this case **Me**. People in collectivist cultures, in contrast, view family not primarily in terms of *relationship* but in terms of *consanguinity*, that is, in terms of a blood connection with a common ancestor. Figure 2.2 will make this clear.

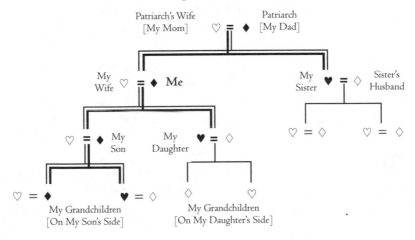

KEY:

♦	represents a male
♥	represents a female

} Filled-in symbols are members of the kin group

=   represents a marriage

| vertical lines coming down from "equals sign" (=) connect parents and offspring

—   horizontal lines connect siblings

Figure 2.2. Mediterranean Family System

Note the difference between our kindred system and the descent group model with respect to how family membership is reckoned. In figure 2.1, the American Family System, all the symbols represent persons whom I consider to be part of my family. On the family tree in figure 2.2, however, only the filled-in figures (♦ ♥) represent family members. Those in outline form (◊ ♡) are not part of my kinship group. This is because only the persons whose symbols are colored in black have the blood of the family's (male) ancestor flowing through their veins.

It will prove helpful to walk through figure 2.2, the Mediterranean Family System, from the top down and see who is "in" and who is "out" with respect to family membership. (You can follow the bloodline down through the double line on the chart.) The individual whose symbol stands at the top of the chart (♦) is the oldest surviving male—the patriarch of the kin group. He is also my father. Notice immediately that his wife is technically *not* a member of his family (her symbol is not filled in). The patriarch's wife does not share his blood because she had a different father. But both of the couple's children (listed on the chart as **Me** and My Sister) *do* belong to the family, since my sister and I have inherited the patriarch's (our father's) blood.

We come now to a defining aspect of PKG orientation. Although my sister and I possess the father's blood, and therefore belong to the same family, *only I can pass on the bloodline to the next generation.* My sister has the blood, but she cannot pass it on (notice that the double line on her side of the chart ends with her). It is for this reason that lineage groups like the one shown here are called "patrilineal"—blood is passed down solely through the male line.[5] An individual must possess the patriarch's blood to be part of the family. Follow the double line from top to bottom and you will notice that it passes from one generation to the next only through sons, not through daughters. The result for my grandchildren's generation, for example, is that my grandchildren on my *son's* side are members of my (and my father's) kinship group. The grandchildren on my *daughter's* side are not, since my daughter cannot pass on my blood.

The patrilineal descent-group family model inevitably generates a characteristic set of relational strategies and family values. In the pages to follow, I will outline those aspects of PKG relationships that are especially important for understanding the surrogate family model which defined social relations among members of the Jesus movement. To illustrate the various aspects of PKG family life, I will draw on a variety of sources from around the Mediterranean, sources both ancient and contemporary.[6]

The Patrilineal Descent Group:
Relational Strategies and Values

Marriage in Ancient Mediterranean Society

The contrast between American kindred systems and descent group families characteristic of the ancient Mediterranean asserts itself most dynamically in the marriage strategies of the respective societies. American kindred groups view marriage in relational terms. Because we are an individualistic culture, relational compatibility and the ensuing happiness of each individual partner constitute our highest conjugal values. This is not the case in descent group societies. The descent group family views marriage not primarily in relational but rather in contractual terms. A recent description of marriage in the New Testament world expands upon this idea: "Marriage . . . is a legal and social contract between two families for (1) the promotion of the status of each [family], (2) the production of legitimate offspring, and (3) appropriate preservation and transferal of property to the next generation."[7] Noticeably absent from this description is any concern for the personal satisfaction of the individuals in the marriage relationship. Energies are passionately directed toward the success and survival of the *group*, in this case the family—not the needs of the *individual*. The most important contribution a marriage can make is to strengthen the descent group of consanguine family members, and this, then, is what is valued. This is not to suggest that persons in descent group family systems are necessarily deprived of relationally satisfying marriages.[8] It is simply to observe that individual marital bliss is generally understood as a secondary by-product, rather than the primary goal, of the institution of marriage.[9] For descent group societies, a good marriage is one that enhances the honor and position of the extended family. Endogamous marriages strengthen the kin group from within by keeping resources within the group. Exogamous marriages serve to build alliances with other families.[10]

Women in the PKG Family System

PKG marriage strategies, in turn, define the role of women in a patrilineal society. A daughter is generally not a free agent in an ancient Mediterranean marriage transaction, nor does she possess the same rights as a son. A daughter belongs to the patriline of her father and lives in her father's household as long as she is unmarried. Daughters provide the opportunity for a PKG to strengthen claims to family inheritance through endogamous marriage, or to build alliances by marrying exogamously. A daughter, however, cannot pass on her family's blood and, therefore, cannot contribute to the ultimate survival of the kin group beyond the present generation. This means that for some, "the birth of a daughter is a loss" (Sir 22:3). It also explains why, in a list of some seventy persons who accompany Jacob to Egypt to live with his son Joseph, we find the names of only two daughters: Dinah, the daughter of Jacob, and Serah, the daughter of Asher (*Jub.* 44:11-34). Genealogies produced in patrilineal societies typically reflect only male offspring (see Ps.-Philo, *Bib. Ant.* 4).

When a daughter marries, she leaves her patrilocal home (unlike her married brother) and moves in with her husband and his father, assuming the latter is still alive. She remains, however, technically an outsider with respect to her husband's family, since she does not share her husband's ancestral blood. Her tenuous position is only ameliorated when she bears a male child and thus provides for the continuance of the patriline. And this is her primary role in the family into which she marries.[11]

Patrilocal Residence and the Family as a Producing Unit

Patrilineal descent ideally manifests itself in some rather specific ways at the level of actual family systems. Daughters are married out; sons are generally kept as close to their father's home as possible. Matthew 10:35-36 provides us with a revealing look at the structural makeup of the typical PKG household: "For I have come to set a man against his father, and a daughter against her mother, and a daughter-in-law against her mother-in-law; and one's foes will be members of one's own household." Notice the assumed residents: a man and his wife (called "a daughter-in-law") who share residence with the man's parents ("father" and "mother" or "mother-in-law") and his unmarried sister ("daughter"). Bruce J. Malina describes such a Mediterranean PKG:

> In the Mediterranean world, the household might include father, mother, the first-born son and his family, along with other unmarried children. These would live in close proximity, perhaps even sharing the same courtyard with other married sons and their families. This sort of family tends to be the effective social, residence, consumption, and production unit.[12]

Patrilocal residence is reflected in a variety of our ancient sources: Enoch (*1 En.* 83:6) and Noah (*Sib. Or.* 1:275); and the Sibyl herself (1:285). It is clear that the Sibyl has married into a patrilineal kin group. She shares residence with a patriarch ("father-in-law"), his wife, the Sibyl's husband, her husband's brothers, and their wives.[13]

Since patrilocal residence is the assumed ideal, it is, conversely, abhorrent for a man to live with his father-in-law (that is, matrilocally). A Syriac version of the

Ahiqar legend reads: "My son, I have carried iron and removed stones; and they were not heavier on me than a man who settles in the house of his father-in-law" (*Syr. Ah.* 2:46).[14] This explains Jacob's desire to leave his mother's brother Laban in order to return with his wives to reside near his father, Isaac (Genesis 29–31; *Jub.* 28:25). In the second-century B.C.E. romance Tobit, Tobias finds his father-in-law highly reluctant to allow him to travel back with his bride, Sarah, to the home of his father, Tobit. Only when his father and mother die, and he has no surviving relatives in his patriline, does Tobias journey with Sarah to take up residence at the home of Sarah's parents (14:11-12).[15]

Closely related to patrilocal residence is the character of the PKG as both a consuming and producing unit. American families typically consume goods as a group but do not work together in a single industry or concern to produce products of some sort. By contrast, the PKG ideal for the family included the collective production of goods of some sort. The Gospel narratives portray two families who shared in a fishing enterprise on the Sea of Galilee:

> As Jesus passed along the Sea of Galilee, he saw Simon and his brother Andrew casting a net into the sea—for they were fishermen. And immediately they left their nets and followed him. As he went a little farther, he saw James son of Zebedee and his brother John, who were in their boat mending the nets. Immediately he called them; and they left their father Zebedee in the boat with the hired men, and followed him. (Mark 1:16-20)

And the *Apocalypse of Abraham* opens with the protagonist working with his father in the manufacture and sale of pagan idols (1:1—2:9; see also *Jub.* 34:1).

Mothers and Sons

The primary role of a woman in a PKG society is to provide male offspring for her husband's family. The centrality of this value for the Mediterranean world can perhaps best be appreciated by examining its mirror opposite: the barren womb. Childlessness—specifically, sonlessness—places a woman in an intensely desperate situation. The barren Rachel exclaims to Jacob, "Give me sons!" (*Jub.* 28:16). Manoah complains to his wife, Eluma, "Behold the Lord has shut up your womb so that you may not bear children, and now let me go that I may take another wife lest I die without fruit" (Ps.-Philo, *Bib. Ant.* 42:1). Particularly revealing is the same author's expansion of the account of Hannah. Hannah is taunted by her husband's other wife because the latter has produced male children and Hannah has not: "I know my husband will love me, because he delights in the sight of my sons standing around him like a plantation of olive trees. . . . For what did it profit Rachel that Jacob loved her? And unless the fruit of her womb had been given to him, his love would have been in vain" (*Bib. Ant.* 50:1-2). Sentiments like these come right out of Old Testament narratives (Gen 29:32-34). We are not surprised, then, at the public exclamation of blessing uttered over a woman who produced one perceived to be a truly exceptional firstborn son: "While [Jesus] was saying this, a woman in the crowd raised her voice and said to him, 'How honorable is the womb that bore you and the breasts that nursed you!'" (Luke 11:27).[16]

When a previously barren women does bear a son, another dynamic comes into play. A unique relationship develops between mother and son(s).[17] The mother, sensing that her son has given her a foothold in an alien family setting, tends to cultivate that relationship in a way that appears odd to Western observers. The story of Rebekah and her son, Jacob, represents perhaps the archetypal expression of the mother-son relationship for Israelites in antiquity. We find a marvelous expansion upon the Old Testament narrative in the second-century B.C.E. book of *Jubilees*. Rebekah expresses her attachment to Jacob: "And I love you very much, my son. And my heart and affection bless you at every hour of the day and (every) watch of the night. And now, my son, heed my voice, and do the will of your mother" (*Jub.* 25:2-3). She then proceeds to lay her hands upon Jacob's head and bless him:

> And may I see, O my son, that you shall have blessed sons in my lifetime; and a blessed and holy seed, may all your seed be. And just as you have given rest to your mother's soul in her lifetime; the womb of the one who bore you likewise blesses you. My affection and my breasts are blessing you; and my mouth and tongue are praising you greatly. (*Jub.* 25:18-20)

Roman historical narratives evidence similar mother-son plotting and positioning. Note, for example, the efforts exercised by Livia in the promotion of her son, Tiberius. Tacitus alludes to Livia's "secret intrigues" and "open suggestions," which result in her son becoming "a colleague in empire and a partner in the tribunician power" alongside his stepfather, Augustus (*Ann.* 1.3). Tiberius's position is later threatened due to the impending death of Augustus and the possibility of an interregnum period during which others might attempt to seize the throne. Livia obviates this potential window of opportunity for other aspirants to the principate by making sure that, when the news of Augustus's death hits the streets, "one and the same report told men that Augustus was dead and that Tiberius Nero was master of the State" (*Ann.* 1.5). Later, Tacitus decries Agrippina the Elder's "ambition to parade her son in a common soldier's uniform, and wish him to be called Caesar Caligula" (1.69). Also to be mentioned in this regard are Agrippina the Younger's notorious efforts to contract what was a technically incestuous marriage to Claudius and thereby ultimately to promote her son, Nero, to the principate (12.3-6).

One Second Temple narrative in particular reflects the special relationship between mother and son(s) in patrilineal society. Fourth Maccabees portrays the martyrdom of a woman who follows her seven sons to death during the persecution suffered at the hands of the Seleucid king Antiochus IV. The mother-son bond gives the story much of its tragic flavor. The narrator's agenda is to demonstrate the superiority of reason over emotions, and the steadfast faithfulness of this mother in the face of the death of her beloved sons provides him an opportunity to extol eloquently his cardinal virtue. The author's editorializing, however, serves to highlight two aspects of the value under discussion: (a) the inseparable bond of mother and son and (b) the utter tragedy of losing one's sons before they have had the opportunity to produce sons themselves. A rhetorically powerful discursus on the affective nature of the mother-son connection fills most of 4 Maccabees 15. The heartache of losing one's sons prematurely is then aptly illustrated in the following chapter:

> Ah, thrice-wretched woman that I am, yes more than thrice-wretched! I have borne seven sons and am the mother of none! How vain were these seven pregnancies, how futile these seven times ten months with child, how fruitless the nursing and wretched the suckling! In vain, my children, did I endure these many pains for you and the even more severe strains of rearing you. Alas for my sons, some unmarried, others married but to no purpose! I shall never set eyes on any children of yours nor shall I know the happiness of being called a grandmother." (16:6-10)

In context (see 16:5), the narrator assures us that the above sentiments were precisely those that did *not* characterize this mother whose "devout reason" took precedence over such "passions" (16:1). For our purposes, however, the point remains—the above exclamation clearly reflects the *expected* reaction of a mother who experiences such a fate.

Sibling Solidarity: The Central Relational Priority

As important as mother-son relationships are to the PKG family matrix, it is yet another relational bond that truly defines what it means to be a part of a patrilineal family group. At the very heart of the PKG ideal is the sibling solidarity so characteristic of Mediterranean families. Indeed, sibling relationships reflect perhaps the most important distinction between ancient PKGs and modern Western kindred systems. And it is the PKG sibling relational model that the followers of Jesus appropriate in their image of the church as family.

SIBLINGS BEFORE SPOUSES

To understand the sibling solidarity that is so fundamental to the PKG, we must first recognize the marked difference between modern and ancient family systems with respect to where the individual experiences his or her deepest sense of emotional bonding and support. Western kindred systems address such affective needs in the marriage relationship. By contrast, for the PKG, the tightest unit of loyalty and affection is the descent group of brothers and sisters. As shown in figure 2.3, the emotional bonding we expect as a mark of a healthy husband-and-wife relationship is normally the mark of sibling relationships.

AMERICAN KINDRED GROUP IDEALS	PATRILINEAL KINSHIP GROUP IDEALS
• Marriage provides offspring and sexual fulfillment • Marriage provides emotional support • Wife's status does not depend on providing heirs	• Marriage provides offspring and sexual fulfillment • Siblings provide emotional support • Wife's status depends on providing heirs

Figure 2.3. Marriage Characteristics

Much in our source material supports the observations shown in figure 2.3. Ben Sira accurately reflects the priorities of his contemporaries (note the order) when he says, "My soul takes pleasure in three things and they are beautiful in the sight of the Lord and of men: agreement between brothers, friendship between neighbors, and a wife and husband who live in harmony" (25:1). Given a choice between "agreement between brothers" and "a wife and husband who live in harmony," the ancient would choose the former hands-down (see 11QT 54.20; Neh 4:14; Tacitus, *Hist.* 5.8). Josephus reflects similar priorities when he lists the individuals after whom Herod named three towers that he built in Jerusalem (again, note the order): "brother, friend, and wife" (*J. W.* 5.162). As Ben Sira elsewhere exhorts, "Do not exchange a friend for money, or a real brother for the gold of Ophir" (7:18). Particularly interesting is a text that compares the father-son relationship to the connection between the father and his brothers. Even the importance of sons to the survival of the patriline cannot unseat the sibling bond from its position of preeminence:

> Rejoice at your sons, father, for they are a (real) joy. However, the position of brothers, the sons do not take for me; see my sons (and) my brothers. For your son prays for your death, since through your death he will receive honor, and will occupy your position, and will live on your goods at will. But your brothers pray to God for your life, because as long as you live they are splendid, but through your death they are handicapped. (*Sent. Syr. Men.* 194-204)

Sibling affective bonds reveal themselves in the PKG practice of sharing important holidays with one's blood family: David's family celebration (1 Sam 20:6, 29);
Job's children's banquet (Job 1:4; *T. Job* 15:1-2); Isaac and Ishmael's celebration of
the harvest (*Jub.* 22:1-2).

The above expressions of the PKG sibling bond are colorfully reflected in the
lives of a young couple whose marriage and subsequent living arrangements are
described by Lloyd and Margaret Fallers in their 1976 ethnography of Edremit, a
village on the west coast of Turkey.[18] The relationship between Azize and Mustafa,
through the whole process of betrothal to marriage, and even afterward, never
assumes a romantic quality. Indeed, wives in Edremit society have no expectations
that their husbands will prove to be "a major source of companionship" in this
regard.[19] By contrast, the bride Azize's relationship with her brother is highly affective in nature. The authors contend that "frequently brother-sister relationships
[have] an almost romantic quality." Even "into later life, the men with whom
women feel most comfortable and upon whom they can most depend are their
brothers." Brothers remain their sisters' primary source of "companionship, advice,
help and defense."[20] For Azize, marriage to Mustafa necessitates a shift in residence
away from her brothers and into the home of her husband's parents in another village (that is, patrilocal residence). After four years of marriage, Azize must still bear
the title "bride" (*gelin*) in her husband's family, for she has produced no offspring.
Day-to-day life reflects the priority of sibling bonds over the marriage relationship
again and again, as the married sisters of Mustafa (Azize's husband) come to the
home regularly (almost daily) to visit Mustafa, while Azize returns to her own village to visit her blood family whenever she finds the opportunity.[21]

Ian Whitaker's study of Gheg society in Albania also confirms the priority of sibling over marital affection and attachment. Not only did a woman retain her membership in the clan into which she was born when she married into another clan, but
long after the wedding ceremony, indeed, "throughout her life, her point of social
identification remained her natal kin group, as represented by her brothers."[22]

DEALING WITH DIVIDED LOYALTIES

We observed above, in our discussion of marriage strategy, that the contractual nature
of marriage in patrilineal society does not necessarily exclude genuine marital affection. An emotionally charged marriage relationship will, however, introduce a degree
of tension into PKG dynamics, since feelings of loyalty and solidarity inevitably
become somewhat divided. Especially engrossing, then, are stories in which the
protagonist is forced to choose between loyalty to a beloved spouse and loyalty to
her or his siblings. To the example of Herod and Mariamme (see note 8, p. 241),

we may add that of Herod's brother Pheroras. Pheroras, too, enjoyed a highly emotionally satisfying attachment to his wife. Ultimately, brother Herod challenges Pheroras to choose sides. He must either align himself with his brother or choose to side with his wife. Pheroras surprisingly opts for the latter, a choice perceived in the narrative to be so utterly countercultural that Herod suggests that Pheroras's wife has bewitched him (Josephus, *J. W.* 1.572). The point is that the sibling bond typically takes precedence whenever one is forced to make a decision regarding family loyalty. Indeed, Herod's sister Salome later draws on this very value when she wants out of her marriage to the Idumaean governor Costobarus after a rather nasty quarrel. She unlawfully divorces Costobarus and then justifies herself by an appeal to consanguinity. Josephus portrays Salome "telling her brother Herod that she had separated from her husband out of loyalty to Herod himself. For, she said, she had learned that her husband . . . was planning to revolt" (*Ant.* 15.260).

Particularly distressing is a blood feud between clans that have previously shared marriage partners. In the event of conflict between her birth family and the kinship group into which she has married, a woman is confronted with an insuperable dilemma, particularly if she has produced children. Roman history offers a tragic example. As discord increases between the two most powerful figures in the Mediterranean world, and civil war looms on the horizon, it is the position of Octavia, the half-sister of Octavian—the future emperor Augustus— and wife of rival Mark Antony, that gives Plutarch's narrative much of its tragic flavor. Her sentiments clearly characterize a woman caught in the middle of divided loyalties:

> She appealed to her brother [Octavius] with tears and passionate entreaties not to make her the most wretched of women after having been the happiest. As it was, she told him, the eyes of the whole world were upon her, since she was the wife of one of its masters and the sister of the other. "If the worst should happen," she said, "and war break out between you, no one can say which of you is fated to conquer the other, but what is quite certain is that my fate will be miserable." (Plutarch, *Ant.* 35)

The historical reliability of Plutarch's account is highly suspect, and scholars generally concur that the role of Octavia has been embellished. Moreover, either Plutarch or his sources, or both, are clearly hostile to Antony.[23] The manner in which Octavia's role has been embellished, however, carries with it implicit assumptions about the sensibilities of Plutarch's audience with respect to family matters. Octavia's "tears and passionate entreaties" concerning her divided loyalties would have resonated with Roman readers, who lived in a society characterized by a high degree of sibling solidarity. That Octavia ultimately ends up back in Rome with her brother (53) is to be expected in light of the priority of the PKG bond in Mediterranean antiquity.

Modern ethnographic research confirms such readings of ancient texts. Mary Durham's study of clan feuding in Gheg society, for example, demonstrates that a woman's loyalty ultimately remains with her descent group of brothers and sisters. The most extreme expression of this loyalty finds women, on rare occasions, seeking to resolve the dilemma of divided loyalties by killing their own children, thereby aligning themselves irrevocably with their families of origin.[24]

Conversely, as we might expect, permanent separation from one's blood relations—especially siblings—represents a much greater sacrifice than separation from one's spouse. Indeed, in the following familiar text, separation from one's spouse apparently is regarded as insignificant among those sacrifices necessary to follow Jesus of Nazareth—it is not even mentioned:

> Peter began to say to him, "Look, we have left everything and followed you." Jesus said, "Truly I tell you, there is no one who has left house or brothers or sisters or mother or father or children or fields, for my sake and for the sake of the good news, who will not receive a hundred fold now in this age—houses, brothers and sisters, mothers and children, and fields with persecutions—and in the age to come eternal life." (Mark 10:28-30)[25]

TREACHERY AND SOLIDARITY AMONG SIBLINGS

PKG sibling solidarity comes into clearest focus when we examine its opposite—treachery and betrayal among brothers. Since Western kindred systems find their strongest affective bonds in marriage relationships, it is hardly surprising to discover that the converse—interpersonal treachery—is epitomized in its archetypal form in stories of spousal betrayal, adultery, and divorce. Stories that captivate the American public and fill the coffers of movie theaters, bookstores, and magazine vendors consistently reflect our preoccupation with relations—often unsuccessful relations—between the sexes. Exactly the opposite is the case for Mediterranean antiquity. Treachery in its most extreme, despised and, therefore, engrossing form is not the breakup of a marriage but strife among blood brothers. John Peristiany notes the close correspondence obtaining between the degree of solidarity expressed when PKG siblings are getting along, on the one hand, and the degree of animosity arising among feuding brothers, on the other:

> Thus, here again, expectations based on a deeply rooted social ideal, an ideal round which a chain of values is co-ordinated, generate, when betrayed, a reaction of the same order as the strength of the ideology forming its inner core. The form of the reaction may have a cultural specificity, but the principle is wide in its application.[26]

Earlier in his essay, Peristiany had observed:

> Indeed, I understand from the literature on the Arabs that few relations are more
> embittered than those between brothers who, through competition, have first
> become rivals then enemies; deep affection and solidarity turning sour and leading
> to equally deep hatred when the all-pervasive ideal of unity has been betrayed and
> shattered by individual or sectional needs. "Who but your brother could have
> gouged out your eye?" is a proverbial rhetorical question asked in northern, eastern
> and southern Mediterranean lands whenever the topic of family friction is dis-
> cussed. "Fighting like brothers sharing an inheritance" is, in Cyprus, the paradigm
> of implacable enmity.[27]

Greek mythology offers a number of examples of hostility among siblings. Eteocles
and Polynices, the sons of Oedipus, murder each other in a power struggle over the
throne.[28] Cicero likens the flight of Mithridates VI to

> the flight in which Medea, according to the myth, once betook herself from this self-
> same country of Pontus. As she fled, the story goes, she scattered the limbs of her
> brother along the route where her father was likely to follow, with the intention that
> his pursuit should be slowed down and delayed by fatherly sorrow, as he collected each
> successive piece of his son's body in one place after another. (*Leg. Man.* 45)

From Roman tradition recall the tragic breakdown of the once harmonious relationship between the twins Romulus and Remus, resulting in the death of the latter
at the hands of the former (Livy 1.3-7).

The Hebrew Scriptures narrate numerous stories of this kind. It is highly
indicative that the first evil act following the expulsion from the Garden of Eden is
not the breakdown of Adam and Eve's marriage relationship but, rather—as we
would expect in PKG society—the murder of Abel by his brother, Cain, a story
that would later become a paradigm for wickedness among Second Temple Israelites
and members of the Jesus movement (Wis 10:3; *Jub.* 4.1-6; 1 John 3:12; Jude 11;
Cyprian, *Jeal. Env.* 5; Theophilus of Antioch, *Auto.* 2.29-30). Other Old Testament
narratives of sibling strife include the stories of Jacob and Esau; Joseph and his
brothers; Aaron, Miriam, and Moses; David and his brothers; the chaos among
Amnon, Tamar, and Absalom; and Solomon and Adonijah.[29]

Later literature reflects much of the same. Among the treacherous individuals
representing the first race of humans, the Sibyl includes "plotters against brothers"
(*Sib. Or.* 1.75). The most regrettable aspect of anger is that it pits father against son
and brother against brother (*T. Dan* 2.3). Noah gravely warns his sons when he
prophecies, "This one will be jealous of that one, and (I see) that you will not be

together, O my sons, each with his brother." Noah proceeds to attribute such an extreme breakdown in PKG solidarity to demonic influence (*Jub.* 7:26-27). Abimelech ultimately dies because he "killed his brothers unjustly" (Ps.-Philo, *Bib. Ant.* 37:4). From the perspective of the author of the *Damascus Document*, the most reprehensible of the acts perpetrated by the despised "Princes of Judah" has to do with betrayal and bloodshed among family members: "They have taken revenge and borne malice, every man against his brother, and every man has hated his fellow, and every man has sinned against his near kin" (CD 8.6-7).

New tales of treachery find new generations of readers. Hyrcanus, son of Joseph ben Tobias, suffers estrangement from and is ultimately forced to kill his own brothers when they attack him (Josephus, *Ant.* 12.190-222). Jason attacks Menelaus in an attempt to regain the priesthood, "not realizing that success at the cost of one's kindred is the greatest misfortune" (2 Macc 5:6). For Josephus, "success at the cost of one's kindred" is precisely Cleopatra's fatal flaw. At the very top of the list of vices that he ascribes to the Egyptian queen is the treacherous killing of her own brother and sister (*Ant.* 15.88-89). The pages of Josephus's works overflow with discord between brothers. Herod and Pheroras are at odds (*Ant.* 17.74-75); Herod's sons continually denounce each other to Herod (*Ant.* 17); Aristobulus I imprisons his brothers and then murders Antigonus (*J. W.* 1.70-83). Josephus's editorial reflections on the latter incident reveal how highly sibling solidarity was valued and, conversely, how intensely treachery was abhorred. For Josephus, the murder of Antigonus by his brother Aristobulus is "sure proof that calumny severs all ties of affection and nature, and that of our better feelings none is strong enough to hold out interminable against envy" (*J. W.* 1.77). If the bond between blood brothers cannot prevail in the face of envy, then nothing can.

Among the Romans as well, brother betrayal constituted the epitome of societal chaos. Ovid, as he heralds the return of the Golden Age, which begins to dawn with Julius Caesar and comes to fruition with Octavian, reflects on the horrors of the Iron Age just previous:

> All manner of crime broke out; modesty, truth and loyalty fled. Treachery and trickery took their place, deceit and violence and criminal greed. . . . War made its appearance. . . . Men lived on what they could plunder: friend was not safe from friend, nor father-in-law from son-in-law, *and even between brothers affection was rare.* . . . All proper affection lay vanquished and, last of the immortals, the maiden Justice left the blood-soaked earth. (*Met.* 1.127-51, emphasis added)

Positive examples of the bond of brotherhood also abound in the literature. The author of 4 Maccabees describes seven Judean brothers martyred under the oppressive rule of Antiochus IV. After all the brothers are executed in their turn, the narrator offers an extended comment upon the solidarity shared by these seven brothers who died for their ancestral faith:

> You are not ignorant of the affection of brotherhood, which the divine and all-wise Providence has bequeathed through the fathers to their descendants and which was implanted in the mother's womb. There each of the brothers dwelt the same length of time and was shaped during the same period of time; and growing from the same blood and through the same life, they were brought to the light of day. When they were born after an equal time of gestation, they drank milk from the same fountains. For such embraces brotherly-loving souls are nourished; and they grow stronger from this common nurture and daily companionship, and from both general education and our discipline in the law of God. (13:19-26)

The Maccabean brothers themselves are probably the epitome of Second Temple brotherhood functioning at its best. When men unrelated by blood to the brothers attempt to lead the battle against Gentile oppression, they are doomed to failure (1 Macc 5:55-62).

Old Testament narratives of sibling interaction continued to maintain their appeal for Second Temple Judeans. The recasting of Old Testament narratives, as well as the testamentary literature so common during the period, rely strongly on themes of sibling loyalty and treachery for their readability. Joseph narrates the various ways in which he refrained from retaliation and protected his brothers' honor even in the face of treachery. Then he concludes:

> So you see, my children, how many things I endured in order not to bring my brothers into disgrace. You, therefore, love one another and in patient endurance conceal one another's shortcomings. God is delighted by harmony among brothers and by the intention of a kind heart that takes pleasure in goodness. (T. Jos. 17:1-3)

In an engaging expansion upon a familiar Old Testament narrative, we find mother Rebekah asking son Esau to forgive his twin, Jacob. Esau's response forms a fitting conclusion to our survey of sibling relationships in Mediterranean society. Esau assures his mother that

> Jacob, my brother, I shall love more than all flesh. And I have no brother in all the earth except him alone. And this is not a great (thing) for me if I love him because he is my brother and together we were sown in your belly and together we came forth from your womb. *And if I do not love my brother, whom shall I love?* (Jub. 35:22, emphasis added)

Clearly, for ancient Mediterranean persons, sibling solidarity and loyalty constitute the apex of intimate human relationships. A treacherous brother is, conversely, the worst of social evils.

SPECIFIC ASPECTS OF SIBLING SOLIDARITY

We must now elaborate upon the PKG concept of sibling solidarity by outlining some of the particulars of its expression in day-to-day family life and, thereby, illustrate what it meant in Mediterranean society to "show love to your kinsman" (*Ps.-Phocylides* 219). To be sure, sibling relationships involved a deep sense of emotional attachment, and treachery among brothers and sisters was abhorred. But there was more. At a bare minimum, an ideally functioning PKG group of siblings shared the following practical responsibilities:

- Protection of family honor vis-à-vis outsiders

- Sharing of resources among insiders

Each of these PKG sibling duties is well evidenced in our sources.

When it comes to choosing sides, brothers must side with brothers regardless of the issue at hand. The following text, portraying the attempt of Archelaus to convince Augustus to confirm Herod's will, illustrates well the ultimate priorities and values that prevailed in a PKG culture. Archelaus's own relatives find themselves torn between kinship loyalty and their disgust with Archelaus as a national leader.[30] They hate Archelaus and are so vehemently opposed to him as king that they refuse openly to cast their lot *with* him. And yet Josephus tells us that "they considered it reprehensible to cast their vote *against* him with the envoys, for they believed that they would be disgraced in the eyes of Caesar if they were willing to act in this way toward a man who was their own kin" (*Ant.* 17.299-302, emphasis added).

Elsewhere in the same context, Augustus is again portrayed as one who highly esteems kinship solidarity. After suppressing a revolt that arose in Palestine while Archelaus was in Rome, the Syrian legate Varus sends the leaders of the insurrection to Caesar. Caesar frees most of them, punishing only those among the rebels who happened to be relatives of Herod "because they had shown contempt for justice in fighting against their own kin" (*Ant.* 17.298). Tacitus, too, credits Augustus with a certain sense of blood loyalty, for he portrays the emperor as one who, despite his ruthless rise to power, "never was hard-hearted enough to destroy any of his kinsfolk" (*Ann.* 1.6). Augustus was, however, ready to use family relations as a pretext for aggression against an enemy. Plutarch suggests that Octavius had permitted his half-sister Octavia to travel east to join her husband, Mark Antony, "not so much to give her pleasure, but rather to give himself a plausible pretext for declaring war, if she were neglected or insulted by her husband" (*Ant.* 53). Whether or not our author accurately identifies the future emperor's motive is immaterial. That such an affront on the part of a brother-in-law could even potentially be adopted as a pretext for war—for Plutarch and his readers, it apparently is plausible—tells us much about common assumptions concerning PKG values in Roman society.

While siblings are expected to defend family honor, it is conversely the case that the failure of a single brother can bring shame upon the whole family. Thus, as the seven brothers are being dragged off, one at a time, to torture and death, we read: "Those who were left behind said to each of the brothers who were being dragged away, 'Do not put us to shame, brother, or betray the brothers who have died before us'" (4 Macc 13:18). Sibling solidarity extends deeply into the consciousness of the PKG mentality.

The PKG commitment to protect family honor most tangibly manifests itself when the group is in some way threatened by outsiders. Judas Maccabees urges his followers to "risk their lives with him to aid their brethren" (2 Macc 11:7). Josephus offers "fraternal affection" as the driving force behind Herod's attempt to acquire money from the Arabs in order to ransom his brother Phasael from Antigonus and his Parthian allies (*J. W.* 1.274-76).

Similar convictions concerning sibling loyalty prevail in Roman literature. Social chaos was particularly pronounced during events surrounding the establishment of the Second Triumvirate. Plutarch discusses several highly regrettable instances of kinship treachery resulting from the ensuing proscriptions. Lepidus, for example, was "given the privilege of having his own brother Paulus executed" (*Ant.* 19). Also among those destined for destruction was Mark Antony's uncle Lucius Caesar, who took refuge in the home of his sister, Antony's mother. Plutarch's description of the ensuing events presents Lucius's sister as a paradigm of what a sibling is to be in PKG society:

> When the murderers broke into her house and tried to force their way into her room, she stood in front of the door barring their entrance, and stretching out her hands, cried aloud, "It was I who brought Antony, your general, into the world, and you shall not kill Lucius Caesar unless you kill me first." By this action she succeeded in getting her brother Lucius out of the way and saved his life. (*Ant.* 20)

To summarize our discussion of sibling solidarity in the face of threats to one's family, in ancient Mediterranean society one should be "ashamed" of "rejecting the appeal of a kinsman" (Sir 41:21).

Another obligation comes into play when an enemy actually succeeds in harming a family member: swift retribution. Stories of revenge exacted on behalf of a sibling captured the minds of ancient Mediterranean readers. Brothers Jonathan and Simon later avenge the blood of their brother John (1 Macc 9:35-42). Herod beheads the rebel general Pappus to avenge the death of his brother Joseph (Josephus, *J. W.* 1.331-42). Unable to apprehend directly brigands who are terrorizing Trachonitis, Herod begins killing off their relatives. This only further aggravates the brigands, who become even more reckless and violent in their raids on Herod's territory because "it is a law among them to take vengeance at any cost on the slayers of their kinsmen" (Josephus, *Ant.* 16.277). Old Testament narratives of kinship retribution found new writers to retell their sagas. Levi and Simeon destroy Shechem and Hamor because of the shame they brought upon the family by defiling Dinah (*T. Levi* 6; *Jub.* 30:1-6). Abraham goes after the kidnappers of Lot, his "brother's son" (*Jub.* 13:22-24).

We find similar cases in Greek and Roman sources. Tacitus records two markedly different popular reactions to Augustus's aggressive assumption of imperial power. Some in Rome gave the emperor the benefit of the doubt, since Octavian was "taking vengeance on his father's murderers" in the war against Antony (*Ann.* 1.9). Others, perhaps reflecting Tacitus's own convictions, cynically replied, "Filial duty and State necessity were merely assumed as a mask" (*Ann.* 1.10). For our purposes the difference is immaterial. The fact that one could appeal, honestly or deceitfully, to filial duty to avenge the murder of a blood relative clearly demonstrates the importance of this value in Roman aristocratic society.

The paramount importance of avenging one's kin in Roman society finds graphic illustration among the restless legions on the perimeter of the empire during the early years of Tiberius's reign. Among the mutinous leaders in Pannonia was one Vibulenus, a common soldier who claimed that Blaesus, his legionary commander, had unjustly put his brother to death and "flung aside his corpse." Vibulenus succeeds in stirring up the indignation of the soldiers, a centurion is murdered, and two legions face off against each other before the uprising is finally quelled when it is discovered that Vibulenus never had a brother at all (Tacitus, *Ann.* 1.22-23).

Another aspect of the preservation of family honor is the concealing of faults and family secrets. The fascinating issue of truth telling and lying in PKG cultures represents an expression of PKG solidarity that is quite foreign to most Westerners. Much evidence suggests that, as the family related to outsiders, preservation of honor was a value held in higher esteem than truth telling in situations in which one or the other had to be compromised. The protagonist in the Ahiqar legend cares for the heir to the throne "as a man would care for his own brother," even employing falsehood and deceit in order to protect and advance his honor (*Ahiqar* 45; 70). And the author of the *Testament of Joseph* goes far beyond his Genesis source material when he portrays Joseph lying about his origins to the Ishmaelites (and again later to Pentephris) in order to protect his brothers' honor (10.6–11.3). Indeed, a large portion of the *Testament of Joseph* is consumed with the theme of safeguarding the reputation of one's brothers (chaps. 10–18). A key part of true brotherhood, concludes Joseph to his sons, is to "conceal one another's shortcomings" (17:2).

Joseph is hardly unique in his sentiments. The *Testament of Gad* similarly enjoins, "In a dispute do not let an outsider hear your secrets" (6:5). In *2 Enoch* 71, brothers Nir and Noe (biblical Noah) conspire together to conceal the untimely death of Nir's wife from the people. One may lie to outsiders, if necessary, in order to preserve family honor, but one must tell the truth to members of the PKG. As Sirach exhorts, "Do not devise a lie against your brother" (7:12). Correspondingly, it is hatred itself that, "if a brother makes a false step, immediately wants to spread the tale to everyone, and is eager to have him condemned" (*T. Gad* 4:3). One of the evil "spirits of error" about which Reuben warns his sons is a spirit that tempts a person to engage in "lying . . . even with his relatives and his household" (*T. Reub.* 3:5).

Incidents such as those described above elicit some rather striking generalizations about the insider-outsider mentality that characterizes patrilineal kinship groups:

> Honor is always presumed to exist within one's family of blood, i.e., among all those one has as blood relatives. A person can always trust his blood relatives. Outside that circle, all people are presumed to be dishonorable, guilty, if you will, unless proven otherwise. It is with all these others that one must play the game, engage in the contest, put one's own honor and one's family honor on the line. Thus no one outside the family of blood can be trusted until and unless that trust can be validated and verified.[31]

Malina's observations are confirmed by Juliet du Boulay in her fascinating study—entitled "Lies, Mockery and Family Integrity"—of a small village located on an island off Greece.[32] The exclusive orientation of each individual's loyalty toward his or her own family members results in a certain adversarial relationship between the families in the village, as each kin group vies to maintain and augment its own honor. The practical result, again, is a value system that is highly foreign to the

Western mind-set, one in which the protection of family honor must take precedence over telling the truth where the two inevitably intersect: "Because the truth of the honour of his family is to the villager a reality much more important than the factual truth of what has actually happened, the lesser truth of the pragmatic event is manipulated to clear the way for the greater truth of family honour to appear."[33] This ultimately entails a redefinition of truth as it is typically understood by Enlightenment-influenced Westerners:

> Thus it appears that the villager lives according to two standards of truth which mirror the two ways in which he experiences honour. Because of the greater reality to himself of his own honour as he experiences it within his family, the truth for himself is that he is always essentially in the right, and his business is to convince others of this. The empirical facts of his own behaviour are in such cases subordinate to the greater reality of his own honour, and may be concealed or manipulated at will.[34]

Deceit, then, is understood as a legitimate means by which family honor is preserved and the prosperity of the home is maintained. Indeed, one villager told the ethnographer that lying can save a house from utter catastrophe. Then she added emphatically, "God wants people to cover things up."[35]

A final value at the heart of Mediterranean convictions about sibling relationships involves the expectation that family members will share their material resources. Ultimately, the term "resources" constitutes a broader category than merely material goods like food, clothing, and shelter. Military power and strength (for example, the ability to meet one's obligation to protect or avenge one's kin) are also resources shared among PKG members. Here, however, we focus more narrowly on the material resources necessary for daily life.

Anthropologists have helpfully organized the exchange of such resources in society—whether among blood relatives or otherwise—under the rubric of reciprocity. Generalized reciprocity, characteristic of the PKG, and the most other-centered form of reciprocity, shares resources without specification of some return obligation in terms of time, quantity, or quality. The converse expression of generalized reciprocity is the willingness to refrain from responding in kind to injustice at the hands of a brother.

Negative reciprocity reflects the other extreme, in which "one party attempts to get something from another without really reciprocating at all."[36] The model shown in figure 2.4, adopted from Malina and slightly edited here, displays how reciprocity functions in various social settings:[37]

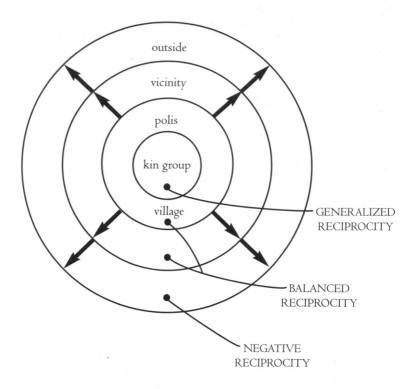

Fig. 2.4. Types of Reciprocity

The model uses two variables to illustrate the context in which various forms of reciprocity are exercised: (1) the quality of persons involved in a given interaction and (2) the place at which the interaction occurs. For our purposes, the first variable is the most important because in Mediterranean society the social network that most consistently reflects generalized reciprocity in the exchange of resources is the patrilineal kin group.[38]

The ancient sources confirm the above model. We are not surprised when Josephus tells us that he sent some of the spoils of his initially successful Galilean campaign to "my kinsfolk in Jerusalem" (*Life* 80-82). Pseudo-Phocylides exhorts his readers not to "fight with kinfolk about possessions" (206). And since community of goods among blood relatives is the assumed norm, to act "arrogantly for the sake of riches and gain" against one's "near kin" is treachery at its worst (CD 8.6-7). By contrast, Jacob is commended in the book of *Jubilees* because "he sent to his father, Isaac, some of all his possessions: clothing, and food, and meat, and drink, and milk, and butter, and cheese, and some dates of the valley . . . everything which he sent to his father and mother from time to time, all of their needs" (29:14-20).

The Book of Tobit provides still more material. The kinship terminology in the passage below identifies the circle of siblings as the assumed social environment in which such generalized reciprocity was exercised:

> In the days of Shalmaneser I performed many acts of charity to my brethren. I would give my bread to the hungry and my clothing to the naked; and if I saw any one of my people dead . . . I would bury him. (1:16-17; see also 2:1-2)[39]

The narrative is full of instances in which Tobit's own blood relatives exercise care and share resources with one another. When Tobit is blinded, his brother's son Ahikar cares for him (1:22; 2:10). Tobit's son Tobias travels to the village of a certain Raguel, a man identified as Tobit's "relative." More "than any other man," Tobias is "entitled to [Raguel's family] inheritance" because of the proximity of the blood relationship (6:9-12). When Raguel first learned of this consanguine bond, he and his immediately family "received them [Tobias and company] very warmly; and they killed a ram from the flock and set large servings of food before them" (7:8).

A most striking example of generalized reciprocity as a PKG value occurs with the alleged treaty made between Areios, King of Sparta, and the Judean priest Onias in the early third century B.C.E. Both Josephus and the author of 1 Maccabees (12:20-23) make it clear that a blood relationship envisioned between Spartans and Judeans demands as its tangible expression the sharing of material resources. Josephus narrates, quoting the Spartan king, "The Jews and the Lacedaemonians are of one race and are related by descent from Abraham. It is right, therefore, that you as our brothers should send to us to make known whatever you may wish. We also shall do this, and shall consider what is yours as our own, and what is ours we shall also share with you" (*Ant.* 12.226-27). The sharing of resources among "brothers" is an assumed norm in PKG culture. In 1 Maccabees, the king is even more specific: "We on our part write to you that your cattle and your property belong to us, and ours belong to you" (12:23).

Generalized reciprocity involves more than just the sharing of resources. As mentioned above, it has a distinct complement—the willingness to refrain from avenging a wrong suffered at the hands of a brother. Just as one expects nothing in return when one *gives* to a brother in need, neither does one *return* in kind an injustice perpetrated by a fellow family member. To be sure, forgiving treachery at the hands of a brother is exceedingly difficult because of the depth of the trust betrayed. When Jephthah's family, which had previously driven him away, seeks his aid, he bemoans, "Does love so return after hatred, or does time conquer all things?" (Ps.-Philo, *Bib. Ant.* 39:4).

The author of yet another rewrite of the Joseph saga would answer Jephthah with a resounding "Yes"—brother must reconcile with brother. The second half of the engaging romance *Joseph and Aseneth* depends greatly on the ideal of PKG sibling solidarity for its narrative appeal. As the reader discovers, the willingness to reconcile with an estranged brother is the very value that provides the narrative with its effective ending (*Jos. and Asen.* 28:9-14). Here, then, is yet another graphic reflection of the generalized reciprocity so central to the PKG family model.

Willingness to refrain from avenging a wrong suffered at the hands of a brother surfaces again and again as a PKG given. One writer, in fact, draws upon this very assumption to warn his readers to keep their distance from sibling quarrels: "For they are brothers, and they will be reconciled; but as for you, they despise you in their minds" (*Syr. Men.* 133-38). The protagonist of *Testament of Zebulon* enjoins, "Do not calculate a wrong done by each to his brothers. This shatters unity, and scatters all kinship" (8:5-6). The power inherent among siblings who have made amends can accomplish nearly anything. According to a second-century collection of sayings, "Jesus said: 'If two make peace with each other in the same house, they shall say to the mountain, Be removed! and it will be removed'" (*Gosp. Thom.* 48). We will see later that Jesus communities, too, assumed this ideal of sibling reconciliation as an important part of their surrogate PKG mentality. The value of generalized reciprocity, then, which guarantees PKG members access to family resources, also assures them that, if they are truly remorseful, they will be forgiven any injustice they perpetrate against their brothers.

Finally, the ultimate expression of weakness or helplessness—death itself—presented blood relatives with a very specific responsibility toward the deceased, namely, a decent burial. Literature from Mediterranean antiquity is full of descriptions of brothers burying brothers, sons burying fathers, and so forth, many at the risk of their own lives (*Jub.* 4:29; 23:107; 36:1-2; Tob. 4:3-4; Jdt 8:3; 2 Macc 12:39; and so forth). Pheroras, for example, attempts to purchase the corpse of his brother Joseph from his archenemy and brother's murderer, Antigonus, so that he can give Joseph a proper burial (Josephus, *J. W.* 1.325). Most of our extant examples of Judean testamentary literature conclude their narratives with the burial of the respective patriarch (*T. Job* 52; *T. Reub.* 7; *T. Sim.* 8; *T. Levi* 19; and so forth). Simon Maccabees went to great lengths to provide an elaborate burial place, fashioned after Hellenistic models, for his family (1 Macc 13:25-30).

To be unable to bury one's kin, on the other hand, was a source of great distress.[40] Josephus underlines the horrors surrounding a riot that broke out in Jerusalem under Florus's governorship by observing that the bodies of the trampled Judean victims "were so disfigured that their relatives could not recognize them to give them a decent burial" (*J. W.* 2.327-28). Later, during the Roman siege of Jerusalem, the breakdown in the social order was such that Zealot tyrants in the city "carried barbarity so far as to grant internment to none" (*J.W.* 4.380).

Finally, even when the opportunity for burial did ultimately present itself, famine-induced weakness prevented people from providing their own with a decent burial (*J. W.* 5.512-14).

Elsewhere, Josephus unequivocally informs us that "the funeral ceremony is to be undertaken by the nearest relatives" (*Ag. Ap.* 2.205). This inviolable duty of burying one's relatives in a PKG society is precisely the background that makes the following passage so radically countercultural: "Another of his disciples said to him, 'Lord, first let me go and bury my father.' But Jesus said to him, 'Follow me, and let the dead bury their own dead'" (Matt 8:21-22).

Ancestors and Inheritance

The last two aspects of patrilineal kin group structure to be examined—ancestor veneration and inheritance practices—are not unrelated to each other. In a helpful attempt to clarify the basic distinctions differentiating American kindred groups from descent group family structures, Sherwood Lingenfelter contrasts the "horizontal focus" so endemic to the West with the "vertical focus" reflected in the kinship orientation of peoples from Mediterranean antiquity.[41] This horizontal orientation of Westerners— Americans in particular—means that we are typically preoccupied with relationships among family members who are living in the present. Members of kindred groups seldom devote any serious reflection to their ancestral origins. Nor are we particularly preoccupied with inheritance, beyond the desire individually to receive our fair share of our parents' estates. The idea of preserving an extended family's estate intact for the next generation is an increasingly rare concern in American society.

The vertical focus of Mediterranean society guarantees a wholly different outlook. Augmenting—at times even supplanting—attention to present family relationships is a preoccupation with the past and the future of the patrilineal kin group. Focus on the past manifests itself in the ubiquitous concern with one's ancestors that is so characteristic of Mediterranean society. Future orientation revolves around making arrangements for the proper distribution of family inheritance. At work in each case is the descent group view of the family as a corporation that takes priority over, and survives the demise of, its individual members. Both the constant appeal to family ancestry and the preoccupation with inheritance reflect the broader concern for the survival of the kin group and the retention of the family's honor in the community.

PREOCCUPATION WITH ANCESTORS

One cannot read far into the pages of any work of ancient literature without encountering information about the ancestry of the protagonist. The Gospel of

Matthew begins with "an account of the genealogy of Jesus the Messiah, the son of David, the son of Abraham" (1:1). The segments of Plutarch's *Parallel Lives* typically begin with an overview of the ancestry of the renowned figure in view (for example, *Sull.* 1; *Mar.* 1–3; *Marc.* 1; *Cat. Mai.* 1; *Ti. Gracch.* 1). The biographies of Suetonius take a similar approach. As Kenneth Hanson properly observes, family honor is the driving force behind the inclusion in the literature of genealogies and all such references to the ancestry of characters in the narrative. His study of the Herodian genealogies is illustrative.[42] By way of example, we find Plutarch discussing the debated patriline of Marcus Brutus, one of the conspirators in the murder of Julius Caesar. For obvious reasons, Brutus's ancestry is traditionally traced back to Junius Brutus, who succeeded in dethroning the Tarquin kings. Plutarch cites Poseidonius as his source in this regard. Some people, however, as Plutarch proceeds to explain to his readers, entertain a different view:

> The people who bear him most hatred and ill will on account of Caesar's murder argue that [his ancestry] cannot possibly be traced back to the Brutus who drove out the Tarquins, because after he had killed his sons he was left without issue. According to them, Marcus Brutus was descended from a plebeian, who was the son of a steward of that name, and had only recently risen to office. (*Brut.* 1)

At stake, of course, is the degree of honor to be ascribed to Brutus as a result of his patriline.

At a higher level of abstraction, however, preoccupation with ancestry—particularly ancestor veneration—highlights yet another important aspect of ancient Mediterranean family systems that contrasts markedly with our contemporary Western approach, namely, the inseparable nature of religion and kinship characteristic of descent group structure and orientation. As anthropologist Roger Keesing notes, "Descent groups are very often religious congregations as well as secular corporations. That is, *lineage ancestors are a spiritual focus of the group.* Often they are propitiated by sacrifice."[43] Note the close connection between family and religion, between one's ancestors and one's religious orientation, reflected in the italicized text above. Our Western tendency to isolate religion from kinship, and correspondingly to understand religious commitment in highly individualistic terms, hinders our ability truly to appreciate the PKG, where we find religion and family inextricably woven together. And more is at work here than simply an obligation on the part of the individual to adopt the religion of her parents. Indeed, the individual has little to say in the matter at all. Rather, one's birth into a particular family guarantees a religious orientation that expresses itself, among other ways, in various degrees of preoccupation with one's ancestors. For some descent group societies, this ancestor focus takes on overtly religious overtones (note Keesing's comments, above, concerning the propitiation of ancestors by sacrifice).

Ancestor worship as such does not seem to have found a place in ancient Mediterranean society, although some have argued that the cult of the *lar familiaris*, a spirit or deity that offered household protection, is to be understood as an expression of a cult of the dead, that is, involving the propitiation of the family's ancestors.[44] It remains the case, however, that both in the Greco-Roman world and among the Judeans of antiquity, religion and kinship are closely bound together, and that this connection is reflected in the fact, as Keesing suggests above, that "lineage ancestors are the spiritual focus of the group." To be sure, this is most apparent in Judean family systems. The Judeans' blood relationship to their ancestor Abraham, and to Abraham's early descendants Isaac, Jacob, and Jacob's sons, assured Judeans that they were truly the people of God.

Nowhere is the connection between ancestor veneration and spiritual orientation more clearly evidenced than in the following text (circa second century C.E.). An angel from the Lord pronounces a blessing upon the patriarch Jacob. The author's intent, however, is obviously to exhort the reader to give her ancestors their proper place:

> Blessed are you, O Israel, and blessed is all your progeny. For all of you will be called "the patriarchs" to the end of the age and of the epochs; you are the people and the lineage of the servants of God. Blessed be the nation which will strive for your purity and will see your good works. Blessed be the man who will remember you on the day of your noble festival. Blessed be the one who will perform acts of mercy in honor of your several names. . . . Such a one shall neither lack any of the good things of this world, nor life everlasting in the world to come. Moreover, whoever shall have caused to be written the stories of your several lives and sufferings at his own expense, or shall have written them by his own hand, or shall have read them soberly, or shall hear them in faith, or shall remember your deeds—such persons will have their sins forgiven and their trespasses pardoned, and they will go on account of you and your progeny into the kingdom of heaven. (*T. Jac.* 2:19-25)

Among the Romans, as well, we find ancestry and religion closely related. Robert Wilken suggests that the Roman value of *pietas* best reflects this connection between family and religion.[45] Carl Koch observes, "Separation of the concept of piety into a familial and a cultic half is clearly a product of modern sensibilities; in antiquity piety formed a unity."[46] Revealing in this regard is the pagan Symmachus's plea to the Christian emperor Valentinian II to restore the altar of Victory in the Senate house in 384 C.E. Extolling the religious rites that made Rome the power she had become, Symmachus exclaims, "We must keep faith with so many centuries and we must follow our fathers, who followed their fathers and therefore prospered" (*Disp. Emp.* 3.8-10). Cicero's comments similarly reaffirm the connection between faith and family: "The preservation of the rites of the family and of our ancestors means preserving the religious rites which, we can almost say, were handed down to us by the gods themselves, since ancient times were closest to the gods" (*Leg.* 2.10.27). One's ancestors and one's ancestral faith, then, are closely intertwined.

The following text aptly illustrates the two key aspects of the PKG focus upon ancestors. Both the appeal to ancestry in defense of family honor and the preoccupation with ancestry as a reflection of the close connection between religion and kinship find striking expression in the course of the following dialogue from the Gospel of John (8:18-44):

> 18 [Jesus speaking] "I testify on my own behalf, and the Father who sent me testifies on my behalf." 19 Then they said to him, "Where is your Father?" Jesus answered, "You know neither me nor my Father. If you knew me, you would know my Father also." . . . 33 They answered him, "We are descendants of Abraham and have never been slaves to anyone." . . . 37 "I know that you are descendants of Abraham; yet you look for an opportunity to kill me, because there is no place in you for my word. 38 I declare what I have seen in the Father's presence; as for you, you should do what you have heard from the Father." 39 They answered him, "Abraham is our father." Jesus said to them, "If you were Abraham's children, you would be doing what Abraham did, 40 but now you are trying to kill me, a man who has told you the truth that I heard from God. This is not what Abraham did. 41 You are indeed doing what your father does." They said to him, "We are not illegitimate children; we have one father, God himself." 42 Jesus said to them, "If God were your Father, you would love me, for I came from God and now I am here. I did not come on my own, but he sent me. 43 Why do you not understand what I say? It is because you cannot accept my word. 44 You are from your father the devil, and you choose to do your father's desires."

Notice, first of all, the appeal to ancestry as a claim to honor. The reader finds Jesus claiming the highest of ancestry and, therefore, the highest of honor—his father is God. His adversaries counter with aspersions concerning his apparent illegitimacy (vv. 19 and 41), thus blatantly challenging his claim to honor. Jesus ultimately responds by assigning to his adversaries an ancestry worse than illegitimacy—their father is "the devil" (v. 44). This public challenge-riposte scenario is a common one in agonistic, honor-shame societies, and it would have been highly engrossing to the Mediterranean reader.[47] Pertinent here, however, is the central focus of the exchange—the appeal to ancestry and family orientation as a basis for public honor.

But there is more. Already the reader begins to sense a connection in the mind of the evangelist between physical lineage and spiritual ancestry. Even at the outset, the interchange alternates quite naturally between comments about Jesus' physical origins ("Where is your Father?"[48]) and his relationship to God ("my Father") (v. 19). Later in the narrative, this bond between kinship and religion becomes patently visible, for underlying the ensuing discussion is the assumption on the part of both parties that to be legitimate children of Abraham is to be legitimate children of God (see v. 39, "Abraham is our father," and v. 41, "we have one father, God himself").

A final aspect of the preoccupation with ancestors comes into view in two of the above citations. In descent group societies, one is expected to emulate the character and deeds of one's ancestors. Indeed, it is expected that a son will naturally be like his father in character and appearance. It is assumed among the peoples of Mediterranean antiquity that "the man who has produced of himself one like him has achieved fulfillment—even more when he sees the other having followed in his footsteps too, in other words, when he has established a child in the same natural place as the father" (Clem. Al., *Strom.* 2.139.5). Thus Brutus acts in accord with his ancestry when he, like Junius Brutus before him, confronts one who would dare to reign as king over the Roman people. Similarly, Jesus tells his opponents, "If you were Abraham's children, you would be doing what Abraham did" (John 8:39).

As a closing illustration, we offer Cicero's appeal to the populace on behalf of Pompey's potential commission to fight Mithridates VI. In a flourish of persuasive rhetoric, Cicero reminds his audience of their ancestors' unwillingness to tolerate foreign aggression and of their corresponding responsibility to act in like manner. He then concludes:

> The verbal infringement of an envoy's privilege caused those ancestors of yours to retaliate. Your envoy, on the other hand, has been subjected to multiple agonies culminating in actual murder—and are you going to pay no attention? Your ancestors won themselves glory by the magnificent empire they handed down to you. See to it that you do not earn a corresponding load of shame by failing to protect and safeguard the heritage you have received as their gift. (*Leg. Man.* 40)

PREOCCUPATION WITH INHERITANCE

Mirroring the past orientation of the PKG value system, which is reflected in the preoccupation with ancestors outlined above, is a concern for the future of the kin group that expresses itself, at one level, in highly formalized rules and guidelines for the distribution of family inheritance. Inheritance is defined by Hanson as "the disposition of movable and immovable property, most commonly at the death of the male head of the family."[49] Dowry is also to be included under the rubric of inheritance, for Jack Goody has shown that dowry is best understood as premortem inheritance given to daughters when they marry.[50]

Hanson provides an insightful overview of the similarities and differences between ancient Israelite, Attic Greek, Hellenistic, Roman, and Mishnaic laws of inheritance. For example, Israelite laws of inheritance, picked up and modified in late Judaism, designated a double portion for the eldest son (Deut 21:17; *m. B. Bat.* 8:3-5). The same was true in Nuzi and Old Babylonia, but not in Greece or Rome, where a more egalitarian approach prevailed.[51] The specifics of inheritance law and practice in ancient societies are somewhat immaterial for our purposes. When used in a metaphorical sense by Jesus' followers, inheritance imagery inevitably becomes rather general in nature. An awareness of the ubiquitous concern about inheritance in the writings of ancient Mediterraneans remains important, however, since the early Christians often employ inheritance terminology as a part of their kin group concept.

Texts dealing with inheritance may be divided into two categories: legal texts and narrative material. Old Testament legislation and narrative, respectively, provide an illustrative example of the interplay between these two genres of literature. Much of the Torah is preoccupied with the division of land among the tribes, clans, and families of Israel during the period of the conquest of Palestine. The semantic concept central to this land division is that of inheritance.[52] For the ancient Israelite, this allotment constituted his ancestral inheritance. It was publicly delineated by means of visible physical boundary markers. Consequently, moving a neighbor's boundary marker to increase one's acreage was forbidden by Israelite law (Deut 19:14). Elsewhere in Deuteronomy we read, "Cursed be anyone who moves a neighbor's boundary marker" (27:17). These sentiments find expression in later literature, as well. Among the revelations granted the scribe-become-seer Ezra is a vision of a man suffering eternal torment because he "transferred boundaries" (*Gk. Ap. Ez.* 5:26).[53]

The desire to retain one's landed inheritance serves as the opening theme for an engaging Old Testament narrative. The story begins with what appears to be a rather innocuous request on the part of Israel's king:

> Naboth the Jezreelite had a vineyard in Jezreel, beside the palace of King Ahab of Samaria. And Ahab said to Naboth, "Give me your vineyard, so that I may have it for a vegetable garden, because it is near my house; I will give you a better vineyard for it; or, if it seems good to you, I will give you its value in money." (1 Kings 21:1-2)

Western Kindred Groups	Patrilineal Descent Groups
How Family Is Defined	
Family viewed in terms of relationship via childbirth and/or marriage. Individual regards as family those living persons who are related to her or him within an arbitrary limit of time (a few generations up or down) and extent (cousins usually included).	Family viewed in terms of consanguinity—sharing the blood of a common ancestor. Individual regards as family all persons—living or deceased—with whom he or she shares a common male ancestor. Only males can pass family blood on to next generation.
Marriage	
Marriage is understood relationally. A good marriage is one that proves mutually satisfying to the two individuals involved.	Marriage is understood contractually. A good marriage is one that enhances the honor of the extended family system.
Women	
A daughter is free to marry as she wishes. She and her spouse together establish a new nuclear family unit. She views herself—and is viewed by others—as a member of her new family.	A daughter is married out of her own kinship group into a family to which she can never truly belong. Her primary role is to bear a son to provide for the survival of her husband's patriline.
Residence	
Persons who marry are expected to leave their parents' home to set up their own (neolocal) residence. Family is a consuming unit but typically does not share together in a corporate economic enterprise.	Members of the patrilineal descent group live together (patrilocal residence): father, sons, and unmarried daughters—along with the father's wife and the wives of his sons. The kinship group is typically a producing and consuming unit.
Key Relationships	
Tightest units of loyalty, affection, and emotional intimacy are husband-wife and parent-child relationships. Sibling relations are not expected to exhibit this degree of affection and emotional intimacy. Relational failure is epitomized in the dissolution of a marriage.	Tightest unit of loyalty and affection is the descent group of brothers and sisters. The emotional bonding characteristic of marriage in Western families is normally a mark of sibling (or mother-son) relationships in the PKG. Relational failure is epitomized in the betrayal of a sibling.
Ancestors and Inheritance	
Little concern for ancestral origins. No convictions that one's value as an individual is contingent upon the honor or achievements of one's ancestor(s). Inheritance understood individually: each child is entitled to his or her share.	Passionate preoccupation with ancestral origins. Personal honor is strongly dependent on one's ancestral lineage. Inheritance understood collectively—it belongs to the patriline as a whole and must be preserved as such.

Figure 2.5. Summary: Family Now and Then

The typical Westerner—for whom kinship and inheritance are not so inextricably intertwined—might inquire further into the precise amount the king is willing to pay for the vineyard. Perhaps the money would suffice to purchase a larger piece of land in a more desirable location. Such is our individualistic, capitalist orientation. Naboth, by contrast, sees the very future of his family at stake in Ahab's inappropriate request. He replies to the king, "The LORD forbid that I should give you my ancestral inheritance" (1 Kings 21:3).[54]

Examples of preoccupation with inheritance are also found in other narrative texts. Abraham doles out the proper allotments to Isaac and Ishmael (*Jub.* 20:11-13). Isaac later divides his belongings between Jacob and Esau (*Jub.* 36:12). Again, examples could be multiplied (for example, *T. Job* 45–47; *Jub.* 8:10–9:15; *Bib. Ant.* 4, 29; *Ahiqar* 14–22; *Ps-Phocylides* 199–200; 1 Esd 5:38-40; Tob 10:10; Jdt 8:4-8, 16:24-25; Sir 33:19-23; and so forth).[55]

It is important to keep in mind the underlying reason for this preoccupation with inheritance in Mediterranean society. Unlike our individualistically oriented Western kindred groups, the PKG model of family exhibits as a central value the survival of the extended family system beyond the demise of an individual family member. The concern for the protection and proper distribution of inheritance, then, constitutes an effort to retain the family's landed wealth and, thereby, preserve the descent group's honor in the community for the next generation.

CONCLUSION

The chart (fig. 2.5) on page 57 summarizes the patrilineal kinship values surveyed in this chapter. A citation from the *Epistle of Aristeas* forms a fitting conclusion to our survey of the common values of Mediterranean family systems. When the Ptolemaic king asks those present at a banquet, "What is the value of family?" a guest responds:

> If we think that we are afflicted with adverse circumstances, and suffer as they do, the great strength of the family bond is manifest, and when that trouble is over, glory and success will be ours in the eyes of such folk, for cooperation when given with good will is of itself indestructible in the face of everything. (241-42)

3

Origins of the Surrogate Kin Group Idea

It will prove helpful to reflect upon the origins of a distinctly Christian conception: a surrogate family whose membership transcended traditional boundaries of ethnicity, generation (patriline), and geography (fatherland).

Origins of the Early Christian Surrogate Family Model

The early Christian idea of the church as a surrogate patrilineal kin group finds its origins in the narrative of Israel's history as interpreted and mediated by Jesus of Nazareth to his first-century followers. This will become clear as we consider each of the following:

1. The concept of the people of God as reflected in the Hebrew Scriptures

2. The concept of the people of God as understood among Second Temple Judeans

3. The concept of the people of God as interpreted and mediated by Jesus of Nazareth.

The People of God in the Hebrew Scriptures

The writers of the Hebrew Scriptures drew upon a number of metaphors to portray the relationship between Yahweh and his people. Israel is pictured as a vineyard,

God as the vineyard's builder-tender (Isa 5:1-7; Jer 12:10); God the shepherd tends his flock, Israel (Pss 28:9, 80:1; Isa 40:11; Jer 31:10); and Israel's tendency to violate her covenant with God finds vivid expression in the image of God as the faithful husband of an adulterous wife (Isa 54:5; Jer 31:32; Hosea).

The concept of a surrogate family of faith—God as father to his sons and daughters, the Israelites—is not a particularly dominant one in Old Testament literature. General references to the Israelites as simply "the people of God" occur much more often (see Deut 27:9). The kin group metaphor does manifest itself, however, in a variety of passages. Those identifying the Israelites as God's children include the following:

> You are children of the LORD your God. You must not lacerate yourselves or shave your forelocks for the dead. (Deut 14:1)

> Know then in your heart that as a man disciplines his son so the LORD your God disciplines you. (Deut 8:5; Ps 82:6; Prov 3:12)

Other passages specifically identify God as the father of his people:

> Do you thus repay the LORD, O foolish and senseless people? Is not he your father, who created you, who made you and established you? (Deut 32:6)

> Father of orphans and protector of widows is God in his holy habitation. (Ps 68:5)

> He shall cry to me, "You are my Father, my God, and the Rock of my salvation!" (Ps 89:26; see also Ps 103:13; Isa 63:16; 64:8)

The image of God as father was prevalent enough that it could serve as a prophetic grounds of appeal to the Israelites to act out the norms of PKG sibling solidarity in their interpersonal relationships: "Do we not all have one father? Has not one God created us? Why do we deal treacherously each against his brother so as to profane the covenant of our fathers?" (Mal 2:10, NASB).[1] The metaphor of family, then, was one of several employed by the authors of the Hebrew Scriptures to describe the relationship of God to his people, Israel.

The relatively limited use of the metaphor of family should not lead us to conclude that a sense of PKG solidarity was lacking in early Israel. Sibling terminology surfaces again and again in Old Testament passages that describe relationships among the Israelites and their ancestors (Gen 9:5; Exod 2:11; 4:18; Num 20:3; and so forth).[2] The use of these terms, reflected in legislation such as the following, however, seems to depend more upon Israel's common blood ancestry through the patriarchs back to Abraham, and upon their shared destiny as Abraham's offspring, rather than upon any expressed idea of a surrogate family of God (Deut 15:1-3, 7-11).[3]

The brotherhood in view above assumes a blood relationship traceable back to Israel's patriarchs.[4] To the degree, however, that such solidarity is here enjoined at a level broader than clan or even tribe—that every Israelite is to treat his fellow as a brother—the sibling terminology in the text takes on a decidedly metaphorical flavor. This, in turn, provides a point of departure for the development of the exclusively metaphorical use of the term "brother"—for persons wholly unrelated by blood or *ethnos*—among the early Christians.

A much more subversive stream of reflection flows through the Old Testament, which, along with the family metaphor and the value of PKG sibling solidarity, contributed powerfully to the conceptual material that the Jesus movement used to construct its own family model. So that the reader may fully appreciate the implications of this recurring theme, I must preface its introduction with a brief discussion of later Judean nationalism.

Old Testament narrative literature concludes with a picture of Israel on the defensive against her pagan neighbors. The postexilic remnant that has reoccupied the land of Judah is acutely aware of a need to identify the people of God as an ethnic Judean assembly whose roots can be traced back by ancestry to the patriarchs. Intermarriage is forbidden (Ezra 9–10). Food laws that serve as boundary markers to facilitate Judean national identification are increasingly stressed (see Daniel 1).

Events during the Greek and Roman periods strongly reinforced this orientation. The watershed events surrounding the Maccabean revolt abruptly attenuated tendencies toward religious and cultural assimilation of Greek beliefs and behaviors, which appeared during the middle decades of the second century B.C.E. Loyalty to God and loyalty to ethnic Israel were increasingly perceived to be inseparable Judean values. To be the children of Abraham was to be the children of God.

These developments, though historically predictable, were highly ironic in light of the Old Testament theme discussed here, a theme that could (and would) serve to undermine the very idea that ethnic Israel by definition constituted the people of God: loyalty to God, for the early Israelite, was to take priority even over loyalty to one's fellow descendants of Abraham. Practically, this meant that the purity of one's ancestry did not, in and of itself, guarantee one a place among God's people.

Nowhere does this value find more graphic expression than in the familiar Exodus narrative of Israel's defection from God to worship the golden calf—a story that was to become central to Israel's self-consciousness as a people redeemed by Yahweh. Soon after Moses returns from Sinai to the camp, the conflict reaches a dramatic crescendo with Moses commanding the Levites to execute those Israelites disloyal to Yahweh (Exod 32:25-29). Here is a value dearer than consanguinity, more important than sibling solidarity: loyalty to the God of the covenant. The question, "Who is on the LORD's side?" (v. 26) could never again be answered entirely by appeal to one's physical ancestry. The sentiment reflected in the above narrative finds more formal expression in later Deuteronomic legal codification:

> If anyone secretly entices you—even if it is your brother, your father's son or your mother's son, or your own son or daughter, or the wife you embrace, or your most intimate friend—saying, "Let us go worship other gods," whom neither you nor your ancestors have known, any of the gods of the peoples that are around you, whether near you or far away from you, from one end of the earth to the other, you must not yield to or heed any such persons. Show them no pity or compassion and do not shield them. But you shall surely kill them; your own hand shall be first against them to execute them, and afterwards the hand of all the people. (Deut 13:6-9)

Again, Israelite blood does not, in and of itself, guarantee one a place among the people of God. But there is more. It is most significant that the very origins of the Israelite people, according to their sacred traditions, are to be traced back to a single individual who opted for loyalty to God over loyalty to his patriline (Gen 12:1-3). The lesson is reinforced for Abraham, in Genesis 22, when God commands him to sacrifice his only son. Isaac represents Abraham's sole hope for kinship continuity in a patrilineal society. His willingness to offer up Isaac is the ultimate testimony to the fact that Abraham's loyalty to Yahweh surpasses his commitment even to the most precious member of his natural family. Yahweh's response is revealing: "Now I know that you fear God, since you have not withheld your son, your only son, from me" (Gen 22:12).

Jesus and his followers, then, had much to work with as they constructed their model of a family of faith from the Hebrew Scriptures and their various Greek translations. The PKG metaphor is at hand. Sibling solidarity is enjoined not just for the local extended family but for all Israelites: they are to treat each other as "brothers." I suggest a conceptual door has been left open to the possibility of a people of God without blood ties to Israel's forefathers. For if a descendent of Abraham could be excluded from the people of God, could not the reverse obtain? Could not one who lacked Israelite ancestry perhaps find a place in God's family? Various prophets certainly envisioned such a day (Isa 60:3, Jer 3:17; Zech 2:11; 8:22-23; 14:16). As John the Baptist would later warn, "Do not presume to say to yourselves, 'We have Abraham as our ancestor'; for I tell you, God is able from these stones to raise up children to Abraham" (Matt 3:9).

The People of God as Understood among Second Temple Judeans

Evidence from the Second Temple period reflects an orientation similar to that uncovered in the Hebrew Scriptures. The surrogate family idea is present as is the general conviction that Jews should treat one another like PKG siblings. Finally, the theme of loyalty to God over family solidarity is even more prevalent than is the case in Old Testament literature.

First, the kinship metaphor of God as a father to his children occurs often in Second Temple literature. Note, for example, the following second century B.C.E. prediction of restoration for Israel, which cites or alludes to several Old Testament passages (Deut 14:1; Jer 31:9; Hos. 1:10):

> But after this they will return to me in all uprighteousness [*sic*] and with all of [their] heart and soul. . . . And I shall be a father to them, and they will be sons to me. And they will all be called "sons of the living God." And every angel and spirit will know and acknowledge that they are my sons and I am their father in uprightness and righteousness. (*Jub.* 1:23-25, circa 150 B.C.E.)

Elsewhere in *Jubilees*, God calls the seed of Jacob "my firstborn son" (2:20). References to God as "father" occur, as well, in 3 Maccabees (2:21) and throughout the Wisdom of Solomon (2:16-18; 5:5; 11:10; 12:19-21). A specific application of the family theme, which we observed in the Old Testament, is echoed again in the *Psalms of Solomon*: "For [the Lord] will admonish the righteous as a beloved son and his discipline is as for a firstborn" (13:9). Examples could be multiplied (see Philo, *Ab.* 12.58; Josephus, *Ant.* 5.93).

Secondly, PKG solidarity, consistently reinforced through the use of sibling terminology, is presented as the behavioral ideal for all who claim Judean ancestry. The author of Second Maccabees, for example, sends greetings from the "Jewish brethren in Jerusalem" to "their Jewish brethren in Egypt" (1:1).[5] Later in the same work, Judas is portrayed urging his soldiers to "risk their lives with him to aid their brethren" (11:7). Judith 8:22-24 also applies brother terminology to the Judean nation as a whole. I cited the Book of Tobit in the previous chapter, but the combination of kinship terms and PKG behavior in the following passage bears repeating in the present context: "In the days of Shalmaneser I performed many acts of charity to my brethren. I would give my bread to the hungry and my clothing to the naked; and if I saw any one of my people dead and thrown out behind the wall of Nineveh, I would bury him" (Tob 1:16-17).

Finally, we find again in Second Temple texts the conviction that loyalty to God must take precedence over loyalty to family in situations in which one or the other must be compromised. The priorities are clearly alluded to by the author of *Pseudo-Phocylides* (circa first century B.C.E. to first century C.E.): "Honor God foremost, and afterward your parents" (8). Josephus similarly observes, "Honour to parents the Law ranks second only to honour to God" (*Ag. Ap.* 2.206). Perhaps scholars are correct to trace the form in which the commandments from the decalogue are combined in these two citations back to corresponding expressions in Greek ethics.[6] But the value itself has already been identified in Old Testament texts. These traditions are now picked up and rewritten by Second Temple authors. The author(s) of Qumran's Temple Scroll (circa first century B.C.E.), in fact, cite verbatim portions of the Deuteronomic legislation (Deut 13:6-9) discussed above (11QT 54.20).

Not only are relevant Old Testament texts rewritten for a new audience, but Second Temple authors spin off new tales acclaiming the great virtue of individuals who choose allegiance to God over commitment to family. And the Judeans are not alone among the faithful. The story of *Joseph and Asenath* (circa first century B.C.E. to second century C.E.) includes at the heart of its narrative the pilgrimage of the proselyte Asenath, who opts for allegiance to Joseph's God over the objections of her Egyptian family. The heroine takes consolation in the fact that she now has a new father, and she implores God to receive her into his family: "Therefore I will take courage too and turn to [the God of the Hebrews]. . . . Perhaps he will . . . see my orphanage and protect me, because he is the father of the orphans." (11:11-13; see also 12:7-8, 15).

Second Temple literature thus reflects the same threefold background that we found in the Old Testament: (1) A number of writers utilize the metaphor of the family of God; (2) sibling solidarity is expected among the Judeans, who regard one another as "brothers"; and finally, (3) the priority of loyalty to God over loyalty to family is reiterated and exemplified again and again. These, then, are the symbolic tools with which Jesus had to work as he hammered out his own vision for the people of God. I now turn to this vision.

The People of God according to Jesus of Nazareth

A discussion of Jesus' understanding of the people of God inevitably runs the risk of digressing into the almost infinite maze of Gospel scholarship produced since the beginning of the Enlightenment. This would take us far afield from the topic at hand. Nevertheless, a word needs to be said here about my convictions concerning the historical reliability of the Gospel traditions.

Two closely related—and hotly debated—issues immediately confront anyone who desires to draw upon the Gospel literature in order to discuss the views of Jesus on the topic at hand. The issues can be framed in question form as follows:

1. Did Jesus ever intend to form a distinct community of followers? Or was the Jesus movement simply a renewal movement that intended to influence the contours of Palestinian Jewish thought and behavior in general?

2. Do the Gospel pericopes relating Jesus' teachings about community reflect the ideas of the historical Jesus? Or do they constitute the creative production of the post-Easter Christ-confessing communities?

These questions, of course, mutually inform each other. For if Jesus did not establish an ongoing community among his followers, then the question of the historicity of the Gospel materials portraying him in such a light must also be answered negatively.

Nearly every conceivable response to these questions can claim a defender among Jesus scholars, and even a cursory survey of the literature is beyond the scope of this book. Instead, I will simply present my own position on the issues in order to clarify my perspective on the Gospel accounts.

I am convinced that Jesus intended to form a distinct community of followers and that the Gospel sayings and narratives that reflect Jesus' understanding of the nature of that community genuinely reflect the convictions of the historical Jesus. It is unfortunately also beyond the scope of this book to adequately deal with the tradition history of the relevant passages on a text-by-text basis. Suffice it to say that numerous scholars take an optimistic approach to the historicity of those texts that reveal Jesus' ideas about community—my position is hardly iconoclastic.[7] We will now reflect upon the social structure of these groups as Jesus envisioned them.

Several Gospel passages are foundational for a proper understanding of Jesus' idea of community. Although already presented in a previous chapter, the following passage is paramount and bears repeating here:

> Then his mother and his brothers came; and standing outside, they sent to him and called him. A crowd was sitting around him; and they said to him, "Your mother and your brothers and sisters are outside, asking for you." And he replied, "Who are my mother and my brothers?" And looking at those who sat around him, he said, "Here are my mother and my brothers! Whoever does the will of God is my brother and sister and mother." (Mark 3:31-35; par. Matt 12:46-50; Luke 8:19-21).

Already we find Jesus adopting and reworking at least two themes found in Old Testament and Second Temple literature: the kinship metaphor and the priority of loyalty to God over commitment to one's family. Our survey of Mediterranean family systems in the previous chapter should render observations about the scandalous nature of the above citation wholly unnecessary. The passage has received appropriate attention from social historians and commentators concerned to highlight the radical nature of Jesus' statements.[8] It will suffice to note that the community Jesus envisions (one that, indeed, he assumes is already gathering around him) constitutes a surrogate kinship group, for which membership depends upon obedience to God, not upon one's patriline. Moreover, according to the example publicly provided by Jesus himself, membership in his faith family demands a group loyalty transcending one's blood family commitment. These emphases reappear throughout the Gospel accounts.[9] For example, the loyalty theme has already confronted Mark's readers in an earlier pericope. Followers of Jesus must be willing to leave their families (Mark 1:14-20).

To abandon one's father ranks right alongside treachery against a sibling as the ultimate in PKG betrayal. Note the position of Mark 1:16-20 in the narrative flow of Mark's Gospel. It stands near the beginning of the work, immediately following Jesus' programmatic call to repentance and faith in verse 15. For Mark, to respond to the basic outline of Jesus' message to Israel is to be willing to leave one's father and one's source of economic security in order to follow Jesus—and to do so "immediately" (v. 20). Moreover, Jesus assumes that such a shift of loyalties will result in significant relational fallout. He foresees the day when "brother will betray brother to death, and a father his child, and children will rise against parents and have them put to death; and you will be hated by all because of my name. But the one who endures to the end will be saved" (Mark 13:12-13).

Elsewhere in Mark, a prominent character in the narrative discovers that his new family of God is intended to provide for his material and relational needs in a manner identical to the very Mediterranean kin group he had left in order to become a follower of Jesus:

> Peter began to say to him, "Look, we have left everything and followed you." Jesus said, "Truly I tell you, there is no one who has left house or brothers or sisters or mother or father or children or fields, for my sake and for the sake of the good news, who will not receive a hundredfold now in this age—houses, brothers and sisters, mothers and children, and fields with persecutions—and in the age to come eternal life" (Mark 10:28-30).

According to the most straightforward reading of the passage, Jesus here assumes his followers will relate to one another according to the standards of solidarity shared by families in Mediterranean antiquity, standards that we surveyed in the previous chapter. Jesus promises Peter, who left his own family to follow him, that Peter will enjoy sibling-like relationships with others who have made such a sacrifice ("brothers and sisters, mothers and children") and find life's necessary physical resources—such as shelter ("houses") and food ("fields")—in the context of the new community.

The basic contours of Jesus' surrogate kinship model, therefore, mirror much of what we uncovered in Old Testament and Second Temple literature. In each case, we find the family metaphor, PKG behavior expressed in generalized reciprocity, and the priority of loyalty to God over loyalty to family explicitly referenced. A brief survey of other Gospel texts reflecting these themes is now in order.

Several passages in Mark, though lacking overt application of kinship terminology in a metaphorical sense, nevertheless reflect an assumed PKG metaphor on the part of Jesus and his followers. The narrative of Jesus' last meal with his disciples in Mark 14 is illustrative. According to Old Testament traditions, the Passover meal was to be celebrated as a family event (Exod 12:3-27; Josephus, *Ant.* 11.109; *m. Pes.* 10.4).

Jesus' celebration of Passover with his disciples is attested in each of the four Gospels (Mark 14; Matthew 26; Luke 22; John 13). The Old Testament and rabbinic sources help us to see the shared meal as a kinship event. The sharing of the meal by Jesus and his disciples clearly reflects their perception of their community as a surrogate family.

The presentation of events surrounding the burial of Jesus, described in Mark 15, also assumes the surrogate PKG idea (Mark 15:43, 45-46). I have previously identified the proper burial of a deceased family member as an indispensable PKG duty. Mediterranean families, ideally, were to bury their own. A kinship relationship between Jesus and Joseph would therefore be assumed by any reader of the above text-segment who shared the cultural values of ancient Mediterranean society.

I close my survey of Jesus' concept of the community he established with some comments about what is perhaps the most obvious evidence for a surrogate family relationship between God, Jesus, and his followers. Again and again, directly and indirectly, Jesus refers to God using father terminology. Much debate has centered around Jesus' use of a particular term of address to God that is reflected in Mark 14:36: *Abba.* The English translation provides a transliteration of the contested term: [Jesus] said, "*Abba,* Father, for you all things are possible; remove this cup from me; yet, not what I want, but what you want." Various writers have commented upon Jesus' personal religious experience based on this passage.[10] More pertinent to my purposes than a reconstruction of the religious affections of Jesus is his repeated usage of the father metaphor to describe God in relationship to Jesus' new community of followers.

The father (*pater*) word group occurs eighteen times in Mark's Gospel. Four times the term is used figuratively to refer to God. The following teaching of Jesus on the subject of prayer is representative: "Whenever you stand praying, forgive, if you have anything against anyone; so that your Father in heaven may also forgive you your trespasses" (Mark 11:25). The idea is even more prevalent in the other Gospel accounts. Perhaps most representative of the ethical teaching of Jesus is what has come to be known as the Sermon on the Mount, found in Matthew 5–7. A computer search uncovers seventeen occurrences of the *pater* word group in the string of connected pericopes. In each case, God is the referent. An overview of this passage tells us much about Jesus' conception of God as father and about how God relates to his community of sons and daughters. God is a father who is to be granted glory or honor (5:16); is to be imitated (5:45, 48); rewards his children (6:1, 4, 6); understands his children (6:8); provides for the needs of his children (6:11, 26, 32); and expects his children to do his will (7:21). Elsewhere in Matthew and Luke, the image of God as father is used in parables (see Matt 17:24-27; 18:7-14; 21:28-32; esp. Luke 15:11-32; and so forth) and in direct teaching (Matt 23:9; Luke 22:28-32; and so forth). The evidence is irrefutable. The model of the surrogate patrilineal kinship group was central to Jesus of Nazareth's understanding of his community of followers.

We may summarize our discussion of the origins of the early Christian model of the church as a patrilineal kin group by reminding ourselves that for each of the sources surveyed—Old Testament literature, Second Temple Judean works, and the Synoptic Gospels—the following characteristics obtain:

1. The metaphor of a surrogate kin group is utilized as one image among several to describe the relationship between the group in question and their God.

2. Behavior appropriate to PKG norms is expected on the part of those who represent, according to the conceptions of the various authors, the true Israel. They are referred to as siblings and are expected to treat one another in a way consonant with this highly charged PKG relationship.

3. When one is forced to choose between loyalty to God and loyalty to one's blood family, the former must prevail.

These characteristics, then, represent aspects of the surrogate kin group model of community shared by ancient Israelites, Second Temple Judeans, and Jesus of Nazareth. But there were differences, as well. We are now prepared to appreciate some important aspects of Jesus' model that serve to render his community—and the early church to which it later gave birth—as distinct among the kin group models of his day.

THE DISTINCTIVE NATURE OF JESUS' PERSPECTIVE

Jesus' concept of his community as a family departs from traditional Israelite ideas in several ways. It is important to recognize at the outset that these are differences of degree and orientation, not of basic substance. As shown above, many similarities exist. Indeed, if Jesus had championed a social ideal totally unique to the culture in which he lived, he would have found no foothold for his message among his contemporaries. Nevertheless, the movement that began with Jesus and his immediate followers, and later spread throughout the Roman Empire, demands that we address the question of innovation. What was it that distinguished Jesus' surrogate family concept from similar options of his day?

Framing the question in this way inevitably invites critique. While scholars are increasingly willing to designate the early Christian conception of community as distinct from Greco-Roman models in Mediterranean antiquity, the idea that Jesus of Nazareth might have been somehow unique in his preaching or praxis is quite unpopular in certain academic circles.[11] We may cite E. P. Sanders's important monograph on the historical Jesus by way of illustration. "History," claims Sanders, ". . . has grave difficulty with the category 'unique.'"[12] Sanders concludes his monograph with the categorical assertion that "we cannot say that a single one of the things known about Jesus is unique: neither his miracles, non-violence, eschatological hope or promise to the outcasts. He was not unique because he saw his own mission as of crucial importance, nor because he believed in the grace of God."[13] Even Sanders, however, must ultimately acknowledge the presence of innovation when he proceeds to suggest that "what is unquestionably unique about Jesus is the result of his life and work." Part of this unique result includes, for Sanders, "the foundation of a movement which endured."[14]

Unique results, in the form of an enduring community of followers that was distinct from the various social models in the ancient world, would seem to suggest at least some innovation on the part of Jesus in his conception of community. Sanders, however, is simply unwilling to draw this connection. He consistently maintains that "we cannot know that the [unique] result springs from the uniqueness of the historical Jesus."[15] To be fair, Sanders does not discuss Jesus' ideas about the people of God. Perhaps, with respect to the topics he chooses to address, it is enough to argue, as Sanders does, that the combination of beliefs and activities elsewhere individually attested in Second Temple Judaism is that which marks out Jesus as unique.[16]

With respect to the topic at hand, however, innovation on the part of Jesus seems patent. To be sure, he drew upon and combined current ideas about the people of God in formulating his conception of a family of faith. But Jesus expanded upon these images and reoriented them in a manner that justly elicits the designation "unique" and thereby serves as a point of departure for attempts to explain the distinctive nature of Pauline and other early Christian congregations.

Jesus' idea of community expanded upon traditional Israelite and Judean models of surrogate kinship in the following three ways:

1. The kinship metaphor is significantly more pervasive in Jesus' teaching than it is in Old Testament and Second Temple literature.

2. PKG solidarity finds more consistent expression among the followers of Jesus than among Israelites and Second Temple Judeans who were not close blood relatives.

3. Jesus emphasized the idea of an exchange of loyalties to a much greater degree and in a much more radical fashion than is the case in contemporary and earlier Israelite literature.

The next sections will discuss these points, followed by a closer look at the similarities and differences between Jesus' family model and that of a Judean sect that was so similar to Jesus' group as to deserve special treatment: the Dead Sea community at Khirbet Qumran.

The Dominance of the Kinship Metaphor

The kinship metaphor was only one of several metaphors used by Jesus and his early community to portray the relationship between God and his followers. Unlike earlier and contemporary Judean perspectives, however, the family model was clearly dominant for Jesus of Nazareth. Mark's Gospel, as we observed earlier, presents the exchange of family loyalties as the initial and ideal response to Jesus' call to join his community (Mark 1:14-20). One of the main collections of Jesus' teachings assumes, for the very cogency and persuasiveness of its instruction, the family model, with God as the father of his followers. That is, it is because God is their father that Jesus can challenge his disciples to live their lives in the ways outlined in Matthew 5–7. Challenge after challenge depends upon the presence and character of God as the disciples' "heavenly Father" (5:48; 6:1, 4, 6, 8, 15, 32; and so forth).

For Jesus, then, family is not simply one among a variety of equally significant metaphors upon which he draws in order to portray the community he envisions. Rather, it is the dominant social model as well as a metaphor that Jesus uses to engender a specific kind of behavior.

The Practice of PKG Solidarity

Here we surmise that, for most ancient Israelites and Second Temple Judeans, the relational solidarity and generalized reciprocity characteristic of PKG family systems were primarily practiced in the context of the extended blood family. Jesus' followers, in contrast, experienced PKG sibling solidarity in their surrogate kin groups. To be sure, the evidence here is more suggestive than conclusive. Nevertheless, although the Israelites referred to one another, across the board, as "brothers" and were to be treated as such (see Deuteronomy 15), we may assume that these values were tangibly experienced most often in the context of the patrilineal kin group.

Times of crisis, of course, demanded exceptions. Thus, we find Judas Maccabeus challenging his followers to "risk their lives with him to aid their brethren" during the Maccabean Revolt (2 Macc 11:7). Typically, however, kinship needs are met in the context of one's immediately family. Thus, for example, Old Testament figures are typically buried by near relatives (Gen 25:9; 50:1-26; Lev 10:1-5). Nowhere do we find the burial of one's father discouraged (as in Matt 8:22). In only one other instance of which I am aware do we read of persons going to the extremes to which Joseph of Arimathea goes in order to bury a person (Jesus) with whom he has no blood ties (Mark 15:42-47; compare Tob 2:1-8).

Also, Jesus and his immediate followers apparently traveled together and operated out of a common purse (Luke 8:1-3). Adding the information provided by these texts to that gleaned earlier, we see that Jesus' concept of the family of God was tangibly realized through the sharing of material resources as he and certain of his followers traveled together. Here, then, is a group of people, unrelated by blood, who nevertheless spent a significant period of their lives together and related to one another according to the standards of PKG solidarity. This moves beyond anything we find operating as normative among the early Israelites or Second Temple Judeans.[17]

Unfortunately, we lack the information necessary to discern the practices of Jesus' sympathizers who remained in their village communities during Jesus' travels through Galilee and Judea. I suspect, however, that the family model operated to a significant degree in the local communities, as well. For although the itinerant nature of Jesus' ministry will not characterize the later church communities as a whole, the surrogate PKG model will. Indeed, the family metaphor becomes even more pervasive in the Pauline communities of the mid-first century C.E., a situation best explained by assuming a similar practice by the early Galilean communities of Jesus' followers.

A Radical Change of Loyalties

Here again the difference is one of degree, but the degree is significant. Circumstances occasionally arose during Israel's history that demanded that the faithful choose loyalty to God over family solidarity. At times, the challenge "Who is on the LORD's side?" could only be answered by publicly disavowing allegiance to one's closest kin (Exod 32:26). But this was the exception and not the norm. For the followers of Jesus, however, the painful reality of having to choose between loyalty to kin and loyalty to God was more than an occasional possibility—it was a common experience.

Also, the way Jesus challenged his followers to make a commitment to him is consistently more forceful than parallels in other Old Testament or Greco-Roman accounts. Take for example the following two statements by Jesus, for which no close parallels exist in Old Testament literature.

The first statement—"Whoever comes to me and does not hate father and mother, wife and children, brothers and sisters, yes, and even life itself, cannot be my disciple" (Luke 14:26)—teaches that one must be prepared to abandon family ties of marriage and consanguinity in order to follow Jesus. Arland Jacobson has recently placed this passage in its proper sociohistorical context:

> Especially shocking is the first [relation] to be mentioned, the father. To be sure, one was to honor both father and mother but Jewish families, like most other Mediterranean families, were strongly patriarchal. Filial obedience was expected. The penalty for the "stubborn and rebellious son" was death by stoning (Deut 21:18-21), though it is not likely this penalty was ever imposed. Q 14:26 is not just radical; it would have been profoundly offensive.[18]

John Nolland rightly rejects attempts to blunt the force of the hatred terminology in the saying with an appeal to a Semitic idiom that means not "hate" but "love less than."[19] Indeed, such an approach is unnecessary, since "'Hate' here probably does not mean 'dislike intensely' but 'sever one's relationship with' the family."[20] It is therefore best to read in the "hate" language the idea of renunciation, drawing for background upon a Hebrew root that has the sense "to leave aside, abandon."[21] Only then does Jesus' saying here cohere with narratives like Mark 3:31-35, in which Jesus renounces his own family ties, and Mark 1:16-20, in which Jesus challenges his followers to do the same.

The burial issue referenced previously is highlighted in a far more pointed way in another pericope that vividly underlines the radical nature of Jesus' call for an exchange of family loyalties. It is universally recognized that refusing to bury a dead relative, especially a parent, constituted for ancient Judeans and Gentiles "an unheard of act of impiety."[22] Mishnaic legislation went so far as to exempt the faithful from their most basic religious duties—reciting the Shema—until their dead were provided with proper burial (*m. Ber.* 3:1).

This is why Wright describes the following response of Jesus to a potential disciple as "quite frankly, outrageous"[23]: "Another of his disciples said to him, 'Lord, first let me go and bury my father.' But Jesus said to him, 'Follow me, and let the dead bury their own dead'" (Matt 8:21-22). A straightforward reading of the passage leads one to assume that the death of the father had just occurred.[24] As Shmuel Safrai relates, "Leaving a corpse unburied through the night, for any reason, was considered sinfully disrespectful."[25] The family relationship involved in the above passage renders Jesus' exhortation particularly insensitive. Jacobson correctly maintains that Jesus' call constitutes "an insult to the most inviolate of all bonds, those of the family."[26] Indeed, the saying simply stands alone in the literature. There are no true parallels to this scandalous saying in the Greco-Roman world.[27]

Sanders identifies Matthew 8:21-22, above, as "the most revealing passage in the synoptics for penetrating to Jesus' view of the law."[28] On the one hand, I agree with Sanders that Jesus here asserts that "following him superseded the requirements of piety and the Torah."[29] But to read this saying solely in terms of Jesus' perspective on the Torah is to miss the powerful sociological dimension of the pronouncement. We must go further and conclude with Wright that "[the] only explanation for Jesus' astonishing command is that he envisaged loyalty to himself and his kingdom-movement as creating an alternative family."[30] The call to exchange one's loyalties is here framed in a manner that goes far beyond anything found among Jesus' contemporaries.[31]

THE COMMUNITY AT KHIRBET QUMRAN: A COMPARISON

Only one other Judean sect can be fairly cited as a social parallel to Jesus and his group of immediate followers.[32] The texts produced by the community at Khirbet Qumran reflect each of the three kin group components uncovered in my survey of Old Testament, Second Temple, and Gospel literature: (1) the surrogate kinship metaphor, (2) the practice of PKG solidarity, and (3) the priority of loyalty to the sect as a high virtue. Moreover, the Qumran community, like Jesus, radicalized the kinship model in a way that went beyond Old Testament and Second Temple conceptions.

Kinship terminology abounds, and the family symbol arguably constitutes the dominant social metaphor in the Qumran library. Additionally, the PKG concept was put into practice in a startling way: the pooling and sharing of material resources was practiced as the community norm. Finally, the Qumran group demanded a PKG type of loyalty that resulted not only in a high degree of commitment to the community but also in a highly polarized stance against others in the land who shared the blood ancestry of Abraham. A brief survey of the common ground shared by the Jesus movement and the Essenes at Qumran is in order before I proceed to highlight important differences.

The Dominance of the Kinship Metaphor

The dwellers at Qumran made extensive use of kinship language to describe their community. Sibling ("brother") terminology occurs in a variety of texts (1QS 6.23; CD 6.20; CD (ms 'B') 2.15-20; 1QSa=1Q28a 1.18; 4Q372 20). The contrasting phrases "sons of light" and "sons of darkness" are particularly prevalent (1QS 1.10 passim; 1QM 1.9-14 passim; 4Q280=4QTohorot D[b] 1; 4Q544=4QAmram[b]; and so forth). Similar expressions include "sons of (His) grace" (1QH 4.33; 1QH 7.21-22), "sons of (His) truth" (1QH 6.29-30), "sons of righteousness" (1QS 9.14), and "sons of the everlasting company" (1QS 2.25).

References to God as the father of the community occur far less frequently, however, in the Dead Sea Scrolls than in the Gospels. Nevertheless, the idea is present in a few documents (11QT=11Q19 48.8; 4Q504 3.5; 4Q372 16-17). The most extensive metaphor occurs in one of the Thanksgiving Hymns:

> Until I am old Thou wilt care for me;
> > for my father knew me not
> > and my mother abandoned me to Thee.
> For Thou art a father
> > to all [the sons] of Thy truth,
> and as a woman who tenderly loves her babe,
> > so dost Thou rejoice in them;
> and as a foster-father bearing a child in his lap
> > so carest Thou for all Thy creatures. (1QH 9.34-38)[33]

Despite the relative paucity in the Dead Sea Scrolls of explicit designations of God as the father of the community, related evidence suggests that the father-children metaphor played an important part in the groups' social self-consciousness. The occurrence of the term "father," followed by the phrase "[the sons] of Thy truth," in the above hymn opens the door to understanding many of the "sons of . . ." phrases, cited above, as oblique references to the father-child relationship. The circumlocutions can be readily attributed to the reticence of Second Temple Judeans to speak and write the various Hebrew words for God. Instead, the authors substitute such words as *light* and *truth* for the divine name.

Other PKG terms and behaviors find their way into the Qumran texts. The metaphorical idea of inheritance arises at a number of places (1QS 11.8-9; 1QH 17.15; 4Q185; 4Q511; 11QMelch=11Q13 line 5). Truth telling in the sect is a high value, as well. Notice the presence of sibling terminology in the following legislation:

> If a malicious witness comes forward against a man to testify against him in a case of a crime, both disputants shall stand before me and before the priests and the Levites and before the judges then in office, and the judges shall inquire, and if the witness is a false witness who has testified falsely against his brother, you shall do to him as he proposed to do to his brother. (11QT=11Q19 61.10-11)

The PKG metaphor is, therefore, a dominant one for the conception of community as it was experienced at Khirbet Qumran.

The Practice of PKG Solidarity

The PKG standards of behavior that governed the Qumran community reflect the covenantors' self-conscious adoption of the family metaphor. Several aspects of Mediterranean family solidarity, as surveyed in chapter 2, are reflected in passages from the Dead Sea Scrolls. In several cases, we find kinship terminology also included in the context. The following excerpt is characteristic:

> But when the second year has passed, he shall be examined, and if it be his destiny, according to the judgment of the Congregation, to enter the Community, then he shall be inscribed among his brethren in the order of his rank for the Law, and for justice and for the pure Meal; his property shall be merged and he shall offer his counsel and judgment to the Community. (1QS 6.23-24; see 1.11-12).

Once the initiate gained full membership in the sect after a two-year novitiate, he was expected to contribute all his material resources to the community's purse. The common property was then used to support the members of the sect. Generalized reciprocity was not merely an option at Qumran—it was the community norm. Strong injunctions were placed upon any who deceitfully betrayed their brothers in the sect by concealing personal property: "If one of them has lied deliberately in matters of property, he shall be excluded from the pure Meal of the Congregation for one year and shall do penance with respect to one quarter of his food" (1QS 6.25-27).

The author of the Temple Scroll makes special provisions for the equal distribution of resources during time of war. When Israel proves victorious and her soldiers capture much booty, "they shall give the king his tithe of this, the priests one thousandth and the Levites one hundredth from everything. They shall halve the rest between the combatants and their brothers whom they have left in their cities" (11QT=11Q19 58.15).

Analysis becomes more complex when we consider the fact that the religious movement known as the Essenes had two branches. In addition to the dwellers at the desert settlement, evidence exists for adherents living in the towns and villages of pre–70 C.E. Palestine. The Damascus Rule (CD) and the Messianic Rule both address the issue of material resources, as, on occasion, does the War Scroll. Geza Vermes cites an important difference between the organization of sympathizers in the towns and the sectarians at Qumran. Sympathizers from the towns did not merge their belongings into a common fund as did the sectarians who settled near the Dead Sea. Unlike the covenantors at Qumran, the village initiates were not required to surrender personal property. Still, they contributed significantly to the needs of their brothers in the sect.[34] Vermes cites the following as an example of pertinent legislation:

> They shall place the earnings of at least two days out of every month into the hands of the Guardian and the Judges, and from it they shall give to the fatherless, and from it they shall succour the poor and the needy, the aged sick and the homeless, the captive taken by a foreign people, the virgin with no near kin, and the maid for whom no man cares. (CD 14.12-16)

Note, as well, the following excerpt, which utilizes sibling terminology in its challenge to PKG solidarity:

> They shall love each man his brother as himself; they shall succour the poor, the needy, and the stranger. A man shall seek his brother's well-being and shall not sin against his near kin. They shall keep from fornication according to the statute. They shall rebuke each man his brother according to the commandment and shall bear no rancour from one day to the next. (CD 6.20–7.3)

The practice of generalized reciprocity therefore occurred among both village Essenes and those at Qumran despite the differences in overall approach to the collection and distribution of resources.

A Radical Change of Loyalties

Finally, as we discovered above, the Qumran community cites and rephrases Deuteronomy 13:6-9 to emphasize the importance of loyalty to the new kin group: "If your brother, the son of your father or the son of your mother, or your son, or your daughter, or the wife of your bosom, or your friend who is like your own self, (seeks to) entice you secretly, saying, 'Let us go and worship other gods whom you have not known,' neither you, (nor your fathers) . . ." (11QT=11Q19 54.20-24). Such loyalty results in a polarization against not only the foreign countries but also various other Judeans and Judean groups who are identified as foes of the sect. The Nahum and Habakkuk commentaries in particular reveal such sentiments. The oracles of judgment against Nineveh from the book of Nahum are applied by the author of the Qumran interpretation of the Old Testament prophecy to apostates among his fellow Jews. The community's interpretation of Nahum 3:4 is quite pointed:

> "Because of the many harlotries of the well-favoured harlot, the mistress of seduction, she who sells nations through her harlotries and families through her seductions." Interpreted, this concerns those who lead Ephraim astray, who lead many astray through their false teaching, their lying tongue, and deceitful lips—kings, princes, priests, and people, together with the stranger who joins them. (4Q169, 2.7-10)

It is clear that for dwellers at Qumran, Judean ancestry is no guarantee of eschatological salvation. Those who will prevail are those who opt for an unmitigated loyalty to the new family of faith. They have experienced (and can expect more) opposition from their fellow Judeans.

Jesus and his community are not alone, then, in their adoption—and radicalization—of the PKG model. Kinship terminology pervades the Qumran literature. The sectarians living at Qumran clearly practiced generalized reciprocity with their community of goods. There was also strong concern for sibling-like loyalty among group members. The distinctiveness of Jesus' conception of the people of God is to be found elsewhere: (a) in his conception of God as the only father for the family of faith and (b) in his orientation toward outsiders, as reflected, in part, in the qualifications for admission to his new community. We will examine these in turn.

God as Father of the Community

We noted the presence among the Qumran sectarians of the metaphor of God as father of the community. There are other texts, however, that have no parallel in the Gospel literature. In these texts, we find not God but a leader in the community portrayed as the sectarians' patriarch. At the beginning of the *Damascus Document*, the author, whom Vermes plausibly identifies as a guardian of the community, addresses his readers as "my sons" (CD 2.14).[35] The document later outlines the role of a "Guardian," who is to act toward the sectarians "as a father loves his children, and shall carry them in all their distress like a shepherd his sheep. He shall loosen all the fetters that bind them so that in his Congregation there may be none that are oppressed and broken" (CD 13.9-10).

In one of the Thanksgiving Hymns, the author adopts a similar perspective when he exclaims in his prayer, "Thou hast made me a father to the sons of grace and as a foster-father to men of marvel" (1QH 7.21-22). The identification of the author of the Thanksgiving Hymns remains an unresolved issue. Much of the content of the hymns could apply to any member of the sect. Certain texts, however, seem to relate the experiences of an author who has endured a degree of betrayal and hardship, that is, "a historical person of significance for the community."[36] Some scholars have explicitly identified him with the "Teacher of Righteousness," a leader of the sect mentioned in other Qumran literature.[37] That the author was a leadership figure of some sort has the general assent of the scholarly community. As such, he perceives himself to be a father figure to the faithful.

We see, therefore, at Qumran, a mixture of metaphors. On the one hand, God is the father and the sectarians are his children (11QT=11Q19 48.8; 4Q504 3.5; 4Q372 16-17; 1QH 9.34-38). Another perspective, however, places the community's leader also in the position of father of the sect. We are now prepared to contrast the Qumran understanding with Jesus' use of the father metaphor:

> Peter began to say to him, "Look, we have left everything and followed you." Jesus said, "Truly I tell you, there is no one who has left house or brothers or sisters or mother or father or children or fields, for my sake and for the sake of the good news, who will not receive a hundredfold now in this age—houses, brothers and sisters, mothers and children, and fields with persecutions—and in the age to come eternal life. (Mark 10:28-30)

I cited this passage previously as evidence of the generalized reciprocity practiced among Jesus' early followers. A closer inspection uncovers a revealing contrast. Among the family relationships to be sacrificed in order to become a member of Jesus' group is the follower's "father." This has already been modeled earlier in Mark's account that portrayed John and James leaving "their father Zebedee" in response to Jesus' call (1:20). But notice in Mark 10:30, above, the absence of "father" among those relationships that one who follows Jesus will gain in return. "Brothers, sisters, mothers, and children" are present. "Fathers" are not. Apparently Jesus' surrogate PKG, unlike that in operation at Qumran, has no human father figure.

Gerhard Lohfink discusses two aspects of the father metaphor in his survey of the Gospel narratives. On the one hand, God is the Jesus community's kind and caring father, who provides for their daily needs (Matt 6:31-33). Those, like the sons of Zebedee, who have left the economic security of their father's home and business must now rely on the graciousness of their heavenly father, mediated through the new community, for the necessities of life. But there is another characteristic of the typical Mediterranean patriarch that, according to Jesus' conception of community, is also reserved for God alone: the authority component.

> If there no longer exist for [the disciples] the kind and caring fathers of the past, but only the one Father in heaven, then it is all the more true that authoritarian fathers exercising power have gone out of existence. It would be paradoxical to leave tender fathers behind and then find authoritarian fathers in the circle of disciples. It was precisely for this reason that Jesus mentioned no fathers in Mark 10:30. The disciples will find everything again in the new family of God, brothers and sisters, mothers and children; but they will find fathers no longer. Patriarchal domination is no longer permissible in the new family, but only motherliness, fraternity and childlikeness before God the Father.[38]

The following paradigmatic passage shows us that the omission of "father" in Mark 10:30 is not an oversight on the part of Jesus or Mark. Moreover, as the context unequivocally indicates, it is precisely the authoritarian aspect of patriarchy that is excluded from the community by Jesus' instruction to his disciples in Matthew 23:

> But you are not to be called rabbi, for you have one teacher, and you are all students.[39] And call no one your father on earth, for you have one Father—the one in heaven. Nor are you to be called instructors, for you have one instructor, the Messiah. The greatest among you will be your servant. All who exalt themselves will be humbled, and all who humble themselves will be exalted. (Matt 23:8-12)[40]

Here, then, we find a significant difference between Jesus' conception of the family of God and that obtaining among the sectarians at Qumran. Among Jesus' earliest followers, the role of father in the community is to be reserved for God alone. We may assume that among the members of the Dead Sea community, the leader exercised his fatherly role in both of the ways Lohfink envisions. He loved them as a father loves his children, assuring the proper distribution of the community's resources (CD 13.9-10, above).[41] And he also wielded strong authority in the community. Studies of the social structure of the sectaries consistently draw our attention to an organizational "hierarchy at Qumran" that was "strict and formal."[42] Leaders were to be recognized as leaders and accorded privilege appropriate to their rank. In several texts, the Guardian of the Community (who functioned, as indicated above, in a surrogate father role) is found at the pinnacle of the leadership hierarchy. He instructs the community on proper life and behavior (1QS 1.1). He presides over assemblies, granting the right to speak to those desiring to do so (1QS 6.11-13). He assesses, along with others, the spiritual progress of the men in his charge and ranks them accordingly (1QS 6.21-22). The Guardian of the Community, then, was undoubtedly both a father who loved and a father who disciplined the faithful. For Jesus, by contrast, God is the sole father who is to fulfill both roles.

Orientation toward Outsiders

Jesus' most radical point of departure from contemporary Judean ideas and praxis regarding the eschatological people of God is Jesus' orientation toward outsiders, which throws into sharp relief the distinct character of his surrogate PKG concept versus the alternative at Qumran.

SECOND TEMPLE JUDAISM AND THE GENTILE PROBLEM

The attitudes of Jesus and the leaders at Qumran cannot be understood apart from an appreciation of the defining problem faced by anyone who would aspire to gather together a group of first-century Judeans as the eschatological people of God: Gentile occupation. Israel's sacred scriptures clearly promised a day when Israel would be politically independent, economically prosperous, and religiously pure as an ethnic entity (Deut 30:4-6, 9-10).

So much for the future ideal. The present reality presented a bleak and striking contrast. Judeans in Palestine at the time of Jesus were under oppressive foreign domination. Many were on the brink of economic disaster. The center of Israel's religious universe—the Jerusalem Temple—was hopelessly polluted in the eyes of some, and probably of questionable spiritual efficacy according to the sentiments of most.[43] In short, three of the most important symbols of the Judean worldview—temple, land, and people—were suffering defilement, or the threat of defilement, in the context of Roman domination. Israel's sacred scriptures repeatedly promised a day when this would no longer be the case.

Possible reactions to the Gentile presence in postexilic Palestine found tangible social expression in the various sects that arose during the period. Different groups responded in different ways to foreign occupation, and the resulting pluriform nature of Second Temple Judaism is now universally recognized by scholars who focus upon first-century Jewish history and culture.[44] Nevertheless, for most of Jesus' contemporaries, including the surrogate kin group at Qumran, which I am contrasting with Jesus' community of followers, agreement obtained on two central issues:

1. One day Israel would once again be independent; promises contained in such passages as Deuteronomy 30 would be fulfilled.

2. During the interim period, the Judeans must, at all costs, maintain their cultural identity as the unique people of God in contrast to the nations of the world.

The second is the salient point. The preservation of Judean national-cultural identity—realized through the practice of circumcision, Sabbath-keeping, and the observance of food purity laws—was a non-negotiable, tenaciously held value for most first-century Judeans, especially the Dead Sea community.

Jewish Purity and the Preservation of Identity

Before we compare Qumran practices with Jesus' attitude toward purity and relate both to the idea of surrogate kinship, we must reflect for a moment on the overarching purpose of the Levitical purity code as understood by Second Temple Judeans. Post-Reformation Protestant scholarship has traditionally misread purity as it functioned during the New Testament period. It has been assumed that one undertook such practices as observation of the food laws and Sabbath-keeping in order to earn one's righteous standing before God and thereby assure oneself of personal vindication at the eschatological court of justice.

This interpretation of Second Temple purity as a "works righteousness" religion has served in turn as the foil against which passages like the following are read—passages that allegedly reflect the radically different perspective of early Christianity (Eph 2:8-9). Recent research has strongly challenged the historical viability of the "works righteousness" explanation of Second Temple purity. The view that individual Judeans obeyed purity legislation solely to earn God's approval has been identified as the anachronistic projection of Western individualism and Reformation concerns back onto Second Temple Judean convictions and praxis.[45]

Drawing upon the findings of cultural anthropologists like Mary Douglas, and rereading Second Temple and Mishnaic literature with a heightened sensitivity to its sociohistorical context, a new generation of historians has shown us that Judean purity had an important and highly informative social component.[46] Specifically, the practice of purity was intended to preserve the identity of the eschatological people of God in a world system that was perceived as compromised and defiled by Gentiles and (for certain sects, such as the Pharisees and the Qumran community) fellow Judeans alike. Purity legislation had, in fact, been framed in precisely these terms in the Hebrew Scriptures:

> I have separated you from the peoples. You shall therefore make a distinction between the clean animal and the unclean, and between the unclean bird and the clean; you shall not bring abomination on yourselves by animal or by bird or by anything with which the ground teems, which I have set apart for you to hold unclean. You shall be holy to me; for I the LORD am holy, and I have separated you from the other peoples to be mine. (Lev 20:24b-26)

Greek and Roman domination rendered passages such as this particularly meaningful to Second Temple Judeans. At stake was the very survival of the Israelite remnant as an ethnic-cultural entity. And purity was the primary vehicle adopted to ensure the preservation of the *ethnos*.

A defensive posture toward Gentile incursion, appearing as early as the reforms of Ezra and Nehemiah, in which intermarriage was discouraged (see Ezra 9–10), only intensified in response to the Syrian king Antiochus IV's attempt to ensure the success of the Hellenization process by forcing Judeans to eat unclean food and prohibiting circumcision. 1 Maccabees 1:41-63 makes this graphically clear:

> Then the king [Antiochus IV] wrote to his whole kingdom that all should be one people, and that each should give up his customs. . . . He directed them to follow customs strange to the land, . . . and to leave their sons uncircumcised. . . . According to the decree they put to death the women who had their children circumcised, and their families and those who circumcised them; and they hung the infants from their mothers' necks. But many in Israel stood firm and were resolved in their hearts not to eat unclean food. They chose to die rather than to be defiled by food or to profane the holy covenant; and they did die.

By the end of the Maccabean crises, the true heroes of the faith were those who had refused to compromise on the purity laws and circumcision, and who consequently suffered death at the hands of the Gentile oppressor. The books of 2 and 4 Maccabees relate a number of stories of the Judean martyrs. The latter work has as its principal subject the death of a mother and her seven sons. In 2 Maccabees, the story of Eleazer, beaten to death on the rack after he spit out pork that had been forced into his mouth by Greek authorities, ends with the following word of praise: "So in this way he died, leaving in his death an example of nobility and a memorial of courage, not only to the young but to the great body of his nation" (2 Macc 6:31). Most honorable, then, is the person who maintains the key markers of Judean identity to the point of death.

More importantly, from the perspective of Jesus' contemporaries, God had resolutely affirmed such Torah-keeping by granting the Maccabees victory and inaugurating the several decades of Judean independence that followed. For one Judean historian, the connection was obvious: "The Jews were invulnerable because they followed the laws ordained by God" (2 Macc 8:36). First-century Judeans were reminded annually at the feast of Hanukkah of this taste of freedom from Gentile domination. More specifically, they were reminded that God honors a people who maintain Levitical purity by observing the commandments of his Torah.[47]

A Maccabean contemporary placed in the mouth of the patriarch Abraham a challenge that would soon resonate positively with Judeans throughout the Mediterranean: "Separate yourself from the Gentiles and do not eat with them" (Jub. 22:16). Indeed, by the first century, some degree of separation from Gentile defilement characterized nearly all who identified themselves as Judeans. Philip Esler, for example, has convincingly documented the universal Judean ban on dining with Gentiles, a ban observed both in Palestine and in the Diaspora.[48] Philo of Alexandria, radically hellenized with respect to his theological and philosophical orientation, nevertheless maintained Judean purity laws. Separation from Gentile defilement was a shared conviction among Second Temple Judeans, and purity was the primary vehicle adopted to ensure the preservation of ethnic Israel.

The proper degree of this separation, however, was the topic of vociferous debate. Some believed that conditions were so serious as to demand separation even from other Judeans who did not (or were unable to) share the group's vision for the renewal of Israel. The Pharisees, for example, encouraged their followers to practice a level of purity that had previously been reserved for the priesthood.[49] Their program necessarily excluded from fellowship at meals individuals who were unwilling or unable to conform to these purity practices (Luke 7:36-50). The covenantors at Qumran were even more radically concerned about purity than were the Pharisees. They separated themselves geographically from both Gentiles and most of their fellow Judeans, whom they felt had been hopelessly corrupted by pagan influence and become part of the enemy (1QS 1.23; 2.5-10).

The above discussion demonstrates that Israelite purity was essentially oriented to group cohesion and survival. The primary question on the minds of first-century Judeans was "How can we maintain our identity as the people of God in the midst of Gentile oppression and defilement?" To the degree that a movement emphasized purity in its efforts to renew Israel, the answer to this vexing question was framed in nationalistic terms. The covenantors at Qumran represent our period's most radical purity sect. They envisioned a victorious future for ethnic Israel, the corollary of which was the utter defeat and destruction of Gentile (and Judean) oppressors.

The Jesus movement situated itself at precisely the opposite end of the purity spectrum. Jesus forcefully challenged the purity practices of his contemporaries and, thereby, raised significant questions for the future of Israel—the people of God—as an *ethnos*. Both groups, however, as we saw above, portrayed themselves conceptually and functioned socially as fictive families. As I will demonstrate next, the surrogate kinship idea was malleable enough to reinforce a strongly nationalistic agenda, in the case of Qumran, or to serve as an alternative to *ethnos* as the defining social category for the people of God, in the case of Jesus and his followers.

PURITY AT QUMRAN

A brief survey of purity practices among the settlers at Qumran begins appropriately with a look at the process of induction into the sect. The initiate went through an orientation process that continued "certainly for two years and possibly for three or more" before he was admitted to purity.[50] During this probation period, the newcomer was forbidden to come into contact with the community's pots, plates, and bowls, and the food that they contained. He was, in effect, excluded from the daily common table that was so central to the sectarians' communal self-understanding.

I will return to the issue of table fellowship in my overview of the contrasting orientation of Jesus of Nazareth below. It will suffice to note here that participation in the Qumran group's communal meal constituted the final and conclusive step in the initiation process (1QS 6.14-24). It was also the first privilege forfeited by a member who failed to maintain the community's standards of purity or ethics (1QS 6.25–7.25). This meant that table fellowship, for the Qumran sectarians, represented the most intense application of the purity system and, correspondingly, the most exclusive practice in the life of the community. Most importantly for our concerns, the community meal at Qumran constituted the preeminent tangible expression of the surrogate family metaphor so central to the sect's social self-definition.

The intense purity focus of the Dead Sea community manifested itself in several other ways. Despite an ongoing debate, most scholars assume that the community consisted of celibate males. Vermes notes the total absence of the word *'ishah* ("woman") in the Community Rule (1QS).[51] The few bones of women and children found on the periphery of the settlement are best explained by assuming that the community hosted occasional events to which they invited their blood family members and sympathizers in the Judean villages. A celibate community was an anomaly in first-century Judaism and is perhaps best explained as an attempt to relive in daily community life the temporary admonition given to Israel just prior to her historic encounter with God at Sinai (Exod 19:10-15).

The final charge in this Exodus passage, "Do not go near a woman," does not constitute a denigration of human sexuality. Rather, the command is to be understood in the context of purity, as the parallel admonitions about consecration and the washing of clothes clearly indicate. Perhaps the dwellers at Khirbet Qumran hoped that if they prepared themselves in a manner deemed appropriate, God would once again visit his people and deliver his remnant.

Finally, those who were accepted into purity at Qumran were prohibited from associating with anyone (Gentile or Judean) outside the group:

> And [the initiate] shall undertake by the Covenant to separate from all the men of injustice who walk in the way of wickedness. For they are not reckoned in His Covenant. . . .They shall not enter the water to partake of the pure Meal of the men of the holiness, for they shall not be cleansed unless they turn from their wickedness: for all who transgress His word are unclean. Likewise, no man shall consort with him with regard to his work or property lest he be burdened with the guilt of his sin. He shall indeed keep away from him in all things: as it is written, *Keep away from all that is false* (Exod xxiii, 7). No member of the Community shall follow them in matters of doctrine and justice, or eat or drink anything of theirs, or take anything from them except for a price; as it is written, *Keep away from the man in whose nostrils is breath, for wherein is he counted?* (Isa ii, 22). (1QS 5.11-19)

JESUS AND PURITY

Jesus' practice of open table fellowship provides the most immediate window through which to view his attitude toward ritual purity and the inclusion of outsiders. Anthropologists have demonstrated the way in which meals, functioning as social institutions, define boundaries in terms of who is excluded or included within a given social group.[52] This was certainly reflected in ancient Mediterranean society, in which mealtime was a highly charged affair affording much more than simply the opportunity to consume nourishment. Scott Bartchy helpfully summarizes the social aspect of shared meals in Mediterranean society:

> Being welcomed at a table for the purpose of eating food with another person had become a ceremony richly symbolic of friendship, intimacy and unity. Thus betrayal or unfaithfulness toward anyone with whom one had shared the table was viewed as particularly reprehensible. On the other hand, when persons were estranged, a meal invitation opened the way to reconciliation. Even everyday mealtimes were highly complex events in which social values, boundaries, statuses, and hierarchies were reinforced.[53]

These broader Mediterranean values took on even more specific form in first-century Palestine. For both the Pharisees and the kin group at Qumran, mealtime was the environment par excellence where purity was practiced—and the place where the impure were correspondingly excluded. We saw this above in the brief discussion of the daily community meal at Qumran.

Moreover, an important relationship obtains between kinship and table fellowship in most societies, and it is not surprising to discover that table fellowship served as a central expression of solidarity both for the covenantors at Qumran and for Jesus' followers. Both groups constituted surrogate families for their respective members. And for both groups, the PKG model found its most tangible expression at mealtime. For, as Bartchy observes, "the extended family was the usual context in which meals were consumed."[54] Family members, of course, were not the only persons who shared meals together. The Greco-Roman symposium, central to the social practices of funeral clubs, trade groups, and philosophical schools, was also an important context for a shared meal. Perhaps Luke's presentation of Jesus at table was influenced by such practices.[55]

At the level of the historical Jesus, however, the kinship background best explains the community's shared meals. The centrality of kinship ideas and behavior both to Jesus' community and to the group at Qumran suggests that the primary imagery brought to the fore by shared meals was the sense of family relationship existing among the participants in the respective communities. Jesus' last meal with his disciples is the final and most representative example of his inclusive table practices.[56] And this meal, as we saw above, was indisputably a family event. We may assume, then, a close relationship between the kinship model adopted by Jesus and his practices at table. We are now prepared to appreciate the radically inclusive nature of Jesus' table fellowship. I will limit my brief survey to an overview of several important passages from Mark's portrayal of Jesus. The first is found in the second chapter of the Markan narrative:

> And as he sat at dinner in Levi's house, many tax collectors and sinners were also sitting with Jesus and his disciples—for there were many who followed him. When the scribes of the Pharisees saw that he was eating with sinners and tax collectors, they said to his disciples, "Why does he eat with tax collectors and sinners?" When Jesus heard this, he said to them, "Those who are well have no need of a physician, but those who are sick; I have come to call not the righteous but sinners." (2:15-17)

In light of the above discussion of the importance of ritual purity for maintaining Judean ethnic identity, we are not surprised to find the Pharisees strongly reacting to Jesus' practice of reclining at table with the ritually impure. Bartchy's comments provide an illuminating interpretative grid through which to view the Markan pericope: "In his message and table praxis, eating with anyone who would eat with him,

Jesus challenged the central role played by table fellowship in reinforcing boundaries and statuses widely believed to be sanctioned by God."[57] Bartchy proceeds to identify "[Jesus'] use of table fellowship as a divine tool for undermining boundaries and hierarchies."[58] In short, Jesus utilized mealtime as a social vehicle to include outsiders in his surrogate kin group. For the faith family at Qumran, table fellowship served precisely the opposite function.

Mark contains other examples of Jesus' approach to ritual purity at table. Mark 7:1-23 contrasts the praxis of Jesus' followers with those who maintained the traditions of the elders by immersing their hands in ritual fashion before eating. The conflict narrative portrays Jesus defending the behavior of his disciples by asserting that "there is nothing outside a person that by going in can defile, but the things that come out are what defile" (7:15). Bartchy, commenting on yet another Gospel tradition, reminds the reader that the only miracle tradition attributed to Jesus in all four Gospels was the feeding of the five thousand (Mark 6:30-44), a meal at which "food was shared with all who were present, without any boundaries or tests of purity."[59] Jesus' last meal with his disciples (14:12-25), discussed above, concludes and strongly reinforces Mark's series of portrayals of Jesus at table.

The attitude of Jesus to ritual purity surfaces not only in the table fellowship passages but also in accounts of various encounters that Jesus had with unclean persons during his itinerant ministry. Jesus receives, touches, and heals a leper who approaches him saying, "If you choose, you can make me clean" (Mark 1:40). Jesus is also remembered by Mark as entering the house in which a dead body was present and proceeding to touch the corpse (5:39-41). Both actions ignored purity injunctions to the contrary (Num 19:11-14). Mark 5:25-34 is especially pertinent in that it combines Jesus' rejection of ceremonial purity with the kinship metaphor so central to our investigation. The woman's illness rendered her unclean according to contemporary purity standards. She would, therefore, have been ostracized to some degree from her village community (Lev 15:19-33; Ezek 36:17; *m. Zab.* 5:1, 6).[60] The purity theme is clearly at the center of the narrative, as illustrated by the presence of an allusion to Old Testament purity legislation in verse 29, where we find the statement "Immediately [the woman's] hemorrhage stopped." Mark's Greek original corresponds almost verbatim to a phrase found in Leviticus 12:7, in the Greek Old Testament, where a woman who has given birth is declared clean after a rite of purification.[61]

It has been argued, however, that the healing that the woman experienced makes the purity issue "moot."[62] But this view overlooks an essential aspect of the pericope. Granted, once the woman is healed of her infirmity, Jesus' interaction with her is no longer problematic from the perspective of purity. At the point in the narrative when the woman took the initiative to touch Jesus, however, she was ritually unclean, and her touch would have rendered Jesus unclean (Lev 15:25-27).[63] This observation provides the interpretive key to the narrative, for in the climactic end of the pericope, Jesus identifies the woman's action—reaching out to him in her impure state—as an act of "faith" (v. 34). Jesus' positive assessment of the woman's behavior thus represents a radical inversion of religious and social conventions, conventions according to which one's faith is normally expressed by maintaining, not violating, the Levitical purity code. Moreover, just as the purity code typically served to exclude unclean persons, like the woman in the narrative, from full participation in local community life, here it is the very violation of the purity code that serves to reintroduce the woman to community, as evidenced by Jesus' final address to her: "Daughter" (v. 34).

Bartchy summarizes Jesus' attitude toward purity with the observation that, for Jesus, "ritual purity of one's body or one's food is irrelevant to God. The important matter is how one treats others."[64] Care must be exercised here to avoid oversimplification. Ethical exhortation is not lacking in the Qumran material. "Truth," "humility," and "charity" are enjoined; "anger," "ill-temper," and "obduracy" are to be avoided (1QS 5.25). Jesus and his followers were hardly alone in their concern for proper treatment of others in their group. As Sanders rightly notes, it is incredible to assume that Jesus was "one of the rare Judeans of his day who believed in love, mercy, grace, repentance, and the forgiveness of sin."[65] Each of the beliefs Sanders mentions can be documented at Qumran. Indeed, various Second Temple Judean groups largely agreed about what constituted the proper treatment of those who were in one's group.

What distinguished Jesus and his followers from contemporary Judean sects was their viewpoint concerning proper treatment of *outsiders*. For most Judean groups of Jesus' day, the keeping of the purity code was precisely the activity that defined the boundary between the group members—Israel as an *ethnos*—and those outside. As we have seen, this was particularly the case for the settlers at Qumran. An overview of the Qumran corpus as a whole gives the impression that when the initiate undertook a "binding oath to return with all his heart and soul to every commandment of the Law of Moses," the purity regulations of the Torah were primarily in view (1QS 5.8-9). Thus the admonition immediately following this citation in the Community Rule requires the initiate to "separate from all men of injustice who walk in the way of wickedness" (1QS 5.10). But these are precisely the kinds of people whom Jesus received, associated with, and ate with, according to the above evidence.

This brings us to the heart of the contrast between the way surrogate family was conceived at Qumran and the way it was expressed in the Jesus movement. The faith family at Qumran remained Judean by blood. As we have seen, for the Qumran covenantors not every descendent of Abraham was, ipso facto, a member of God's eschatological remnant. But it remained the case that every member of the remnant was a descendent of Abraham. Judean blood flowed pure at Qumran.

This also was true for most Second Temple groups that maintained a defensive posture vis-à-vis the Gentile world. As a result, the field of potential candidates for inclusion among the eschatological people of God increasingly narrowed as one moved along the purity continuum from Old Testament legislation to Pharisaic standards and, finally, to the more demanding strictures in operation at Qumran. This meant, finally, that at Qumran the family metaphor functioned to delineate a *subset* of ethnic Israel that in the view of the covenantors constituted the eschatological people of God. Purity and surrogate kinship were thus united in the service of a markedly nationalistic agenda, and this union of ritual purity and family imagery was tangibly reinforced on a daily basis at Qumran in the form of the communal meal.

Among Jesus and his followers, on the other hand, surrogate kinship functioned as an *alternative* to (not a *subset* of) *ethnos* as the defining social category for God's eschatological people. As we saw in chapter 1, the Jesus movement's lack of a national-ethnic identity proved to be a significant liability in the early Roman Empire. This radical redefinition of what it meant to be religious in the ancient world finds its roots in the historical Jesus. Jesus' rejection of purity inevitably brought into question the whole identification of ethnic Israel with the eschatological people of God. No longer was it clear that God's people were co-equal with ethnic Israel. By calling into question the ongoing validity of the traditional markers of national identity—the Sabbath, food laws, and the temple economy—while at the same time maintaining exclusive allegiance to Yahweh, Jesus prepared his followers to redefine the people of God as a transnational surrogate kinship group— one that would welcome not only unclean Judeans into the family, but Gentiles as well. Figure 3.1 may prove helpful in contrasting Qumran with the Jesus movement.

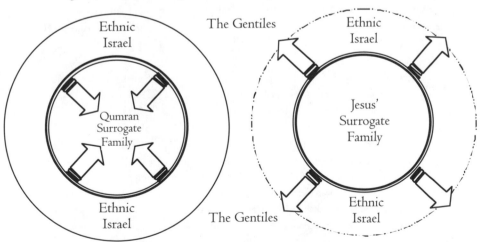

Fig. 3.1. Surrogate Families according to Qumran and Jesus

As the diagrams illustrate, the family construct at Qumran served a defensive purpose, expressed preeminently in the exclusive daily meal shared by members of the sect. Jesus utilized the surrogate kinship model inclusively, as a trans-ethnic alternative to competing Second Temple definitions of the eschatological people of God, which were typically nationalistic in orientation.

Finally, the contrasting function of surrogate kinship among Jesus and his followers, on the one hand, and the covenantors at Qumran, on the other, must be framed in broader terms. The two social orientations ultimately reflect two irreconcilable perspectives on the consummation of Israel's history in eschatological blessing and renewal. Bartchy rightly sees Jesus' practice of "radically inclusive and non-hierarchical table fellowship" not simply as a social alternative to current purity standards but, rather, as "a central strategy in his announcement and redefinition of the inbreaking rule of God."[66]

For the first-century Judean, the "inbreaking rule of God" meant, of course, an end to the dark reality of Gentile oppression and defilement of God's people. Old Testament literature is, however, relatively ambiguous concerning the manner in which God would ultimately address the Gentile problem. On the one hand, the judgment of God against the nations is a common theme in prophetic literature (see, for example, Isaiah 14–23). Second Temple Judeans did not have to look far to find passages that reinforced the idea of an ethnically pure Israel, separated from the Gentiles forever: "Awake, awake, put on your strength, O Zion! Put on your beautiful garments, O Jerusalem, the holy city; for the uncircumcised and the unclean shall enter you no more" (Isa 52:1). It only made sense, in light of prophetic challenges like the above, to maintain a standard of purity and separation that anticipated what God himself would do at the end of the age—thus, the social experiment at Qumran.

Another strain of prophetic tradition, however, looked to a future time when foreigners would be included among—not excluded from—the eschatological people of God:

It is too light a thing that you should be my servant to raise up the tribes of Jacob and to restore the survivors of Israel; I will give you as a light to the nations, that my salvation may reach to the end of the earth. (Isa 49:6)

3 Do not let the foreigner joined to the LORD say, "The LORD will surely separate me from his people"; and do not let the eunuch say, "I am just a dry tree." 4 For thus says the LORD: To the eunuchs who keep my sabbaths, who choose the things that please me and hold fast my covenant, 5 I will give, in my house and within my walls, a monument and a name better than sons and daughters; I will give them an everlasting name that shall not be cut off. 6 And the foreigners who join themselves to the LORD, to

minister to him, to love the name of the LORD, and to be his servants, all who keep the sabbath, and do not profane it, and hold fast my covenant— 7 these I will bring to my holy mountain, and make them joyful in my house of prayer; their burnt offerings and their sacrifices will be accepted on my altar; for my house shall be called a house of prayer for all peoples. (Isa 56:3-7)

This second strain of prophetic tradition provided Jesus of Nazareth and his followers with the foundation for a concept of community that differed radically from social practices at Qumran: an inclusive, rather than exclusive, surrogate kinship group.

For Jesus, a new age had dawned, and God was once and for all intervening for the salvation of his people and the establishment of his rule. This meant a different approach to purity and the Gentile problem. Wright's remarks about Jesus and his rejection of the Pharisaic purity code form an apt summary to my overview of the contrast between the Jesus community and the Essenes living at Khirbet Qumran:

> The rigorous application of the law in the way in which we have observed, as a defence against Gentiles and hence as a reinforcement of national boundaries and aspirations, had become, in Jesus' view, a symptom of the problem rather than part of the solution. The kingdom of the one true god was at last coming into being, and it would be characterized not by defensiveness, but by Israel's being the light of the world; not by the angry zeal which would pay the Gentiles back in their own coin (as Mattathias had advised his sons) but by turning the other cheek and going the second mile. The command to love one's enemies, and the prohibition on violent revolution, constituted not an attack on Torah as such but a radically different interpretation of Israel's ancestral tradition from those currently on offer. Jesus, precisely in affirming Israel's unique vocation to be the light of the world, was insisting that, now that the moment for fulfillment had come, it was time to relativize those god-given markers of Israel's distinctiveness.[67]

In short, it was time for the people of God to make the epoch-breaking transition to family—from *ethnos* to a trans-ethnic surrogate family of God.

4

The Communities of Paul of Tarsus

PAUL'S LETTERS ARE GENERALLY RECOGNIZED as our earliest evidence of Christian beliefs and behaviors.[1] My analysis will focus upon those documents that are universally assigned to Pauline authorship.[2] For each of Paul's epistles, I will be sensitive to the presence of kinship terminology in the text and evidence of (or a challenge to exercise) the kind of sibling solidarity characteristic of a Mediterranean family.

The outset of 1 Thessalonians reveals Paul's conception of community as he wished it to function among his converts. I will examine the letter more thoroughly later in the chapter, but it is important to note at this point that already in 1 Thessalonians, probably the first extant letter of Paul's that we have, the kinship model is deeply embedded in the text.[3] Nineteen occurrences of sibling terminology sprinkled throughout the epistle reflect a kinship metaphor that is in turn reinforced by the references to God as the father of the community and by the expressions of family-like affective intimacy that are found elsewhere in the letter (see below). We will discover that the PKG social model reflected in Paul's first extant letter is not unique to 1 Thessalonians. Rather, the idea of the church as family is ubiquitous in Paul's writings and is, therefore, central to Paul's understanding of the manner in which interpersonal relationships are to function in the communities to which he writes.

A computer search of the broader Pauline corpus for the presence of three important kinship ideas yields the following data:[4]

> sibling terminology—118 occurrences
> father terminology—40 occurrences
> inheritance terminology—14 occurrences

The frequency with which these terms appear in Paul's writings (ranging from 3.29 occurrences per thousand words in 2 Corinthians to 15.54 per thousand in Philemon) is all the more striking when we consider that the overwhelming majority of occurrences reflect a surrogate kinship model. Seldom does Paul have occasion to use such terminology for blood relationships (for example, 1 Cor 9:5: "the brothers of the Lord"). The following passages are important for gaining a basic structural understanding of Paul's conception of the church as family (God as Father, adoption, ancestral line, inheritance, and so forth): Rom 4:1-18; 8:12-29; Gal 3:26—4:7; and 1 Thess 2:7-12.

For Paul, moreover, the family idea represents much more than terminology and conceptual structure. Paul expects his readers to live out the metaphor in their day-to-day relationships. Insights from cultural anthropology reveal a correlation between specific types of language and the social order, a correlation that enhances our appreciation of the power inherent in Paul's kinship metaphor. Paul's employment of family language is more than a stylistic formality. It represents a strategically crafted attempt to challenge (and sometimes shame) the communities to which he writes to behave in a manner consistent with the PKG value system.

LANGUAGE AND THE SOCIAL ORDER

Much attention has been given in recent years to the role of language in establishing and affirming the social order. Three observations in particular prove relevant to the study of Paul and his writings. A central function of language in strong-group societies like those of Mediterranean antiquity is to reaffirm the social order; language in such cultures exhibits a solidarity-making function. The primary linguistic metaphor Paul employs to reaffirm the social order is the Mediterranean family. Paul, however, uses family language rather unevenly in several of his epistles. Some sections of his letters contain much in the way of family language, while other parts of the same letters are relatively devoid of kinship terms. A few comments will prove helpful regarding the first and third observations (the second will become clear as this chapter unfolds).

Mary Douglas's important work on ritual and symbolism underlines the role of language in establishing and affirming the social order. Douglas contends that groups reflecting a high level of social solidarity tend to exhibit a correspondingly restrictive linguistic code. She then describes the function of this "insider language":

> The [dynamic] arises in a small-scale, very local social situation in which the speakers all have access to the same fundamental assumptions; in this category every utterance is

pressed into service to affirm the social order. Speech in this case exercises a solidarity-maintaining function closely comparable to religion as Durkheim saw it functioning in primitive society.[5]

Robert Wuthnow elaborates:

> A restricted code, because of its very restrictiveness, forces others to utilize their commonly held group assumptions to decode what is said, and this, in turn, brings these assumptions to life, and as such reaffirms the group which they constitute. If groups are comprised of shared assumptions among individuals—a common culture—then the activation of that culture is an activation of the group.[6]

The manner in which Paul uses kinship terminology appears highly consonant with the speech strategies associated with strong-group social settings in the above analysis. Paul often deliberately employs kinship terms to reaffirm commonly held group assumptions, particularly when his communities are falling short of the Mediterranean family ideal of social solidarity.

What is surprising, in view of the above observations, is the rather uneven distribution of family language in Paul's letters. This corresponds to the fact that family vocabulary is actually used rather rarely in our everyday speech. Roger Keesing explains why:

> In many societies, kin terms are apparently used only rarely. A common pattern seems to be to refer to a person's kinship relation to you not in everyday conversation, but in situations when that person is violating the norms of kinship; or in situations when you are trying to manipulate him (lend me a dollar, brother. . .). Use of kin terms often turns out to be a political strategy, not an everyday social nicety.[7]

Keesing's remarks provide an enlightening interpretive window through which to view Paul's rhetorical strategies. As mentioned above, the kinship metaphor, so dominant with Paul, is nevertheless distributed rather unevenly in several of his letters. Romans and 1 and 2 Corinthians, in particular, contain clusters of family language at specific points in Paul's argument. Keesing's observations lead us to suspect that the increased density of kinship language in these passages corresponds to a concern on Paul's part to reestablish PKG values where such values have been ignored or violated on the part of the readers. Robert Banks rightly maintains, therefore, that Paul's "brother" terminology "has not lost its basic meaning and become a mere formal description."[8] Paul deliberately employs "brother" and other kinship terms in order to encourage his readers to live out the family metaphor in their day-to-day relationships, for he has intentionally crafted his letters precisely to that end. We turn now to the Pauline corpus.

1 CORINTHIANS

The Corinthian correspondence provides a fitting point of departure for a survey of Paul's use of the kinship metaphor. The first epistle constitutes the most detailed expression in the Pauline corpus of the author's application of theology to practical problems of day-to-day life in a local church group. Specifically, 1 Corinthians reveals a church divided. Paul responds by bringing to bear upon the situation in Corinth all of his extensive linguistic and rhetorical resources in a manner that radically inverts common assumptions about social status and the body politic.

Scholarly treatments of the Corinthian correspondence have traditionally focused upon the problem of identifying Paul's opponents. Scholars who grapple extensively with this question inevitably find themselves preoccupied with the relationships between Paul and his various adversaries.[9] Such works also attend more to the theological concerns of the parties involved rather than to the social relationships among the Corinthian church members.[10] A more recent approach, which better serves my purposes in the present discussion, draws upon the social sciences in order to understand the nature of the discord besetting the Jesus movement in Corinth. Literary criticism is then employed to elucidate the manner in which Paul addresses these divisions.[11]

Discord in the Corinthian Community

Dale Martin aptly summarizes current thinking about the Corinthian problem as revealed in Paul's first epistle: "The Corinthian church was for the most part split along one major 'fault line,' with wealthier, higher-status Christians (along with their dependents or ideological allies) on one side and lower-status Christians on the other."[12] Martin, and others who argue similarly, follows Paul in designating the two parties with the terms "Strong" and "Weak."[13]

Evidence for the convictions and value system characteristic of the Strong in Corinth may be gleaned from the few fragmentary quotations Paul provides of the Corinthians' own comments concerning various controversial issues. Among those found in 1 Corinthians are the following:

> All things are lawful for me. (6:12; 10:23)

> Food is meant for the stomach and the stomach for food [and God will destroy both one and the other]. (6:13)[14]

> All of us possess knowledge. (8:1)
> No idol in the world really exists, and . . . there is no God but one. (8:4)

Slogans like these originated in the "general marketplace of popular, moral philosophy."[15] The values reflected found their primary expression in the philosophical schools and, most importantly, in the homes of the empire's high-status elites, who could afford the luxury of a household philosopher. This means that the Strong in Corinth, whose sentiments are reflected in the above quotations (and whose social values are so powerfully challenged by Paul), constituted an elite social class.

Understanding divisions in the community along the lines of social class has generated new and convincing readings of various passages in 1 Corinthians. Gerd Theissen, in an important series of articles, utilized the Strong-Weak interpretive grid to demonstrate that controversies over both the Lord's Supper (11:17-34) and the eating of meat sacrificed to idols (chaps. 8 and 10) had split the community along status lines.[16] Martin maintains that problems concerning lawsuits in the congregation, Paul's defense of his means of self-support, and the divisive issue of glossalalia also had their roots in the different values and social expectations of the Strong and the Weak.[17]

Paul's Rhetorical Strategy

So much for the identity of the problems and opposing parties at Corinth. I am particularly concerned here with Paul's strategy for addressing this split in the community. Margaret Mitchell has recently identified 1 Corinthians as an epistolary version of a Greco-Roman concord speech (Gr. *homonoia*; Lat. *concordia*), a subcategory of the broader genre of deliberative discourse that finds both oral and written expression in antiquity.[18] The concord speech was designed to challenge a divided people, typically the people of a *polis*, to set aside their differences and become united once again. Rhetoricians delivered concord speeches to cities and their leaders at times of crisis. Historians also utilized the genre in their narratives. Others, like Paul, sought to diffuse factional behavior through epistolary appeal. Laurence Welborn summarizes: "Their authors, generally philosophers or rhetoricians, seek to calm the outbreak of faction, within cities or between cities, by dissuading from strife (*stasis*) and exhorting to concord (*homonoia*)."[19]

As Mitchell has shown, 1 Corinthians contains a number of the specific terms and broader rhetorical strategies characteristic of concord speeches. The letter's first exhortation sets the tone immediately: "Now I appeal to you . . . that all of you be in agreement and that there be no divisions among you, but that you be united in the same mind and the same purpose" (1:10). The theme is again picked up in chapter 12, in which Paul applies his body metaphor: "But God has so arranged the body, giving the greater honor to the inferior member, that there may be no dissension within the body, but the members may have the same care for one another"

(12:24-25). Paul thus employs a variety of terms from vocabulary common to concord speeches, and the overall thrust of the letter concerns the unity and harmonious functioning of the Corinthian congregation.[20]

Martin has expanded upon Mitchell's insights with the striking suggestion that "Paul uses homonoia rhetoric to an ideological end that is the opposite of that normally advocated by such rhetoric."[21] To understand the significance of Martin's remark, we must first grasp the manner in which homonoia rhetoric typically functioned in the ancient world. The ideological purpose of concord speeches was almost universally to mitigate conflict by reaffirming and solidifying the *strongly hierarchical* nature of the ancient *polis*. Martin offers an excerpt from a Pseudo-Aristotelian work in which the *cosmos* is compared with the *polis*, a typical homonoia strategy, and the status quo is thereby reaffirmed:

> It is as if men should wonder how a city survives, composed as it is of the most opposite classes (I mean rich and poor, young and old, weak and strong, bad and good). They do not recognize that the most wonderful thing of all about the harmonious working (*homonoias*) of a city-community is this: that out of plurality and diversity it achieves a homogeneous unity capable of admitting every variation and degree. (*On the Cosmos*, 5.396b)[22]

Martin perceptively observes:

> It is worth noting that in the joining of these hierarchically arranged opposites, the hierarchy itself is not challenged. In fact, since opposites are necessary for each other's existence, it would appear that the weak and poor are necessary to balance the strong and rich—in the city as well as the cosmos. Homonoia has as its aim not equality or strength for all members but the preservation of the "natural" relation of strength to weakness.[23]

Martin acknowledges that the upper class was forced to yield at times in order to preserve harmony in the *polis*. Such concessions, however, constituted no challenge to the normal and natural hierarchy of the political body.

The conciliatory speech by Menenius Agrippa, who, in order to dissuade the Roman plebeians from rebellion, relates the famous fable about the body that is destroyed because the different members rebelled against the belly, is a classic example of a homonoia speech that seeks to preserve the "benevolent patriarchal ideology" of the upper class.[24] Agrippa's speech is flanked in the narrative by the democratic speech of Lucius Junius (a leader of the plebeians) and by the oligarchic speech of Senator Appius Claudius, who suggests that a dictator should be appointed (compare Dionysius of Halicarnassus 6). Agrippa's presentation mediates between the two extremes reflected in the speeches of Lucius Junius and Appius Claudius, extremes representing democracy and tyranny respectively. Martin comments:

In Greco-Roman political writings and speeches, democracy is portrayed as the excessive freedom of the masses and the enslavement of the upper class (the "natural" leaders) to the lower class, resulting in chaos. Tyranny, at the other extreme, is portrayed as an excessively harsh and unbending rule whereby the upper class, an oligarchic faction, or a dictator rules without taking into account sufficiently the interests of the entire political body, including the masses. But when the stronger rules the weaker with restraint and the weaker submits to the stronger in self-control, the interests of the entire city are protected, and everybody lives happily ever after.[25]

The benevolent patriarchalism regularly affirmed in homonoia speeches was therefore consistently conservative—geared, as Martin appropriately concludes, "to maintaining the class structure by advocating only *moderate* exploitation of the lower class."[26]

Paul, in stark contrast, employs the concord genre to a different end. Instead of reinforcing the social hierarchy, Paul challenges the Strong among his readers to a self-lowering status reversal that flies in the face of traditional concord rhetoric. First, he puts forward a crucified criminal as the honored, central figure of the community's devotion ("the cross of Christ," 1:17). This radical inversion of common assumptions provides Paul with a point of departure to introduce a view of reality that is diametrically opposed to that of the dominant culture. He contrasts the two opposing realms:

For the message about the cross is foolishness to those who are perishing, but to us who are being saved it is the power of God. . . . For Jews demand signs and Greeks desire wisdom, but we proclaim Christ crucified, a stumbling block to Jews and foolishness to Gentiles, but to those who are the called, both Jews and Greeks, Christ the power of God and the wisdom of God. (1:18, 22-24)

Paul then identifies his readers as examples of God's alternative *cosmos*:

Consider your own call, brothers and sisters: not many of you were wise by human standards, not many were powerful, not many were of noble birth. But God chose what is foolish in the world to shame the wise; God chose what is weak in the world to shame the strong; God chose what is low and despised in the world, things that are not, to reduce to nothing things that are, so that no one might boast in the presence of God. He is the source of your life in Christ Jesus, who became for us wisdom from God, and righteousness and sanctification and redemption, in order that, as it is written, "Let the one who boasts, boast in the Lord." (1:26-31)

Paul proceeds to use this paradigm to address the various problems in the Corinthian community, each time challenging the Strong to voluntarily reverse their status and lower themselves to serve the Weak for the common good. As Martin concludes, "This move marks a radical break with traditional homonoia speeches, which invoke a unified, stable cosmos. Paul, by contrast, opposes 'this cosmos' with an 'anti-cosmos' whose value and status system is an inversion of what the Corinthians see all around them."[27]

I wish to develop the thinking of Mitchell and Martin yet further. Kinship terminology is generally absent from homonoia speeches in antiquity, which is not surprising in light of Martin's contention that the concord speech was targeted to affirm the status hierarchy of ancient society.[28] There was simply no place in homonoia rhetoric for a social model—family—whose most basic relational values included affective intimacy and generalized reciprocity. Such values were not exercised across the dividing line of social class, and the kinship terminology with which they were associated would have undermined, rather than reinforced, the purpose of the traditional concord genre. What is remarkable in this regard, then, is the juxtaposition of family language and concord terminology in 1 Corinthians. Indeed, Paul introduces his first appeal to concord with a challenge for his readers to behave like PKG siblings in the family of God:

> Now I appeal to you, brothers and sisters, by the name of our Lord Jesus Christ, that all of you be in agreement and that there be no divisions among you, but that you be united in the same mind and the same purpose. For it has been reported to me by Chloe's people that there are quarrels among you, my brothers and sisters. (1:10-11)[29]

Paul had already referenced the symbolic world of discourse that he shares with his readers in the first sentence of his epistle. He there referred to his coauthor as "our brother Sosthenes" (1:1).[30] With the twofold repetition of the vocative "brothers and sisters" in verses 10 and 11, Paul now makes it immediately clear that the "divisions" and "quarrels" that characterize the Corinthian community are unacceptable among a people who refer to themselves with sibling terms of endearment.[31]

To summarize, Paul indeed employs the concord genre in a unique way. Through his use of kinship terms and the PKG metaphor, Paul repeatedly challenges his readers to live out a social model whose values form a stunning contrast to the hierarchical matrix of the *polis*: a family of brothers and sisters who have God as their father. Paul turns the conventions of rhetoric on their head in order to invert the social expectations of the Strong among his readers.[32]

Family Terminology in 1 Corinthians

That Paul and his Corinthian readers shared the conception of the church as family can hardly be challenged. Kinship expressions, including, especially, sibling terminology, are sprinkled throughout the epistle. The word group *adelphos* (sibling terms *brother/sister*) occurs forty-one times in the course of the epistle. In every case but one, the term is used for the surrogate family of God.[33] Among the many passages in which Paul addresses his readers as siblings are the following:

> Consider your own call, brothers and sisters: not many of you were wise by human standards, not many were powerful, not many were of noble birth. (1:26)

> When I came to you, brothers and sisters, I did not come proclaiming the mystery of God to you in lofty words or wisdom. (2:1)

> And so, brothers and sisters, I could not speak to you as spiritual people, but rather as people of the flesh, as infants in Christ. (3:1)

The multiple appearance of "brother(s)" in Paul's final series of greetings reflects the affective bond characteristic of siblings in a PKG family system:

> Therefore let no one despise him. Send him on his way in peace, so that he may come to me; for I am expecting him with the brothers. Now concerning our brother Apollos, I strongly urged him to visit you with the other brothers, but he was not at all willing to come now. He will come when he has the opportunity. (16:11-12)

> Now, brothers and sisters, you know that members of the household of Stephanas were the first converts in Achaia, and they have devoted themselves to the service of the saints. (16:15)

> All the brothers and sisters send greetings. Greet one another with a holy kiss. (16:20)

Paul introduces his most succinct summary of the early Christian *kerygma* (message of proclamation) with the same term of familial affection (*adelphos*): "Now I would remind you, brothers and sisters, of the good news that I proclaimed to you." (15:1) Fatherhood imagery—the identity of God as the father of the community—is another aspect of the family model encountered on several occasions in the letter. The following passages are illustrative:

> Then comes the end, when he hands over the kingdom to God the Father, after he has destroyed every ruler and every authority and every power. (15:24)

> Yet for us there is one God, the Father, from whom are all things and for whom we exist, and one Lord, Jesus Christ, through whom are all things and through whom we exist. (8:6)

Chapter 2 explored the vertical focus of Mediterranean family systems, which results in a preoccupation with the past and the future of the patrilineal kin group. Focus on the past manifests itself in concern with one's ancestors. Future orientation finds expression in the constant awareness of family inheritance and the concern for long-term survival of the extended family. Early Christian writings reflect both an awareness of one's ancestors—in this case, of course, ancestors in the faith—and a concern with inheritance, albeit at a high level of abstraction.

The inheritance *topos* (theme) is reflected in the following text-segment from 1 Corinthians: "Do you not know that wrongdoers will not inherit the kingdom of God? Do not be deceived! Fornicators, idolaters, adulterers, male prostitutes, sodomites, thieves, the greedy, drunkards, revilers, robbers—none of these will inherit the kingdom of God" (6:9-10). Elsewhere, the Corinthians' forefathers in the faith come into view. In 1 Corinthians 10:1-6, Paul instructs his readers concerning the spiritual heritage they share with their ancestors and reminds them that most of their ancestors proved less than faithful. Near the end of the letter, the reader encounters sibling terminology and inheritance imagery in the same sentence: "What I am saying, brothers and sisters, is this: flesh and blood cannot inherit the kingdom of God" (15:50).

So far we are in familiar territory, since each of the above ideas finds expression in Jesus of Nazareth's conception of community, surveyed in the previous chapter. We encounter innovation, however, in the following excerpt:

> I am not writing this to make you ashamed, but to admonish you as my beloved children. For though you might have ten thousand guardians in Christ, you do not have many fathers. Indeed, in Christ Jesus I became your father through the gospel. I appeal to you, then, be imitators of me. For this reason I sent you Timothy, who is my beloved and faithful child in the Lord, to remind you of my ways in Christ Jesus, as I teach them everywhere in every church. (4:14-17)

As explained in chapter 3, the surrogate kin group of followers gathered together by Jesus of Nazareth had no earthly father. Because of their identity as God's offspring, Jesus instructed his disciples to regard one another as siblings and to call no man father (Matt 23:9). Neither did Jesus promise a replacement in the human faith family (that is, among fellow community members) for the blood fathers who had been left behind by those who became members of Jesus' group (Mark 10:29-30).

In contrast, Paul here refers to himself as the Corinthians' "father through the gospel," literally, "I begat you" (4:15). This represents marked innovation in the use of the family metaphor. Various writers refer to conversion as a new birth (see John 3:3; 1 Pet 1:3, 23; 1 John 4:7). God, the surrogate father of the community, is usually identified as the agent effecting this spiritual birth (see Titus 3:5; 1 Pet 1:3; 1 John 4:7). Here, however, it is Paul who claims he "begat" his readers. The alteration of the metaphor is easily explained. The Corinthians, and most other members of Paul's communities, are now at least one generation removed from the earliest followers of Jesus. They had responded to the gospel under the preaching of those who had preceded them in the family of faith. Paul therefore refers to his converts at Corinth as "my beloved children" (4:14).[34]

Timothy, too, is Paul's "beloved and faithful child in the Lord" (v. 17). In the present context, Timothy, the "faithful child," is to remind children whose behavior is less than ideal (the readers) of the lifestyle of their common spiritual progenitor. The Corinthians are then to "be imitators" of Paul. Imitation of the behavior of one's father is, of course, a cross-cultural family value and is hardly unique to Paul's society. The value is particularly emphasized, however, in cultures that take a conservative approach to social change and exhibit descent group kinship systems, such as the world of Mediterranean antiquity. In contrast to contemporary American practices, the ideal son in the ancient world was typically expected to adopt his father's general lifestyle, including, among other things, his father's religious orientation, means of livelihood, and place of residence.

Although Clement of Alexandria will proceed to argue for a different perspective, he accurately describes the sentiments of the great majority of his peers in second-century Alexandria: "The man who has produced of himself one like him has achieved fulfillment—even more when he sees the other having followed in his footsteps too, in other words, when he has established a child in the same natural place as the father" (*Strom.* 2.139.5). Thus Paul's challenge for his children in the faith to imitate his behavior would have powerfully resonated with the family sensibilities of his Mediterranean readers.

Since Paul in 1 Corinthians 4 places the emphasis of his exhortation primarily upon imitation of his behavior—and only secondarily upon obedience to his fatherly directives—the reader does not sense a strongly authoritative, patriarchal flavor in the above passage. Paul addresses his readers in rather endearing terms: "my beloved children" (v. 14). And although the Greek participle translated "to admonish" in the verse is a strong term and refers to fatherly authority in other contexts (Eph 6:4), it was also a word Paul could use of activity that he deemed appropriate between siblings in the family of God.

The immediately ensuing context of 1 Corinthians 4:14-17, however, contains one of Paul's strongest warnings to his readers:

> But some of you, thinking that I am not coming to you, have become arrogant. But I will come to you soon, if the Lord wills, and I will find out not the talk of these arro-

gant people but their power. For the kingdom of God depends not on talk but on power. What would you prefer? Am I to come to you with a stick, or with love in a spirit of gentleness? (vv. 18-21)

The Greek term translated "stick" is the term used in the Septuagint to refer to the rod with which a father disciplines his children (Prov 22:15; 23:13; 24:14). One cannot help but think that the Corinthians would have read verses 14 through 21 as a unit, with the *topos* of Paul's role as the readers' spiritual father linguistically framed by an *inclusio* in verses 14 ("I am . . . writing . . . to admonish you as my beloved children") and 21 ("Am I to come to you with a stick?").[35] The authoritative aspect of Paul's role as the Corinthians' spiritual father is, then, clearly in view.

On the other hand, plurality leadership apparently prevailed in Paul's communities. In none of Paul's epistles can we identify a single authoritative leader, let alone one who is referred to as the father of the community. Philippians specifically addresses groups of leaders ("bishops and deacons," 1:1), and Paul generally refers to the leaders of his various churches in the plural ("those who labor among you, and have charge of you in the Lord and admonish you," 1 Thess 5:12). Apparently, then, the image of Paul as his converts' spiritual father was not replicated at the level of local community leadership during his lifetime. In fact, the metaphor is rather fluid in Paul's hands, for he can address his readers with sibling terminology while in the same sentence referring to them as "infants in Christ": "And so, brothers and sisters, I could not speak to you as spiritual people, but rather as people of the flesh, as infants in Christ" (1 Thess 3:1). Nevertheless, Paul's modification of the surrogate kinship structure that we saw reflected in the practices of Jesus of Nazareth, combined with the sharp warning of 1 Corinthians 4:21, provides a foundation upon which later writers will erect a church family structure characterized by highly authoritative one-man leadership in individual community settings (see Ignatius of Antioch, chap. 5).

I move now from the structural aspects of Paul's familial ecclesiology in 1 Corinthians to the ways in which he expected the model to find expression in the day-to-day life of the community. We saw above that kinship terminology typically serves a solidarity-making function, and that it is generally employed when the speaker (or writer) perceives that the norms of kinship have been violated. Paul's first extant letter to the Corinthians reflects this at the outset: "Now I appeal to you, brothers and sisters, by the name of our Lord Jesus Christ, that all of you be in agreement and that there be no divisions among you, but that you be united in the same mind and the same purpose" (1:10). The assumption that a PKG group of blood "brothers and sisters" would be "in agreement" on important family issues is foundational. We are reminded of the pleasure Ben Sira's soul found in "agreement between brothers" (25:1). And Paul's rhetorical strategy is most apparent when he brings the emotive force of kinship terminology to bear upon specific problems in the church. Two PKG values in particular are underscored by Paul in 1 Corinthians.

Generalized Reciprocity

It is hardly a coincidence that the kinship metaphor pervades Paul's admonition to refrain from taking fellow members of the community before pagan tribunals (1 Corinthians 6). We observed in chapter 2 that it is a contradiction of PKG generalized reciprocity to seek to avenge a wrong suffered at the hands of a sibling. An even more serious breach of PKG norms arises when a family member appeals to outsiders for support against his kin. Paul shames the Corinthians for taking family disputes to civic court.[36] Note, again, the concentration of the *adelphos* word group—and the rhetorical power of the final clause of verse 8 ("even your own brethren"):

> When one of you has a grievance against a brother, does he dare go to law before the unrighteous instead of the saints? . . . I say this to your shame. Can it be that there is no man among you wise enough to decide between members of the brotherhood, but brother goes to law against brother, and that before unbelievers? To have lawsuits at all with one another is a defeat for you. Why not rather suffer wrong? Why not rather be defrauded? But you yourselves wrong and defraud, and that even your own brethren. (1 Cor 6:1-8 RSV)

Paul, in the verses following, maintains the family metaphor, shifting from the theme of sibling solidarity to that of inheritance, as he brings his exhortation on the topic to a close (6:9-11).

Paul's "grocery list" of vices in verses 9-10 is, of course, stock material utilized in ancient literature for deviant labeling.[37] But his point is not to be missed. A so-called brother who wrongs or defrauds a member of his own family through recourse to the Greco-Roman legal system is no true brother at all. He is, therefore, excluded from the inheritance shared by the children of God.

Only recently have the social-status implications of litigation in antiquity been factored into the interpretation of 1 Corinthians 6. The insights gained provide an enlightening framework within which to discuss Paul's use of sibling terminology in the passage. Roman courts were, of course, biased in favor of members of the upper class. Bruce Winter observes, "The right to prosecute was not granted to all. If the defendant was a parent, patron, magistrate, or a person of high rank, then charges could not be brought by children, freedmen, private citizens and men of low rank respectively."[38]

Additionally, judges and jurors came almost exclusively from the well-to-do, and lower-status persons typically lacked the funds to hire an advocate. Bribery was rampant. A character in Petronius's *Satyricon* reveals the common expectations of his day: "Of what avail are laws where money rules alone, and the poor suitor can never succeed? . . . A lawsuit is nothing more than a public auction, and the knightly juror who sits listening to the case approves, with the record of his vote, something bought" (*Satyricon* 14).[39] Lower-status persons who found themselves involved in litigation were thus at a serious disadvantage. This meant, of course, that people of higher status were much more likely than those of lower status to initiate litigation.

Even more important for the present discussion is a further observation by Alan Mitchell. Drawing upon the insights of legal anthropologists, Mitchell maintains, "People of the same rank are more likely to work out a compromise rather than go to court. The further away they are on the social scale the less likely they are to settle out of court. An increase in stratification predicts a decrease in conciliation."[40] Adding this insight to the advantage that higher-status persons had in the Greco-Roman legal system, Mitchell summarizes, "One can conclude from these basic principles that people of higher status are favored in the legal process and are more likely to litigate against those of lower status and are less likely to litigate against one another."[41] It seems likely, then, that the lawsuits referred to in 1 Corinthians 6 involved higher-status members of the community defrauding their lower-status "brothers" in the courts of Corinth. Paul forcefully challenges the probity of such behavior.

Mitchell proceeds to locate the primary rhetorical thrust of Paul's argument in a theme common to Hellenistic philosophy which maintained that the truly "wise" person would never initiate litigation.[42] The idea is certainly present in 1 Corinthians 6:5: "Can it be that there is no man among you wise enough to decide? . . ." Paul's rhetorical sword, however, has more than a single edge. Given a legal context in which "[persons] of the same rank are more likely to work out a compromise rather than go to court," Paul's sibling terminology gains great rhetorical force.[43] For who in ancient Mediterranean society should reflect more same-rank solidarity than the Corinthian "brethren"?

My understanding of the generalized reciprocity characteristic of Mediterranean family systems leads me to conclude that the primary thrust of Paul's rhetoric lies in his repeated recourse to the *adelphos* word group in the passage. Yes, it is out of character for those who claim to be "wise" to litigate. But it is utterly shameful for a sibling to do so. As Paul himself exclaims at the crescendo of his argument, "even your own brethren" (6:8).[44] Paul's challenge, "Why not rather suffer wrong?" (v. 7), finds its primary locus of resonance here. PKG generalized reciprocity demands that a family member refrain from avenging a wrong suffered at the hands of a brother. Paul's readers were violating this PKG norm, thus the density of sibling terminology in the text-segment.

Familial Loyalty

In the previous chapters, I emphasized the centrality of familial loyalty to Mediterranean kinship groups. I specifically discussed the priority of loyalty to one's family of origin over loyalty to the family to which one belongs solely by marriage. In 1 Corinthians 7:12-16, Paul addresses the problem of divided loyalties that occurs for a Christian brother or sister who is married to an unbeliever. His rhetorical strategy involves the use of the PKG value of sibling loyalty to argue for the priority of the surrogate family relationship. The primary thrust of the chapter relates to the place of sex and marriage in the Christian community. The literature on 1 Corinthians 7 is immense, interpretive problems remain, and no attempt will be made here to evaluate all the options. I will simply draw attention to the kinship terminology in the context and offer some observations about the insight it provides for understanding Paul's argument.

First Corinthians 7 begins with Paul's perspective on marriage in general, a passage that has received much attention in the scholarly literature:

> Now concerning the matters about which you wrote: "It is well for a man not to touch a woman." But because of cases of sexual immorality, each man should have his own wife and each woman her own husband. The husband should give to his wife her conjugal rights, and likewise the wife to her husband. For the wife does not have authority over her own body, but the husband does; likewise the husband does not have authority over his own body, but the wife does. Do not deprive one another except perhaps by agreement for a set time, to devote yourselves to prayer, and then come together again, so that Satan may not tempt you because of your lack of self-control. This I say by way of concession, not of command. I wish that all were as I myself am. But each has a particular gift from God, one having one kind and another a different kind. To the unmarried and the widows I say that it is well for them to remain unmarried as I am. But if they are not practicing self-control, they should marry. For it is better to marry than to be aflame with passion. (7:1-9)[45]

Paul here discusses marriages involving two believers (see "devote yourselves to prayer," v. 5). He proceeds to conclude his general comments with more specific instructions regarding separation and divorce. Most scholars agree that in verses 10 and 11, Paul paraphrases Jesus' teaching about divorce and remarriage:[46] "To the married I give this command—not I but the Lord—that the wife should not separate from her husband (but if she does separate, let her remain unmarried or else be reconciled to her husband), and that the husband should not divorce his wife." Sibling terminology has been noticeably absent from the text since the last occurrence of *adelphos*, some twenty-four verses previous, in 6:8. In 1 Corinthians 7:12, however, Paul introduces a new but related issue, that of marriages between believers and unbelievers. He also reintroduces sibling terminology into the text at this juncture, in order to buttress his argument.

The conversion of whole households to the Jesus movement was not uncommon in antiquity, and believers were expected to marry other believers (7:39 and, by implication, 2 Cor 6:14). The result was that many Christians were married to others who shared their faith. Nevertheless, it remained the case that at times only one spouse would convert. The reality of such divided households left Paul and other early Christian leaders with an issue that was apparently not addressed in the teachings of Jesus. I noted earlier in the present study that loyalty to one's siblings typically took precedence over loyalty to one's spouse in Mediterranean society in situations in which one had to choose between them. Tensions were particularly high when serious conflict arose between a person's family of origin and the family into which she married. The constitution of the early churches as surrogate kinship groups introduced a whole new factor into the loyalty equation, since the conflict between "the children of God and the children of the devil" (1 John 3:10) was of a most foundational nature according to the worldview championed by the Jesus movement. Inevitable problems would arise in marriages involving parties from both "families."

For Christians who were married to believing spouses, divided loyalty was, of course, a moot issue—one's marriage partner was at the same time a sister or brother in the faith. To be loyal to one's spouse was to be loyal to one's surrogate sibling. For believers married to unbelievers, however, divided loyalties were inevitable. Paul now turns his attention to this issue, drawing upon the PKG value of family loyalty by reintroducing sibling terminology into his argument in 1 Corinthians 7:12-16. We will see that Paul lands precisely where our studies of PKG family values would lead us to expect him to land—he affirms the priority of sibling loyalty over spousal loyalty.

Paul begins the section by forbidding divorce in the case of an unbelieving spouse who consents to remain in the marriage:

> To the rest I say—I and not the Lord—that if any believer [Gr. *adelphos*] has a wife who is an unbeliever, and she consents to live with him, he should not divorce her. And if any woman has a husband who is an unbeliever, and he consents to live with her, she should not divorce him. For the unbelieving husband is made holy through his wife, and the unbelieving wife is made holy through her husband [Gr. *adelphos*]. Otherwise, your children would be unclean, but as it is, they are holy. (1 Cor 7:12-14)

Although he claims to be offering his own view ("I and not the Lord," v. 12), Paul's directives at this point in his argument appear to be a logical extension of the teachings of Jesus that Paul himself cited in the previous context. Already, however, Paul introduces a "brother"/"unbeliever" antithesis into his argument. The antithesis then serves as the foundation for striking innovation in the verse immediately following, in which Paul considers a much different situation: "But if the unbelieving partner separates, let it be so; in such a case the brother or sister is not bound. It is to peace that God has called you" (1 Cor 7:15). The innovation is in the phrase "is not bound." Similar terminology in Romans 7:1-6, along with the absence of an explicit prohibition of remarriage here as compared with Paul's instructions for two believers who separate (see "let her remain unmarried or else be reconciled to her husband," v. 11), suggests that Paul deems wholly acceptable the remarriage of a "brother or sister" whose unbelieving spouse chooses to depart.

In allowing remarriage in the case of the departure of an unbelieving spouse, Paul is self-conscious of the fact that he assumes a position not reflected in the teachings of Jesus. Indeed, he faces a problem that Jesus of Nazareth apparently did not confront. By importing sibling terminology into his argument at precisely this point, Paul assumes a paradigm that will have long-standing implications for Christians in the ancient world: unbelievers are not truly family to begin with.[47] And all marriages involving a "brother" or a "sister" with an unbeliever are necessarily and ultimately tentative: "For how do you know, O wife," Paul concludes, "whether you will save your husband? Or how do you know, O husband, whether you will save your wife?" (v. 16a NASB).

The PKG value that demands loyalty to blood relations (especially siblings) over loyalty to one's spouse is thus appropriated and subtly reinterpreted by Paul to apply to a Christian's loyalty to her siblings in the faith. Indeed, Paul expresses his sentiments even more directly, as he summarizes his arguments in 1 Corinthians 7. Apparently, even the marriage relationship between believing spouses must take second place to the priority of sibling solidarity in the family of faith: "I mean, brothers and sisters, the appointed time has grown short; from now on, let even those who have wives be as though they had none" (7:29).

Other unexamined passages of 1 Corinthians that contain PKG language must be bypassed in order to maintain the broad historical focus of this study (see 4:6; 5:11; 8:11-13; 11:33; 14:6, 20, 26). The above survey suffices to demonstrate the centrality of family among Paul's various metaphors for the Corinthian community. Kinship terminology is sprinkled throughout the epistle, and Paul powerfully uses the shared metaphor to challenge his readers to exercise the essential values characteristic of Mediterranean sibling relations.

2 Corinthians

Paul's second extant letter to his congregation at Corinth contains proportionally less kinship terminology than 1 Corinthians. The metaphor is present, however, and it takes on particularly pointed application at the very place in the letter where Paul challenges his readers to participate in the famine-relief gift he is collecting for the churches of Judaea.

Family Language in 2 Corinthians

Sibling terms occur twelve times in 2 Corinthians. Timothy is introduced as "our brother" in 1:1, and the readers are addressed as "brethren" in 1:8 and 13:11. The context in which the latter reference occurs reflects the social solidarity Paul desires for the Corinthian family: "Finally, brothers and sisters, farewell. Put things in order, listen to my appeal, agree with one another, live in peace; and the God of love and peace will be with you" (13:11). Mutual agreement and harmony are, of course, among the basic expectations for behavior among members of a patrilineal kinship group.

Earlier in the epistle, the affective nature of brotherhood in Mediterranean antiquity finds graphic expression in Paul's comments about his feelings toward his fellow missionary Titus. Notice, again, the presence of the sibling term in the passage: "When I came to Troas to proclaim the good news of Christ, a door was opened for me in the Lord; but my mind could not rest because I did not find my brother Titus there. So I said farewell to them and went on to Macedonia" (2:12-13). The sharing of material goods among brothers is illustrated in 11:9: "And when I was with you and was in need, I did not burden anyone, for my needs were supplied by the friends [*adelphos*] who came from Macedonia."

The fatherhood of God is reflected at the outset of the epistle where, in the course of two verses, God is variously identified as "our Father" (1:2), "the . . . Father of our Lord Jesus Christ" (1:3), and "the Father of mercies" (1:3). The image returns in an Old Testament quotation in the sixth chapter of the letter:

> I will live in them and walk among them, and I will be their God, and they shall be my people. Therefore come out from them, and be separate from them, says the Lord, and touch nothing unclean; then I will welcome you, and I will be your father, and you shall be my sons and daughters, says the Lord Almighty. (6:16b-18)

The father metaphor appears a fifth and final time near the end of the letter: "the God and Father of the Lord Jesus Christ" (11:31).

Finally, Paul alludes again in 2 Corinthians to the fact that he is the spiritual progenitor of the community:

> In return—I speak as to children—open wide your hearts also. (6:13)

> Here I am, ready to come to you this third time. And I will not be a burden, because I do not want what is yours but you; for children ought not to lay up for their parents, but parents for their children. (12:14)

The family metaphor thus remains at the forefront of Paul's thinking about the church in Corinth, since sibling terminology and the father metaphor surface at various places in Paul's argument. Paul uses PKG terminology less frequently, however, in his second extant letter than he does in his first. And *adelphos*, in particular, is distributed through the epistle in a highly uneven manner. These observations serve to make the density of sibling terminology in 2 Corinthians 8–9 all the more striking and demanding of explanation.

Paul's Collection for the Jerusalem Community

Second Corinthians 8–9 deals with the collection that Paul was gathering from his Gentile congregations in order to meet pressing material needs among the churches of Judaea. The origins of the collection can be traced to Paul's second visit to Jerusalem, recorded in Galatians 2:1-10. The leaders of the Jerusalem congregation affirmed his ministry to the Gentile world (vv. 7-9). Almost as an aside, Paul relates to his Galatian readers a final request made by the Jerusalem "pillars": "They asked only one thing, that we remember the poor" (2:10a). Paul concludes by assuring his readers that remembering the poor "was actually what I was eager to do" (2:10b). This final clause becomes an understatement in light of the importance that the collection for Judaea takes on for Paul's later life and ministry.[48]

Second Corinthians 8–9 constitutes our most important line of evidence for the collection. The project is also referred to in 1 Corinthians 16:1-4 and Romans 15:27. By the time Paul finally delivered the gift to Jerusalem, he had apparently elicited support from churches in nearly every region he had visited during the previous two decades. Congregations from Galatia had been instructed to put aside a weekly allotment (1 Cor 16:1-4), and the Macedonian churches became an example to others in their generosity (2 Corinthians 8–9). Achaian churches joined in, as well (Rom 15:26).[49]

The historical occasion for the collection was, of course, the economic situation in the Jerusalem church. Possible reasons for the poverty besetting the Jesus movement in Jerusalem include (1) a relief fund for widows, which became overburdened as the church grew; (2) pilgrimages to Jerusalem by Galilean followers of Jesus who came to the Holy City to await the return of the Messiah and thereby taxed the resources of the community; (3) potential problems resulting from Jerusalem's practice of pooling of resources, as illustrated in Acts 4:32-37; and (4) economic hardships caused by famine (Acts 11:27-30).[50] In view of the general economic condition of Roman Palestine during the first century C.E., it is hardly surprising to find a community led by a number of displaced Galileans (Peter, John, and James) struggling with poverty. For whatever reason, the Jerusalem Christians were in severe economic distress, and Paul was determined to alleviate their suffering using the collection provided by his Gentile congregations.

Paul uses a number of different words to describe his Jerusalem collection. The presence of this variety of terms is one factor that has motivated commentators to postulate a broader theological purpose behind what appears at one level to be a simple act of charity.[51] Noticeably absent from studies discussing Paul's collection, however, are attempts to account for the density of kinship terminology in 2 Corinthians 8–9. I observed above that 2 Corinthians contains only twelve occurrences of the *adelphos* word group. It is especially important to note, then, that half of these occurrences are found in the text-segment in which Paul discusses the collection. The relative density of the PKG terminology in 2 Corinthians 8–9 suggests that Paul at this point in his argument is particularly aware of the need to provoke his readers to behavior consonant with the Mediterranean family values that he shares with the Corinthians. The six instances of sibling terminology are most helpfully viewed through the interpretative lenses of three PKG values surveyed previously (chap. 2).

The first value is perhaps the most obvious: generalized reciprocity. Paul introduces his exhortation concerning the collection with the first use of *adelphos* since the second chapter of the letter: "We want you to know, brothers and sisters, about the grace of God that has been granted to the churches of Macedonia; for during a severe ordeal of affliction, their abundant joy and their extreme poverty have overflowed in a wealth of generosity on their part" (8:1-2). Paul proceeds to call upon the Corinthians to join the Macedonians and renew their involvement in the project (8:6-7). Then, in an important passage, Paul clarifies his perspective about access to resources among the Gentile and Israelite churches. His comments reflect precisely the practice of generalized reciprocity:

> I do not mean that there should be relief for others and pressure on you, but it is a question of a fair balance between your present abundance and their need, so that their abundance may be for your need, in order that there may be a fair balance. As it is written, "The one who had much did not have too much, and the one who had little did not have too little." (8:13-15)

Paul expected Christians, as members of a surrogate Mediterranean family, to administer material resources in such a way that "provision and need ought to be matched."[52]

A second PKG value reflected in Paul's use of sibling terminology as he discusses the collection consists in the honesty and truthfulness expected among members of a Mediterranean family. As I mentioned in my survey of PKG values in a previous chapter, a person in a society comprised of lineage family groups can expect to wholly trust her blood relatives—but only her blood relatives. "No one outside the family of blood can be trusted until and unless that trust can be validated and verified."[53] This explains why Paul uses *adelphos* five times to refer to the persons overseeing the transport and delivery of the financial gift to the church at Jerusalem (8:18-24; 9:3-5).

Paul is clearly concerned to distance himself from any accusations of fraud or dishonesty in his administration of the collection. As another ancient writer had observed, "The chief thing in all public administration and public service is to avoid even the slightest suspicion of avarice" (Cicero, *Off.* 2.21.75).[54] To this end, Paul enlists messengers of proven worth (8:22). One is universally known "among all the churches" (8:18), and two are valued by Paul as trusted colleagues in ministry (8:17, 22-23). Most importantly, they are "brothers," and as such they can be trusted completely with the community's resources.

The common behavior expected of individuals who are related by blood, another familiar expression of Mediterranean family solidarity, represents a third and final PKG value surfacing in 2 Corinthians 8–9. I explained in an earlier chapter that members of lineage kinship groups are expected to emulate the behavior of their ancestors. We saw this illustrated above in Paul's challenge to his readers to imitate his behavior as their spiritual father (1 Cor 4:14-16). The value applies to behavior among family members belonging to the same generation, as well.

Paul draws upon this value in 2 Corinthians 8–9 when he offers the congregations of Macedonia as examples in order to encourage the Corinthians to renew their efforts for the collection:

> We want you to know, brothers and sisters, about the grace of God that has been granted to the churches of Macedonia; for during a severe ordeal of affliction, their abundant joy and their extreme poverty have overflowed in a wealth of generosity on their part. For, as I can testify, they voluntarily gave according to their means, and even beyond their means, begging us earnestly for the privilege of sharing in this ministry to the saints—and this, not merely as we expected; they gave themselves first to the Lord and, by the will of God, to us, so that we might urge Titus that, as he had already made a beginning, so he should also complete this generous undertaking among you. (8:1-6)

The Corinthians are strongly encouraged to match the zeal of their Macedonian siblings in the faith by fulfilling their commitment to participate in the collection for the Jerusalem saints. Paul could just as easily have exhorted his readers in a manner identical to the mother of the seven brothers in 2 Maccabees: "Prove worthy of your brothers" (7:29). The sentiments are the same.

Later in his argument, Paul draws again upon the value of common sibling behavior in an even more pointed manner. As we saw above, Paul sent Titus to Corinth, along with others apparently chosen to represent their respective congregations in the distribution of the offering. It is one thing to be challenged with a secondhand report of the liberality of one's Macedonian siblings (8:1-6). Now Paul informs his readers that representatives from Macedonia are coming to Corinth in person. The physical presence of "brothers" from other contributing congregations will only serve to increase the pressure upon the Corinthian congregations to participate in the collection. Paul thus uses his announcement of the impending visit to draw upon his readers' concern to preserve their honor as part of the broader family in Christ, for he exhorts them to behave in a manner similar to the behavior of the churches represented by these emissaries: "Therefore openly before the churches, show them the proof of your love and of our reason for boasting about you" (8:24). The first four verses of the following chapter provide Paul with a final opportunity to engage in a similar rhetorical strategy:

> Now it is not necessary for me to write you about the ministry to the saints, for I know your eagerness, which is the subject of my boasting about you to the people of Macedonia, saying that Achaia has been ready since last year; and your zeal has stirred up most of them. But I am sending the brothers in order that our boasting about you may not prove to have been empty in this case, so that you may be ready, as I said you would be; otherwise, if some Macedonians come with me and find that you are not ready, we would be humiliated—to say nothing of you—in this undertaking. (9:1-4)

To paraphrase: "The Macedonians are your brothers. They have contributed. I expect you to do likewise."

We see, then, that the kinship metaphor is central to Paul's linguistic strategy as he seeks to engage the Corinthian community in the great undertaking of his collection for the poor saints in Jerusalem. Paul draws upon sibling terminology in order to (1) elicit expressions of generalized reciprocity, (2) provide assurance of honest administration of the funds, and (3) challenge his readers to respond in a manner worthy of the sibling bond that they share with other Christians who have already demonstrated their generosity.

Romans

The letter "to all God's beloved in Rome" finds Paul drawing again upon the kinship metaphor as his dominant model for the Christian community.[55] Of the twenty undisputed occurrences of sibling terminology in the epistle, eighteen refer to surrogate kin relationships. The term first appears in a passage in which Paul expresses his desire to visit the readers. The themes of (a) mutual encouragement that occurs when siblings are gathered and (b) the corresponding sense of longing when they are separated are powerfully wedded together in Romans 1:11-13:

> For I am longing to see you so that I may share with you some spiritual gift to strengthen you—or rather so that we may be mutually encouraged by each other's faith, both yours and mine. I want you to know, brothers and sisters, that I have often intended to come to you (but thus far have been prevented), in order that I may reap some harvest among you as I have among the rest of the Gentiles.

Sibling terminology surfaces elsewhere in the epistle as Paul's standard manner for addressing his fellow believers in Rome (7:1; 10:1; 11:25).

The reader encounters a final concentration of sibling terminology in the last chapter of the epistle, in which Paul refers to a number of his fellow Christians by name:

> I commend to you our sister Phoebe, a deacon of the church at Cenchreae. (16:1)

> Greet Asyncritus, Phlegon, Hermes, Patrobas, Hermas, and the brothers and sisters who are with them. (16:14)

> Gaius, who is host to me and to the whole church, greets you. Erastus, the city treasurer, and our brother Quartus, greet you. (16:23)

Francis Watson plausibly suggests that Paul in Romans 16 challenges his readers to greet one another in order to ameliorate a division existing between Israelite and Gentile Christians in Rome.[56] We may assume that Paul draws upon the *adelphos* word group in order to better accomplish this goal.

Surrogate father language is found more often in Romans than in any of Paul's other epistles. In several passages, God is the referent (1:7; 6:4). The metaphor of God as father also comes into play in corresponding references to followers of Christ as God's offspring. For example, Paul looks forward to a future day when "the creation itself will be set free from its bondage to decay and will obtain the freedom of the glory of the children of God" (8:21).

Paul also uses father terminology in Romans to refer to the readers' ancestors in the faith. Abraham is a particular focus of attention along these lines (Rom 4:11-18). Elsewhere, other Israelite patriarchs are identified as fathers of the Christian community. We find a reference to "Isaac our father" in 9:10 (see also 15:8, "the promises given to the patriarchs").

The various strands of family language and imagery converge in an especially noteworthy manner in the eighth chapter of Romans:

> So then, brothers and sisters, we are debtors, not to the flesh, to live according to the flesh—for if you live according to the flesh, you will die; but if by the Spirit you put to death the deeds of the body, you will live. For all who are led by the Spirit of God are children of God. For you did not receive a spirit of slavery to fall back into fear, but you have received a spirit of adoption. When we cry, "Abba! Father!" it is that very Spirit bearing witness with our spirit that we are children of God, and if children, then heirs, heirs of God and joint heirs with Christ—if, in fact, we suffer with him so that we may also be glorified with him. (8:12-17)

Combined in this brief excerpt are (1) sibling terminology (v. 12); (2) the father-children metaphor (note the variety of expressions: "children of God," v. 14; "adoption," "Father," v. 15; "children of God," vv. 16-17); and (3) inheritance imagery ("heirs . . . joint heirs," v. 17). Most expressive is Paul's use of "Abba," a transliterated Aramaic term addressed to God as father (v. 15). The sonship theme arises again in verse 19 ("the children of God"), and adoption terminology appears a few verses later: "and not only the creation, but we ourselves, who have the first fruits of the Spirit, groan inwardly while we wait for adoption, the redemption of our bodies" (8:23). Finally, the idea that Christians are Jesus' siblings, implied in the appellation "joint heirs with Christ" (v. 17), finds confirmation in 8:29: "For those whom he foreknew he also predestined to be conformed to the image of his Son, in order that he might be the firstborn within a large family" (literally "among many brethren"). According to Paul's understanding of the surrogate family matrix, Jesus is in some sense perceived to be the readers' firstborn brother.

In view of the plethora of kinship terms in the letter, it is not surprising to find Paul strongly emphasizing PKG values as the accepted standard for relations among his Roman readers. The most apparent example of Paul's strategy of utilizing the *adelphos* word group in order to encourage family solidarity is Romans 14. At issue is the struggle between Christian factions in Rome over the acceptability of various kinds of foods for members of the Jesus movement:

> Welcome those who are weak in faith, but not for the purpose of quarreling over opinions. Some believe in eating anything, while the weak eat only vegetables. Those

who eat must not despise those who abstain, and those who abstain must not pass
judgment on those who eat; for God has welcomed them. Who are you to pass judgment on servants of another? It is before their own lord that they stand or fall. And
they will be upheld, for the Lord is able to make them stand. (14:1-4)

Before commenting upon the sibling terminology that appears in the verses immediately following the above excerpt, I must outline what I believe to be the most
cogent explanation of the background of the Book of Romans. The interpretation
of Paul's paraenesis in Romans 14:1—15:13 is directly affected by our understanding
of the historical situation that produced the letter.

What follows represents a reconstruction of the situation among Christians and
Israelites living in Rome that takes into account not only the biblical materials but
also epigraphic sources and evidence from secular historians.[57] The general framework unfolds chronologically as follows:

EARLY 30s–49 C.E.

> The Jesus movement begins in Rome as a Judean movement attached to the
> synagogues.

49 C.E.

> Edict of Claudius drives all Judeans (including Judean followers of Jesus) out
> of Rome, due to increasing discord that erupts between Judeans who under-
> stand Jesus to be their Messiah and the majority, who do not.

49–54 C.E.

> The Jesus movement in Rome is exclusively in the hands of Gentiles, who
> now meet in homes instead of synagogues. The complexion and social struc-
> ture of the church change accordingly.

54 C.E.

> Claudius dies, and the Judeans and Judean Christians are free to return to
> Rome. The long-absent Judean Christians, now in the distinct minority, must
> relate to a church whose theology and social structure have changed substan-
> tially. Conflict inevitably erupts, and the Christians at Rome are fragmented
> into as many as eight house churches.

MID- TO LATE 50s C.E.

> Paul writes Romans to address specific problems arising among the Roman
> Christians as a result of the above events.

The above reconstruction explains Paul's desire in Romans to warn his predominantly Gentile readership against any feelings of superiority over their Judean fellows (see 11:17-21). The events also provide the appropriate background for appreciating the density of sibling terminology found in chapter 14 of the letter. Specifically, it is the change in social milieu from a synagogue environment to home-based meetings, necessitated by Claudius's decree of 49 C.E., that contributes significantly to the rhetorical persuasiveness of Romans 14:1—15:6.[58]

Moreover, understanding the food conflict as a debate about the relevance of Mosaic purity regulations for the Roman Christians remains the most cogent reading of the text in light of the historical background cited above. Polarization had erupted in the Jesus movement between those who chose to observe Israelite purity laws and others who did not. Paul refers to the two groups as the "weak" and the "strong," respectively.[59]

We are now ready to appreciate the manner in which Paul suddenly draws upon the kinship metaphor in order to challenge his readers to PKG solidarity. The above historical scenario suggests that the Gentile Christians at Rome likely took great pride in their independence from the synagogue. The alternative they adopted—meeting in various homes in the city—came to represent the most tangible evidence of the transition of the Jesus movement in Rome from an almost exclusively Israelite to a predominantly Gentile phenomenon.[60] Every house-church meeting would have reminded the Gentile Christians of what they had gained through Claudius's decree of 49 C.E.

Returning Israelite Christians, however, undoubtedly struggled with the changes that had occurred during their absence. For them, the social matrix of the weekly home meetings would have been a painful reminder of what had been lost in 49 C.E. Moreover, the Israelite Christians were now a vulnerable minority. And as a minority whose identity was increasingly threatened, it is likely that they increased, rather than ameliorated, their emphasis upon the Mosaic purity code.[61] The resulting situation rendered the gathering together of both parties in homes, and sharing the sacred meal as a key element of such a gathering, impossible—thus the fragmentation of the Jesus movement in Rome at the time Paul wrote his letter.[62]

Banks helpfully identifies in Paul two categories of family-related words. The first set of terms comes from "the business side of family affairs" (kinship economics), and includes such words such "household" (the *oikos* word group), "slave" (*doulos*), and "servant" (*hupēretēs*). A second category of terms Banks situates in "the intimate side of family affairs"—the very words with which we have become familiar in the present study ("brother," "father," and so forth).[63]

Different rhetorical strategies call for different language, and when Paul desires to call his readers to PKG solidarity, he consistently turns to the more intimate kinship terminology to elicit the intended behavior. Romans 14 is a case in point. Paul begins his challenge to the "weak" and "strong" in faith by employing a "lord-servant" (*kurios-oiketes*) metaphor—words from kinship economics. The picture is of two domestic slaves, each answerable individually to the master of the household (v. 4). But note the striking shift of metaphor in verse 10: "Why do you pass judgment on your brother or sister? Or you, why do you despise your brother or sister? For we will all stand before the judgment seat of God." The word *adelphos* appears for the first time since 12:1, and the reader is dramatically ushered into a conceptual arena loaded with the various expectations and emotions associated with PKG sibling solidarity.[64] Paul proceeds to capitalize on this connection:

> Let us therefore no longer pass judgment on one another, but resolve instead never to put a stumbling block or hindrance in the way of another [*adelphos*]. . . . If your brother or sister is being injured by what you eat, you are no longer walking in love. Do not let what you eat cause the ruin of one for whom Christ died. . . . Let us then pursue what makes for peace and for mutual upbuilding. Do not, for the sake of food, destroy the work of God. Everything is indeed clean, but it is wrong for you to make others fall by what you eat; it is good not to eat meat or drink wine or do anything that makes your brother or sister stumble. (Rom 14:13-21)[65]

Paul is not unaware of the importance of the house-church environment for his Gentile readers. He carefully crafts his paraenesis in Romans 14 to challenge "the strong" in his audience to live out the sibling relationships suggested by the very social context of their meetings. To paraphrase: "Independent of the synagogue, are you? Meeting in homes instead? Then act like brothers and sisters who live under the same roof." To "put a stumbling block or hindrance in the way of," "cause the ruin of," "do anything . . . that makes your brother or sister stumble"—such behavior has no place in the PKG environment realized on a weekly basis in the house-church setting.

Yet another passage from Paul's letter to the churches at Rome draws upon the family metaphor for much of its persuasive effect:

> Let love be genuine; hate what is evil; hold fast to what is good; love one another with mutual affection; outdo one another in showing honor. Do not lag in zeal, be ardent in spirit, serve the Lord. Rejoice in hope, be patient in suffering, persevere in prayer. Contribute to the needs of the saints; extend hospitality to strangers. (12:9-13)

The phrases found in verse 10 are particularly relevant to the present study. The first command—"love one another with mutual affection"—is better translated "in brotherly love showing family affection to one another."[66] The kinship metaphor is thus at hand in Paul's exhortation.

Although perhaps not as immediately obvious to the Western reader, the second expression in verse 10—"outdo one another in showing honor"—also strongly implies a family environment.[67] Paul's point is that his readers should place concern for the honor of others ahead of concern for the protection and augmentation of their own honor. Attempts to interpret the phrase theologically prove less than satisfying. Charles Cranfield grounds Paul's challenge in the fact that Christ is mystically present in each believer.[68] More satisfying is an interpretation of verse 10b that assumes that Paul is capitalizing upon the family model introduced in the previous command. Studies of honor-shame societies identify the patrilineal kinship group as the key environment in which agonistic efforts to retain and gain honor become, in fact, dishonorable. Among brothers, the male competition for honor and esteem that is so characteristic of the broader Mediterranean world is discouraged. Rather, brothers are to defer to one another and prefer one another in honor.

PHILEMON

A survey of Paul's use of the PKG model would be incomplete without mention of the short epistle to Philemon. Paul persuasively draws upon the social networks of both patronage and kinship to challenge Philemon to live out his Christian convictions in his relationship with his newly converted slave Onesimus.[69] As observed above, more kinship terminology obtains proportionally in Philemon than in any other portion of the Pauline corpus. The letter is addressed "to the church in your house" (v. 2). Paul refers to Philemon as his "brother" twice in the course of his brief appeal (vv. 7, 20). The fatherhood of God is highlighted (v. 3). Paul has "begotten" "his child" Onesimus in prison (v. 10). Finally, Paul's rhetorical aside in verse 19 ("I say nothing about your owing me even your own self") is likely a reference to Paul's role as the spiritual father of Philemon.

Given such a conceptual framework, Paul's overt challenge to sibling solidarity renders the following passage climactic:[70] "so that you might have him back forever, no longer as a slave but more than a slave, a beloved brother—especially to me but how much more to you, both in the flesh and in the Lord" (vv. 15b-16). Bartchy maintains that Paul is challenging Philemon to manumit Onesimus. Paul gives Philemon "the choice either of continuing to regard himself as Onesimus' owner or of becoming his 'brother' and 'partner' (v. 17) in a new social reality."[71] Thus, it is Philemon's newly acquired surrogate kin relationship with Onesimus as a brother in

Christ that serves as the most persuasive lever in Paul's argument. Onesimus is now Philemon's brother. Will Philemon respond in kind? As Bartchy concludes, Philemon was presented with a major decision: "Would he deny his Christian identity by acting first of all with the prerogatives of an angry slave owner, or would he strengthen it by doing all in his power as Onesimus' patron to make him his 'beloved brother'? His house church was watching, and Paul hoped to be there soon to see for himself."[72]

GALATIANS, 1 THESSALONIANS, AND PHILIPPIANS

The analysis of Paul's employment of the family model concludes with an abbreviated look at the remaining letters of undisputed Pauline authorship: Galatians, 1 Thessalonians, and Philippians. The constraints of the project render impractical any detailed exegesis of specific passages in these letters. I must also refrain from an extended discussion of the occasion and purpose of the epistles. I will limit myself, instead, to an approach that simply (1) identifies the presence of the PKG metaphor in the texts and (2) offers brief summary statements where appropriate.

The letter to the churches in Galatia reflects the PKG metaphor in the variety of ways that we have come to expect from a work penned by Paul. The term *adelphos* occurs eleven times. In every case but one (1:19, "James the Lord's brother"), the family of believers is in view. The first occurrence finds the apostle identifying himself and his companions as siblings: "Paul an apostle . . . and all the members of God's family [*adelphos*] who are with me, To the churches of Galatia" (Gal 1:1-2). Throughout the epistle, Paul uses the same word group as the standard vocative appellation for his readers. Representative text-segments include the following:

> For I want you to know, brothers and sisters, that the gospel that was proclaimed by me is not of human origin. (1:11)

> Brothers and sisters, I give an example from daily life: once a person's will has been ratified, no one adds to it or annuls it. (3:15)

> But my friends [*adelphos*], why am I still being persecuted if I am still preaching circumcision? In that case the offense of the cross has been removed. (5:11)

In the following passage, Paul draws upon several PKG values as he appeals to his Galatian readers:

> 12 Friends [*adelphos*], I beg you, become as I am, for I also have become as you are. You have done me no wrong. 13 You know that it was because of a physical infirmity that

I first announced the gospel to you; 14 though my condition put you to the test, you did not scorn or despise me, but welcomed me as an angel of God, as Christ Jesus. 15 What has become of the good will you felt? For I testify that, had it been possible, you would have torn out your eyes and given them to me. (4:12-15)

Reflected in the text-segment are (1) the assumption that siblings will behave in like manner (v. 12) and (2) Paul's recollection of a striking expression of generalized reciprocity that he experienced while among the Galatian Christians (v. 15).

Paul's argument in Galatians also relies heavily upon the father-children metaphor. God is identified as the father of Paul and of the readers three times in the first four verses of the letter (1:1, 3-4). The image becomes central to Paul's reasoning in the middle portion of the epistle. In the following passage, for example, Paul draws together a number of terms from the PKG linguistic storehouse to highlight the nature of his and his Galatian readers' relationship to God their father:

My point is this: heirs, as long as they are minors, are no better than slaves, though they are the owners of all the property; but they remain under guardians and trustees until the date set by the father. So with us; while we were minors, we were enslaved to the elemental spirits of the world. But when the fullness of time had come, God sent his Son, born of a woman, born under the law, in order to redeem those who were under the law, so that we might receive adoption as children. And because you are children, God has sent the Spirit of his Son into our hearts, crying, "Abba! Father!" So you are no longer a slave but a child, and if a child then also an heir, through God. (4:1-7)

The inheritance *topos* returns again in 5:21: "I am warning you, as I warned you before: those who do such things will not inherit the kingdom of God."

Finally, Paul begins and ends what has come to be known as the last chapter of Galatians by addressing his readers as "brothers" (6:1, 18). Included in the chapter are exhortations to behavior that could be fairly read in terms of PKG family solidarity:

My friends [*adelphos*], if anyone is detected in a transgression, you who have received the Spirit should restore such a one in a spirit of gentleness. Take care that you yourselves are not tempted. Bear one another's burdens, and in this way you will fulfill the law of Christ. . . . So then, whenever we have an opportunity, let us work for the good of all, and especially for those of the family of faith. (6:1-2, 10)

The letter to the Galatians, then, consistently reflects the kinship metaphor. Once again, the family predominates as Paul's preferred social model for community as he envisions it.

I turn now to 1 Thessalonians, where the nineteen occurrences of *adelphos* are sprinkled throughout the letter. Most of the examples reflect the now-familiar use of sibling terminology as Paul's standard term of address:

> For we know, brothers and sisters beloved by God, that he has chosen you. (1:4)

> You yourselves know, brothers and sisters, that our coming to you was not in vain. (2:1)

> But we do not want you to be uninformed, brothers and sisters, about those who have died, so that you may not grieve as others do who have no hope. (4:13)

The imitation theme occurs, in conjunction with sibling terminology, in at least two passages:

> For we know, brothers and sisters beloved by God, that he has chosen you, because our message of the gospel came to you not in word only, but also in power and in the Holy Spirit and with full conviction; just as you know what kind of persons we proved to be among you for your sake. And you became imitators of us and of the Lord, for in spite of persecution you received the word with joy inspired by the Holy Spirit, so that you became an example to all the believers in Macedonia and in Achaia. (1:4-7)

> For you, brothers and sisters, became imitators of the churches of God in Christ Jesus that are in Judea, for you suffered the same things from your own compatriots as they did from the Jews. (2:14)

It may also be in view later in the epistle:

> Finally, brothers and sisters, we ask and urge you in the Lord Jesus that, as you learned from us how you ought to live and to please God (as, in fact, you are doing), you should do so more and more. (4:1)

First Thessalonians, more than any of Paul's epistles, reflects the strong affective relationship between Paul and the Jesus community in this Macedonian *polis*. This is likely due to the brief time that had elapsed between Paul's visit to Thessalonica and the penning of the letter. Paul left Macedonia rather suddenly, went to Achaia, and ultimately settled in Corinth for about eighteen months (Acts 17–18). Some weeks or months later, concerned about the long-term results of his efforts in Macedonia, Paul sent Timothy north to obtain information about the status of the nascent work in Thessalonica.[73] Paul's response to the good news he has now received from Timothy makes up 1 Thessalonians. Paul expresses his emotional attachment to the readers most pointedly in the following extended citation. Note that the text-segment begins and ends with the vocative "brothers and sisters":

> As for us, brothers and sisters, when, for a short time, we were made orphans by being separated from you—in person, not in heart—we longed with great eagerness to see

you face to face. For we wanted to come to you—certainly I, Paul, wanted to again and again—but Satan blocked our way. For what is our hope or joy or crown of boasting before our Lord Jesus at his coming? Is it not you? Yes, you are our glory and joy! Therefore when we could bear it no longer, we decided to be left alone in Athens; and we sent Timothy, our brother and co-worker for God in proclaiming the gospel of Christ, to strengthen and encourage you for the sake of your faith, so that no one would be shaken by these persecutions. . . . For this reason, when I could bear it no longer, I sent to find out about your faith; . . . But Timothy has just now come to us from you, and has brought us the good news of your faith and love. He has told us also that you always remember us kindly and long to see us—just as we long to see you. For this reason, brothers and sisters, during all our distress and persecution we have been encouraged about you through your faith. For we now live, if you continue to stand firm in the Lord. (2:17–3:8)

Earlier in the letter, Paul had expressed similar feelings toward the Thessalonians, using the metaphor of himself as the readers' father:

As you know, we dealt with each one of you like a father with his children, urging and encouraging you and pleading that you lead a life worthy of God, who calls you into his own kingdom and glory. (2:11-12)

Again, I do not sense a strongly patriarchal flavor in the above passage. This judgement is reinforced by a complementary image occurring in the immediately preceding context: "But we were gentle among you, like a nurse tenderly caring for her own children. So deeply do we care for you that we are determined to share with you not only the gospel of God but also our own selves, because you have become very dear to us" (2:7b-8).

Nevertheless, when Paul refers to himself with paternal terminology, he is innovating vis-à-vis the family model we observed with Jesus of Nazareth who commanded his disciples, "Call no one your father on earth, for you have one Father—the one in heaven" (Matt 23:9). Later Christian writers will further extend the metaphor in ways that will serve to invert the intentions of Jesus in a manner in which Paul does not.

I conclude my overview of 1 Thessalonians with references to the idea of God as the readers' surrogate father. The letter contains four explicit references to the fatherhood of God (1:1, 3; 3:11, 13). An allusion to the filial relationship of the readers to their heavenly father occurs in 5:5: "For you are all children of light and children of the day; we are not of the night or of darkness." We are reminded of references in the Dead Sea Scrolls to members of the Qumran community as "sons of light" (1QS 1.10 passim).

My overview of Paul's writings concludes with the letter to the Christians at Philippi. Few surprises await the reader who has become sensitive to Paul's use of the kinship metaphor. Sibling terms are used nine times, rather evenly apportioned over the course of the letter. God is called "Father" in three places (1:2; 2:11; 4:20). In 2:15, the Philippians are called "children of God." Noticeably absent from Philippians, however, are the high concentrations of family language at specific points in the argument that we uncovered in Romans and in the Corinthian correspondence. It is fair to infer that the rhetorical edge characteristic of Paul's use of the family metaphor in, for example, 1 Corinthians 6, 2 Corinthians 8–9, and Romans 14, is lacking in Philippians. Paul is apparently not as concerned in Philippians to use sibling terms in order to precipitate a change in his readers' behavior in which he believes kinship norms to be violated. Rather *adelphos* appears as a general term of address, an expression of family endearment, evenly distributed throughout the four chapters of the letter.

The explanation for this is patent. Paul's letter to the Philippians is directed to a church that is a positive reflection of the family model Paul values so highly. What little polemic the reader does encounter in Philippians is aimed not at perceived behavioral flaws among the readers but rather toward outsiders (see 3:1-4, 18-19). John Fitzgerald summarizes the important aspects of Paul's relationship with his Philippian converts:

> By his own account, Paul had a unique relationship with the church in Philippi. Departing from his usual practice of refusing compensation from his converts (1 Corinthians 9), Paul accepted financial support from the Philippian church while he was in Thessalonica, and he did so on more than one occasion (Phil 4:15-16). Funds were also supplied to him later when he was in Corinth (2 Cor 11:7-9), and Paul's receipt of still another monetary gift occasioned at least part of his correspondence with the Philippians (4:10-20). Since the Philippians shared in the Macedonians' abject poverty (2 Cor 8:2), such largess was not a sign of their affluence, but of their genuine affection for the apostle and of their support of his labors (Phil 1:5; 4:10; see also Rom 15:26). These gifts served to solidify the bond between Paul and the Philippians and to nurture their special relationship.[74]

Paul, aware of no conspicuous violations of the PKG value system among his readers, therefore found no need to utilize concentrations of sibling terminology in the particular manner in which he did in Romans and 1 and 2 Corinthians.

Still, the family model surfaces throughout Philippians, and it is appropriate to cite several examples as I bring to a close my cursory examination of the letter. In light of the above discussion, the reader is not surprised to find expressions of Paul's special relationship with the Philippians in the epistle. Note the sibling term of address in the second excerpt:

I am confident of this, that the one who began a good work among you will bring it to completion by the day of Jesus Christ. It is right for me to think this way about all of you, because you hold me in your heart, for all of you share in God's grace with me, both in my imprisonment and in the defense and confirmation of the gospel. For God is my witness, how I long for all of you with the compassion of Christ Jesus. (1:6-8)

Therefore, my brothers and sisters, whom I love and long for, my joy and crown, stand firm in the Lord in this way, my beloved. (4:1)

Similar PKG solidarity, reflected in the deep emotional attachment obtaining between siblings, apparently existed between the Philippians and their emissary to Paul, Epaphroditus. Indeed, the reader encounters in the following passage a three-way family bond between Paul, Epaphroditus, and the Philippian addressees:

Still, I think it necessary to send to you Epaphroditus—my brother and co-worker and fellow soldier, your messenger and minister to my need; for he has been longing for all of you, and has been distressed because you heard that he was ill. He was indeed so ill that he nearly died. But God had mercy on him, and not only on him but on me also, so that I would not have one sorrow after another. I am the more eager to send him, therefore, in order that you may rejoice at seeing him again, and that I may be less anxious. (2:25-28)

The expectation that siblings should behave in like manner also manifests itself in this short epistle: "Brothers and sisters, join in imitating me, and observe those who live according to the example you have in us" (3:17). The image of Paul as the spiritual progenitor of Timothy appears as another now-familiar theme: "But Timothy's worth you know, how like a son with a father he has served with me in the work of the gospel" (2:22). Moreover, in view of (a) the kinship terms occurring throughout the text and (b) the ideal of generalized reciprocity so central to the PKG value system, it is reasonable to view the financial support Paul received from the Philippians at least in part through the lens of Paul's family ideology (1:3-8; 4:10-19).[75] Finally, although lacking kinship terms in the near context, the orientation to interpersonal relationships reflected in the following exhortation is most consonant with what we have observed concerning PKG solidarity:

If then there is any encouragement in Christ, any consolation from love, any sharing in the Spirit, any compassion and sympathy, make my joy complete: be of the same mind, having the same love, being in full accord and of one mind. Do nothing from selfish ambition or conceit, but in humility regard others as better than yourselves. Let each of you look not to your own interests, but to the interests of others. (2:1-4)

CONCLUSION

My survey of Paul's epistles reveals the indisputable centrality of the family model for Paul's conception of Christian community. Kinship terminology is found throughout each of the letters that are generally assigned to Paul. The epistles are replete with sibling words, the father-children metaphor surfaces in each letter, and the inheritance theme is found in a number of passages. Moreover, Paul employs the kinship metaphor in a rhetorically powerful way in order to challenge the members of his communities to live with one another in a manner consonant with Mediterranean family values. PKG values upon which Paul draws include (1) generalized reciprocity (1 Cor 6:1-11; 2 Cor 8-9; Gal 4:15); (2) the priority of sibling loyalty over spousal loyalty (1 Cor 7:12-16); (3) truthfulness and honesty (2 Cor 8-9); and (4) the common behavior expected of siblings and offspring (1 Cor 4:14-17; 2 Cor 8–9; 1 Thess 1:4-7; 2:14). One gets the distinct impression that, for Paul of Tarsus, to live with one's fellow believers as an exemplary member of a Mediterranean family constituted the epitome of faith in Jesus as experienced in the arena of interpersonal relationships. Next I will explore how the family model received continued and markedly different expression at the hands of later Christian writers.

5

Second-Century Christian Writers

In 165 c.e., a Cynic philosopher named Peregrinus committed suicide by throwing himself on the flames at the Olympic Games. Originally from Parium in Mysia, Peregrinus had associated himself for some time with the Jesus movement in Palestine. He apparently became a recognized Christian leader and was imprisoned for his activities in this regard. After his release, Peregrinus had a falling out with the Christians and went to Egypt, where he studied under the Cynic Agathobulus. A lifestyle of itinerant preaching characterized the rest of Peregrinus's life, leading him through Italy and then on to Greece.

Peregrinus was classed by some with Epictetus, but Lucian of Samosata, our sole eyewitness to Peregrinus's demise, was more than mildly skeptical of the self-proclaimed Cynic's integrity as a wandering teacher. In Lucian's eyes, Peregrinus was hardly an esteemed philosopher. Rather, he was a con artist who would don any religious disguise necessary to exploit the naive and gullible—especially Lucian's ever-multiplying Christian contemporaries. In the course of Lucian's castigation of Peregrinus (whom he also calls "Proteus"), the reader gains great insight into the manner in which members of the Jesus movement were perceived by pagan elites:

> When [Peregrinus] had been imprisoned, the Christians, regarding the incident as a calamity, left nothing undone in the effort to rescue him. Then, as this was impossible, every other form of attention was shown him, not in any casual way but with assiduity; and from the very break of day aged widows and orphan children could be seen waiting near the prison, while their officials even slept inside with him after bribing the guards. Then elaborate meals were brought in, and sacred books of theirs were read aloud, and excellent Peregrinus—for he still went by that name—was called by them "the new Socrates." (Lucian, *Peregr.* 12)[1]

Lucian's purpose here is not to commend Christians for their social solidarity. Indeed, Lucian portrays Peregrinus's supporters as highly gullible "simple folk," who were an easy mark for the charlatan. This, however, renders the information that he provides all the more valuable for understanding the social fabric of the second-century churches. In the excerpt cited above, Lucian recounts the specific efforts that Palestinian Christians exerted on behalf of Peregrinus. In what follows, the author broadens his account to include a description of Christian practices in general. Lucian was widely traveled in the East and was, therefore, familiar with Christian practices in Palestine, Asia, and Egypt.[2] His background—along with his obvious lack of sympathy for the Jesus movement—makes him a reliable witness to early Christian social solidarity:

> Indeed, people came even from the cities of Asia, sent by the Christians at their common expense, to succour and defend and encourage the hero. They show incredible speed whenever any such public action is taken; for in no time they lavish their all. . . . The poor wretches have convinced themselves, first and foremost, that they are going to be immortal and live for all time, in consequence of which they despise death and even willingly give themselves into custody, most of them. Furthermore, their first lawgiver persuaded them that they are all brothers of one another after they have transgressed once for all by denying the Greek gods and by worshipping that crucified sophist himself and living under his laws. Therefore they despise all things indiscriminately and consider them common property, receiving such doctrines traditionally without any definite evidence. So if any charlatan and trickster, able to profit by occasions, comes among them, he quickly acquired sudden wealth by imposing upon simple folk. (*Peregr.* 13)

For Lucian, the favor extended to Peregrinus is hardly unique; it is typical of Christian social practices. It is, moreover, reflective of an important PKG value discussed in previous chapters of the present work—the value of generalized reciprocity expressed in the sharing of material resources. Most interesting is the fact that Lucian, although an outsider, is nevertheless aware that the activities he describes have their roots in the Christians' conception of themselves as a surrogate kinship group. Lucian draws attention to the sibling mind-set among the Christians ("they are all brothers"). He traces such a conception back to Jesus of Nazareth ("their first lawgiver persuaded them") and then identifies the surrogate sibling relationship as the logical explanation (see "Therefore") of the early Christian practice of generalized reciprocity realized in the sharing of material resources ("common property").

We are already, therefore, on firm historical ground in asserting that the faith-family concept survived, flourished, and found tangible expression among the members of second-century churches in the Roman East. The balance of the present chapter will survey the works of several Christian writers, works that continue to reflect a kinship understanding of Christian social organization. I will cast a rather broad geographical net in order to demonstrate that the family concept is widely attested among second-century Christians. We will examine in some detail the works of Clement of Rome, Ignatius of Antioch, and Justin Martyr (Rome), since these three writers are especially liberal in their employment of the kinship metaphor. Moreover, the writings of Clement, Ignatius, and Justin each reflect certain permutations that the family model experienced at the hands of a new generation of Christian writers. Selected portions of the writings of Clement of Alexandria and Irenaeus (Gaul) will occupy the balance of the chapter.

The addition of Clement of Alexandria and Irenaeus significantly expands the geographical provenance of the second-century evidence that I cite for the kinship idea. I will again be sensitive to (a) the presence of the kinship model, as evidenced by PKG terminology, (b) the use of such terminology to encourage or sustain family-like behavior, and (c) activities that can fairly be construed as representative of ancient Mediterranean family practices (for example, the care extended to Peregrinus, above). In the course of our survey, we will repeatedly and indisputably confirm Lucian's observations concerning the family orientation of the Jesus movement during the second century.

CLEMENT OF ROME

The letter to the church at Corinth traditionally assigned to Clement of Rome constitutes a fitting point of departure for a survey of second-century Christian literature.[3] Indeed, 1 Clement, as the epistle has come to be known, may have been written near the end of the first century, but this is uncertain.[4] At any rate, Clement's work represents one of our earliest vantage points for viewing Christian social practices during the post-apostolic era. The letter became widely known in the East and was included in the canon of Christian scripture for a time in Egypt and Syria.[5] It therefore expresses convictions concerning both ideology and social behavior that warmly resonated with a significant number of the author's second-century Christian contemporaries.

A schism among the Corinthian Christians occasioned 1 Clement. Apparently a group of young persons rose up and deposed the ruling presbyters. In the following passage, the author intersperses his own descriptive phrases with quotations from the Old Testament as he relates the origins of the "sedition" in Corinth: "Thus 'the worthless' rose up 'against those who were in honour,' those of no reputation against the renowned, the foolish against the prudent, the 'young against the old'" (3.3). Later in his letter, Clement is even more explicit:

> We consider therefore that it is not just to remove from their ministry those who were appointed by them, or later on by other eminent men, with the consent of the whole Church, and have ministered to the flock of Christ without blame, humbly, peaceably, and disinterestedly, and for many years have received a universally favourable testimony. For our sin is not small, if we eject from the episcopate[6] those who have blamelessly and holily offered its sacrifices. . . . For we see that in spite of their good service you have removed some from the ministry which they fulfilled blamelessly. (44.3-4, 6)[7]

The conflict reflected in this excerpt occupies Clement throughout his rather lengthy epistle to the Corinthian congregation.

Like Paul before him, Clement draws upon the surrogate kinship model to encourage his readers to restore their rightful leaders and put an end to the conflict that has arisen among them. Clement also extensively uses the rhetoric of concord to achieve this end. Significant differences obtain, however, between the approaches of Paul and Clement, differences best explained by an inevitable transition toward increasing institutionalization that characterizes the early second-century Christian communities Clement reflects.

Family Language in 1 Clement

The reader of Clement's letter to the church at Corinth encounters frequent uses of kinship terminology, such as "brother" (adelphos) (4.7; 13.1; 14.1; 33.1; 37.1; 41.1-4; 45.16; 46.1; 52.1; 62.1); "brotherhood" (adelphotēs) (2.4); "fratricide" (adelphoktonia) (4.7); and "love for the brethren" (philadelphia) (47.5). Clement addresses his Corinthian recipients as "children" (tekna) (22.1), quoting Psalm 33 (LXX). In the next chapter, God is described as "the all-merciful and beneficent Father" who "has compassion on those that fear him, and kindly and lovingly bestows his favours on those that draw near to him with a simple mind" (23.1). Later, in 29.1, God is called "our gracious and merciful Father."

In 8.3, Clement cites a text, whose origins are obscure, which portrays God's willingness as a loving Father to receive those who return to him: "Repent, O house of Israel, from your iniquity. Say to the sons of my people, If your sins reach from the earth to Heaven, and if they be redder than scarlet, and blacker than sackcloth, and ye turn to me with all your hearts and say 'Father,' I will listen to you as a holy people." Clement later draws upon the image of God the father disciplining his sons in order to persuade those "who laid the foundation of the sedition" to "submit to the presbyters, and receive the correction of repentance" (56.2—57.1).

Themes of family loyalty and concern for ancestry also make their appearance in 1 Clement. Like Paul before him, Clement appropriates Abraham, the blood patriarch of the Israelites, as "our father," that is, the father of the Christian family of faith (31.2). Abraham is offered as an example of one who "in obedience went forth from his country and from his kindred and from his father's house, that by leaving behind a little country and a feeble kindred and a small house he might inherit the promises of God" (10.2). Abraham is thus introduced as a model to be emulated by those who must sacrifice loyalty to their families of origin in order to join the family of God.

Abraham is not the only Old Testament figure understood to be an ancestor of the Christian community. At one point in the letter, Clement exhorts, "Let testimony to our good deeds be given by others, as it was given to our fathers, the righteous" (30.7). A discussion of a number of Old Testament patriarchs, including Abraham, Jacob, and others, follows. Then, after extolling their behavior (chaps. 31–32), Clement begins the next chapter with the challenge, "What shall we do, then, brethren?" (33.1). The kinship term "brethren" and the strong inferential conjunction ("then") combine to suggest that Clement is here challenging his readers to act in a way appropriate to siblings who share such ancestors as Abraham and Jacob.

The ancestor theme surfaces elsewhere, where the reader encounters a reference to "our father Adam" (6.3). In yet another text-segment, Clement specifically challenges his readers to imitate the behavior of their spiritual ancestors. As we have seen, such an expectation is characteristic of the PKG value system: "Let us also be imitators of those who went about 'in the skins of goats and sheep,' heralding the coming of Christ; we mean Elijah and Elisha, and moreover Ezekiel, the prophets, and in addition to them the famous men of old" (17.1). Clement includes among his "famous men of old" Abraham (17.2), Job (17.3), Moses (17.5), and David (18.1). Finally, Clement weaves together sibling terms, the inheritance theme, and the idea of emulating the examples of one's spiritual ancestors in 45.6—46.1:

> For what shall we say, brethren? Was Daniel cast into the lions' den by those who feared God? Or were Ananias, Azarias, and Misael shut up in the fiery furnace by those who ministered to the great and glorious worship of the Most High? God forbid that this be so. . . . But they who endured in confidence obtained the inheritance of glory and honour; they were exalted, and were enrolled by God in his memorial for ever and ever. Amen. We also, brethren, must therefore cleave to such examples.

As the above overview demonstrates, 1 Clement reflects a PKG self-consciousness on the part of its author. And there is evidence that Clement expected the metaphor to find tangible expression in community life.

Family Activity in 1 Clement

Two passages, in particular, reflect the kind of solidarity we have come to expect among siblings in Mediterranean antiquity. Most striking is the author's claim that "many among ourselves have given themselves to bondage that they might ransom others. Many have delivered themselves to slavery, and provided food for others with the price they received for themselves" (55.2). The first comment in the above excerpt may refer to "a Christian's self-substitution for a person imprisoned for debt."[8] The activity described in the final sentence is patently clear: Christians are sacrificing their freedom in order to meet the material needs of their brethren in the community. "Many," according to Clement, have exercised each of the two options reflected in the above quotation.[9]

Clement reveals his own ideal of family solidarity, presumably shared by his readers, when he instructs the Corinthians, "Let the strong care for the weak and let the weak reverence the strong. Let the rich man bestow help on the poor and let the poor give thanks to God, that he gave him one to supply his needs" (38.2). The sibling term occurs in the verse immediately following the above excerpt: "Let us consider, then, brethren, of what matter we were formed." (38.3). The kinship model is thus at the forefront of Clement's thinking when, in the preceding context, he enjoins the rich to "bestow help on the poor."

In most of the passages in which kinship terminology occurs, Clement uses the family metaphor as part of his attempt to address the schism and power struggles in Corinth. He makes it clear at the outset of his letter that sedition and brotherhood are mutually exclusive, when he compares past behavior with present problems. First, Clement extols the readers' former reputation:

> Day and night you strove on behalf of the whole brotherhood that the number of the elect should be saved with mercy and compassion. You were sincere and innocent, and bore no malice to one another. All sedition and schism was abominable to you. You mourned over the transgressions of your neighbours; you judged their shortcomings as your own. (2.4-6)[10]

Then (chap. 3), the author censures the Corinthians for the "jealousy and envy, strife and sedition, persecution and disorder" that have arisen in their midst. Important for our purposes is the biblical imagery Clement chooses to adopt in order to castigate his readers in the ensuing argument. After recounting the Cain and Abel story (4.1-6), he concludes:

> You see, brethren,—jealousy and envy wrought fratricide. Through jealousy our father Jacob ran from the face of Esau his brother. Jealousy made Joseph to be persecuted to

the death, and come into slavery. Jealousy forced Moses to fly from the face of Pharoah, King of Egypt, when his fellow countryman said to him, "Who made thee a judge or a ruler over us? Wouldest thou slay me as thou didst slay the Egyptian yesterday?" Through jealousy Aaron and Miriam were lodged outside the camp. (4.7-11)

Notice the profuse employment of the sibling betrayal motif in the above text-segment. We saw that treachery among siblings comprised a most engaging topic for readers in Mediterranean antiquity. Old Testament narratives, in particular, contain much about brother discord, and captivating narratives—such as those describing Cain and Abel, Jacob and Esau, and Joseph and his brothers—find repeated citation in the literature of Second Temple Judaism and the Jesus movement. Cain's murder of Abel represents the first tangible expression in relational terms of the alienation from God experienced by Adam and Eve, according to the story of the "fall" of humankind in Genesis 3.

Abel's misfortune, therefore, becomes the paradigmatic example of fratricide for those who esteemed Old Testament narratives. Here, in his editorial commentary on the Genesis account (see 4.7: "You see, brethren,—jealousy and envy wrought fratricide"), the author of 1 Clement implicitly associates the activities of those who had fomented rebellion against the Corinthian presbyters with this most prominent example of Old Testament sibling betrayal. Clement then augments his argument with reminders of the struggles experienced among the twins Jacob and Esau, Joseph and his brothers, and Moses and his brother (Aaron) and sister (Miriam). For Clement, the sibling solidarity that should be reflected in the Corinthians' conception of their community as a surrogate kin group has been sacrificed to schism and sedition. The two are mutually exclusive, as he later explicitly observes (14.1).

Like Paul of Tarsus, then, Clement makes liberal use of PKG language throughout his letter to the church at Corinth. Also like Paul, he uses the kinship metaphor as a rhetorical device to dissuade his readers from behavior he deems inappropriate for persons who view one another as members of a common family of God. Paul and Clement differ, however, in their respective goals for community orientation. Because of this difference in goals, Clement's rhetorical use of the kinship metaphor is at times less than persuasive.

Innovation in Clement's Use of the Family Metaphor

Nearly everyone who studies the early history of the Jesus movement recognizes that a change occurs with respect to church structure and organization as one moves from the epistles of Paul to the works of writers like Clement and Ignatius. Paul's churches reveal a rather dynamically oriented approach to day-to-day community

life: local congregations operate in a manner that is much more relational than institutional in nature. Although order and recognized leadership are not lacking in
these early communities (see 1 Corinthians 12–14; Phil 1:1-2), the primary emphasis
is upon the movement of the Spirit among a group of people who are expected to
defer graciously to one another after the examples of Jesus of Nazareth and their
founder, Paul of Tarsus (Phil 2:1-11; 1 Thess 2:1-12). At times, this mutual deference
is located in the PKG model: "love one another with mutual affection" (literally
"brotherly love"; *tē philadelphia*); "outdo one another in showing honor" (Rom 12:10).
The use of kinship terminology to encourage mutual deference in the community
is understandable, since family was the one social sphere in which the honor game
was radically redefined (see chap. 4). Correspondingly, authority in the early Pauline
communities is legitimized in the spheres of character and behavior; there is little
emphasis on community structure and positions of leadership, as such. Thus, challenges to submit to the directives of church leaders are rarely based solely on appeal
to a recognized hierarchy of ecclesiastical authority.

A different picture emerges with Clement and his second-century contemporaries. Although we must not exaggerate the cleavage between Paul and Clement in
the area of ecclesiology, it is widely recognized that Clement emphasizes the
authority of church leaders in a way that Paul does not.[11]

Social theorists have long recognized the proclivity of a movement that might be
characterized as a dynamic organism to change, over time, into what could be
termed a static organization. The tendency has been variously defined as (a) a transition from sect to church,[12] (b) the routinization of charisma,[13] (c) the transformation of a social matrix characterized by leadership-focused reciprocity into a stable, manager-focused centricity structure,[14] or (d) the transition of an intentional
community into a natural (or, in the case of second-century Christian churches,
seminatural) community.[15]

The mind-set reflected in *1 Clement* situates itself well along the path toward
institutionalization. Clement's solution to rebellion against established church leaders is to enforce submission to those leaders based upon their position and upon
their appointment by those who came before them. Accordingly—and unlike
Paul—the author appropriates the concord genre of deliberative discourse in a
manner consonant with its normal use, namely, to reinforce the hierarchical social
system. We saw how Paul employed the genre in a way that was radically opposed
to its typical usage. He used concord rhetoric to invert the expectations of the
Strong in Corinth, expectations that informed them (wrongly from Paul's perspective) that the social hierarchy of the *polis* was to be replicated in the Christian
church.

Clement takes precisely the opposite approach.[16] He appropriates concord rhetoric, and employs it much more thoroughly than Paul,[17] in order to challenge the perceived originators of the sedition to return to their proper places in the pecking order of church life—in short, to "bow the neck, and take up a position of obedience" (63.1). A necessary corollary of this is that Clement, in contrast to Paul, primarily addresses the low-status members of the now hierarchically oriented community to encourage them to submit to recognized leaders. Paul, as the reader will recall, typically addressed the Strong in his appeals.[18]

One writer, elaborating further upon Clement's strategy, suggests that the intervention of the Roman church is modeled on the actions of the Roman senate and emperor. Just as leadership at Rome (senate or emperor) sent out emissaries (often philosophers or orators well-versed in concord rhetoric) to quell discord (stasis) in important cities in the provinces, so Clement, as a representative of the Roman church, appeals to the Corinthians.[19] Such a conceptual background for Clement's appeal to the Corinthians situates the author in a position of authority vis-à-vis his readers and coheres quite well with Clement's traditional use of concord rhetoric. For as we learned in the previous chapter, the benevolent patriarchalism regularly affirmed in homonoia speeches was consistently conservative in nature—geared "to maintaining the class structure by advocating only *moderate* exploitation of the lower class."[20]

The questions of how much exploitation, moderate or otherwise, occurred when concord rhetoric was appropriated and employed in the traditional way by the early Christians is probably unanswerable. Indeed, in the present instance, the offenders' reasons for initiating the sedition against their presbyters in Corinth are strikingly absent from *1 Clement*. The formal and social constraints characteristic of concord rhetoric generally excluded detailed descriptions of the causes of strife (see Dionysius of Halicarnassus, *Rhet.* 10.14; Quintilian, *Inst. Orat.* 3.8.6-10).[21] One wonders, however, what the rebels themselves would have said had Clement given them a voice in the discussion. The agitators may have had legitimate reasons to complain. As one commentator notes, "The unrest of the 1st and 2nd centuries almost always had economic causes," and asks, "Were the established presbyters accused of embezzlement?"[22] The question is, of course, unanswerable, since we hear only Clement's side of the debate. The rebels, for their part, are simply enjoined, through concord rhetoric, to submit to their appointed leaders.

Clement's desire to preserve the established community hierarchy, as well as his utilization of the concord genre in its traditional manner, significantly diminishes the effectiveness of the kinship metaphor as it appears in certain portions of Clement's epistle. I noted above that Clement's kinship terminology is sometimes less-than-persuasive in its rhetorical appeal. I must now be more specific. When Clement juxtaposes kinship terminology with *general* admonitions to desist from sedition and schism, and instead to pursue peace and concord, the metaphor carries a degree of persuasive power.

A number of the passages I cited above are representative (2.4-6; 4.1-11; 14.1). In these texts, Clement employs the kinship model, with all its implications of family solidarity, as a foil against which to view the sedition in the Corinthian community. The discord is thereby exposed as clearly inappropriate among members of a Mediterranean family. When, however, Clement uses kinship terms in the passages that outline his *solution* to the sedition—namely, the restoration of the recognized hierarchy—the reader is inevitably confronted with a degree of symbolic dissonance that takes the wind, so to speak, out of the sails of Clement's family rhetoric. The following passage reflects this phenomenon. Clement describes the order and hierarchy that characterized the Old Testament priesthood and then employs the Israelite model to enjoin submission to the hierarchy in Corinth. Note the three occurrences of "brethren":

> For to the High Priest his proper ministrations are allotted, and to the priests the proper place has been appointed, and on Levites their proper services have been imposed. The layman is bound by the ordinance of the laity. Let each one of us, brethren, be well pleasing to God in his own rank, and have a good conscience, not transgressing the appointed rules of his ministration, with all reverence. Not in every place, my brethren, are the daily sacrifices offered or the free-will offerings, or the sin-offerings and trespass-offerings, but only in Jerusalem; and there also the offering is not made in every place, but before the shrine, at the altar, and the offering is first inspected by the High Priest and the ministers already mentioned. Those therefore who do anything contrary to that which is agreeable to his will suffer the penalty of death. You see, brethren, that the more knowledge we have been entrusted with, the greater the risk do we incur. (40.5—41.4)

The kind of mutuality and solidarity typically associated with sibling relations in Mediterranean family systems finds little expression in Clement's solution to the sedition, which consists in maintaining a hierarchy of "rank," order, and "the appointed rules of [one's] ministration." The "brother" terminology in the above excerpt thereby loses much of its rhetorical energy. The same is the case in the following text-segment, in which the author draws upon another strongly hierarchical model—the Roman army—in order to make his case:

> Let us then serve in our army, brethren, with all earnestness, following his faultless commands. Let us consider those who serve our generals, with what good order, habit-

ual readiness, and submissiveness they perform their commands. Not all are prefects or tribunes, nor centurions, nor in charge of fifty men, or the like, but each carries out in his own rank the commands of the emperor and of the generals. The great cannot exist without the small, nor the small without the great; there is a certain mixture among all, and herein lies the advantage. (37.1-4)[23]

The implication, of course, is that the seditious in Corinth should similarly exhibit "good order, habitual readiness, and submissiveness" as they "perform [the] commands" of their church presbyters. The citation thus constitutes a classic example of concord rhetoric as traditionally employed in the Greco-Roman cities of antiquity. Again, however, the image portrayed flies in the face of the PKG metaphor suggested by the address "brethren" with which the author opens his appeal.

Clement's reasoning takes another interesting turn when he offers the spiritual ancestors of the readers as examples to be followed in dealing with the problems at hand. As we have seen, the idea of emulating the behavior of one's ancestors is a common theme in literature produced by lineage-group societies. Early Christians who adopted the PKG model and applied it to their communities included among its components the idea of ancestor imitation. Clement, as I noted above, is representative, as is Paul of Tarsus. When Paul uses the imitation *topos*, however, the theme invariably finds its point of application in the readers' relationship with God. So, for example, in Romans Paul cites "our father Abraham" (4:12) as the consummate example of one who was justified by faith. The point of application: Paul's readers must relate to God in similar fashion; they, too, must be justified by faith.

The parallel obtains in a negative sense, as well. In 1 Corinthians 10, Paul presents Old Testament "fathers" as an example of disobedience: "God was not pleased with most of them" (v. 5). In this instance Paul challenges his readers to relate to Christ in the opposite way: "We must not put Christ to the test, as some of them did, and were destroyed by serpents. And do not complain as some of them did, and were destroyed by the destroyer" (1 Cor 10:9-10). The parallel is thus drawn between the interaction between the Corinthians' spiritual ancestors and God, on the one hand, and the relationship between the readers and God, on the other. Paul's approach may be diagrammed as shown in figure 5.1.

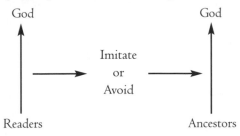

Fig. 5.1. Relationship to God

Clement, too, at times employs the imitation idea in the same way as Paul. Thus, after enumerating a list of spiritual ancestors who obeyed God, in chapters 9–12, he enjoins, "Therefore it is right and holy, my brethren, for us to obey God rather than to follow those who in pride and unruliness are the instigators of an abominable jealousy" (14.1). The readers must obey God as their ancestors obeyed God. Elsewhere, however, Clement applies the imitation *topos* differently. His desire to elicit from his readers submission to recognized leadership encourages him to alter the parallel and use the idea of ancestor emulation as shown in figure 5.2.

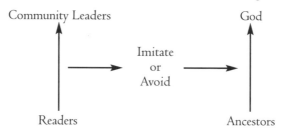

Fig. 5.2. Relationship to Leaders

Note that the recognized leadership of the Corinthian community replaces God in the diagram. Clement's readers are to behave toward their presbyters as their spiritual forefathers acted toward God. The connection is implied in chapters 44–45 of the letter. In 44.4-6, Clement specifically identifies the deposition of the presbyters as a "sin" that is "not small." He then introduces several Old Testament heroes as examples of those who "served God with a holy and faultless purpose" and are, therefore, to be received as "examples" (45.1—46.1). Though he does not explicitly state it in these terms, for Clement, to serve God "with a holy and faultless purpose" clearly consists in reinstating the presbyters in their rightful position of leadership and submitting to their authority.

The same is true of an earlier portion of Clement's letter. In 17.1, he encourages his readers, "Let us also be imitators of those who went about 'in the skins of goat and sheep.'" Elijah and Elisha are mentioned, along with Abraham, Moses, Job, and David. In each case, the character quality of humility toward God is proffered as exemplary. Clement concludes by observing that the "humility and obedient submission of so many men of such great fame, have rendered better not only us, but also the generations before us, who received his oracles in fear and truth" (19.1). Given the context of the letter, it is fair to assume that Clement offers the example of the "humility and obedient submission" of these Old Testament saints to God in order to challenge the Corinthian rebels to submit to their presbyters. Later, when Clement summarizes his appeal at the close of his letter, the application reflected in figure 5.2 is expressed in much clearer terms:

We have now written to you, brethren, sufficiently touching the things which befit our worship, and are most helpful for a virtuous life to those who wish to guide their steps in piety and righteousness. For we have touched on every aspect of faith and repentance and true love and self-control and sobriety and patience, and reminded you that you are bound to please almighty God with holiness in righteousness and truth and long-suffering, and to live in concord, bearing no malice, in love and peace with eager gentleness, even as our fathers, whose example we quoted, were well—pleasing in their humility towards God, the Father and Creator, and towards all men. . . . It is therefore right that we should respect so many and so great examples, and bow the neck, and take up a position of obedience, so that casting from vain sedition we may gain without any fault the goal set before us in truth. (62.1—63.1)

The "humility towards God" exemplified in the behavior of the readers' spiritual ancestors is to find tangible expression not only in the attitude of the Corinthian "brethren" "towards God, the Father and Creator" but also "towards all men." The specific application is as follows: "bow the neck, and take up a position of obedience" before established community leaders. Our next second-century author, Ignatius of Antioch, will make the connection between obedience to God as father, on the one hand, and submission to church leadership, on the other, even more explicit when he identifies the community's bishop as "a type of the Father" (*Trall.* 3.1) and commands his readers, "Be subject to the bishop . . . as Jesus Christ was subject to the Father" (*Magn.* 13.2).

IGNATIUS OF ANTIOCH

Ignatius of Antioch makes his first appearance on the stage of early Christian history during the final weeks of his life. He wrote his seven extant letters as he was being led to Rome to be martyred for his faith. Among the epistles of Ignatius that have been generally acknowledged as authentic are letters to the Christians at Ephesus, Magnesia, Tralles, Rome, Philadelphia, and Smyrna, along with a letter to Smyrna's bishop, Polycarp.[24] Ignatius wrote the first four letters from Smyrna and the final three from Troas, as he journeyed toward Rome, "bound to ten leopards," as he called his Roman military escort, who "became worse for kind treatment" (*Rom.* 5.1). Ignatius was likely martyred in the capital during a celebration marking Trajan's victories in the East (circa 110 C.E.).[25] Ignatius's letters, therefore, constitute the Christian leader's last opportunity to exhort his fellow believers to live in a manner befitting their calling as followers of Jesus.

The degree to which Ignatius was acquainted with the writings of his early Christian predecessors is debated. He may have possessed a copy of Matthew's

Gospel, but that is less than certain.[26] There is even less indication that Ignatius knew Mark, Luke, or John firsthand.[27] Ignatius was clearly familiar with at least a portion of the Pauline corpus, for he directly alludes to a passage from 1 Corinthians (*Rom.* 9.2; 1 Cor 15:8-9). Moreover, Ignatius, as overseer of the church at Antioch, served in "the congregation in which the apostle had ministered and which the author of Acts regarded as his base of operations."[28] One would expect, then, close affinity between Paul and Ignatius on a variety of issues. Instead, such distinctive Pauline ideas as justification by faith through grace, the relationship between law and gospel, and the conflict between the flesh and the spirit find no place in the Ignatian epistles. Paul's preoccupation with the concept of sin is also notably absent from Ignatius. Walter Wagner concludes that "Paul was regarded as a hero but disregarded as a shaper of Christian teaching, at least in Syria and Asia."[29]

Ignatius's lack of literary dependence on New Testament materials, combined with his relative disregard for key aspects of Paul's theology, renders all the more striking his adoption of the social pattern that was central to Jesus' and Paul's concept of community. Although the consistent preoccupation with the family model so common with Paul is not as evident in the Ignatian epistles, the overseer of Antioch did share Paul's model of the church as a surrogate patrilineal kinship group. Evidence from the seven letters demonstrates that relatively uniform social practices coexisted among the early Christians (see Lucian's generalizations earlier in this chapter) alongside differences in theological orientation. Let us turn, then, to the Ignatian corpus.

Ignatius's Use of Family Language

Ignatius employs kinship terminology in each of his letters. Sibling terminology surfaces on numerous occasions (*Eph.* 10.3; 16.1; *Phild.* 3.3; *Rom.* 6.2; *Trall.* 9.2; *Smyrn.* 12.1; 13.1; *Pol.* 5.1). The following passages are representative. Note the affection expressed in the first:

> Brethren, I am overflowing with love to you, and exceedingly joyful in watching over your safety. (*Phild.* 5.1)

> The love of the brethren at Troas salutes you; and I am writing thence to you by the hand of Burrhus, who was sent with me by the Ephesians and Smyrnaeans as a mark of honour. (*Phild.* 11.2)

> Suffer me, my brethren; hinder me not from living, do not wish me to die. Do not give to the world one who desires to belong to God, nor deceive him with material things. (*Rom.* 6.2)

> The love of the brethren who are at Troas salutes you, whence I am writing to you by
> Burrhus, whom you together with the Ephesians your brothers sent with me, and he
> has in every way refreshed me. Would that all imitated him, for he is a pattern of the
> ministry of God. (*Smyrn.* 12.1)

The last passage cited contains both sibling terms and the imitation theme. Natural
kinship relationships and the faith-family metaphor intersect in Ignatius's letter to
Polycarp, overseer of the Christian community at Smyrna: "Speak to my sisters
that they love the Lord, and be content with their husbands in flesh and in spirit.
In the same way enjoin on my brothers in the name of Jesus Christ, 'to love their
wives as the Lord loved the Church'" (*Pol.* 5.1). Especially pervasive in Ignatius are
references to the fatherhood of God (*Eph.* 1.1; 2.1; 4.2; 5.1; 15.1; 21.2; *Magn.* 1.1 passim). The bishop's farewell address to the Trallians is illustrative: "For I am still in
peril, but the Father is faithful in Jesus Christ to fulfil both your and my prayer, in
which you may be found blameless" (13.2). Ignatius also discusses Jesus, "who was
truly raised from the dead, when his Father raised him up, as in the same manner
his Father shall raise up in Christ Jesus us who believe in him, without whom we
have no true life" (*Trall.* 9.2).

Even when Ignatius switches from the family metaphor to that of the church as a
building, the image of God as father of the community still finds its way into the text:
"You are as stones of the temple of the Father, made ready for the building of God
our Father, carried up to the heights by the engine of Jesus Christ, that is the cross,
and using as a rope the Holy Spirit" (*Eph.* 9.1). Sibling and father references occur
together in *Letter to the Smyrnans* 13.1: "I salute the families of my brethren with their
wives and children, and the maidens who are called widows. Farewell in the power of
the Father." Other aspects of the PKG model, such as inheritance imagery and the
expectation that family members will imitate one another's behavior, are found in several passages that will be discussed in more detail below (*Eph.* 16.1; *Phild.* 3.3).

Family Activity in the Ignatian Epistles

For Ignatius, as for Paul, the PKG model, reflected in the use of family terminology,
carried with it an indispensable behavioral component. A number of text-segments
make it clear that Mediterranean family values found tangible expression among the
congregations that Ignatius addressed; to some degree, metaphor corresponded to
reality. The first chapter of the letter to the church in Ephesus begins with several
references to God as father. The author informs his readers that they are "imitators
of God." He proceeds to remind them of their past behavior: they "kindled [their]
brotherly task by the blood of God" and they "completed it perfectly" (*Eph.* 1.1).

Ignatius then elaborates on the particulars: "For when you heard that I had been sent a prisoner from Syria . . . you hastened to see me" (1.2). Caring for one's fellow Christians when they are imprisoned, as if for an incarcerated family member, is another theme common to literature written during times of persecution. Like Lucian's Peregrinus, above, Ignatius received care from his fellow Christians while under guard as a prisoner of Rome.[30]

PKG sibling solidarity is also alluded to in *Letter to the Smyrnans* 6:2. Ignatius warns against "those who have strange opinions concerning the grace of Jesus Christ." His description of his adversaries here assumes that the opposite is the case among the community that he addresses: "For love they have no care, none for the widow, none for the orphan, none for the distressed, none for the afflicted, none for the prisoner, or for him released from prison, none for the hungry or thirsty." Again, in *Letter to Polycarp* 4, he addresses the community's ministry to the weak. Widows are not to be neglected (v. 1). Polycarp is challenged not to be "haughty to slaves, either men or women" (v. 3), followed by an admonition not to set slaves free at the church's expense (v. 3). The implication is that Polycarp's community did engage in such a practice, one that clearly reflects generalized reciprocity among the persons involved.[31] Ignatius, however, disapproves.[32]

Ignatius is not fully satisfied with the activities by members of the communities he addresses. There is need for improvement, and Ignatius, like Paul, uses kinship language as a rhetorical device to correct the behavior of his readers where he perceives that such correction is necessary. Here the bishop adopts the family metaphor in order to exhort his readers to beware of schismatic teachers: "Do not err, my brethren; they who corrupt families shall not inherit the kingdom of God. If then those who do this according to the flesh suffer death, how much more if a man corrupt by false teaching the faith of God for the sake of which Jesus Christ was crucified?" (*Eph.* 16.1-2).

Innovation in the Ignatian Corpus

Like Clement, Ignatius found new application for the family metaphor. One passage, in particular, merits extended citation:

> Now for other men "pray unceasingly," for there is in them a hope of repentance, that they may find god. Suffer them therefore to become your disciples, at least through your deeds. Be yourselves gentle in answer to their wrath; be humble minded in answer to their proud speaking; offer prayer for blasphemy; be stedfast [*sic*] in the faith for their error; be gentle for their cruelty, and do not seek to retaliate. Let us be proved their brothers by our gentleness and let us be imitators of the Lord, and seek who may

suffer the more wrong, be the more destitute, the more despised; that no plant of the
devil be found in you but that you may remain in all purity and sobriety in Jesus
Christ, both in the flesh and in the Spirit. (*Eph.* 10.1-3)

The text-segment contains a constellation of family images, including brother
terminology, the imitation idea, and a strong emphasis upon the kind of nonretal-
iatory behavior that characterized ideal sibling relations in Mediterranean family
systems. As we have seen, in honor-shame societies such as that of Mediterranean
antiquity, the patrilineal kinship group constituted the sole social matrix, in which
the basis for acquiring honor was redefined.[33] Among strangers, honor was to be
acquired at the expense of the honor of others. Correspondingly, retaliation in the
face of a challenge to one's honor was itself the only honorable response in an
extrafamily social encounter. The family context inverted such values, however, as
brothers were expected to extend honor to their siblings and, correspondingly, to
resist responding in kind to an honor challenge from a family member. Accordingly,
Ignatius exhorts "brothers" to "be gentle" and "do not seek to retaliate." Ignatius,
however, is not here addressing relations as they obtained in the Christian surrogate
family. Indeed, the most striking aspect of the above citation lies in the author's
conviction that it is non-Christians who are to be treated as "brothers."

Paul of Tarsus drew a categorical distinction between "those outside" and the
members of the Christian brotherhood, a distinction that was often crucial to his
argument (1 Cor 5:9—6:11). At times, Paul could envision extending the resources of
the family of God beyond the boundaries of the community (Gal 6:10).[34] Never,
however, does Paul use the term "brother" to refer to pagans. For Ignatius, though,
the evangelistic thrust of the Jesus movement meant that every pagan was to be
viewed—and treated—as a potential brother in the faith.[35] Although the idea of
extending family-like treatment to outsiders is hardly new to early Christian thinking (see Matt 5:43-48; Rom 12:17), Ignatius is the first leader who uses and expands
upon the kinship metaphor to spell out in detail the practical implications for such
an outlook in Christian-pagan relations: Christians are not to respond in kind to
injustice perpetrated against them by their pagan neighbors. They are to respond
with gentleness—like brothers.

As shown above, Ignatius utilizes the PKG metaphor in a rather pointed way to
address the problem of schismatic teachers. Like Paul, he weds sibling terminology
to the image of inheritance to warn his readers: "Be not deceived, my brethren, if
any one follow a maker of schism, he does not inherit the kingdom of God" (*Phild.*
3.3). Ignatius departs markedly, however, from the Pauline model in his determina-
tion to use the authoritative position of local church leadership as a key weapon in
his struggle against teachers who oppose established community leaders.[36]

As outlined in the previous chapter, Paul's basic model for the church family consisted of siblings without an earthly father. According to the Pauline image, God was to be the father of the community. Leadership structure (where such existed in a formal sense at all in Pauline circles) appears to have intersected the PKG metaphor such that no single leader emerged in a given community. Rather, leadership was shared among several persons, variously called "elders" or "overseers" interchangeably. Thus, Paul addresses "overseers" and "deacons" in Philippians 1:1.

Plurality leadership, moreover, was not unique to Paul's communities. The author of Hebrews challenges the readers, "Remember your leaders, those who spoke the word of God to you; consider the outcome of their way of life, and imitate their faith" (13:7). The Book of Acts also assumes plurality leadership in the Gentile churches (14:23; 20:17). The model is reflected in other documents found among New Testament literature (Jas 5:14; 1 Pet 5:1-6). Plurality leadership for the family of faith can be traced back to the conceptions of Jesus of Nazareth (see chapter 3).

In this regard, the writings of Ignatius reflect a notable innovation. For the first time in early Christian literature, the community is led by a single individual. The term "bishop" or "overseer" (*episcopos*) is now distinguished from "elder" (*presbuteros*)—a single overseer presides over a group of elders. Much has been written (often fueled by strong confessional convictions) about the appearance of the monepiscopate in Ignatius. A Platonic element has been observed. Unlike Irenaeus, who derives the authority of the Jesus movement and its teaching from a chain of teaching chairs, Ignatius finds the authority of church leaders rooted in the fact that their offices constitute an earthly antitype of a heavenly pattern.[37] The parallels are as follows:

HEAVEN	EARTH
God	overseer
apostles	elders
Christ	deacons

With this model as his point of departure, Ignatius proceeds to use kinship terminology in a new way in his attempt to elicit obedience and unity from his followers. In striking contrast to the Pauline model, the bishop becomes the father of the local community: "the bishop is also a type of the Father" (*Trall.* 3.1). Ignatius takes full advantage of the idea of authority so closely associated with PKG patriarchy as he challenges his readers to an obedience appropriate to the child-father relationship: "Be subject to the bishop . . . as Jesus Christ was subject to the Father" (*Magn.* 13.2). William Schoedel acknowledges that ministerial authority has been "significantly enhanced by Ignatius" but nevertheless claims "it is difficult to show that it has been legitimated in a fundamentally new way."[38] Schoedel, however, has overlooked the rhetorical power of the family metaphor and Ignatius's use of the model to undergird episcopal authority in a truly innovative way:

> But flee from divisions as the beginning of evils. See that you all follow the bishop, as Jesus Christ follows the Father. . . . Let no one do any of the things appertaining to the Church without the bishop. Let that be considered a valid Eucharist which is celebrated by the bishop, or by one whom he appoints. . . . It is not lawful either to baptise or to hold an "agapé" without the bishop. (*Smyrn.* 7.2—8.2)

It appears that the idea of a surrogate patrilineal kin group without a human father figure (for example, Jesus, Paul, and Clement) was difficult to maintain, particularly in a culture in which every community member came from a family with a human patriarch, and in which families and social structures were almost universally characterized by authoritative patriarchal leadership. It was only natural that, given the pressure of schismatic teachers, Christian communities like those addressed by Ignatius would inevitably adopt a family model more closely approximating family as they knew it from their surrounding culture. An intangible heavenly father had to give way to his corporeal, earthly antitype.

Justin Martyr

With Justin Martyr, I turn to our most important second-century Christian apologist. Born around 90 C.E. to Gentile citizens of a Roman colony in Samaria, Justin joined the Jesus movement as a young man, after an intellectual quest that had driven him to examine various systems of thought, including Stoicism, Pythagoreanism, and Platonism. Justin was making great progress in the latter school of philosophy when an aged man confronted him and directed him to the study of Scripture. Examination of the Scriptures, involvement with Christians, and admiration for Christian martyrs combined to persuade Justin emotionally and intellectually that Christianity was the only true philosophy. Justin soon became the first philosopher of and for Christ.

Three of Justin's literary productions have survived: the *First Apology*, the *Second Apology*, and the *Dialogue with Trypho the Jew*. All were written near the middle of the second century.[39] Unlike the works of Clement and Ignatius, Justin's writings are ostensibly directed to those outside the community of faith. They seek to offer a defense of the Jesus movement to literate and educated pagans. The two apologies, originally a single work, are addressed to Antoninus Pius and his two adopted sons.[40]

The apologetic nature of his writings means that, in contrast, for example, to Clement of Rome, Justin focuses primarily upon the Christian belief system and less upon social interaction as it occurred in the Christian communities with which he was familiar. We will not be surprised, then, to discover less in the way of kinship terminology than we have observed with Paul, Clement, and Ignatius, each of whom addressed local Christian churches. Justin, unlike Paul and Clement, does not address behavioral problems among the faithful in a specific Christian community. Correspondingly, he does not utilize family language as a rhetorical device to shame his readers into PKG behavior.

The PKG model is still present, however, in Justin's writings. Indeed, Justin's ideological orientation renders the references to the kinship metaphor that do occur in his works all the more noteworthy as evidence for the centrality of this early Christian social model. Additionally, as I shall demonstrate, the philosophical and apologetic nature of Justin's approach necessitates a degree of innovation on Justin's part in his use of the now-familiar kinship theme.

Kinship Terminology in Justin's Writings

A search through Justin Martyr's three extant writings uncovers a significant amount of family terminology. Sibling terms appear twice in one passage as a designation for the group into which newly baptized converts are admitted (*1 Apol.* 65). "Brethren" is also used for Justin's fellow Christians in the *Dialogue with Trypho* (47). The image of God as father of the Christian family is found in various places in Justin's writings (*2 Apol.* 9, 10, 13; *Dial. Tryph.* 7, 17, 25-26, 119, 126). The corresponding idea that Christians are "children of God" also finds expression (*Dial. Tryph.* 123-24). Another aspect of the kinship model that surfaces repeatedly in the *Dialogue* is that of inheritance, often appearing with the related idea that Israel's patriarchs constitute the Christian community's surrogate ancestors. This is only to be expected in a work in which the author is defending the early Christians' appropriation of the Old Testament (Septuagint) narratives as their own literary and historical heritage.

Part of the debate with Trypho centers around the future of the Judeans in God's plan for salvation history. At issue at one point is the interpretation of a phrase from Isaiah 63:18 that Justin cites as follows: "that we may inherit for a little Thy holy mountain" (25). Trypho in turn inquires, "Do I understand you to say that none of us Jews will inherit anything on the holy mountain of God?" (25). The inheritance theme remains in the foreground in Justin's response:

> I didn't say that, but I do say that those who have persecuted Christ in the past and still do, and do not repent, shall not inherit anything on the holy mountain, unless

they repent. Whereas the Gentiles, who believe in Christ and are sorry for their sins, shall receive the inheritance, along with the Patriarchs, and Prophets, and every just descendant of Jacob, even though they neither practice circumcision nor observe the sabbaths and feasts. They shall undoubtedly share in the holy inheritance of God. (*Dial. Tryph.* 26)

Another excerpt from the *Dialogue* combines the three family images of inheritance, fatherhood, and ancestry: "And we shall inherit the Holy Land together with Abraham, receiving our inheritance for all eternity, because by our similar faith we have become children of Abraham. . . . Thus, God promised Abraham a religious and righteous nation of like faith, and a delight to the Father" (*Dial. Tryph.* 119).

The issue of ancestry appears elsewhere in the *Dialogue*, as well (44, 113, 122, 130, 139). Most interesting is a passage that reveals a problem faced inevitably by the early Christians as they appropriated the Old Testament patriarchs as their spiritual ancestors, on the one hand, but dispensed with the Mosaic law, on the other. Justin cites and then comments on a passage from the Psalms:

These words show . . . that the Word of God speaks to His faithful . . . as to a daughter, namely, the Church which was established by and partakes in His name (for we are all called Christians). That this is so, and that we are instructed to forget the ancient customs of our ancestors, the following words imply: "Hearken, O daughter, and see, and incline thy ear, and forget thy people and thy father's house. And the king shall greatly desire thy beauty, for He is thy Lord, and Him thou shalt adore" [Ps 44:11-12]. (*Dial. Tryph.* 63)

Justin must resort to some rather fanciful exegesis to justify the patent fact that the Christians lived their lives in a manner much different vis-à-vis the Mosaic Law than did their alleged ancestors.

Justin and Family Behavior

Justin Martyr, like the writers examined previously, expects the kinship metaphor to be reflected in day-to-day Christian life. Indeed, his writings contain evidence that the values associated with Mediterranean family systems found tangible expression in the communities with which Justin was familiar. The sharing of material resources, associated with the PKG value of generalized reciprocity, is clearly expressed in the following description of Christian practices: "We who once took most pleasure in the means of increasing our wealth and property now bring what we have into a common fund and share with everyone in need; we who hated and killed one another and would not associate with men of different tribes because of their different customs, now . . . live together" (*1 Apol.* 14). Later in the same work, Justin describes the means by which community resources are collected and distributed on a weekly basis:

> Those who have more come to the aid of those who lack, and we are constantly together. . . . Those who prosper, and so wish, contribute, each one as much as he chooses to. What is collected is deposited with the president, and he takes care of orphans and widows, and those who are in want on account of sickness or any other cause, and those who are in bonds, and the strangers who are sojourners among [us], and, briefly, he is the protector of all those in need. (67)

Yet another aspect of the PKG metaphor may be in view in the two excerpts cited immediately above. In the course of Justin's descriptions of the sharing of community resources, the author claims that he and his fellow believers "live together" (14) and "are constantly together" (67). The reader will recall the identification, in chapter 2, of patrilocal residence as an important characteristic of Mediterranean family systems. Keeping family members in close geographical proximity—typically under the same roof or around the same courtyard—was a high priority for ancient patrilineal kinship groups. The indisputable presence of one PKG value in the above text-segments (generalized reciprocity) suggests that Justin's comments about community members being "together" also finds its locus in the family metaphor. Similarly, Justin elsewhere refers to Christians as "those who have shown to God by their actions that they follow him and long to dwell with him, where no evil can disturb" (*1 Apol.* 8).

I also identified the practice of loyalty as central to the solidarity inherent in Mediterranean family systems. The divided loyalties that resulted from the Christian convert's commitment to her natural family, on the one hand, versus her attachment to her new surrogate family, on the other, produced tensions that find expression in the writings of a variety of early Christian authors, including Justin.[41] The first indication of the presence of this central PKG value among Justin's contemporaries is found near the middle of the first *Apology.* Justin here attempts to explain the willingness of Christians to die for their faith. Observe his analogy:

> It would be ridiculous when soldiers whom you have recruited and enrolled stick to their loyalty to you before their own life and parents and native land and all their families, though you have nothing incorruptible to offer them, for us, who desire incorruption, not to endure all things in order to receive what we long for from Him who is able to give it. (39)

Just as the emperor's soldiers "stick to their loyalty" to him at the cost of life, parents, and family, it is correspondingly logical, Justin implies, for Christians to make the same family sacrifices as an expression of their loyalty to God.[42]

In his second *Apology*, Justin presents a real-life example of the practical implications of PKG loyalty as it worked itself out in the family of faith. He narrates the story of a woman who became a Christian to the dismay of her pagan husband. Justin describes the man as "a husband who sought in every way those means of sensual pleasure contrary to the law of nature and in violation of every right." For some time, the woman adhered to the advice of Christian friends who urged her to continue in the relationship in the hope that her husband would ultimately convert to the Jesus movement. Finally, when she could endure no more, "she, in order not to participate in his sinful and impious acts by continuing to live with him by sharing his table and his bed, gave him what you term a bill of divorce and left him." The incident then escalated into the public arena when the husband "brought a charge against her, claiming that she was a Christian." In the course of events that followed, the woman's tutor in the faith, a certain Ptolemaeus, along with another Christian who attempted to intercede on his behalf, were "ordered to be led to execution by the magistrate Urbicus" (2 *Apol.* 2).

The radical change of loyalties reflected in the above narrative was not an uncommon expression of family-like commitment to the Christian community. It is interesting to note, in this regard, that stories of this nature typically relate the activities of converted women as they seek to relate as Christians to their pagan husbands. I cannot recall a story of a husband converting apart from his spouse. Given the hierarchical nature of patrilineal family systems, this is understandable. A household typically followed the religious practices of its male head. If the patriarch joined the Jesus movement, the household converted, as well. The opposite, however, would not necessarily, or even typically, be the case. Indeed, wives were not to convert to an alien religion in the first place. As Plutarch opines:

> A wife ought not to make friends of her own, but to enjoy her husband's friends in common with him. The gods are the first and most important friends. Where it is becoming for a wife to worship and to know only the gods that her husband believes in, and to shut the front door tight upon all queer rituals and outlandish superstitions. (Plutarch, *Advice to the Bride and Groom* 140D)[43]

A woman who attempted to follow religious practices alien to her husband's household would inevitably find herself in a tenuous position in her family—unless, of course, the new religion offered her an alternative family in which to find the security and material resources necessary for survival in ancient Mediterranean society.[44]

This alternative family, as we have seen, is precisely what the Jesus movement offered, and it is hardly surprising to see women exercising their option in this regard and leaving unreasonable or abusive pagan husbands to join the Christian family of faith.

I now examine a final aspect of PKG behavior in Justin that received attention in an earlier chapter. One of the more tangible expressions of PKG solidarity in ancient Mediterranean families was the sharing of meals together. For Justin, this applies to the family of God, as the following text-segment indicates. The issue of contention addressed by this passage consists of the status of Judean Christians who persist in observing the precepts of the Mosaic Law. Justin had just responded in the affirmative to Trypho's inquiry as to whether or not such Christians would be saved. Trypho is rather surprised at Justin's liberality in this regard, for he is clearly aware of other Christians who, he claims, "hold a different opinion." Justin responds:

> Yes, Trypho, there are some Christians who boldly refuse to have conversation or meals with such persons. I don't agree with such Christians. But if some, due to their insta-bility of will, desire to observe as many of the Mosaic precepts as possible—precepts which we think were instituted because of your hardness of heart—while at the same time they place their hope in Christ, and if they desire to perform the eternal and nat-ural acts of justice and piety, yet wish to live with us Christians and believers, as I already stated, not persuading them to be circumcised like themselves, or to keep the Sabbath, or to perform any other similar acts, then it is my opinion that we Christians should receive them and associate with them in every way as kinsmen and brethren. (*Dial. Tryph.* 47)

The passage constitutes a key piece of evidence for the history of Judean and Christian relations in antiquity.[45] For our purposes, however, it is important to note the association in Justin's mind between the idea of the church as a family and the practice of table fellowship. Those who are "kinsmen and brethren" share "conver-sation or meals."

The linguistic data and PKG solidarity evidenced in the above excerpts from the writings of Justin Martyr reflect what has now become a familiar pattern. Like the previous writers surveyed, Justin employs the family metaphor, and he also gives evidence of tangible expressions of the PKG value system in the Christian commu-nities with which he is familiar. Justin's philosophical orientation and apologetic purposes, however, lead him occasionally to use kinship terminology in a manner that differs markedly from the practices of the writers previously surveyed. It is to Justin's innovations of the family metaphor that we now turn.

Innovation in Justin's Use of Father and Sibling Language

Perhaps the best example is Justin's expansion of the concept of the fatherhood of God to apply not only to Christians but to all human beings and, indeed, to all of creation. He refers to God as "the Father and Fashioner of all things" (*1 Apol.* 8; see *Dial. Tryph.* 58), "the Father of all" (*1 Apol.* 45; *Dial. Tryph.* 32, 74, 133), and "Universal Father" (*Dial. Tryph.* 75). Elsewhere Justin observes that "all authors call God [the] father of men and gods" (*1 Apol.* 22). In yet another passage, he calls God the "Father of righteousness and temperance and the other virtues" (*1 Apol.* 6).

To appreciate the innovative nature of Justin's father language, it will help to contrast the above citations with a passage that reflects a more typical Christian understanding of the father metaphor. The following text-segment finds Jesus of Nazareth in a heated dialogue with his opponents in the Gospel of John. After his adversaries claim God for their father, the narrator portrays Jesus responding as follows:

> Jesus said to them, "If God were your Father, you would love me, for I came from God and now I am here. I did not come on my own, but he sent me. You are from your father the devil, and you choose to do your father's desires. He was a murderer from the beginning and does not stand in the truth, because there is no truth in him." (John 8:42-44)[46]

The author of this work and the community he represents would surely have had a problem with Justin's conception of God as the "Universal Father" (*Dial. Tryph.* 75). Justin's approach, however, is easily explained. The idea of a cosmic father of all, who is creator of all, is not uncommon in antiquity (Plato, *Tim.* 28C, 37C, 41A; Philo, *Spec. Leg.* 2.165; 3.189; *Corp. Herm.* 5.9; 11.6-8; 12.15b; 14.4). Before Justin's time, however, the image is generally limited to non-Christian works whose orientation is philosophical.[47] Second-century Christian apologists, seeking common ground on which to erect arguments against the views of their educated pagan opponents, appropriate images such as the universal fatherhood of God in order to persuade the opposition of the credibility of the Jesus movement (see also Minucius Felix, *Oct.* 19.1; 33.1). Justin's background and training (see, especially, his extensive background in Platonism), combined with the apologetic purpose of his corpus, adequately account for the innovative use of the father metaphor when compared with what we have observed with Paul, Clement, and Ignatius.

Justin's expansion of the semantic field typically covered by sibling terminology in early Christian literature may be similarly explained. We saw above that Ignatius, unlike Paul, used sibling terminology to refer to pagans. For Ignatius, pagans were potential converts, and as such, they were to be treated like "brethren" (*Eph.* 10.1-3).

Justin's broad use of the sibling metaphor is best explained along other lines. In the following passage, the idea of pagans as possible converts to the Jesus movement is wholly absent from the discussion. Rather, Justin appeals to the Roman Senate on the basis of a common philosophical notion—the universal brotherhood of humankind: "you Romans who are men of feelings like ours and are our brethren, even though you fail to realize it or refuse to admit it because of your pride in your so-called dignities" (2 *Apol.* 1). The reader encounters a similar use of "brethren" in at least two other passages (*Dial. Tryph.* 58; 96).

Here then is a summary of the ways in which Justin's appropriation of the PKG metaphor is similar to, and differs from, the practices of the authors surveyed previously. His designated audience guaranteed that Justin, unlike our previous authors, would not use the kinship model as a rhetorical device to engender proper Christian behavior, since Justin addressed not Christians but pagan elites and Trypho, a Judean. More importantly, Justin's training in Hellenistic philosophy led him occasionally to use certain aspects of the family model—specifically, father and brother terminology—in a broad and innovative way. In fact, these passages taken in isolation might lead us to the conclusion that for Justin the concept of the family of God has taken on such broad application as to become essentially meaningless as a defining model for day-to-day Christian social interaction. I demonstrated above, however, that the more traditional application of the metaphor—to the Christian community as such—remains paramount with Justin, and that it is expressed both in his extensive use of kinship terminology and in passages which show that the early Christians with which Justin was familiar practiced PKG values such as generalized reciprocity and family loyalty on a regular basis.

We will conclude with the works of two late second-century writers: Clement of Alexandria and Irenaeus of Gaul. The evidence provided by these widely separated authors significantly expands our awareness of the geographical distribution of the family model among Christians. This evidence confirms my contention that, despite variety in theological orientation, the early Christians shared the central social ideal reflected in the PKG metaphor.

CLEMENT OF ALEXANDRIA

Clement of Alexandria constitutes our first reliable witness to the social ideals and practices that characterized an important cross section of Alexandrian Christianity.[48] The evidence Clement provides is important to the present study because, despite the theological diversity that may have characterized the early Jesus movement in Egypt, the family metaphor remains central to Clement's understanding of Christian social organization and behavior.[49] Indeed, this first undisputed source of evidence for the social organization of the Alexandrian Jesus movement reflects the model of the church as family at every turn.

Clement's surviving corpus is extensive. The major treatises include the *Instructor (Paidagogos)*, *Exhortation (Protreptikos)*, and *Miscellanies (Stromateis)*. The PKG metaphor appears often in each of these works, as an overview of their contents would demonstrate. In order to demonstrate the centrality of the kinship model to Clement's thinking about Christian community, however, it will prove most instructive to limit my examination to yet another, shorter, treatise of Clement's: *Who Is the Rich Man Being Saved?*[50] The work consists of an exposition of Mark 10:17-31 and concludes with a narrative about a young man who was baptized, lost, and restored to the Jesus movement by the apostle John.

The central issue of *The Rich Man* is the place of riches—and of those who possess them—in the Christian community. The topic was hardly theoretical for the author of our treatise, for Clement apparently encountered high-status Christians on a daily basis in his role as director of the catechetical school at Alexandria. The reader of Clement's corpus of writings inevitably senses that Clement is addressing his works to an audience of some means. As Wagner notes, "The tone and extent of [Clement's] advice to Christians who were wealthy, accustomed to luxury, and owned slaves indicates that he moved often and comfortably among successful merchants and aristocrats."[51] Christians with extensive material resources, however, inevitably experienced a serious tension between their own lifestyles and the ideals reflected in passages, like the following one, from the Jesus traditions:

> Then Jesus looked around and said to his disciples, "How hard it will be for those who have wealth to enter the kingdom of God!" And the disciples were perplexed at these words. But Jesus said to them again, "Children, how hard it is to enter the kingdom of God! It is easier for a camel to go through the eye of a needle than for someone who is rich to enter the kingdom of God." (Mark 10:23-25)

It is this tension that our author seeks to resolve, and the task necessarily beckons Clement, who is otherwise often taken to theological and philosophical abstractions, to create a dialogue in highly practical terms about Christian social responsibility. Specifically, *The Rich Man* allows Clement to expound upon the Markan passage, and his discussion of the spiritual condition of the wealthy inevitably includes such issues as the role of the church's high-status members as patrons of the community and the corresponding distribution of their wealth to the community's poor and destitute. Moreover, as we shall see, the kinship idea proves to be the most appropriate rhetorical metaphor for Clement to draw upon in order to legitimate his challenge to the rich man to use his riches "for his brothers' sakes rather than his own" (16).[52]

I begin my examination of *The Rich Man* with a general survey of its kinship terminology and then proceed to highlight the PKG value of generalized reciprocity as Clement expected it to function among the Alexandrian Christians. Clement uses the PKG metaphor at the very beginning of his treatise when he refers to God as the one who "accords such gifts (that is, riches) to his children" (1). References to God as father appear throughout the work (6, 27, 29, 31, 37, 39, 41). The following text-segments concern the nature of the father-children relationship as Clement envisions it:

> God Himself our Father, through whom all things have come into being and exist . . . by the very act of loving the Father to the limit of our personal strength and power we gain incorruption. (27)

> For to every one who turns to God in truth and with his whole heart the doors are opened and a thrice-glad Father receives a truly penitent son. . . . And if we, being evil know how to give good gifts, how much more does the Father of mercies. (39)

> He does not withstand His children when they beg His mercies. (41)

The last half of the second excerpt is a conflation of several biblical references (see Matt 7:11; 2 Cor 1:13). Other references to Christians as God's children also appear at various points in Clement's argument (5, 22-23, 29, 31). Given the centrality of the father-children metaphor to Clement's conceptual universe, the reader is not surprised to find sibling terminology throughout the work, as well (4, 16, 30, 37, 38, 40). Indeed, it is the "love of the brethren" that is to motivate the faithful to embrace the very task Clement undertakes in the penning of his treatise: "to help the rich members of the church to salvation" (3). Characteristic of Clement's style is a passage that includes in a single sentence father-children imagery, the sibling metaphor, and inheritance terminology: "Those who perfectly observe the Father's will He makes not slaves, in the manner of a slave, but sons and brothers and joint-heirs" (9).

The issue of loyalty to the family of God surfaces in an important passage in which Clement elaborates upon this central PKG value. Clement cites a saying of Jesus and then offers commentary. The text-segment is quoted at length here:

> "He that hates not father and mother and children, yes and his own life also, cannot be My disciple." . . . If, for instance, a man had a godless father or son or brother, who became a hindrance to his faith and an obstacle to the life above, let him not live in

fellowship or agreement with him, but let him dissolve the fleshly relationship on account of the spiritual antagonism. Think of the matter as a lawsuit. Imagine your father standing by you and saying, "I begat you and brought you up, follow me, take part in my wrong-doing and do not obey the law of Christ," and whatever else a man who was a blasphemer and in nature dead might say. But from the other side hear the Savior; "I gave you new birth, when by the world you were evilly born for death; I set you free, I healed you, I redeemed you. I will provide you with a life unending, eternal, above the world. I will show you the face of God the good Father." "Call no man your father upon earth." "Let the dead bury their dead, but do you follow Me." "For I will lead you up to a rest and to an enjoyment of unspeakable and indescribable good things" "which eye has not seen nor ear heard, nor have they entered into the heart of man, which angels desire to look into and to see what good things God has prepared for His saints and for His children that love Him." . . . When you have listened to these appeals from each side pass judgment on your own behalf and cast the vote for your own salvation. Even though a brother says the like, or a child or wife or any one else, before all let it be Christ that conquers in you; since it is on your behalf He struggles. (22-23)

The kinship metaphor is obviously central to Clement's argument. The passage contains references to the "new birth," God as "Father," "His children." Juxtaposed against these kinship terms are references to blood-family relations: "father," "son," "brother," "child," "wife." The courtroom scene further accentuates the polarization between the two spheres of familial loyalty. Clement, of course, urges the reader to opt for loyalty to God the father over loyalty to those relations considered most important in Mediterranean family systems (see, for example, line 2: "father or son or brother"). Moreover, the citation demonstrates that the demands for such a transfer of loyalties find their legitimation, for Clement, in the words of Jesus of Nazareth.

The loyalty idea surfaces again a few paragraphs later in the text. Here Clement considers the situation of a believer who has a selfish attitude toward "lands and riches and houses and brothers." He advises: "If joined with such persecution [Clement defines "persecution" here as the tendency to hoard one's possessions and to express inordinate loyalty toward one's family of origin] you have visible wealth and brothers by blood and all other separable possessions, abandon your sole enjoyment of these which leads to evil" (25).

The PKG practice of patrilocal residence is yet another Mediterranean family characteristic echoed in Clement's understanding of the family of faith. Twice in one text-segment, Clement refers to Christians as those who have "an eternal habitation from the Father" (31). The reader encounters a similar idea earlier in the writing, at which point the rich Christian is challenged to discipline himself to become a "victor, admitted to be worthy of the fatherland above" (3).

Clement's primary rhetorical purpose for drawing upon the family metaphor is to answer the question posed by the title of his treatise, known more widely in Latin as *Quis Dives Salvetur?* For Clement, the rich man who is saved is the one who understands that his riches are not his own: they have been entrusted to him by God for the benefit of his Christian brothers and sisters. Clement faces his greatest hermeneutical dilemma in the course of his exposition of Mark 10:17-31 when he wrestles with the sentence that we now designate verse 21. Here the reader is confronted with Jesus' categorical statement to the rich ruler in dialogue with Jesus concerning eternal life: "You lack one thing; go, sell what you own, and give the money to the poor, and you will have treasure in heaven; then come, follow me" (10:21).

Clement's solution is a creative one, which has been employed, with some variation, by countless interpreters throughout the centuries. For Clement, Jesus' words are not to be taken literally and then applied to all of his subsequent followers.[53] The command's ultimate application is to be found not in the disowning of one's possessions but rather in one's attitude toward—and use of—one's possessions. Indeed, it would be senseless for Christians to relieve themselves of all worldly resources. For, as Clement observes,

> How could we feed the hungry and give drink to the thirsty, cover the naked and entertain the homeless, with regard to which deed He threatens fire and the outer darkness to those who have not done them, if each of us were himself already in want of all these things? . . . It is on this condition that He praises their use, and with this stipulation,—that He commands them to be shared, to give drink to the thirsty and bread to the hungry, to receive the homeless, to clothe the naked. (13)

Moreover, such administration of one's wealth only makes sense, for Clement, in the context of the generalized reciprocity characteristic of the family model. The rich man who shares God's perspective on his riches "holds possessions and gold and silver and houses as gifts of God, and from them ministers to the salvation of men for God the giver, and knows that he possesses them for his brothers' sakes rather than his own. . . . [He is] a ready inheritor of the kingdom of heaven" (16). Note the presence in the above citation of both sibling and inheritance terminology.

The idea of the rich man sharing his bounty with needy brethren in the context of the Christian surrogate kin group surfaces again in two other important passages in Clement's treatise:

> Those who believe in Him He calls children and young children and babes. . . . He declares that all possessions are by nature unrighteous, when a man possesses them for personal advantage as being entirely his own, and does not bring them into the common stock [*koinon*] for those in need; but that from this unrighteousness it is possible

to perform a deed that is righteous and saving, namely, to give relief to one of those who have an eternal habitation from the Father. (31)

But if we owe our lives to the brethren, and admit such a reciprocal compact with the Saviour, shall we still husband and hoard up the things of the world, which are beggarly and alien to us and ever slipping away? Shall we shut out from one another that which in a short time the fire will have? Divine indeed and inspired is the saying of John: "He that loveth not his brother is a murderer," a seed of Cain, a nursling of the devil. (37)

Once again, the reader encounters the Cain-and-Abel archetype of sibling treachery. By drawing upon the powerful imagery of Cain in the last excerpt cited above, Clement essentially demonizes any member of the community who would hesitate to practice the central PKG value of generalized reciprocity in the sharing of his riches with those in need. "'Love,'" Clement concludes shortly thereafter, citing Paul of Tarsus, "'seeketh not its own,' but is lavished upon the brother" (38).

IRENAEUS

The Jesus movement in Gaul first appears in history with the pogrom instigated against Christians at Lyons (then Lugdunum) in 177 C.E. By the second century, Lyons and nearby Vienne had become thriving trade centers attracting colonists from various regions in the empire. Among the foreign settlers in Gaul was a group of merchants from Asia and Phrygia who had established themselves on an island in the Rhone below the original Celtic fort of Lugdunum, opposite an area now (in 177 C.E.) decorated with a temple to Augustus. Like other merchant groups, the Asians and Phrygians had brought their religion—the Jesus movement— with them to Lyons. The colonists had apparently prospered commercially, acquired slaves, learned Latin, and had some success attracting local residents to the Christian faith.[54]

Lyons was an important center of Gallic paganism, and tensions were inevitable between indigenous Gauls and recently arrived foreigners. An annual gathering in the city brought together representatives of the various Gallic tribes, who elected a high priest and sacrificed to the Celtic deity Lud, as well as to Rome and Augustus. In a society that understood the favor of the gods to be directly dependent upon proper attention to cult and sacrifice, foreigners who rejected Gallic and Roman gods, defied the emperor's decrees, and sought converts for their way of life were badly out of sync with sociocultural norms. It is not unusual, however, for socially marginal groups to thrive unmolested alongside the dominant culture during times

of economic prosperity and regional security. Such was apparently the case for
some time among Christians and pagans in Lyons. In the 170s, however, German
invaders crossed the northern borders, and the emperor Marcus Aurelius soon
called for sacrifices, unity, and a ban on secret societies. Local Christians soon experienced the indirect but severe consequences of the emperor's decrees.[55]

The resulting persecution took the lives of some forty-eight Christians, who
perished in prison or in the amphitheater in August 177 (see Eusebius, *Hist. Eccl.* 5.1,
5.2.2-8). The behavior of the Christians of Lyons during the events surrounding the
persecution provides helpful insights into the social practices characterizing early
Gallic Christianity; I will consider Eusebius's account below. That the pogrom
proved to be the occasion of Irenaeus's accession to the bishopric of Lyons is
important to our discussion. Born to a Christian family in Asia, Irenaeus went (or
was sent) to Lyons, perhaps as an emissary to expatriate Asian Christians. During
the late 170s, Pothinus, the Bishop of Lyons, dispatched Irenaeus from Gaul to
Rome in order to advise the Roman bishop, Eleutherus, about Montanism. While
Irenaeus was in Rome, the Gallic persecution erupted and Pothinus was martyred.
Irenaeus returned to a quieter Gaul and was duly elected the church's bishop (Eusebius, *Hist. Eccl.* 5.3-4).

Irenaeus has left us two complete works, along with various fragments ascribed
to him by Eusebius and others. Most extensive is his five-book treatise, *Against Heresies* (as the *Refutation and Overthrow of Knowledge Falsely So-Called* is commonly known),
a reply to the Valentinian and Marcionite Gnosticism that had challenged and influenced the Jesus movement in Gaul.[56] The other surviving work is a smaller handbook of Christian apologetic, the *Proof of the Apostolic Preaching.* Irenaeus crafted his
writings neither to address behavioral problems in specific Christian communities
(see Paul of Tarsus) nor to provide a general prescription for acceptable Christian
social organization and activity. Rather, Irenaeus's purposes are ideological, and
he is remembered primarily for his responses to the various streams of gnostic
thinking of his day.[57] This means that much of the kinship terminology found
in Irenaeus's writings occurs in the context of gnostic mythological speculation
and finds no social referent in the gnostic (or Christian) communities Irenaeus
discusses. The description Irenaeus provides of gnostic teaching about the post-
mortem ascent is representative:[58]

> And they instruct them, on their reaching the principalities and powers, to make use
> of these words: "I am a son from the Father—the Father who had a pre-existence, and
> a son in Him who is pre-existent. . . ." And they affirm that, by saying these things, he
> escapes from the powers. He then advances to the companions of the Demiurge, and
> thus addresses them: "I am a vessel more precious than the female who formed you. If

your mother is ignorant of her own descent, I know myself, and am aware whence I came, and I call upon the incorruptible Sophia, who is in the Father, and is the mother of your mother, who has no father, nor any male consort." (*Adv. Haer.* 1.21.5)[59]

The citation is characteristic of extensive portions of Irenaeus's treatise in which he relates the viewpoints of his opponents. In passages such as these, kinship terms are used in the context of gnostic mythology and they find no expressed application in the sphere of human relationships (see *Adv. Haer.* 1.30.1-15; 3.15.2). Thus, in the survey that follows, I ignore these mythological usages of family language and discuss only those kinship terms and ideas that Irenaeus applies to the Christian church. Even here, however, most of the evidence is ideological rather than sociological. Irenaeus is concerned to demonstrate that the Christians are God's true adopted sons and daughters, but he frames his argument in conceptual, rather than behavioral, terms. Nevertheless, in the course of his exposition, he does at times make it a point to contrast what he perceives to be the godless behavior of his opponents with the family-like relationships among his fellow Christians.[60] These brief but pointed comments leave the reader with the impression that there was a social corollary to Irenaeus's persistent assertion that Christians "are children in God's household" (4.13.2).

The family model surfaces throughout Irenaeus's five-volume work. He does not use sibling terminology often, but it does occur (1.13.5). Certain heretical groups, such as the Encratites, are said to "hold themselves aloof from the communion of the brethren" (3.11.9). The church is referred to as a "brotherhood" on several occasions (2.31.2; 4.28.3-4; 5.6.1). One of the occurrences of "brother" found in Irenaeus's writings draws upon the now-familiar theme of sibling treachery, citing again the Cain-and-Abel narrative from Genesis 4. In a discussion of proper sacrifices and oblations, the author first quotes Matthew 5:23-24 ("first be reconciled to your brother, then go to the altar") and then offers Cain and Abel as archetypal examples of acceptable and unacceptable sacrifice. God, claims Irenaeus, "had not respect unto the offering of Cain, because his heart was divided with envy and malice, which he cherished against his brother" (4.18.1-3).

Much more common than text-segments employing sibling imagery in *Against Heresies* are passages that focus upon the fatherhood of God and its implication for Irenaeus's theology (2.9.1; 3.6.1; extensively in 3.16.7-8 and 4.1.1; see also 4.8.2; 4.16.5; 4.36.4).[61] Irenaeus is highly concerned to limit the fatherhood of God to the sphere of orthodoxy and to demonstrate that the heretics "have been deserted by the paternal love" (3.12.12). The reader gains insight into Irenaeus's understanding of the implications of the father metaphor for the divine–human relationship when the author compares the idea of God as father with other familiar designations for the deity: "Now this being is the Creator, who is, in respect of His love, the Father; but in respect of His power, He is Lord; and in respect of His wisdom, our Maker and Fashioner" (5.17.1). The imitation *topos* appears in association with the father metaphor when Irenaeus asserts that the "grace of the Spirit" will "accomplish the will of the Father, for it shall make man after the image and likeness of God" (5.8.1).

Inextricably bound to the father metaphor is a related kinship concept that Irenaeus draws upon more often than any writer before him. Frequently in *Against Heresies*, the reader encounters the idea, variously expressed, that the Christians are the adopted sons and daughters of God the father, that they are "partakers of the adoption as sons" (3.18.7; see 3.6.1; 3.20.2; 4.1.1; 4.16.5; 4.33.4; 4.34.2; 5.12.2; 5.18.2). At one point Irenaeus cites Galatians 4:4-5, observing that the Pauline text-segment plainly indicates "one God, who did by the prophets make promise of the Son . . . the Son of God being the Son of man, that through Him we may receive the adoption" (3.16.3).

Elsewhere, Irenaeus offers the following as a central reason for the incarnation of the Son of God: "For it was for this end that the Word of God was made man, and He who was the Son of God became the Son of man, that man, having been taken into the Word, and receiving the adoption, might become the son of God . . . that we might receive the adoption of sons" (3.19.1). As a result of adoption by God, Christians "are children of God's household" (4.13.2), which is for Irenaeus a fulfillment of Old Testament prophecy: "Bring My sons from far, and My daughters from the ends of the earth" (4.14.1, citing Isa 43:5). The idea of spiritual generation also comes into play among the constellation of images that reflect the belief that Christians are God's children (4.33.4). At one point, Irenaeus prays that heretics might return to the church, and that they, "being converted to the Church of God, may be lawfully begotten" (3.25.7).

The themes of sonship and adoption are central to Irenaeus's argument, and they occasion one of the most extensive theological explanations of the family metaphor found anywhere in early Christian literature. Note the manner in which our author carefully attempts to preserve the unique relationship shared by Christians with their divine father, while at the same time allowing for the broader conception of God as universal father to all humankind:

> Since, therefore, all things were made by God, and since the devil has become the cause of apostasy to himself and others, justly does the Scripture always term those who remain in a state of apostasy "sons of the devil" and "angels of the wicked one." For "son," as one before me has observed, has a twofold meaning: one [is a son] in the order of nature, because he was born a son; the other, in that he was made so, is reputed a son, although there be a difference between being born so and being made so. For

the first is indeed born from the person referred to; but the second is made so by him, whether as respects his creation or by the teaching of his doctrine. For when any person has been taught from the mouth of another, he is termed the son of him who instructs him, and the latter [is called] his father. According to nature, then—that is, according to creation, so to speak—we are all sons of God, because we have all been created by God. But with respect to obedience and doctrine we are not all sons of God: those only are so who believe in Him and do His will. And those who do not believe, and do not obey His will, are sons and angels of the devil, because they do the works of the devil. And that such is the case He has declared in Isaiah: "I have begotten and brought up children, but they have rebelled against Me" [Isa 1:2]. And again, where He says that these children are aliens: "Strange children have lied unto Me" [Ps 18:45]. According to nature, then, they are [His] children, because they have been so created; but with regard to their works, they are not His children.

For as, among men, those sons who disobey their fathers, being disinherited, are still their sons in the course of nature, but by law are disinherited, for they do not become the heirs of their natural parents; so in the same way is it with God—those who do not obey Him being disinherited by Him, have ceased to be His sons. Wherefore they cannot receive His inheritance. . . . But when they should be converted and come to repentance, and cease from evil, they should have power to become the sons of God, and to receive the inheritance of immortality which is given by Him. For this reason, therefore, He has termed those "angels of the devil," and "children of the wicked one," who give heed to the devil and do his works. But these are, at the same time, all created by the one and the same God. When, however, they believe and are subject to God, and go on and keep His doctrine, they are the sons of God; but when they have apostasized, and fallen into transgression, they are ascribed to their chief, the devil—to him who first became the cause of apostasy to himself, and afterwards to others. (4.41.2-3)

Other facets of the kinship metaphor appear elsewhere in *Against Heresies*. The conviction that the Old Testament patriarchs are the Christians' spiritual ancestors was an important one to Irenaeus, since he sought, against Marcion and others, to preserve Old Testament narratives as inspired texts for the Christian community. Abraham, in particular, is mentioned at various points in the work (3.10.2; 4.7.1-2; 4.21.1; 5.32.2). Irenaeus elaborates in the Fourth Book of his treatise:

Vain, too, is Marcion and his followers when they exclude Abraham from the inheritance, to whom the Spirit through many men, and now by Paul, bears witness, that "he believed God, and it was imputed unto him for righteousness." And the Lord, in the first place, indeed, by raising up children to him from the stones, and making his seed as the stars of heaven, saying, "They shall come from the east and from the west, from the north and from the south, and shall recline with Abraham, and Isaac, and Jacob in the kingdom of heaven;" and then again by saying to the Jews, "When ye shall see Abraham, and Isaac, and Jacob, and all the prophets in the kingdom of heaven, but you yourselves cast out." This, then is a clear point, that those who disallow his salvation, and from the idea of another God beside Him who made the promise to Abraham, are outside the kingdom of God, and are disinherited from incorruption, setting at naught and blaspheming God, who introduces, through Jesus Christ, Abraham to the kingdom of heaven, and his seed, that is, the Church, upon which also is conferred the adoption and the inheritance promised to Abraham. (4.8.1)

Abraham is later used, along with Jesus' earliest disciples, as an illustration of yet another PKG value: loyalty to the family of God over loyalty to one's family of origin:

Righteously, therefore, having left his earthly kindred, [Abraham] followed the Word of God, walking as a pilgrim with the Word, that he might [afterwards] have his abode with the Word. Righteously also the apostles, being of the race of Abraham, left the ship of their father, and followed the Word. (4.5.3)

The loyalty issue comes to the fore again in Book Five, in which Irenaeus quotes Matthew 10:25: "He came to divide a man against his father, and the daughter against the mother, and the daughter-in-law against the mother-in-law" (5.27.1).

As the above survey indicates, most of Irenaeus's kinship terminology appears in an ideological framework. Irenaeus seeks to identify the Christians as the true children of God versus the false claims of his gnostic opponents. The day-to-day behavior of the children of God in local Christian communities is not a central concern to Irenaeus in *Against Heresies*. Perhaps the social ramifications of Irenaeus's theology of the church as family find implicit expression in text-segments reflecting the loyalty *topos*. Even here, however, the reader encounters no specific examples of Christians in the Gallic communities who have opted for loyalty to their church family and who have suffered the consequences of such convictions. Given this author's subject, we might expect an absence of information concerning social practices in his circle of influence. Yet one passage, in particular, at least alludes to a connection between ideology and social practices in the Gallic communities. I will conclude my examination of *Against Heresies* with a look at this important text-segment.

In Book Two of his treatise, Irenaeus compares the miracles and exorcisms performed by Simon and Carpocrates with those performed by Christians with whom he is acquainted. Initially, Irenaeus chooses a rather predictable avenue of argument to discredit his opponents: he claims his opponents are deceivers who work no miracles at all. Perhaps they perform some genuine exorcisms, but they can chase away only those demons "sent into others by themselves" (2.31.2).

Irenaeus then subtly moves his argument to another level. The Christian miracles, unlike the alleged wonders worked by their opponents, are "done in the brotherhood on account of some necessity" (2.31.2). They cure those who "are distressed," who are suffering some "bodily infirmity." This the heretics fail to accomplish.

Finally, our author contrasts his opponents' "magical illusions," "impiously wrought in the sight of men," with the "sympathy," "compassion," and "aid and encouragement of mankind" characteristic of the church. He concludes that such benefits "are not only displayed without fee or reward, but we ourselves lay out for the benefit of others our own means; and inasmuch as those who are cured (by miraculous healing) very frequently do not possess the things that they require, they receive them from us" (2.31.3). The presence of the sibling term "brotherhood," in conjunction with the information Irenaeus provides about the sharing of material resources, suggests a kinship background for the above text-segment.[62] Moreover, the contrast our author draws between the behavior of the Christian "brotherhood" and the practices of the heretical wonder workers is central to Irenaeus's argument, for it is precisely in this contrast that "these men [Simon and Carpocrates] are . . . undoubtedly proved to be utter aliens from the divine nature, the beneficence of God, and all spiritual excellence" (2.31.3). This suggests that the family metaphor, with which Irenaeus is preoccupied at the ideological level throughout his treatise, found practical expression among the Christians with whom this author associated. Eusebius's account of the persecution in 177 C.E. confirms this observation.

Eusebius narrates the course of events in Gaul by quoting a letter sent from the survivors of the persecution to Christians in Asia and Phrygia. A kinship connection is established at the outset: "The servants sojourning in Vienne and Lyons in Gaul to the brethren in Asia and Phrygia, who have the same faith and hope of redemption as you. Peace, grace, and glory from God the Father and Jesus Christ our Lord" (*Hist. Eccl.* 5.1.3). The similarity of the above greeting with the opening words of several New Testament epistles (see Rom 1:7; 1 Cor 1:3; Col 1:1-2) might suggest wholesale adoption of earlier language on the part of the letter's authors, which would in turn serve to attenuate the symbolic force of the kinship terms in the passage and reduce the rhetorical effect of the metaphor to mere formal imitation. That this is not the case can be demonstrated by the repeated recurrence of family language in the ensuing portions of the letter that Eusebius quotes. The Christians in Lyons and Vienne are referred to as "brethren" in several text-segments (*Hist. Eccl.* 5.1.9-10; 5.1.33; 5.2.3-8; 5.3.4). The martyr Blandina is twice called "sister" (5.1.41, 54). The shedding of "tears" among the "brethren" at one point in the narrative suggests a tangible experience of the emotive power of the PKG sibling bond among the Christians at Lyons (5.2.3). The metaphor of God as father appears on at least five occasions in the letter (5.1.3, 23, 34, 36; 5.2.6).

Elsewhere, the narrative draws upon the idea that conversion to the Jesus move-ment can be understood as childbirth into the family of God. The authors of the epistle describe the activities of ten persons who renounced their Christian faith in the face of persecution. The ten are identified as "those born out of due time" (5.1.11). They appear in the letter again when the reader is informed that "those who had denied," inspired by the example of the faithful, again confessed Christ. The result was that "there was great joy to the Virgin Mother who had miscarried with them as though dead, and was receiving them back alive. For through them [that is, the faithful] the majority of those who had denied were again brought to birth and again conceived and quickened again." (5.1.45-46).

The restoration to the church family of those who had denied faith in Christ left only two classes of persons in the Gallic cities: faithful Christians and pagans. The narrative draws on the kinship metaphor to describe the latter as follows: "Those indeed remained without who had never had any vestige of faith, nor perception of the bridal garment, nor idea of the fear of God, but even through their behavior blasphemed the Way—they are the sons of perdition—but all the rest were added to the church" (5.1.48). A final reference to the restoration of those who denied Christ emphasizes the sibling-like attitude of the more steadfast believers toward their weaker brethren. Note the extensive use of family language in the excerpt:

> For their [the faithful martyrs'] greatest contest, through the genuineness of their love, was this, that the beast [the Devil] should be choked into throwing up alive those whom he had at first thought to have swallowed down [that is, those who denied and later confessed Christ]. For they did not boast over the fallen, but from their own abundance supplied with a mother's love those that needed, and shedding many tears for them to the Father, they prayed for life, and he gave it to them, and they divided it among their neighbors, and then departed to God, having in all things carried off the victory. . . . For their mother they left behind no sorrow, and for the brethren no strife and war, but glory, peace, concord, and love. (5.2.6-8)

Eusebius at this point interrupts his citation of the letter to insert his own com-mentary: "Let this profitable extract suffice concerning the love of those blessed ones for their brethren who had fallen" (5.2.8.).

Most informative is a portion of the letter that narrates the intervention of one Christian on behalf of others who had been arrested. During the legal pro-ceedings, a certain Vettius Epagathus spoke up, intending to offer a defense of his fellow Christians. He is described as "one of the brethren, filled with love towards God and towards his neighbor" (5.1.9). After extolling the excellence of Vettius Epagathus's character, the narrative proceeds as follows:

His character forbade him to endure the unreasonable judgement given against us, and, overcome with indignation, he asked to be heard in defence of the brethren to the effect that there was nothing atheistic or impious among us. He was howled down by those around the judgement-seat, for he was a man of position, and the governor would not tolerate the just requests which he had put forward but merely asked if he were a Christian himself. He then confessed in clear tones and was himself taken into the ranks of the martyrs. He was called the 'Comforter of Christians,' but had the Comforter in himself, the spirit of Zacharias which he had shown by the fulness of his love when he chose to lay down even his own life for the defence of the brethren, for he was and is a true disciple of Christ, and he follows the Lamb wheresoever he goes. (5.1.9-10)

The narrative implies that Vettius Epagathus was himself in no danger until he took the initiative to intervene "in defence of the brethren." Aiding a family member in danger, even at the risk of one's own life, was, of course, a standard expression of solidarity among the patrilineal kinship groups of Mediterranean antiquity. Vettius Epagathus's actions cost him his life, and it is clear that those who crafted the letter understood his sacrifice as an example of family solidarity. The letter contains other evidence suggesting that the PKG metaphor found practical application among Gallic Christians. Local authorities took precautions to guarantee that the surviving Christians could not provide the bodies of the martyrs with proper burial. The result was that "great grief obtained" among the Christians (5.1.61). The reader will recall that burial of one's relatives was a central component of PKG family solidarity.

The evidence from second-century Gaul, then, supports the contention that expatriate Asian and Phrygian Christians understood their communities in terms of the family model. The PKG metaphor fills the pages of both the works of Irenaeus and the letter penned by the survivors of the Gallic pogrom. It is reasonable, moreover, to conclude from the evidence that the metaphor found practical expression in the interpersonal behavior of members of Christian communities in Lyons and Vienne. Such activities are alluded to by Irenaeus and confirmed by the narrative of Eusebius.

CONCLUSION

In each of the works examined in this chapter, the family model takes pride of place among the symbolic and linguistic resources that the writer draws upon to formulate his conception of Christian community. During the second century, Mediterranean kinship values continued to represent the ideal for day-to-day relationships among surrogate siblings in the communities of faith. Many of the now-familiar aspects of the PKG metaphor consistently found their way into the texts; the most important are the image of the fatherhood of God, sibling terminology, preoccupation with inheritance and ancestry, and exclusive family loyalty. There can be little question that Clement of Rome, Ignatius, Justin Martyr, Clement of Alexandria, and Irenaeus, along with the authors of the letter to Asia from Gaul, were indeed "persuaded," as one perceptive outsider has observed, that Christians were "all brothers of one another" (Lucian, *Peregr.* 13).

As I have demonstrated, however, the kinship metaphor received somewhat different treatment at the hands of the writers surveyed in the present chapter from that of earlier authors. Increasing emphasis upon hierarchy and office in second-century congregations inevitably resulted in various modifications of the concept of the local church as a family. This is particularly apparent among writers who continue to address the needs of individual Christian communities. In the letter of Clement of Rome, for example, the juxtaposition of kinship terminology with traditional homonoia reasoning generates a certain disharmony in the argument, which at times undermines the rhetorical effectiveness of Clement's family language.

Ecclesiastical institutionalization affected Ignatius of Antioch differently. In his letters, the reader encounters for the first time a single figure—the bishop—described in father language and identified as the sole leader of a local Christian community. As the reader will recall, Paul of Tarsus had placed himself in a paternal role and had taken a correspondingly authoritative stance vis-à-vis his readers in 1 Corinthians 4:14-21 (chapter 4). No evidence exists, however, to suggest that this role was replicated by local leaders in Paul's churches. Ignatius's use of the kinship model to legitimate ministerial authority at the local level therefore presents a distinct innovation in the employment of the metaphor in the history of the Jesus movement.

The desire to enter into dialogue with pagan elites constitutes another factor that changed the manner in which second-century authors used the family metaphor. The image of God as father, for example, takes on universal connotations in the writings of the apologist Justin Martyr. With Justin, not only Christians but all human beings are understood to be offspring of God the father. Justin also expands the semantic field of sibling language when he refers to the Roman senators he addresses as "our brethren" (2 *Apol.* 1). In both instances, the innovation is accounted for by Justin's adoption of Hellenistic philosophical ideas in an attempt to create a dialogue with an educated pagan audience. Irenaeus, on his part, is not unaware of the conceptual dissonance that results from affirming the universal fatherhood of God, while at the same time retaining the idea that, in some special sense, God is the father only of the Christians. In an extended discussion, Irenaeus explains the difference between the two ideas—and preserves both—in terms of the doctrines of creation and redemption, respectively (*Adv. Haer.* 4.41.2-3).

For both Justin and Irenaeus, then, the universal fatherhood of God is an important aspect of the kinship metaphor. This was not the case among the first-century authors who preceded them. Finally, it is reasonable to assume that the desire to appeal to educated, high-status readers also accounts for certain innovations in Clement of Alexandria's use of the family model, specifically, his assignment of Jesus to the role of the household *paidagogus* and his appropriation of maternal language to refer to God and to the church.

Nevertheless, much remains the same, particularly regarding interpersonal relationships. Clement of Rome, Ignatius, Justin Martyr, Clement of Alexandria, and Irenaeus all attest to a relational solidarity in their local communities, which finds its primary explanation and legitimation in the family model. The sharing of material resources and a concern for exclusive loyalty to the family of God are but two of the PKG values that surface on numerous occasions in the works which I have examined. My survey of second-century Christian literature has clearly confirmed Lucian of Samosata's contentions (a) that his Christian contemporaries were persuaded that they were "all brothers of one another" and (b) that this conviction found practical expression in day-to-day community life (*Peregr.* 13).

Moreover, the evidence rests upon a broad geographical base. Whether an individual such as Lucian found himself in second-century Italy (see the evidence from Clement of Rome), Palestine (Lucian), Syria (Ignatius), Gaul (Irenaeus), Asia (Ignatius), or Alexandria (Clement), the Christians he encountered in these regions would have understood their communities to be surrogate patrilineal kinship groups, and they likely would have behaved accordingly. For the Jesus movement during the second century, the church remained a family.

6

North African Christianity

My survey concludes with an examination of the North African conception of Christian community as reflected in the writings of Tertullian and Cyprian of Carthage. I will also examine an African Christian document of a rather different literary genre, the *Passion of Perpetua.*

African Christians march onto the scene of history as a church of martyrs. The first Christian document from North Africa, the *Acts of the Scillitan Martyrs* (180 c.e.), reveals a Christian community highly polarized against Roman religion and mores.[1] The work foreshadows the radical rejection of secular values, both religious and intellectual, that would characterize Christianity in Carthage throughout its history. A corresponding preoccupation with discipline and the purity of the church in Carthage resulted in various conflicts with the Roman See, disputes that lasted for more than a century.

The Jesus movement spread quickly in North Africa. In the *Passion of Perpetua* (203 c.e.) and in the works of Tertullian, the reader encounters a widespread and well-organized North African church. A half-century later, when he became Bishop of Carthage, Cyprian (circa 250 c.e.) had authority over more than one hundred bishops.[2] The social composition of this well-established African church remains "obscure," although there is some evidence that the expansion of Christianity in Carthage had extended into the upper classes of society.[3]

Nevertheless, even though the precise social location of individual Christians along the continuum of the status hierarchy of North African society is less than clear, the social model according to which these Christians understood their communities to function is patently evident in the writings to be examined below. The surviving literary output of the third-century Carthaginian church contains ample data to support my contention that Christians in third-century North Africa continued to view themselves as members of a surrogate patrilineal kinship group. The *Passion of Perpetua*, extolled as "the archetype of all later Acts of the Christian martyrs," constitutes a fitting point of departure for my survey of the North African conception of the church as a family.[4]

PASSION OF PERPETUA

In 202 C.E., the Roman emperor Septimius Severus forbade conversion to Christianity. A result was that a socially prominent North African woman named Perpetua,[5] twenty-two years of age, and several other catechumens suffered imprisonment and were later condemned to execution in the arena at Carthage, as a part of a celebration of the birthday of Geta Caesar, the younger son of Septimius Severus.[6] The *Passion* purports to be a contemporary account, perhaps edited by Tertullian, which chronicles Perpetua's martyrdom and also relays various visions of Perpetua and of a priest identified as Saturus. Perpetua's prison diary, which constitutes the centerpiece of the work, has been aptly described as "one of the most intimate of all early Christian texts."[7]

Although the kinship metaphor surfaces in various portions of the broader narrative, the diary in particular attests to the conflict of loyalties that inevitably arose for Christians whose family relations remained pagan. Indeed, the family tensions surrounding Perpetua's commitment to the Christian faith infuse the narrative with much of its dramatic power. The *Passion of Perpetua* demonstrates that the Christians at Carthage viewed themselves as a surrogate kinship group, and Perpetua's first-person account graphically illustrates the price paid by one young woman who opted for loyalty to her family of faith over loyalty to her family of origin.[8]

The first two sections of the *Passion* introduce the work and are framed in the third person. The reader encounters the kinship motif at the outset, as the unidentified narrator addresses his audience as "my brethren and little children" (1.6). He then proceeds to introduce Perpetua by detailing her family relations. At the time of the heroine's imprisonment, her mother and father were still alive, and "one of her two brothers was a catechumen like herself" (2.2). The other brother, we may assume, was not a Christian. The potential for a divided family is thus introduced early in the work. It will be developed as a central theme as the story unfolds. The narrator concludes his opening remarks with the rather foreboding observation that Perpetua also "had an infant son at her breast" (2.2).

The perspective then switches to the first person, as Perpetua offers an account of the events leading up to her martyrdom. The theme of family loyalty, alluded to in the previous lines, immediately captures the reader's attention: "While we were still under house arrest [she said] my father out of love for me was trying to persuade me and shake my resolution" (3.1). Perpetua proceeds to tell how she refused to be called "anything other than what I am, a Christian." The comments that follow reflect the increasing estrangement that resulted between pagan father and Christian daughter, as Perpetua continued to stand her ground:

> At this my father was so angered by the word "Christian" that he moved towards me as though he would pluck my eyes out. But he left it at that and departed, vanquished along with his diabolical arguments. For a few days afterward I gave thanks to the Lord that I was separated from my father, and I was comforted by his absence. (3.3)

The sense of comfort and gratitude that Perpetua derives from the absence of her father during the most serious crisis of her life is highly anomalous in view of PKG relational values. The ancient Mediterranean reader, expecting reciprocal expressions of kinship support and solidarity in the face of a threat to the physical well-being of a family member, instead encounters a divided kin group.

Several days later, Perpetua is scheduled for a hearing, and her father again attempts to persuade her to deny her Christian faith. Initially, he addresses Perpetua as "Daughter," pleading with her as follows:

> Have pity on my grey head—have pity on me your father, if I deserve to be called your father, if I have favoured you above all your brothers, if I have raised you to reach this prime of your life. Do not abandon me to be the reproach of men. Think of your brothers, think of your mother and your aunt, think of your child, who will not be able to live once you are gone. Give up your pride! You will destroy all of us! None of us will ever be able to speak freely again if anything happens to you. (5.2-4)

Perpetua remains unmoved, however, and claims that soon "he no longer addressed me as his daughter but as a woman" (5.5). In a final, desperate attempt to dissuade his daughter, Perpetua's father appears on the scene with her child in his arms and boldly interrupts the procurator Hilarianus's interrogation: "Have pity on your father's grey head; have pity on your infant son. Offer the sacrifice for the welfare of the emperors" (6.3). For his trouble, the procurator orders Perpetua's father to be "thrown to the ground and beaten with a rod" (6.5).[9] Perpetua persists in her confession and is condemned, along with the rest of the prisoners, to the beasts.

The rift between daughter and father widens in the ensuing narrative. At one point during her imprisonment, Perpetua had received permission to have her nursing baby with her (3.9). This arrangement apparently continued for some time, for as she describes the fateful day of her sentencing Perpetua observes, "My baby had got used to being nursed at the breast and to staying with me in prison" (6.7). Her father's public humiliation before the governor, however, effected a change. As had been her practice, Perpetua again sent the deacon Pomponius to her father to bring back the baby. This time, however, "Father refused to hand him over" (6.7).

Some days shortly thereafter, as "the day of the contest was approaching," Perpetua's father visits his daughter for the last time. The scene is a tragic one: "My father came to see me overwhelmed with sorrow. He started tearing the hairs from his beard and threw them on the ground and began to curse his old age and to say such words as would move all creation. I felt sorry for his unhappy old age" (9.2-3). The sorrow that Perpetua feels for her father is, however, insufficient to persuade her to abandon her confession.

In her persistent refusal to give in to the wishes of her father, Perpetua dares to "reject all the traditional pieties and loyalties in which she had been brought up."[10] The primary focus of traditional piety and loyalty in Mediterranean society is, of course, one's patrilineal kinship group. In rejecting her father's pleas and his authority, Perpetua radically disassociates herself from the most pivotal values of the world in which she lives. The young woman's natural father now disappears entirely from the narrative. There is no reference to him in the visions Perpetua experiences, nor does his character reappear in the climactic scene of his daughter's martyrdom near the end of the work. Indeed, during the final occasion on which Perpetua is visited by her family, her brothers are present but her father is noticeably absent (16.4). Perpetua is not fatherless, however, for her "trainer"—who clearly symbolizes God in Perpetua's final vision of her victorious contest with the devil—says to her, "Peace be with you, my daughter!" (10.13).

Metaphorical family language and behavioral reflections of kinship solidarity surface elsewhere in the *Passion of Perpetua*. Sibling terms appear in various contexts. Saturus, for example, claims that during his vision of paradise, he and Perpetua "began to recognize many of our brethren" (13.8). One of Perpetua's visions portrays her drawing upon her unique spiritual resources as a confessor to pray her deceased brother out of hell and into heaven. Reflecting back on his death at age seven after a battle with cancer, Perpetua refers to Dinocrates as "my brother according to the flesh" (7.5). The implication, of course, is that Perpetua has an additional family consisting of siblings according to the Spirit.

The father metaphor also finds expression in the *Passion*. Perpetua's first vision finds her at battle with "a dragon of enormous size." Upon her victory, she enters a large garden and encounters "a grey-haired man" in "shepherd's garb" who welcomes her to paradise with the words, "I am glad you have come, my child" (4). The idea that God is the father of his children in the faith is thereby reflected in the imagery of the vision. The work closes with another, final reference to "God the Father" (21.11).

In addition to the conflict of family loyalties which Perpetua faced, the *Passion* contains other evidence that PKG family values found practical expression among the circle of Christians who associated with the confessors. At one point in the account, Perpetua's personal slave and fellow confessor gives birth to a daughter in prison. Since Perpetua is identified as "a newly married woman" (2.1), it is reasonable to assume that she acquired her slave, Felicitas, before marriage. Upon the death of Perpetua and Felicitas, the slave's infant daughter would have been the legal property of Perpetua's father. It is singularly striking, then, to discover that "one of the sisters (that is, a Christian) brought [Felicitas's newborn child] up as her own daughter" (15.7).

I observed earlier that persons typically cared for imprisoned family members in ancient Mediterranean society. In Perpetua's case, both her natural family and her Christian siblings share concern for her comfort in prison. The reader encounters this situation on several occasions. At one point in the narrative, two deacons, Tertius and Pomponius, bribe the prison guards so that, as Perpetua gratefully observes, she and the other confessors could "go to a better part of the prison to refresh ourselves for a few hours" (3.7). In the near context, Perpetua is visited by her brother and mother. Later in the narrative, the officer in charge "allowed her brother and other persons to visit, so that the prisoners could dine in their company" (16.4). Elsewhere in the text, it is noted that the confessors are allowed many visitors who gave and received much comfort (9.1).

In each of these passages, it is fair to assume that the visitors, representing Perpetua's natural and surrogate families, provided for the material needs of the confessors, in accordance with ancient Mediterranean kinship norms. Indeed, Tertullian, a contemporary of the confessors, confirms this assumption in his introduction to a treatise that he directed to Christians about to become martyrs. Note the presence of both sibling terminology and PKG behavioral solidarity in the following excerpt: "Blessed martyrs elect, along with the nourishment for the body which our Lady Mother the Church from her breast, as well as individual brethren from their private resources, furnish you in prison, accept also from me some offering that will contribute to the sustenance of the spirit" (*Ad Mart.* 1.1). The metaphor of the church as a family thus found both conceptual and practical expression among the Christians who wrote and lived through the events chronicled by the *Passion of Perpetua*.

TERTULLIAN

Tertullian (circa 160–225 C.E.) gave reasoned and passionate expression to the uncompromising nature of the Christian movement in North Africa. Although much of Tertullian's work has survived, the thirty-eight extant treatises reveal little about his life.[11] Evident throughout his writings, however, are his erudition and his strongly polemical stance in the face of pagan thought and culture.[12] Tertullian's involvement with the Montanist movement in Carthage, post–207 C.E., only intensified an already highly disciplined approach to Christian morality. Increasingly, his writings began to take issue not only with paganism but also with the behavior of non-Montanist Carthaginian Christians whom he perceived to be compromising with the pagan world.[13]

Tertullian's works contain much kinship terminology. Various passages from his writings demonstrate that the North African Christians with whom he was familiar exercised PKG values in their relationships with one another. Tertullian shares with his fellow Carthaginian Christians the idea that the church is "our own household" (*Apol.* 7.3).[14]

The reader encounters sibling terms throughout Tertullian's various treatises (*De Spec.* 3.1; *De Virg. Vel.* 1.1.1; 2.1.1; 2.4.1; 2.5.5; 2.9.4; 2.13.5; *De Orat.* 18.1-2; 26.1-2; *De Test. Anim.* 1.1). It is important to recognize that Tertullian includes among his surrogate siblings those who view certain aspects of the Christian faith differently than he does: "There are some brethren, who being either too naive or overparticular in their faith, demand a testimony from holy Scripture, when faced with giving up spectacles" (*De Spec.* 3.1). Tertullian's generosity in this regard extends even into his Montanist period. Tertullian opens his discussion concerning the proper response to persecution with a sibling term of address, thereby extending his conception of the Christian family to include those catholic Christians who did not share his increasingly Montanist convictions. From Tertullian's perspective, such an individual remains a "brother," even though he is "guilty in not accepting the Paraclete, the guide to all truth" (*De Fuga* 1.1). His extension of brother terminology to his non-Montanist readers suggests that the theological dissension between Montanist and catholic Christians had not yet resulted in wholesale social alienation between the two camps during Tertullian's time.[15]

Father imagery also surfaces on numerous occasions in Tertullian's writings, and Tertullian reserves this paternal imagery for God alone. God is referred to as the father of Jesus (*De Fuga* 2.5; 8.1; 13.1). He is more commonly the father of the Carthaginian Christians (*De Orat.* 11.2; *De Pat.* 2.3; *De Cor.* 14.4; *Apol.* 35.9). Tertullian's exposition of the Lord's Prayer provides him with an opportunity to elaborate upon the father concept:

> Our Lord very frequently spoke to us of God as a Father; in fact, He even taught us to call none on earth "father," but only the one we have in heaven. Therefore, when we pray like this we are observing this precept, too. Happy are they who know the Father! This is the reproach made against Israel, when the Spirit calls heaven and earth to witness saying, "I have begotten sons and they have not known me." Moreover, when we say "Father," we also add a title to God's name. This form of address is one of filial love and at the same time one of power. (*De Orat.* 2.2-4)

Tertullian then proceeds to draw from the appellation of God as father further kinship implications:

> In the Father, the Son is also addressed. For Christ said, "I and the Father are one." Nor is Mother Church passed over without mention, for in the Son and the Father the Mother is recognized, since upon her the terms "Father" and "Son" depend for their meaning. With this one form then, or word, we honor God with His own, we heed His precept, and we reproach those who are unmindful of the Father. (*De Orat.* 2.5-7)

The metaphor "Mother Church" appears sparingly in Tertullian's works. I will examine the image in my discussion of Cyprian of Carthage, later in this chapter, since Cyprian utilizes the idea of the church as a mother of the Christians quite often. More pertinent to my present argument is Tertullian's strong emphasis on the father metaphor, reflected in each of the passages cited above.

Among the character qualities exhibited by God in his paternal role is that of patience with outsiders who reject him and persecute his children: "He endures ungrateful peoples who worship the trifles fashioned by their skill and the works of their hands, who persecute His name and His children, and who, in their lewdness, their greed, their godlessness and depravity, grow worse from day to day" (*De Pat.* 2.3). Tertullian devotes to the virtue of patience the treatise from which the above excerpt is taken. The passage cited portrays God as a father whose behavior is to be emulated by his children. The patience that God extends to those who mistreat him is to be replicated in the behavior of Tertullian's readers, as they interact with one another and with their pagan neighbors. Father imitation is, as I have noted, a familiar theme in Mediterranean family systems.

It is already clear, then, that for Tertullian, the idea that the church is a family involves more than symbols and terminology. Tertullian is adamant in his contention that the family model must find practical expression in the life of the community. The tangible realization of kinship values manifests itself in three ways. First, Tertullian expects his readers to exercise a loyalty toward their church family that takes priority over every other bond of society. Secondly, he uses the sibling idea as a rhetorical device to challenge his readers to live with their fellow Christians in peace and harmony. Finally, Tertullian's writings show us that the PKG value of generalized reciprocity operated among the Carthaginian Christians, as the church distributed material resources to imprisoned confessors and to the weak and the poor in their local community.

Tertullian on Family Loyalty

Several passages in Tertullian's writings suggest that the Christian demand for total allegiance to the family of faith engendered a significant degree of disharmony in certain Roman families in North Africa. Tertullian's treatise on the appropriateness of wearing the soldier's crown provides a helpful point of entry for my examination of family loyalty. In the text-segment to follow, Tertullian reveals his convictions about the proper loyalties to be accorded by the Christian to the state, to family, and to God, respectively. The family idea appears near the end of the citation. The passage begins with Tertullian expanding his consideration of military attire into a broader discussion of the validity of military service itself for a Christian:

> Now, to come to the very heart of this question about a soldier's crown, should we not really first examine the right of a Christian to be in the military service at all? In other words, why discuss the merely accidental detail when the foundation on which it rests is deserving of censure? Are we to believe it lawful to take an oath of allegiance to a mere human being over and above the oath of fidelity to God? Can we obey another master, having chosen Christ? Can we forsake father, mother and all our relatives? By divine law we must honor them and our love for them is second only to that which we have toward God. The Gospel also bids us honor our parents, placing none but Christ Himself above them. (*De Cor.* 11.1)

Tertullian's main point, of course, is that allegiance to the military is incompatible with a Christian's "oath of fidelity to God." Moreover, the main thrust of the passage is family-friendly, since Tertullian sets family loyalty, which he values, in opposition to the military oath, which he disallows. He expects a negative reply to his rhetorical query, "Can we forsake father, mother and all our relatives?" Honoring one's blood relatives constitutes, for Tertullian, a practical expression of a believer's fidelity toward God.[16]

Nevertheless, as the passage intimates, the Christian's allegiance to God must take precedence not only over the state but also over his blood family. For Christians in Carthage, there were times when commitment to God and loyalty to family were mutually incompatible. Tertullian subtly anticipates such conflicts when he concludes his comments in the above excerpt with the observation that love for family "is second only to that which we have toward God" (11.1). Conversion to Christianity in Carthage often put a person at odds with her own family members, and the resulting discord sometimes necessitated a painful choice of loyalties.

Tertullian lived in a world in which such choices were made on a regular basis. Although he asserts that "the Gospel . . . bids us to honor our parents," he is quick to add that it nevertheless places "Christ Himself above them" (11.1). This latter conviction, which situates loyalty to God above allegiance to one's blood kin group in the Christian's hierarchy of relational priorities, is only briefly referenced in the above quotation. It surfaces elsewhere in Tertullian's writings as a central theme of the Carthaginian Christian conception of the church as a surrogate family.

The incompatibility of blood-family loyalty with allegiance to the Jesus movement, central to the *Passion of Perpetua*, is a recurrent theme in Tertullian's works. Moreover, his works give the sense that Tertullian is even more adamant about the priority of loyalty to God than is the author of the *Passion*. The *Passion* does not present Perpetua's relations with her family of origin in a wholly negative light. In his attempts to dissuade Perpetua from her Christian confession, Perpetua's father, of course, occupies the role of an antagonist in the narrative. Perpetua's relationship with her family of origin, however, receives positive treatment, as well. As noted earlier, Perpetua receives aid in prison from her blood family, as well as from her fellow Christians. The point here is that the author of the *Passion* apparently failed to see anything incongruous about Perpetua's continuing contacts with members of both her natural and surrogate families.[17]

Tertullian's perspective is different. As will be shown below, he extols the church's practice of caring for the imprisoned confessors. He takes a less positive view, however, of the continued association of the martyrs with their families of origin. Tertullian concludes his discussion of the burdens and worldly attachments from which the confessors need to be released with the following observation: "Other attachments, equally burdensome to the spirit, may have accompanied you to the prison gate; so far your relatives, too, may have escorted you" (*Ad Mart.* 2.1).

For Tertullian, then, blood relatives are "burdensome" to the spirit of the confessors. Tertullian would certainly have congratulated Perpetua on her faithfulness to her confession in the face of her father's repeated pleas to the contrary. I suspect, however, that he also would have cautioned her against her continued association with other members of her natural family during their regular visits to her prison cell. Here we see Tertullian revealing his priorities in a way only hinted at in the excerpt from *On Military Service* cited earlier in this chapter. In the context of his comments about military service, Tertullian extolled the act of honoring one's blood family. Now we discover that family loyalty represents a value that is only provisionally consonant with commitment to Christ. When a confessor's relatives begin to exercise their potential ability to distract her confessor from her higher calling, blood family members become "burdensome to the spirit."

The strife that at times resulted from the partial conversion of a Roman household finds expression in another important text-segment. Apparently, certain Christians, slave and free, were forced to leave their pagan families. Tertullian marvels at the expulsion of these household members, persons who through conversion to Christianity experienced an improvement in moral character. He attributes such illogical behavior to a hatred toward Christians, an attitude that rendered the pagan household head incapable of appreciating the potential contributions of a newly converted family member:

> Some, even, at the expense of their own advantage [that is, the advantage of having a spouse or family member improve in character through conversion to Christianity], bargain with their hatred, satisfied to suffer a personal loss, provided that their home be freed from the object of their hatred. A wife who has become chaste is cast out by her husband now that he is relieved of his jealous suspicions of her. A son, now docile, is disowned by a father who was patient with him in the past. A servant, now trustworthy, is banished from the sight of a master who was formerly indulgent. (*Apol.* 3.4)

One wonders just how extensive such discord was between Christian and pagan family members in early third-century Carthage. Perhaps Tertullian is drawing upon the experiences of but a single family as his background for the above polemic. The correlation of this passage with the information provided by the *Passion of Perpetua*, however, suggests that the experience of divided loyalties was more typical than exceptional for Christian converts who belonged to pagan families. The uncompromising nature of the North African Jesus movement likely produced crises of family loyalty for the faithful on numerous occasions.

Harmony among Siblings

The responsibility of siblings to live with one another in harmony and accord is another practical theme that surfaces repeatedly in the writings of Tertullian. The topics of patience and prayer offer Tertullian two fitting thematic backgrounds against which to display his conception of Christian sibling solidarity. In the course of his treatment of both topics, he draws upon examples of sibling discord in Old Testament narratives to illustrate his argument and to encourage his Christian sisters and brothers in their relationships with one another.

During his discussion of the virtue of patience, Tertullian joins other early Christian writers who, as we have seen, cite the Cain-and-Abel narrative as the archetypal example of breakdown in sibling relations:

> Since [impatience] had plunged Adam and Eve into death, it taught their son also, to commit the first murder. Vain were it for me to ascribe this sin to impatience, had Cain, the first homicide and the first fratricide, accepted it with equanimity and without impatience when his offerings were refused by the Lord; if he had not been angry with his brother; if, in fine, he had killed no one. Therefore, since he could not commit murder unless he were angry, and could not be angry unless he were impatient, it proves that what he did in anger is to be referred to that which prompted the anger. (*De Pat.* 5.15-17)

The role of impatience in the Cain-and-Abel affair is not as obvious to the modern reader as it was to Tertullian. In fact, patience is an idea wholly absent from the Hebrew narrative (Gen 4:1-8), and Tertullian must extrapolate the patience idea from the theme of anger, which drives the Genesis account (see Gen 4:5: "Cain was very angry"). Tertullian's general point, unconvincing though his exegesis may be, remains pertinent, however, to the present discussion—he uses the Old Testament story to challenge his readers to exercise patience in their relationships with their brothers and sisters in the Carthaginian church. In doing so, Tertullian demonstrates that he intends the sibling metaphor to find tangible application in the daily lives of his audience.

The relationship between impatience and sibling discord surfaces again in another passage from the same treatise:

> What man, completely given over to impatience, will forgive his brother, I will not say seven times and seventy times seven times, but even once? . . . No one whose mind is violently disturbed against his brother will complete his offering at the altar unless first he has been reconciled to his brother through patience. (*De Pat.* 12.1, 3)

The second sentence in the above excerpt makes reference to a passage from the Gospel of Matthew in which the evangelist quotes Jesus as follows: "So when you are offering your gift at the altar, if you remember that your brother or sister has something against you, leave your gift there before the altar and go; first be reconciled to your brother or sister, and then come and offer your gift" (Matt 5:23-24). According to Matthew's Jesus, there is an intrinsic connection between

(a) acting toward one's surrogate siblings in a manner consonant with ancient Mediterranean family sensibilities and (b) one's relationship with God, the father of the community.

Tertullian elaborates upon this connection between relating to God the father and relating to one's surrogate siblings in the course of his exposition of the Lord's Prayer:

> The remembrance of these teachings paves the way for our prayers to reach heaven, and the first of these is not to approach the altar of God without settling any controversy or quarrel we may have contracted with our brethren. For how can one approach the peace of God without peace, or the forgiveness of sin, when he nurses a grudge? How will he please his Father if he be angry with his brother, when all anger had been forbidden us from the beginning? For, Joseph, sending his brothers home to bring their father, said: "Do not quarrel on the way!" He was in fact admonishing us—for elsewhere our manner of life is called our "way"—that on the way of prayer that has been set up we must not approach the Father if we are angry. Furthermore, our Lord, clearly enlarging upon the Law, adds anger with one's brother to the sin of murder. He does not permit even an evil word to be expressed; even if one must experience anger, it should not outlast the setting of the sun, as the Apostle reminds us. How foolhardy it is, moreover, either to pass a day without prayer, while you fail to give satisfaction to your brother, or to pray to no avail since your anger persists! (*De Orat.* 11.1-3)

This passage is an important one, since it demonstrates that the various images associated with the kinship model are not understood by Tertullian to function in isolation. Rather, they constitute a constellation of interrelated ideas. Here, as in the passage cited previously, the reader discovers that sibling and father relationships are inseparably connected with one another for a member of God's faith family: "How will he please his Father if he be angry with his brother?" (11.1).

Notice how Tertullian introduces the Old Testament Joseph narrative into his argument in order to illustrate this dynamic. As I observed in a previous chapter, Joseph's betrayal by his brothers and his gracious forgiveness of their treachery sharply reflect, respectively, the worst and best in PKG sibling interaction. For this reason, the story remained popular among both Judeans and Christians in antiquity. Tertullian, however, extends the application of the narrative through some rather creative exegesis: Joseph's admonition to his brothers not to "quarrel on the way" home to their father teaches that the Christian must not approach God the father if he is angry with his brother. He must not harbor bitterness toward a brother while he is "on the way" to meet his heavenly father in prayer. The unconvincing exegetical gymnastics to which Tertullian must resort in order to draw such a conclusion from the Genesis account only reinforce the point I am making in the present discussion, since Tertullian's application lies precisely in the inseparable connection between the Christian's relationship to God the father, on the one hand, and her relationship with her brothers and sisters in the faith, on the other.

Tertullian and Generalized Reciprocity

PKG sibling solidarity, as Tertullian expected it to function in the Christian community, includes more than simply the absence of discord. The positive expression of the family bond manifests itself in the now-familiar exercise of generalized reciprocity evidenced in the sharing of material goods among the Christians in North Africa. Tertullian claims that Christians are "bound together by such intimate ties," a claim vindicated by the repeated examples of the sharing of tangible resources found in Tertullian's writings (*Apol.* 37.3).

Persecution provided one opportunity for Carthaginian Christians to minister in a practical way to their siblings in the faith. Tertullian informs his readers that the needs of the imprisoned confessors were met both institutionally, by "Lady Mother the Church," and personally, by "individual brethren from their private resources" (*Ad Mart.* 1.1). The assertion is reiterated later in the same document:

> Let us compare the life in the world with that in prison to see if the spirit does not gain more in prison than the flesh loses there. In fact, owing to the solicitude of the Church and the charity of the brethren, the flesh does not miss there what it ought to have, while, in addition, the spirit obtains what is always beneficial to the faith. (2.6-7)

The reader will note that in each of the two excerpts just cited, the material help provided to the martyrs is understood to function in the context of the sibling bond that exists between the imprisoned confessors and their Christian "brethren" (1.1, 2.7). Indeed, it is Tertullian's conviction that persecution is good for the church, since it stirs the faithful to "mutual charity and love" (*De Fuga* 1.6).

There are limits, however, to the extent to which Christians should exert themselves on behalf of their imprisoned sisters and brothers in the faith. Apparently, some were securing release from prison for their fellow Christians by bribing the authorities. Tertullian offers his opinions on the practice in two passages found in a treatise in which he considers the proper response to persecution:

> Just as Christ laid down His life for us, so should we do the same for Him, and not only for Him, but for our brethren, for His sake. It is the teaching of St. John not that we should pay for our brethren, but that we should die for them. (*De Fuga* 12.7)

> It is better that sometimes you do not see the vast crowds of your brethren than that you submit to the payment of ransom. (14.1)

It is striking that Tertullian must place limits upon the material sacrifices that Christians are willing to make to reduce the suffering of their brothers and sisters in the family of God. Carthaginian Christians were apparently quite willing to live out the family metaphor in their relations with their suffering brethren. Moreover, generalized reciprocity is not extended only to imprisoned confessors. Elsewhere, Tertullian claims that "orphans . . . and the needy" also receive aid from the church (*Ad Scap.* 4).

For Tertullian of Carthage, the church is a family. PKG terminology occurs throughout his writings, and Tertullian expects his fellow North African Christians to behave in a manner consonant with Mediterranean family norms. The texts cited above would constitute ample evidence that Tertullian conceived of the Carthaginian church as a surrogate kinship group. I will conclude my analysis of Tertullian's use of the family metaphor, however, with yet another quotation from the *Apology*. The text-segment that follows constitutes one of the most thorough descriptions of the church as a family in all of early Christian literature. It serves as a fitting summary to my survey of Tertullian's writings. The passage begins with a description of the various kinds of practical care the Christians exercised toward those in need:

> Each man deposits a small amount on a certain day of the month or whenever he wishes, and only on condition that he is willing and able to do so. No one is forced; each makes his contribution voluntarily. These are, so to speak, the deposits of piety. The money therefrom is spent not for banquets or drinking parties or good-for-nothing eating houses, but for the support and burial of the poor, for children who are without their parents and means of subsistence, for aged men who are confined to the house; likewise, for shipwrecked sailors, and for any in the mines, on islands or in prisons. Provided only it be for the sake of fellowship with God, they become entitled to loving and protective care for their confession. The practice of such a special love brands us in the eyes of some. "See," they say, "how they love one another;" (for *they* hate one another), "and how ready they are to die for each other." (They themselves would be more ready to kill each other.) (*Apol.* 39.5-7)

Tertullian then confronts the reader with a polemical description of the specific social context in which such an exchange of material resources naturally functions. That context is, of course, the church family of surrogate brothers and sisters:

> Over the fact that we call ourselves brothers, they fall into a rage—for no other reason, I suppose, than because among them every term of kinship is only a hypocritical pretense of affection. But, we are your brothers, too, according to the law of nature, our common mother, although you are hardly men since you are evil brothers. But, with how much more right are they called brothers and considered such who have acknowledged one father, God, who have drunk one spirit of holiness, who in fear and wonder have come forth from one womb of their common ignorance to the one light

of truth! Perhaps this is why we are considered less legitimate brothers, because no tragic drama has our brotherhood as its theme, or because we are brothers who use the same family substance which, among you, as a rule, destroys brotherhood. So, we who are united in mind and soul have no hesitation about sharing what we have. Everything is in common among us—except our wives. (*Apol.* 39.8-11)

It would be easy to stumble over Tertullian's wholesale dismissal of the integrity of pagan family relations (39.8) and thereby fail to appreciate the valuable information about Christian social organization provided in the above text-segment. Gerhard Lohfink has rightly observed that Tertullian here presents the reader with "a magnificent theological justification for the Christian use of 'brother' as a form of address."[18] In addition, I would stress that Tertullian also provides a "magnificent" sociological explanation for the behavior outlined in the previous excerpt: the Carthaginian Christians "have no hesitation about sharing" what they possess because they conceive of themselves as a genuine Mediterranean family. As Tertullian proudly relates, "We call ourselves brothers" (39.8).

Cyprian

In the extensive writings of Cyprian of Carthage, the student possesses source material invaluable not only for inquiry into the nature of third-century Christianity but also for more general historical analysis of the period.[19] From Cyprian's writings—along with the *Acta Proconsularia*, Pontius's *Vita Cypriani*, and Jerome's *De Viris Illustribus*—one may deduce the following outline of the Carthaginian Christian leader's life.

Cyprian was a high-status, property-owning pagan rhetorician who converted to Christianity circa 246 c.e.[20] Just two years later, he was elected overseer of the Christian community in Carthage, in the face of significant clerical opposition.[21] During his episcopate, which ended with his martyrdom in Carthage in September 258 c.e., Cyprian wrestled with a variety of issues both practical and theological, which inevitably resulted from the persecutions instituted by Decius (249 c.e.) and, later, by Valerian (257 c.e.).

At the center of the controversies was the question of readmission to church life of those Christians who had apostasized in the face of persecution. Determining the corresponding status of clergy who had lapsed proved to be a particularly divisive task. Yet another point of contention related to the validity of baptism administered at the hands of those deemed heretic priests. Rome and Carthage at times adopted markedly different positions on each of these issues. Christians were polarized in each of the two great cities, as well.

As the preeminent leader of North African Christianity, Cyprian found himself at the forefront of every controversy. His response to the debates is graphically reflected both in his treatises and in the eighty-two extant letters. Cyprian's convictions concerning the relevant ideological issues will be touched upon in the course of the discussion to follow. My approach, however, will be primarily sociological in nature. For centuries, scholars have appreciated Cyprian's contribution to the theology of the church. For my purposes, it is more pertinent to recognize that the challenges facing Cyprian, as the pastor of a large urban church, were of an eminently practical nature. As a result, Cyprian addressed the most pressing issues affecting day-to-day relations among Christians in Carthage. As Graeme Clarke has recently observed about Cyprian's epistolary corpus:

> The letters ought to prevent us from forgetting that we are studying not a theologian but a pastoralist who had to deal, by force of circumstances, with theological problems embedded in the practical decisions of his administration. The poor and the suffering of Carthage—as with victims of the plague—and the financial back-up needed to support them and the clergy who were the ministers of his care are deep and real concerns of his.[22]

Clarke's commentary deals exclusively with the epistles, but his remarks could equally be applied to Cyprian's treatises. The happy result is that the historian of early Christianity possesses in Cyprian's writings a veritable gold mine of information from which to piece together a picture of social relations among mid-third-century Christians in North Africa.[23] Indeed, Cyprian's surviving works provide more evidence for the family model of church social organization than do the works of any other ancient Christian author.[24] In the discussion that follows, I will first examine a selection of Cyprian's eighty-two extant epistles and then augment my analysis with a number of excerpts from the rest of his writings.[25]

Cyprian's writings are so extensive—and they contain so much evidence for my thesis—that what follows must necessarily represent only a sample of the North African leader's thinking about Christian community. Along with such a profusion of source material comes the inevitable methodological temptation to cite only those excerpts from the corpus that best support my contention that the family model was central to Cyprian's thinking. Indeed, some selectivity is unavoidable due to space limitations.

In an effort to provide a fair reading of Cyprian's works, however, I will combine the selective approach with more thorough and exhaustive analysis as follows. I will initially examine in detail the first nine extant letters that Cyprian wrote during his tenure as overseer of the community at Carthage. The letters will be surveyed in order, and I will cite and comment upon all the information they provide about

Cyprian's model of the church as family. In this way, the reader will receive at the outset a fair picture of what is typical of Cyprian's perspective on community, as reflected in nine epistles chosen simply for their position at the beginning of the epistolary corpus. A more selective survey of the remaining letters and the treatises will then conclude my overview of the works of Cyprian of Carthage.

Examination of Specific Epistles

The traditional ordering of Cyprian's epistles fails to correspond to the letters' respective dates of composition. The task of arranging the letters into chronological sequence, based on the internal evidence that Cyprian incidentally provides, has occupied scholars for many generations. Now, as Clarke observes, the place of most of the letters can be confined within a reasonably narrow time frame.[26] I will follow Clarke in his chronological (and often, as a result, topical) ordering of the letters as I now begin my survey of Cyprian's conception of the Carthaginian church as a surrogate patrilineal kinship group.[27]

EPISTLES 1–4

Epistles 1–4, which Clarke groups together as nonpersecution epistles, provide a revealing introduction into Cyprian's idea of Christian community. The kinship theme finds its way into Cyprian's epistles at the beginning of the collection, when Cyprian addresses the leaders and members of the church in the town of Furnos as "my very dear brothers." He also refers to the subject of the letter as "our brother Geminius Victor" (1.1).[28] Cyprian will continue to use sibling language as his primary terms of opening address throughout the epistolary corpus (1.1.1; 2.1.1; 3.1.1; 4.1.1; 5.1.1; 6.1.1; and so forth). Cyprian also typically closes his letters with a "farewell" to his siblings in the faith (1.2.2; 3.3.4; 4.5.2; 5.2.1; 6.4; and so forth).[29]

The tangible expression among North African Christians of the PKG values typically associated with sibling solidarity greatly concerned Cyprian in his capacity as Carthage's bishop. Letter after letter attests to Cyprian's efforts to ensure that the material resources of the community are properly distributed to those in need.[30] Early in the corpus, the reader is impressed by the variety of circumstances that could render such assistance necessary.

In *Epistle* 2, mentioned briefly above, Cyprian addresses a colleague named Eucratius, who served as bishop in the town of Thena. Eucratius had apparently written to inquire about an ethical dilemma facing his local Christian community. A former actor in Eucratius's congregation had, in good Christian fashion, ceased to practice his profession after converting to Christianity. He continued to earn his living, however, by teaching others the art of acting. Eucratius had written to ask, in Cyprian's words, "whether such a man ought to remain in communion with us" (2.1.1).

Cyprian's response is unequivocal: "On this question, my personal view is that it is not in keeping with the reverence due to the majesty of God and with the observance of the gospel teachings for the honour and respect of the Church to be polluted by contamination at once so degraded and so scandalous" (2.1.2). The reader who is acquainted with the early-Christian attitude toward the Greco-Roman stage, in general, and the conservative nature of North African Christianity, in particular, finds nothing surprising in the above admonition. The church was universally hostile to the contemporary stage. Cyprian himself expounds upon the evils of theatrical vice elsewhere, in a more lengthy treatise (*Ad. Donat.* 8) (see also Novatian, *De Spec.*; Minucius Felix, *Oct.* 37.12; Tertullian, *De Spec.*).

Cyprian is not satisfied, however, simply to censure the unacceptable behavior of the former actor by reiterating typical Christian convictions relating to the theater. He apparently is aware of the hardship that will inevitably ensue if the individual in question responds to Cyprian's admonition to cease from teaching his craft. Cyprian therefore proceeds to offer the offender a way to leave his profession and still acquire the material resources necessary for daily living. As Cyprian's comments clearly demonstrate, complementing the North African church's hard-line position on morality and involvement with the pagan world was a genuine concern for those whose livelihood might be adversely affected by the community's demanding standards:

> If such an instructor pleads poverty and straitened circumstances, his needs can be alleviated along with those of others who are supported by the provisions of the Church—on condition, of course, that he can be satisfied with more frugal, and harmless, fare and does not consider that he ought to be bought off by means of a pension, so as to break away from his sins, for he is the one to benefit from such a break, not us. . . . Accordingly, you should do your utmost to call him away from this depraved and shameful profession to the way of innocence and to the hope of his true life; let him be satisfied with the nourishment provided by the Church, more sparing to be sure but salutary. (2.2.2-3)

Should the resources of the church at Thena, however, be overburdened by such an outlay, Cyprian offers yet another alternative: "But if your church is unable to meet the cost of maintaining those in need, he can transfer himself to us and receive here what is necessary for him in the way of food and clothing" (2.2.3). Not only does Cyprian deem it perfectly appropriate for the Thenan church to meet the material needs of the unnamed actor, but the sense of brotherhood extends beyond the boundaries of the local community (as Cyprian's identification of Eucratius as "my dearest brother" already implies), since the Carthaginian bishop is more than willing to take on the support of the individual in question should Eucratius's church lacks sufficient funds.[31]

The next passages in which Cyprian draws directly upon the kinship metaphor to address the practical problems of community life are found in *Epistle* 4. The letter outlines the proper disciplinary action to be taken in the case of dedicated virgins who occupy the same sleeping quarters as men in the church. The family model surfaces at the beginning of the letter, when Cyprian and his visiting episcopal colleagues in Carthage (whom Cyprian includes as his coauthors) address their fellow overseer, to whom they write, as "their brother Pomponius." Yet another vocative—"brother"—follows in the first sentence of the letter's introduction (4.1.1). Then, before tackling the issue at hand, Cyprian prefaces his advice with a two-part reminder of the responsibility incumbent upon church leaders to properly discipline their people. Notice the PKG terminology:

> We want you to know that we do not depart from the precepts handed down by the evangelists and the apostles which prescribe that we take counsel with courage and firmness for the well-being of our brothers and sisters. (4.1.2)

> And so, our dearest brother, our foremost endeavour, for leaders and for laity alike, must be, fearing God as we do, to adhere with utmost scrupulousness to these divine ordinances on discipline and not allow our brothers to go astray and live according to their personal caprice and whims. (4.2.1)

Elsewhere, the author again employs the sibling metaphor, challenging Pomponious as follows:

> Accordingly, our dearest brother, you must ensure that the unruly do not die or perish, by guiding the brethren, as best you can with saving advice and by taking counsel for the salvation of each individually. (4.5.1)

As is clear from these citations, the context of church discipline is the surrogate kinship group. The goal of church discipline is "the well-being of our brothers and sisters" (4.1.2). For North African church leaders, sibling solidarity must extend to a sense of personal responsibility for the moral behavior—and the corresponding spiritual plight—of their brothers and sisters in the faith.

Moreover, as a careful reading of the epistle demonstrates, it is not only the erring whose well-being Cyprian has in view. The high-group orientation of the Mediterranean family means that the spiritual health of others in the community is in danger of being compromised, as well. The sins of a few affect the whole kinship group. To be sure, the central advice Cyprian offers in the epistle concerns those individuals who have stepped beyond the boundaries of proper Christian behavior by cohabiting with unmarried brothers and sisters of the opposite sex.[32] In this regard, he enjoins, "Acting faithfully to these precepts we should take counsel for the life of each person; we should not allow virgins to dwell with men—I do not mean sleep together, but they should not even live together" (4.2.1). Again, in classic North African fashion, Cyprian refuses to compromise: Pomponius is to prohibit such behavior among his flock for the well-being of those individuals whose behavior is being censured. PKG solidarity, however, includes the assumption that the sins of the few have potential to affect the many adversely. For this reason, the rest of the community will derive great benefit from the discipline, as well. Cyprian traces such reasoning back to Paul of Tarsus. The transgressors, in Cyprian's view, "must avoid causing any scandal for their brothers and sisters, since it is written: 'If the food scandalized my brother, I will not eat of meat while this world lasts, for fear I may cause him to stumble'" (4.2.3; see 1 Cor 8:13). Near the end of the letter, the reader encounters similar sentiments. Those who have made a vow of chastity, and who have then proceeded to engage in questionable behavior, "must not make of themselves a cause for scandal to their brethren throughout the Church" (4.5.1).[33]

Notice that, in every instance, the passages I have cited contain sibling terminology. From Cyprian's perspective, the family model, so central to the North African conception of Christian community, demands a concern for the brotherhood tangibly expressed in the exercise of church discipline, the goals of which are twofold: (1) the restoration of erring siblings, and (2) the protection of faithful siblings from temptations to sin brought on by the unacceptable behavior of others.

The brief letter contains yet another passage relevant to my survey, one that draws upon a different aspect of kinship conceptualization for its rhetorical persuasiveness. Early in the history of Christian literature, the church was viewed as the bride of Christ. The imagery is present at one point in Paul's writings, but it is not nearly as important to Paul's thinking as is the much more common constellation of images discussed earlier, in chapter 4 (that is, God as father of a community of siblings): "I feel a divine jealousy for you, for I promised you in marriage to one husband, to present you as a chaste virgin to Christ. But I am afraid that as the serpent deceived Eve by its cunning, your thoughts will be led astray from a sincere and pure devotion to Christ" (2 Cor 11:2-3). The metaphor was adopted and reworked by another writer several decades later:

> "Let us rejoice and exult and give him the glory, for the marriage of the Lamb has come, and his bride has made herself ready; to her it has been granted to be clothed

with fine linen, bright and pure"— for the fine linen is the righteous deeds of the saints. And the angel said to me, "Write this: Blessed are those who are invited to the marriage supper of the Lamb." (Rev 19:7-9)

The increasing practice of sexual continence in the service of Christian spirituality opened the door to the expansion and reworking of the image of the church as the bride of Christ. Common sentiments increasingly held that the dedicated virgin was betrothed to Christ in some special way, a perception that gave rise to a variety of expressions of the metaphor. In *Epistle* 4, Cyprian employs the idea as a rhetorical device to threaten those brothers who are cohabiting with unmarried Christian women with the judgment of Christ the betrothed:

> If a husband should come along and see his own wife lying with another man, is he not outraged, is he not incensed, in grief and jealousy perhaps even seizing a sword in his hand? Christ is our Lord and our Judge: when He observes His own virgin who has been vowed to Him and dedicated to His holy estate lying with another man, imagine His rage and His fury and the punishments He threatens to exact for such unchaste associations. (4.3.2)[34]

The brother is not simply cohabiting with a sister. He is sleeping with another's wife. He must be warned of the danger, and the responsibility for such admonition lies with his faith family of siblings. For as Cyprian immediately proceeds to enjoin, "It is our duty to take pains to ensure by every possible means that every one of our brothers can escape His spiritual sword and the approaching day of His judgment. All are obliged to uphold the discipline without fail" (4.3.3).

Cyprian's *Epistle* 4, then, is particularly rich both in kinship terms and in challenges to family-like solidarity. Indeed, the words "brother," "brothers," "brethren," and "sisters" occur seventeen times in the course of the brief letter. The centrality of the sibling idea is further reinforced by Cyprian's understanding of his own position in the community. In view of the strong emphasis that he places upon episcopal authority, it is striking that Cyprian identifies himself, and his fellow bishops, as siblings of the Christians in their communities.

Cyprian is certainly unequivocal about disobedience to established ecclesiastical authorities: "And [persistent offenders] should not think that there is still hope of life and salvation for them if they have refused to obey their bishops and priests" (4.4.2). Passages like this lead Clarke to refer to Cyprian as our first clear example of "a dominating type of 'metropolitan' incumbent."[35] Given Cyprian's strong monarchical leanings, one might expect him to adopt a paternal role and to address his congregants in filial terms. The stage would then be set for him to draw upon

the rich *topos* of fatherly discipline so common to Mediterranean family sensibilities. Instead, Cyprian consistently refers to himself as a "brother" in his writings,
reminding leaders and community members alike that they are siblings of one
another and that they should, therefore, exhibit proper concern toward their brothers and sisters who have gone astray (see 4.3.3: "It is our duty. . . . *All* are obliged to
uphold the discipline without fail") (italics added).

EPISTLES 7, 5–6, AND 13–14

The next block of epistles finds Cyprian in hiding and the Decian persecution
increasingly threatening the Carthaginian church.[36] Practical pastoral concerns
addressed in the letters include (a) the need in Cyprian's absence for continued
attention to the ongoing distribution of material resources to the indigent (7.2;
14.2.1); (b) the task of administering alimentary aid to imprisoned confessors (5.2;
14.2.2); (c) the high visibility of church members who visit the confessors in great
numbers and who thereby attract undue attention to an already besieged community
(5.3); (d) the need for perseverance unto death on the part of the imprisoned confessors (6.2.1-6.4.1; 14.2.2-3); and (e) unresolved relational and moral disputes that
had broken out among the prisoners (13.5.1-2; 14.3.2).

Cyprian opens his earliest surviving letter written during the Decian persecution
with the familiar greeting "my dearest brothers."[37] At this stage of events, North
African Christians have yet to experience the full effects of imperial policy, and
Cyprian expects to "return soon" to the presbyters and deacons whom he addresses
in the letter (7.1). He makes reference in his introduction to a mutual *desiderium*
("longing") between himself and the leaders he addresses. Cyprian places such
affection in the context of sibling relations: "I send greetings to you, my dearest
brothers, by the grace of God in safety but anxious to return soon to you and thus
assuage my longing as well as yours and that of all our brothers (7.1)."[38] The reader
is reminded of the similar fraternal affection expressed by Paul of Tarsus toward his
fellow Christians in Thessalonica (1 Thess 2:17—3:8; see chapter 4).

The central admonition of *Epistle* 7 addresses the need for ongoing support for
the community's indigent in the absence of the supervising bishop. Cyprian offers
the following challenge to the clergy in Carthage:

> I urge that you be scrupulous in your care for the widows, the sick, and all the poor,
> and further, that you meet the financial needs of any strangers who are in want out of
> my own personal funds which I have left in the care of our fellow presbyter Roga-
> tianus. In case these funds have already been completely expended, I am sending to
> Rogatanius by the acolyte Narcissus a further sum, to ensure that the work of charity
> amongst those in difficulty may be carried out the more generously and readily. (7.2)

The exhortation finds itself firmly situated in a context that reflects family self-consciousness, for Cyprian immediately follows his above charge concerning "the work of charity" with a closing desire, one that, again, draws upon family imagery: "I wish that you, my dearest brothers, may ever fare well" (7.2).

Among those deemed worthy of family assistance in the above citation are "the widows, the sick, and all the poor." The addressees are also to provide for the "financial needs of any strangers." Strong Christian pressure against remarriage, along with malnutrition (among the poor) and high rates of mortality, served to increase chances of widowhood in Christian groups in the ancient world. Widows were grouped in Carthage by this time into a formal Christian order (see Tertullian, *De Virg. Vel.* 9.2; *De Praesc. Haer.* 3.5). Christian communities had been in the practice of singling out widows for alimentary aid for generations (Acts 6:1; Hermas, *Sim.* 9.27.2; Justin, 1 *Apol.* 67; Cornelius, according to Eusebius, *Hist. Eccl.* 6.43.11). Strangers, as well, could count on family treatment at the hands of their fellow Christians. Indeed, it was the overseer's role to dispense hospitality to Christian travelers, a responsibility that the bishop might carefully guard against usurpation by wealthy laymen.[39]

The text-segment quoted above juxtaposes the sharing of material resources as an expression of kin group solidarity with another important ancient Mediterranean social construct, that of patronage and the various relationships and obligations that it entailed. Cyprian instructs his readers to meet the financial needs of strangers "out of my [Cyprian's] personal funds." The phrase is taken to refer not to Cyprian's official portion of the church's income but, rather, to privately owned funds.[40] Cyprian thus functions in the role of patron to the Christian community in Carthage.[41]

The next two letters focus more specifically upon the situation of those who had publicly confessed Christ and were imprisoned as a result. *Epistle 5* is written to Cyprian's presbyters and deacons. The companion letter (*Epistle 6*) addresses the confessors themselves.[42] The latter epistle contains several kinship terms of address and description but lacks illustrations of the specific application of Mediterranean family values in the life of the local Christian community. Cyprian is primarily concerned in *Epistle 6* to exhort the imprisoned believers to remain steadfast in their confession. The family language that does appear includes references to the readers as the author's "dearest and most blessed brothers," an expression found at the beginning and at the end of the letter (6.1.1; 6.4.1). One of the confessors is elsewhere referred to as "our brother" (6.4.1).

Cyprian does, however, draw upon a family passage from Paul's letter to the Romans, as he reminds the confessors of the eternal glories that will follow their martyrdom for Christ: "'We are,' [Paul] says, 'sons of God: but if sons, heirs of

God and joint-heirs with Christ—if, indeed, we share in His sufferings so that we may share in His glory'" (6.2.1). The point is an obvious one: a glorious family inheritance awaits those who persevere unto death in their confession. Cyprian does not, however, capitalize upon the *topos* in the ensuing context. He fails to elaborate on the glories to come in terms of family inheritance, as one might expect after reading the above citation from Romans.

Epistle 5 more pointedly reflects the practice of family solidarity among the Christians at Carthage. Cyprian opens the letter with the now-familiar address "dearest brothers" (5.1.1). Sibling terms surface elsewhere four times in the short work (5.1.1, 5.2.1 [3x]). At the heart of *Epistle* 5, the reader encounters yet another challenge to live out tangibly the PKG value of generalized reciprocity. The imprisoned confessors are among those concerned. Cyprian writes, "I ask that there be nothing wanting in furnishing supplies to those who have confessed the Lord with words of glory and who are now to be found in prison" (5.1.2).[43]

Cyprian proceeds to expand his charge to include other indigent persons in the community, as well: "as equally to those who are suffering from need and want but yet continue faithful in the Lord. For all the funds collected have been distributed amongst the clergy in Carthage precisely to meet emergencies of this kind, thus putting a number in the position to ease individual cases of hardship and necessity" (5.1.2). Clarke makes much of a shift in Cyprian's terminology, from his exhortation to care for "*all* the poor," without qualification, in *Epistle* 7 (see above for discussion of this earlier epistle), to the more limiting language found here in *Epistle* 5 (written later), in which alimentary assistance is apparently to aid only "those who are suffering from need and want but yet continue faithful in the Lord." The implication, for Clarke, is that "there are some who have lapsed between times."[44] Little evidence exists, however, according to Clarke's own analysis, of a general apostasy as early as *Epistles* 5–6.[45] The phrase may be otherwise explained.

The reminder to care for the needs of poor persons in the church who had not yet been arrested by authorities may simply have been necessary in view of the zeal with which church members and their leaders attended to their imprisoned siblings in the faith. As Cyprian notes in the following context, again employing fraternal language, "Our brethren in their charity are very anxious to visit and meet the noble confessors" (5.2.1). Indeed, the resulting activity in the vicinity of the prisons brought so much unwanted attention to the Carthaginian Christian community that Cyprian warns his readers to "act with caution, avoiding visits in crowds and meeting in large numbers together" (5.2.1). In an atmosphere in which imprisoned confessors were accorded such respect and attention, there was a corresponding danger of ignoring the needs of equally faithful persons who remained in the community. This, in turn, adequately explains the need Cyprian feels to remind his flock that these individuals, too, "continue faithful in the Lord," and that they should receive resources from the community purse (5.1.2). No generalized apostasy need be assumed this early in the persecution (contra Clarke, above) in order to account for Cyprian's language in the above citation.

The final two letters contained in the present group of epistles evidence a marked change in the situation in Carthage. In *Epistles* 13–14, we encounter a church under siege: "Losses are by now heavy."[46] The two letters are, again, companion epistles. *Epistle* 13 addresses imprisoned confessors; *Epistle* 14, the now-beleaguered clergy in the city. The former letter finds its author reminding the confessors that they have only begun their spiritual battle. They must remain humble and faithful until they complete the course. The confessors are called "my dear and courageous brothers," and the broader church population is identified in the same context by Cyprian as "all of the brethren" (13.1.1).

Near the end of the letter, sibling terminology appears again, as the author once more refers to the church at large as "our brothers," and to the chief addressee, confessor, and presbyter Rogatianus as "my dearly loved brother" (13.7.1). The body of the epistle generally lacks references to the kinship metaphor, the only exception being the phrase "your Father in heaven," taken from Matthew 5:16, an expression decidedly peripheral to Cyprian's argument at the point at which it appears in the letter.

In the final paragraph of the epistle, however, Cyprian informs the confessors of the directions he previously gave to the clergy, namely, to provide for the confessors' needs during their imprisonment. Here the family model is pivotal:

> To our clergy I wrote very explicitly both recently when you were still in prison and I have written to them similarly again now. I have asked that you be supplied with everything you find needful in the way of food and clothing. Nevertheless I am also sending to you myself 250 sesterces from the meager resources which I brought with me (this is in addition to another 250 sesterces which I sent previously). Victor the deacon and former lector who is with me here is also sending you 175. And I am delighted to hear that in their charity our brothers vie with each other in large numbers to alleviate your difficulties with contributions of their own. (13.7.1)

The role of the overseer as patron is again manifest. Both Cyprian and the deacon Victor appear to function in this capacity. Their activity in this regard is clearly complemented, however, by the enthusiastic kinship behavior exercised by other "brothers" who "vie with each other in large numbers" to meet the pressing material needs of the confessors.

In the above quotation, the nature of the needs of the confessors is spelled out in detail: "food and clothing." In his previous correspondence, Cyprian only alluded to the purpose for which the crowds of Carthaginian Christians visited their brethren in the prison (Cyprian offered only a general descriptive expression: "in their charity," 5.2.1). The last sentence in the above excerpt clearly demonstrates the highly practical nature of the visits to the prisons by large companies of the faithful. They came, Cyprian reminds the confessors, "to alleviate your difficulties with contributions of their own" (13.7.1).[47]

My detailed examination of a sample of Cyprian's epistles concludes with an analysis of *Epistle* 14. The epistle amply reflects Cyprian's family self-consciousness, as he writes again to the clergy in Carthage. The seven occurrences of the sibling word group include application of fraternal language (a) to the addressees (*incipit*; 14.1.1; 14.4.1), (b) to Cyprian's emissary Tertullus (14.1.2), (c) to the church at large (14.2.2; 14.4.1), and (d) to the confessors (14.3.1). Cyprian's "ardent yearning" for his readers may be read in the context of PKG affective solidarity (14.1.2). The situation in the church has clearly deteriorated since the previous correspondence (that is, *Epistles* 5–6). Now, "this hostile tempest has overwhelmed not only the majority of our people . . . it has involved in its devastating wake even a portion of the clergy" (14.1.1).[48]

Cyprian informs his clergy that he is relying on their "charity and devotion." He then provides details concerning the expected exercise of these virtues. The reader is not surprised once again to encounter the theme of alimentary aid, here designated both for the indigent and for the confessors. First, the poor are in view:

> The poor, in the meantime, must be cared for to the extent that it is possible and in whatever way that it is possible, provided, that is, they remain standing with faith unshaken and have not forsaken the flock of Christ. You should take earnest care that they are provided with the means of alleviating their poverty; otherwise necessity may force them to do in their difficulties actions which faith prevented them from doing in the storm. (14.2.1)

The persecution has accelerated and, as noted earlier in this chapter, many persons in the community have compromised with paganism. Now Cyprian clearly does draw a distinction between the poor who had remained faithful to the community and other needy individuals who had recently abandoned the church in the face of pagan pressure. Only the former merit the support of the church.

For the first time in Cyprian's letters, the imprisoned confessors are similarly divided into two groups. Only those confessors who submit to the discipline of the church are provided for by the faithful:

> To the glorious confessors likewise you must devote especial care. I know that very many of them have been supported by the devotion and charity of our brethren.

> Nevertheless there may be some in need of clothing or provisions; they should be supplied by whatever is necessary, as I also wrote to you previously when they were still in prison. But there must be this proviso: through you they must be informed, instructed, and taught what the discipline of the Church, based on the teaching authority of the Scriptures, requires of them. They must conduct themselves humbly, modestly, and peaceably. (14.2.2)

Cyprian proceeds to offer biblical examples of persons who remained humble despite great spiritual accomplishments. There are lessons to be learned in this regard from the lives of Paul of Tarsus and Jesus of Nazareth. Indeed, it is the clergy's responsibility to "bring each of these lessons home to our brothers" (14.2.3).

The letter goes on to describe in more detail certain recalcitrant confessors, now released from prison, whose behavior must be censured. They are "running about, conducting themselves viciously and arrogantly; . . . polluting the members of Christ, even after their confession of Christ, by unlawful cohabitation, refusing to be ruled by the deacons or presbyters" (14.3.2). Such individuals are to receive no alimentary aid at the hands of the Carthaginian clergy (see 14.2.2, earlier in this chapter).

This concludes my examination of Cyprian's first nine epistles. Before I proceed to a more selective survey of the remaining writings, it will help to summarize the analysis of the letters chosen above. The intention has been to provide a fair introduction into Cyprian's view of Christian social relations by simply examining the first nine epistles in the order in which Clarke has arranged them. It is clear that the family model is central to Cyprian's conception of social organization for the North African church. Like the writers examined before him, Cyprian both frequently employs kinship terminology and consistently expects the members of his North African Christian churches to relate to one another in a manner appropriate for members of a Mediterranean family.

I will continue my analysis of Cyprian with a more selective collection of excerpts taken from the remaining letters and treatises. After a brief general overview, my approach will be topical in nature, examining, in turn, various aspects of the family model as reflected in Cyprian's works.

Survey of Cyprian's Other Works

Cyprian's commentary on the prayer that Jesus of Nazareth is remembered to have taught his disciples aptly reflects the family metaphor as Cyprian conceived it. Many aspects of the passage that follows will prove familiar to the reader. Here are Cyprian's comments on the prayer's opening address, "Our Father":

A new man, reborn and restored to his God by his grace says in the first place "Father,"
because he has now begun to be a son. . . . He, therefore, who has believed in His name
and has become the son of God, thereafter should begin to give thanks and to profess
himself the son of God, when he declares that his father is God in heaven. . . . [He
should] testify . . . that he has begun to know and to have as father Him only who is
in heaven, as it is written: "Those who say to their father and mother: I do not know
you, and who do not recognize their children, these have kept thy words, and observed
thy covenant" [see Deuteronomy 33:9]. Likewise the Lord in His Gospel has bidden us
to call not [sic] our father upon earth, because one is our Father, who is in heaven. And
to the disciple who made mention of his dead father, He replied: "Let the dead bury
their own dead." For he had said that his father was dead, when the father of believers
is living. (Dom. Or. 9)[49]

This text-segment contains several important aspects of the kinship model as we
have come to understand it. God is the father of those who have become his children through a second birth (see "reborn," line 1), and the believer's allegiance to his
new family necessarily involves a loosening of ties to his family of origin. Cyprian
cites both Old and New Testament traditions to support his contention that the
child of God "has begun to know and to have as father Him only who is in heaven"
(my emphasis). As I will demonstrate later in this chapter, this value of family loyalty serves Cyprian well as a rhetorical device with which to castigate perceived
heretics for abandoning their siblings in the faith.

Cyprian continues his commentary on Jesus' prayer with observations that situate
him at the center of typical North African convictions concerning the relationship
between the church and the pagan world. Absent from Cyprian's writings is the
expansion of the sibling metaphor to include unbelievers in a broader circle of
brothers who are related because they belong to the common stock of humanity.
This elaboration of the family metaphor was, as I noted earlier, characteristic of
Christian writers of a more philosophical orientation, such as Justin Martyr. By contrast, North African Christian leaders are preoccupied with preserving intact the distinct social and ideological boundaries between the church and the non-Christian
world, a focus reflected in a general unwillingness to adopt pagan philosophical reasoning. The reader is hardly surprised, then, to find the idea of the universal brotherhood of humankind noticeably absent from the Cyprianic corpus. Cyprian instead
insists upon recognizing only Christians as the children of God. Continuing his
commentary on the phrase "Our Father," he writes:

We join in saying "Our Father" . . . of those who believe, of those who, sanctified
through Him and restored by the birth of spiritual grace, have begun to be sons of
God. And this voice also reproaches and condemns the Jews, . . . who now cannot call

the Lord father, since the Lord confounds and refutes them, saying: "You are born of the devil as father, and you wish to do the desires of your Father. He was a murderer from the beginning. . . ." [see John 8:44]. And through Isaiah the prophet God exclaims with indignation: "I have begotten and brought up sons, but they have despised me. . . . Woe to the sinful nation . . . a wicked seed, ungracious children" [see Isaiah 1:2]. And in condemnation of these we Christians say, when we pray, "Our Father," because He now has begun to be ours and has ceased to be of the Jews, who have forsaken Him. (*Dom. Or.* 10)

Judeans are not the only persons excluded from the family of God. The same is the case for those who have been baptized by heretics. In another work, Cyprian asserts: "That nativity generates not sons for God but for the devil" (*De Cath. Eccl.* 11). Family language thus serves Cyprian as a useful rhetorical tool, reflecting the polarization that characterized North African Christianity's relationship with the non-Christian world.

Other components of the family model that appear throughout Cyprian's writings include (a) the affection characteristic of Mediterranean siblings (*Laps.* 2); (b) the expectation that one will emulate the behavior of one's relatives (*Laps.* 2; *Ep.* 39.5); (c) patrilocal residence (*De habitu virginum* 23; *Dom. Or.* 8, 10; *De Cath. Eccl.* 8); (d) preoccupation with ancestral lineage (*De Mort.* 12, 26); and (e) the inheritance *topos* (*De Cath. Eccl.* 24). These now-familiar applications of the kinship metaphor have received much attention in the course of the present study, and they will be explored further in the discussion to follow. In a striking way, Cyprian expands upon one aspect of the metaphor that has remained peripheral for the writers surveyed to this point, namely, the image of the church as the mother of the faithful.

When Cyprian returned to Carthage in the spring of 251 c.e., he read an important treatise on the unity of the church to a council that met in April to consider divisions that had erupted in the church during the months of the Decian persecution. In several places, Cyprian uses the metaphor of the church as the mother of the faithful to argue that schismatic leaders and their followers have situated themselves squarely outside the family of God. For Cyprian, "the Church . . . is the one mother copious in the results of her fruitfulness. By her womb we are born; by her milk we are nourished" (*De Cath. Eccl.* 5). In the following text-segment, he alternates between two metaphors, that of the church as the spouse of Christ, and that of the church as the mother of Christians. In each case, Cyprian's goal is to marginalize those who teach and baptize without submitting to recognized community leadership:

The spouse of Christ cannot be defiled; she is uncorrupted and chaste. She knows one home, with chaste modesty she guards the sanctity of one couch. She keeps us for God; she assigns the children whom she has created to the kingdom. Whoever is separated from the Church and is joined with an adulteress is separated from the promises of the Church. (*De Cath. Eccl.* 6)

Cyprian summarizes the above argument with the categorical assertion, "He cannot have God as a father who does not have the Church as a mother." (*De Cath. Eccl.* 6)

When the mother image surfaces elsewhere in Cyprian's writings, it is almost exclusively used, as in the above citations, as a rhetorical device to denounce opposition leaders and their adherents.[50] Christians who are deceptively swept away by the schismatics "are being separated from their mother through the attacks made by members of a wilful and heretical faction" (45.3.2). Leaders of the opposing party "must realize that it is an act of impiety to abandon their mother" (44.3.2).

The mother metaphor surfaces in another letter, in which Cyprian reflects upon the plight of some who had lapsed during the pogrom and who were now receiving readmission to communion outside of normal ecclesiastical channels. The schismatic confessors who claim to remit their sins are guilty of matricide: they "go and leave the Church and take up murderous arms against her, their mother" (59.13.1). In the paragraph that follows, Cyprian elaborates. Notice the expansion of the mother metaphor: "True reconciliation they destroy by their false and fallacious reconciliation; the stepmother impedes them from reaching their true mother's healing embrace, anxious to prevent her from hearing any sobbing and weeping coming from the hearts and lips of those who have fallen" (59.13.2). Cyprian juxtaposes the mother metaphor with the opposing kinship image of the stepmother in yet another attempt to condemn his opponents and thereby dismiss the efficacy of the forgiveness that they claim to offer to the lapsed penitent.

Cyprian was not alone in his appropriation of the mother metaphor in debates with schismatic leaders. The epistolary corpus contains a letter written to Cyprian from Firmilian, a renowned church leader from Cappadocia. In the letter, Firmilian sides with Cyprian in a heated controversy with the Roman overseer Stephen. At issue is the admission policy for persons who had been baptized by Novatianist leaders but who now wished to join (or return to) the catholic church. Stephen had insisted, against Cyprian, on the validity of Novatianist baptism. He refused to rebaptize those returning to his fold. Cyprian argued the contrary, asserting that baptism performed outside recognized ecclesiastical channels could not effect spiritual birth. Like Cyprian, Firmilian alternates between the two interrelated family metaphors of spouse and mother as he marginalizes those who operate independently of established church leadership:

Now if the baptism of heretics is to have the regenerative effect of the second birth, then those who are baptized among them are to be reckoned not as heretics but as sons of God. But if the bride of Christ, that is to say, the catholic Church, is one, then she alone is the one who gives birth to the sons of God. For Christ does not have a number of brides, as the Apostle says: "I have betrothed you to Christ as a chaste virgin to her one husband." . . . But the synagogue of heretics is by no means one with us, because the bride is neither adulteress nor whore—hence that synagogue is unable to produce children of God. Unless, perhaps (as Stephen seems to think), heresy does produce them but exposes them; and the Church then takes up these exposed children and rears as her own those whom she has not produced herself, whereas, in fact, she cannot be the mother of alien children. (75.14.1-2)

Firmilian employs a whole constellation of kinship imagery in order to make his point. The excerpt contains references to believers as "sons of God," to "the second birth," and to the church as "the bride of Christ" who, as a mother, "gives birth to the sons of God." Firmilian, like Cyprian, uses bride imagery and the mother metaphor to draw a sociological line in the sand, so to speak, between orthodox and heterodox believers in local Christian communities.

To summarize, Cyprian and Firmilian use the image of the church as the mother of the faithful to situate opposition leaders such as Novatian in Rome and Felicissimus in Carthage outside the true family of God. The metaphor of the church as mother will find various applications in Christian writings in the decades to follow (see Eusebius, *Hist. Eccl.* 5.1.45; 5.2.8).[51]

As has already been demonstrated in my analysis of the first nine epistles, Cyprian's conceptual image of the church as a family carries with it an inseparable behavioral component. At the heart of Cyprian's conception of Christianity is his conviction that the family metaphor must find tangible expression in social relations among Christians in local communities. As he himself exhorts, "So, most beloved brethren, we ought to remember and to know that, when we speak of God, we ought to *act* as sons of God, so that just as we are pleased with God as Father, so too He may be pleased with us" (*Dom. Or.* 11, italics added).

For Cyprian, the admonition to "act as sons of God" (see the imitation *topos*) includes among its central components two important aspects of the PKG value system: (1) undivided loyalty to the family of God, and (2) the sharing of material resources. These two behaviors constitute the primary tangible expressions of the Mediterranean family model as Cyprian envisioned it functioning among Christians in North Africa. I will now deal with each in some detail.

Loyalty to the Family of God

Cyprian draws upon the loyalty *topos* in order to address problems that arose both directly and indirectly from the Decian persecution. The emperor's edict, which demanded that his subjects sacrifice to the pagan gods, necessitated a choice of allegiance on the part of Christians in North Africa. Cyprian uses the idea of sibling solidarity to challenge believers to continue unmoved in their faith, and his writings demonstrate that a number of individuals did, indeed, maintain loyalty to one another—and to God their father—to the point of death.

Moreover, the theme of family loyalty remained important to Cyprian long after the persecution had subsided. After the immediate dangers of the pogrom had ended, the effects of the Decian persecution continued to be experienced among Christians. Various controversies erupted over (a) the readmission of the lapsed and (b) the efficacy of baptism administered by those who operated outside the recognized church. Cyprian's pen again proves to be a powerful and persuasive weapon, as he defends the majority North African position on both points of contention in a number of epistles and treatises. Here the theme of family loyalty is no longer employed primarily to encourage the faithful. Instead, it becomes a powerful rhetorical device that Cyprian and others adopt in order to castigate their opponents. This is particularly true with respect to the rebaptism controversy. Treachery against the brotherhood is a charge continually leveled at those who teach and baptize without submitting to the authority of recognized church leaders. I will now provide evidence for these various applications of the theme of family loyalty.

The Decian persecution brought with it many opportunities for Christians in various regions of the empire to opt for loyalty to God's family over loyalty to their families of origin. That the confessors understood their actions in precisely these terms is aptly illustrated by an excerpt from a letter in which four imprisoned Roman clerics—Moses, Maximus, Nicostratus, and Rufinus—describe to Cyprian their impending martyrdom: "To this battle the Lord rouses us with the trumpet call of His Gospel, in these words: 'He who loves his father or his mother more than Me is not worthy of Me . . . and brother will deliver up brother to death and father son'" (*Ep.* 31.4). The confessors trace back to a saying of Jesus the conviction that their refusal to sacrifice is to be understood in the context of family loyalty.

In another letter, Cyprian offers to the North African congregation at Thibaris a challenge to remain loyal to God and his church in the face of coming persecution. The epistle, addressed to Cyprian's "dearly beloved brethren," draws upon the kinship model in several places to encourage the local Christians to persevere in their faith. In one text-segment, Cyprian combines the family metaphor with imagery from the arena, as he assures his readers that "it is God who now watches us as we compete, and as He surveys with His gaze those whom He vouchsafed to make His sons He takes delight in the spectacle of our encounter" (*Ep.* 58.8.1). Elsewhere in the letter, Cyprian reinforces his call to loyalty with now-familiar citations from New Testament literature:

> We are sons of God, but if sons, heirs of God also and joint heirs with Christ—if, indeed, we share in His sufferings so that we may share in His glory (cf. Rom 8:16-17). (58.1.3)[52]

> There is no man who leaves home and land, family and brethren, wife and children for the sake of the kingdom of God who shall not receive seven times more in this present time, and in the world to come life everlasting (cf. Luke 18:29-30). (58.2.3)

The Christians from Thibaris must remain true to their confession, for they belong to an alternative family with a patrimony that, when received in full, will more than compensate for present sacrifices of family and property.

The priority that Cyprian places upon family loyalty leads him to use the theme as a rhetorical device to denounce the treachery of those who apostasized when faced with pagan antipathy. In the following text-segment, Cyprian regretfully considers the effects that the behavior of the lapsed has had upon their infant children. Note the centrality of the kinship metaphor in the second half of the passage:

> But for many their own destruction was not enough. . . . [I]nfants also, placed in the arms of parents or led by them, lost as little ones what they had gained at the very first beginning of their nativity (i.e., when they were baptized). When the day of judgment comes, will they not say: "We have done nothing; we have not abandoned the Lord's bread and cup and of our own accord hastened to profane contaminations. The perfidy of others has ruined us; we have found our parents parricides. They have denied us the Church as Mother, God as Father." (*Laps.* 9)

Such betrayal of God and the abandonment of his family are inexcusable. Instead, as Cyprian proceeds to contend, one must jettison earthly belongings and family ties for the cause of Christ:

> There is not, alas, any just and serious reason which excuses so great a crime. The fatherland should have been abandoned, the loss of personal property suffered. For what man, who is born and dies, does not at some time have to abandon his fatherland and suffer the loss of personal property? Let not Christ be abandoned; let the loss of one's salvation and one's eternal home be the object of fear. (*Laps.* 10)

The convictions expressed in the above citation are echoed in a passage from another treatise. After presenting the patriarch Abraham as one who viewed loyalty to God as more important than allegiance either to his earthly father or to his son, Isaac, Cyprian exhorts his readers to embrace a similar attitude:

The fear of God and faith ought to make you ready for all things. Though it should be the loss of private property, though it should be the constant and violent affliction of the members by wasting diseases, though it should be the mournful and sorrowful tearing away from wife, from children, from departing dear ones, let not such things be stumbling blocks for you. (*De Mort.* 12)

Cyprian thus effectively uses the loyalty theme to encourage his fellow Christians to remain faithful to their surrogate family during the Decian persecution.

Cyprian had no monopoly on the powerful rhetorical resources inherent in the theme of sibling solidarity. Elsewhere in the epistolary corpus, the loyalty *topos* appears in a letter addressed to Cyprian that challenged his own commitment to the family of God. No longer is Cyprian on the offensive, urging others to remain faithful to their surrogate Christian family. Now, Cyprian is confronted with persons who question his own loyalty to the Carthaginian community. While Cyprian is in hiding and the See at Carthage is ostensibly vacant, a letter of concern arrives from the clergy in Rome.

The first metaphor used by the authors of the letter is that of a shepherd and his sheep: Cyprian is wrong to have abandoned his flock. It is the leader's "duty to keep watch over the flock" (*Ep.* 8.1.1). The overseer, like Christ, should be willing to lay down his life for his sheep (*Ep.* 8.1.2). The Roman authors then interject the family metaphor into their argument, extolling their own behavior and, by implication, censuring Cyprian as one who has abandoned the brotherhood:

And so, dearly beloved brothers, our desire is that you are found to be not hireling but good shepherds. You are aware that there is the risk of extreme peril should you fail to exhort our brothers to stand steadfast in the faith; otherwise they may rush headlong into idolatry and be totally ruined. And it is not by words alone that we exhort you to do this. You will be able to learn from the many travellers who come to you from us that, with the help of God, all these things we not only have done ourselves but we continue to do them with unremitting zeal in the face of worldly dangers. . . . We do not abandon our brothers but we exhort them to stand firm in the faith, and as is their duty, to be in readiness to walk with the Lord. (*Ep.* 8.2.1–2)

The church leader is responsible to exhort others "to stand steadfast in the faith." The authors of the epistle locate this duty in the context of family obligations— those in need of encouragement are Cyprian's "brothers." The implication is that Cyprian, by retiring from his post, has abandoned his siblings.

The censorious correspondence from Rome occasioned a pointed letter of response in which Cyprian defends his behavior. First, Cyprian defers to the "beloved brethren" to whom he writes by assuming that they have perhaps received information about him that is "not completely candid or accurate" (*Ep.* 20.1.1). He then proceeds to inform his readers of the true reasons for his departure from Carthage:

> Right at the very first onset of the troubles, when the populace clamoured for me violently and repeatedly, I followed the directives and instructions of the Lord and withdrew for the time being. I was thinking not so much of my own safety as the general peace of our brethren; I was concerned that if I brazenly continued to show myself in Carthage I might aggravate even further the disturbance that had begun. And yet, though absent in body, I have not faltered in spirit, action, or the advice I have given, endeavouring to look after the interests of our brothers in conformity with the Lord's precepts in so far as my meager abilities have allowed. (*Ep.* 20.1.2)

Cyprian assures his critics that he is acting in accordance with the teachings of Jesus of Nazareth (that is, "in conformity with the Lord's precepts"; see Mark 13:14).

Cyprian is not satisfied, however, simply to defend his behavior with an allusion to a biblical injunction. He must forcefully refute the scandalous charge of sibling betrayal. It is hardly the case, Cyprian retorts, that he is deserting the brotherhood. Rather, his retirement has in view precisely "the interests of [the] brothers." His loyalty to his siblings in the faith, then, is unassailable. Indeed, his own well-being was hardly in view. Rather, he has left his post to preserve "the general peace of the brethren."

It will help to summarize the material I have presented to this point surrounding Cyprian's use of the loyalty *topos.* As I have demonstrated, Cyprian draws upon the *topos* to encourage his fellow Christians to resist the pressures of pagan persecution. He also employs the loyalty idea to defend his own flight from Carthage in response to those who accuse him of abandoning the brethren. I conclude from the above passages that the PKG value of family loyalty constituted Cyprian's primary conceptual matrix for viewing the various responses to pagan persecution in Carthage, circa 250–51 C.E. The loyalty *topos* remained highly useful to Cyprian, however, long after the dangers of the Decian era had subsided.

The persecution left in its wake a series of issues that were hotly debated by Christians in the following decades. The theme of kinship loyalty regularly appears in the context of Cyprian's response to each of these debates.

One of the controversies involved a dispute that resulted upon the consecration of the schismatic overseer Novatian in Rome in 251 C.E. The end of the Decian persecution brought with it the need to choose a new leader for the church at Rome, since the community's beloved overseer, Fabian, had been martyred in January 250 C.E. Cornelius was chosen in Fabian's stead by a group of church leaders who had been hastily convened for the election. Other Italian clerics quickly challenged the election on several grounds. Most troubling was the charge, later proven untrue, that Cornelius had lapsed during the persecution. An influential group of Roman confessors who had recently been released from prison refused to recognize Cornelius. They participated instead in a rival consecration at which the Roman presbyter Novatian was elected overseer. Supporters rallied around the two opposing bishops, and a long-lasting schism resulted, which affected the church throughout the empire.

By the mid–250s C.E., Novatian's influence had expanded far beyond the confines of the Roman church, with Novatianist activists baptizing converts in North Africa. As events unfolded, however, many in Rome and Carthage who had initially aligned themselves with the schismatic party sought to be readmitted to the recognized church. The church became divided over whether or not those who had been baptized by the Novatianist camp needed to be rebaptized upon admission to the Christian community.

Cyprian found himself immersed in the schism, as he corresponded with local leaders and with others elsewhere in the empire. His letters constitute our most important source material for the Novatianist controversy. One can reconstruct from various passages in Cyprian's epistles a course of events that ultimately saw a number of Novatian's key supporters returning to the church at Rome. The relevant letters reveal ongoing communication between Cyprian, Cornelius, and the Roman confessors who initially sided with Novatian. The epistolary interchange is deeply situated in the conceptual universe of the church as a family. I will cite several highlights from the dialogue.

Cyprian first writes to Maximus and Nicostratus, confessors who, at the time the letter was written, were aligned with the *pseudepiscopus* Novatian. Cyprian's perspective on the schism is clear, as he draws upon the image of sibling betrayal in order to underline his convictions:

> My dearest friends, you will have perceived many times from my letters the high esteem I have professed for your confession and the love I have expressed for brothers who are united to us. . . . I am weighed down with grief, I am overwhelmed with unendurable distress, I am stricken and almost prostrate with sadness: I have learnt that you in Rome have given your consent to the appointment of another bishop. . . . I do beg of you that, at least as far as you are concerned, this unlawful rending of our brotherhood should not persist. . . . It is rather up to you to return to the Church, your mother, and to your brothers. (*Ep.* 46.1.1; 46.1.2; 46.1.3; 46.2.2)

The sibling form of address, characteristic of nearly all of Cyprian's epistles, is noticeably lacking here. Instead of being identified as "dearest brethren," the readers are simply referred to as the author's "dearest friends."[53] Cyprian proceeds to accuse the schismatic confessors of that behavior which is most deplorable to PKG sensibilities: they are, Cyprian claims, "rending our brotherhood" (*Ep.* 46.1.3). The PKG metaphor thus becomes in the hands of Cyprian a powerful rhetorical tool with which to marginalize those who have joined the Novatianist party in Rome.[54] In a companion letter, in which Cyprian informs Cornelius that he has written the above letter to Maximus and Nicostratus, Cyprian twice identifies Cornelius as his "dearest brother" and again refers to the schism in kinship terms: "My purpose is to induce [Maximus and Nicostratus] out of fraternal affection to return to their own true mother, that is, to the Catholic Church" (*Ep.* 47.1.1).

Nicostratus refuses to recant. Happily for Cyprian and Cornelius, however, Maximus and a group of his followers ultimately submit to Cornelius's leadership in Rome and formally denounce Novatian. The events that follow read like a family reunion. Exultation abounds in North Africa and in Rome upon Maximus's return to the community. From Carthage, Cyprian writes:

> We can get a sense of the excitement of that day [when Maximus and others returned] from our own feelings. Here the letter itself which you sent about their declaration caused our entire community to rejoice [literally, "the whole number of brethren"], and they eagerly welcomed with open arms the news of universal joy it contained. How much greater must have been the excitement there where the joyful events were actually taking place. (*Ep.* 51.2.1)

The sibling terminology situates the above expressions of joy and affection in the context of surrogate family relations.

The correspondence concludes with yet another pair of letters, consisting of an interchange between Cyprian and the Roman confessors themselves. The confessors write Cyprian to personally inform him of their return to the fold (*Ep.* 53). Cyprian immediately responds to them with a letter of his own. Now that Maximus has left Novatian and reestablished his allegiance to Cornelius and the Roman community, he and his party are once again addressed as Cyprian's "dearly beloved brothers" (compare *Ep.* 46.1.1, above). Cyprian's general response to the group is characterized by sibling affection:

> I have read, dearly beloved brothers, your letter which you wrote to me bringing news of your return to the Church, of the peace you have made with her as well as of your reunion with your brethren. I must confess that my delight on reading this letter of yours was as great as it had been previously when I first learned of your glorious confession. (*Ep.* 54.1.1)

For Cyprian, the Novatianist schism is clearly a highly charged social conflict, as his profuse employment of the kinship metaphor in his epistolary rhetoric clearly indicates.

A second controversy that erupted among mid-third-century Christians centered upon the troubling issue of penitential discipline. During the persecution, the majority of the Carthaginian community apostasized. Some sacrificed to the pagan gods. Others refused to sacrifice but, instead, purchased *libelli*, certificates testifying that they had done so. Most of the lapsed eventually begged for forgiveness and sought readmission to the church. The terms upon which the penitent were to be restored to the community occasioned much bitterness and dissension.

Cyprian was amenable to the return of the lapsed, but he insisted that they wait until the end of the persecution. He allowed an exception, however, for those about to die of natural causes. They were to be absolved immediately. In his convictions, Cyprian occupied a middle ground between (a) those who resisted making any concessions to persons who had compromised with paganism, and (b) others who opted for receiving straightaway all who desired to be reunited with the church. As Cyprian himself relates, "We have no right to be so hardhearted and unyielding as to knock back their repentance, but, on the other side, neither ought we to be so soft and easygoing as to slacken the rules and let all and sundry return to communion" (*Ep.* 55.19.1). Cyprian had to defend his mediating position against Christians who held more extreme views at both ends of the spectrum.

In *Epistle* 55, Cyprian is particularly concerned to respond to the rigorist position, which generally denied readmission to the Christian community for persons who had lapsed in any way during the Decian era. Novatian, the schismatic Roman bishop, was a primary representative for the rigorist camp, and he had sympathizers in North Africa. Cyprian employs much family imagery in his appeal for a measure of mercy and compassion in dealing with the lapsed. Specifically, he argues (a) from the character of God as father and (b) from the concern siblings should feel for one another, that the genuinely penitent lapsed ought to be readmitted to communion.

Father imagery comes into play in the following text-segments. First, Cyprian quotes a familiar Gospel text:

> The Lord also illustrates the compassion of God the Father when He says in the Gospel: "What man is there among you who if his son should ask for bread would hand him a stone, or if he should ask for a fish would hand him a snake? If you, then, evil as you are, know how to give good gifts to your sons, how much more will your heavenly Father give good things to those who ask Him?" (cf. Matt 7:9-11). (*Ep.* 55.23.1)

He then applies the text to the plight of the lapsed. An earthly father, Cyprian argues, would gladly welcome back a wicked son who demonstrates true remorse and repentance through a change of behavior (*Ep.* 55.23.2). Certainly, God can be expected to exhibit even more compassion:

> But how much more must that one, true Father who is kind and merciful and compassionate, indeed who is Himself kindness and mercy and compassion, how much more must He take joy in the repentance of his own sons and no longer threaten them with His wrath if they are repentant or with punishment if they weep and mourn, but promise to them instead His pardon and forgiveness. (*Ep.* 55.23.2)

Cyprian's point is that Christians, as God's children, should reflect these same character qualities and exercise mercy and compassion toward their fallen but now remorseful brethren: "Bearing in mind this kindness and mercy which He shows, we have no right ourselves to be overrigid or harsh and callous in caring for our brothers. Rather we ought to mourn with those who mourn and weep with those who weep" (*Ep.* 55.19.1). The theme of sibling affective solidarity is thus juxtaposed with the *topos* of paternal imitation, as our author pleas for compassion in dealing with the penitent lapsed.

Immediately following the above excerpt in the letter, Cyprian draws upon yet another aspect of Mediterranean sibling solidarity, namely, the responsibility to come to the aid of a sibling in times of danger and distress:

> See, your injured brother lies there before you on the battlefield, wounded at the hands of our foe. On the one side is the devil, striving to have killed the man he has already wounded; on the other side is Christ, urging that the man whom He has redeemed should not be wholly lost. Which of these two do we assist? On whose side do we stand? Do we lend our support to the devil so that he can destroy him; do we simply walk past our brother lying there half-dead, like the priest and levite in the Gospel? Or rather, being priests of God and of Christ, do we imitate Christ's teaching and example, snatch our wounded brother from the jaws of our foe? (*Ep.* 55.19.2)

For persons steeped in Mediterranean family values, only one answer to Cyprian's question is even conceivable—a brother must deliver a brother from the "jaws of [a] foe."[55]

Cyprian's viewpoint was resisted not only by those of more rigorist persuasions but also, at the opposite end of the spectrum, by highly influential persons who believed that Cyprian's mediating position was still much too harsh. A number of African confessors demanded immediate and unconditional reconciliation for all who desired it. The confessors' status in the community was significant because they had proven their faithfulness to God in the face of persecution. Representing the laxist party was the deacon Felicissimus. He surrounded himself with a group of Cyprian's opponents whose number included several presbyters who had originally resisted Cyprian's election as overseer. The appointment of a rival Carthaginian bishop, Fortunatus, exacerbated the animosities (circa summer 252 C.E.).

Soon after Fortunatus's election, a delegation headed by Felicissimus went to Rome to seek Cornelius's support. Cornelius resisted their entreaties, maintaining his loyalty to Cyprian. Cyprian reflects upon this conflict in several of his writings. The family metaphor finds particularly pointed application in a letter that Cyprian wrote to Cornelius. Felicissimus and his party treacherously seek "all over the province brethren they may ensnare and despoil" (*Ep.* 59.16.2). But this, in Cyprian's view, should not come as a surprise to him or to his brother Cornelius. Indeed, sibling betrayal has characterized the lives of the faithful for generations:

> We can see that our Lord Himself was seized by His own brethren and betrayed by a man whom He had Himself chosen to be one of the apostles. So it was, too, in the very beginning of the world. The just Abel was slain by none other than his own brother; Jacob was pursued in flight by his enraged brother; Joseph as a boy was put up for sale with his very own brothers as traders. In the Gospel, too, we read it foretold that it will chiefly be from our own household that our enemies will come, that those who have previously been united together by the sacred bond of fellowship will betray one another. . . . It can bring no disgrace upon us to suffer at the hands of our own brethren just as Christ Himself suffered. (*Ep.* 59.2.4)

The Old Testament illustrations of sibling discord that Cyprian uses are now familiar to the reader. Notice, though, how Cyprian's rhetoric leads him to remove the New Testament sayings of Jesus from their original context and apply them in an innovative way to the problems at hand. In the Gospels, Jesus' predictions of family division apply to individuals who choose allegiance to Jesus' community vis-à-vis their families of origin. Those who followed Jesus would open themselves up to enmity from members of their own blood families.

Cyprian instead applies the prediction to discord and betrayal among members of the family of faith. According to Cyprian's interpretation of the saying, Jesus predicted "that those who have previously been united together by the sacred bond of fellowship [would] betray one another" (*Ep.* 59.2.4). It remains for Cyprian and his "dearly beloved brother" Cornelius to stand fast and "preserve unshakable strength of faith, and a courage that is unyielding" (*Ep.* 59.2.3).

The North African schism between Cyprian and his colleagues, on the one hand, and the party of Felicissimus and Fortunatus, on the other, also receives attention in another important treatise. In the following passage, Cyprian again appropriates family imagery from both Old and New Testament materials in his attempt to demonstrate that the members of the opposing camp are behaving in a manner totally inappropriate for siblings who claim to appeal to the same father:

> So too when He gave the law of prayer, He added, saying: "And when you stand to pray, forgive whatever you have against anyone, that your Father also who is in heaven

may forgive you your offenses." And He calls back from the altar one who comes to the sacrifice with dissension, and He orders him first to be reconciled with his brother and then return with peace and offer his gift to God, because God did not look with favor upon the gifts of Cain; for he could not have God at peace with him, who through envious discord did not have peace with his brother. What peace then do the enemies of the brethren promise themselves? What sacrifices do the imitators of priests believe that they celebrate? (*De Cath. Eccl.* 13)

Cyprian here uses the Cain-and-Abel narrative to illustrate the teaching of Jesus in order to suggest that the "imitators of priests" (that is, the schismatic leaders) cannot "have God at peace" with them because they remain "enemies of the brethren." Indeed, for Cyprian, the schismatic is worse than one who succumbs to pagan threats during times of persecution, for the former deceives not only himself but others as well: "That one, swelling in his sin and taking pleasure in his very crimes, separates children from their Mother" (*De Cath. Eccl.* 13).

The themes of family loyalty and betrayal thus appear often in the writings of Cyprian of Carthage. He uses the loyalty idea both to encourage Christians to remain faithful to God during times of persecution and as a rhetorical device to marginalize schismatic leaders and their followers. I will now conclude my examination of Cyprian's writings with a discussion of another central PKG value that often surfaces in the North African overseer's letters and treatises: generalized reciprocity.

THE SHARING OF MATERIAL RESOURCES

The second practical aspect of Cyprian's conception of proper behavior among those who understand God to be their Father (see "act as sons of God," *Dom. Or.* 11, above) is generalized reciprocity expressed in the sharing of material resources. Cyprian closes *Epistle* 12, written from his place of hiding during the Decian persecution (circa April–May 250 C.E.), with the following exhortation to the clergy at Carthage:

> As I have by now frequently written, be unsparing also in the care and attention you give to the poor—that is to say, the poor who, standing steadfast in the faith and fighting valiantly on our side, have not deserted the battlements of Christ. They are now deserving of even greater love and concern from us, for they have been neither constrained by poverty nor overthrown by the storm of persecution, but by remaining faithful servants of the Lord they have, besides, set the rest of the poor an example of faith. I wish that you, my most dear and cherished brothers, may ever fare well and be mindful of us. Greet our brothers in my name. Farewell. (*Ep.* 12.2.2)

Meeting the needs of the impoverished among the brotherhood is central to Cyprian's theology of Christian community. Nowhere is this more clearly illustrated than in a treatise in which Cyprian attributes the Decian persecution directly to a failure on the part of certain members of the community to practice this Mediterranean family value in their relations with their less fortunate brethren. The excerpts that follow were read at a church council that met in Carthage in 251 C.E., soon after Cyprian's return to the city. Reflecting upon the suffering of the previous year, the North African bishop observes:

> Nevertheless, most beloved brethren. . . . If the cause of the disaster is known, the remedy for the wound also is found. The Lord wished his family to be proved, and, because a long peace had corrupted the discipline divinely handed down to us, a heavenly rebuke has aroused a prostrate and, I might say, sleeping faith, and, although we deserved more on account of our sins, the most merciful Lord has so moderated all things, that all that has happened seemed an examination rather than a persecution. (*Laps.* 5)

Cyprian's theology apparently demands that he somehow locate "the cause of the disaster" in God's orchestration of human events: the church had grown lax and "the Lord wished his family to be proved." Cyprian proceeds to outline those areas of "the discipline divinely handed down" that the faithful had abandoned in the years leading up to the persecution. Among them is the responsibility of the rich in the community to meet the practical needs of the poor. Instead of doing their Christian duty, the wealthy "wandered through the foreign provinces and sought the market places for gainful business; while their brethren in the church were starving, they wished to possess money in abundance" (*Laps.* 6). Notice the centrality of the kinship metaphor in each of the above excerpts. God's "family" had to be "proved," because certain high-status community members failed to meet a family obligation to help their starving "brethren in the church."

It is not enough to explain and mourn past failings. Later in the same treatise, Cyprian employs the power of his pen in an effort to prevent a return to the "sleeping faith" that, regrettably, characterized the church before the outbreak of the persecution (*Laps.* 5). In view of the above, the reader is not surprised to find Cyprian particularly skeptical of the sincerity of allegedly penitent high-status Christians. Their unbrotherly administration of their goods had contributed to the onset of the persecution; they then denied the faith; and now they wish to be readmitted to the Christian community. For Cyprian, traditional acts of penitence are insufficient evidence of a change of heart:

> Do we think that he laments with a whole heart, implores the Lord with fastings, weepings, and mournings, who from the first day of his crime daily frequents the baths, who, feeding on rich banquets and distended by fuller dainties, belches forth the undigested food on the next day, and does not share his food and drink with the needy poor? (*Laps.* 30)

It is only in the equitable distribution of the basic necessities of life that Cyprian recognizes the genuine expression of Christian brotherhood.

I will cite a final example from Cyprian's writings of PKG solidarity tangibly expressed in the sharing of material resources. Sometime between his return from exile (Easter 251 C.E.) and his relegation to Curubis (August 257 C.E.), Cyprian received a letter from eight Numidian bishops requesting moneys to ransom church members who had been captured during raids by barbarians.[56] Cyprian's remarkable reply deserves extended citation, since it places Carthage's generous response to the Numidians' request squarely in the context of the social matrix of the church as a family:

> It has caused us the gravest anguish in our hearts, dearly beloved brothers, and indeed it brought tears to our eyes to read your letter which in your love and anxiety you wrote to us about our brothers and sisters who are now held in captive hands. Who would not be distressed at such a calamity or who would not reckon the distress which his brother feels as his own, remembering the words which the apostle Paul speaks: "If one member suffers, the other members also suffer with it; and if one member rejoices, the other members also rejoice with it" [1 Cor 12:26]. And in another place he asks: "Who is weak and I am not weak also?" [2 Cor 11:29]. We must now, accordingly, reckon the captivity of our brethren as our captivity also, and we must account the distress of those in peril as our own distress; for, I need hardly remind you, in our union we form but one body and, therefore, not just love but our religion ought to rouse and spur us on to redeem brethren who are our fellow members. (*Ep.* 62.1.1-2)

The affective sibling bond, so characteristic of family relations in ancient Mediterranean society, clearly serves as the driving rhetorical image for the above text segment.

The family metaphor is not, however, the only image Cyprian draws upon to illustrate solidarity as it ideally should function among North African Christians. The captive Christians should also be redeemed (a) because they are temples of God, and (b) because in redeeming their fellow Christians they are redeeming Christ who indwells them (*Ep.* 62.2.1-2). Nevertheless, the family image remains central, since it is the metaphor with which Cyprian opens and closes his epistle. Indeed, sibling terms appear sixteen times in the short letter. The following passages describe the Carthaginians' generous response to the request of their Numidian brethren:

> And so [our brethren] all forthwith contributed most willingly generous financial aid for their brothers. Being of such robust faith, they are ever ready to do the works of God; but on this occasion they were more than usually fired to perform such works of mercy by their awareness of these distressing circumstances. (*Ep.* 62.3.1)

Accordingly, we are sending in cash one hundred thousand sesterces which have been collected from the contributions of the clergy and the laity who reside here with us in the church over which, by God's favour, we have charge. This is for you to distribute with your wonted diligence. Our fervent wish is indeed that nothing similar should happen in the future and that our brothers, under the protection of the Lord's majesty, may be kept safe from all such perils. If, however, in order to test and examine the faith and charity in our hearts, anything of the kind should befall you, do not hesitate to write word of it to us; you can be fully confident and assured that whilst our church and all of the brethren here do pray that this should never occur again, yet, if it does, they will willingly provide generous assistance. (*Ep.* 62.3.2—62.4.1)

Cyprian then informs his readers that he is appending a list of the "brothers and sisters" who participated in the collection so that the Numidians can remember them in their prayers. He concludes by writing, "We wish that you, dearly beloved brothers, may ever fare well in the Lord and be mindful of us" (*Ep.* 62.4.2).

CONCLUSION

Christianity in North Africa, as evidenced in the writings examined in the course of this chapter, consistently emphasized the indelible social boundary that separated the faithful from the pagan society which surrounded them. In the writings of Tertullian, as Frend observes, "[The North African] church was set irrevocably against paganism and against a Christianity that would compromise with the pagan world."[57]

Much the same could be said for the other writers surveyed in this chapter. In such a polarized social context, the family metaphor proved to be an especially useful idea for illustrating and reinforcing North African convictions about Christian community, in terms readily understood by the faithful. Family loyalty and the responsibility of siblings to meet one another's material needs—the two behavioral aspects of the PKG metaphor most evidenced in North African Christian literature—were values with which persons in antiquity were eminently familiar. They were also values particularly suitable to an alternative community that understood itself to be surrounded by a hostile pagan world and that experienced treatment at the hands of local authorities which served to reinforce such convictions. The family metaphor, then, served to define and reinforce the boundary between the North African church and the non-Christian world of Roman Carthage, and it helped remind the faithful of their obligations to their siblings in the family of God.

The kinship metaphor also found another important application, in the writings of Cyprian of Carthage. Along with the boundary between Christians and pagans, mentioned above, the communities of North African Christians were significantly polarized. Cyprian found himself at odds with a number of Christian leaders who failed to share his convictions concerning rebaptism and the reconciliation of the lapsed. In these cases, the family image proved itself a powerful rhetorical weapon in Cyprian's conflicts with those who chose to operate outside the approved channels of ecclesiastical hierarchy. As I demonstrated, Cyprian often drew upon the *topoi* of sibling loyalty and betrayal in order to stigmatize schismatic leaders and their misled followers.

To summarize my discussion of Christian North Africa, the evidence outlined in the course of the above survey leads me to conclude that among Christian writers in third-century Carthage, the predominant social model for community, as reflected both in terminology and in interpersonal behavior, continued to be the Mediterranean patrilineal kinship group. For Tertullian, Cyprian, and others whose surviving works inform us of North African social convictions, the church was a family.

7

Summary and Evaluation

Scholars have devoted much attention in recent years to the social history of the Jesus movement, including the highlighting of various aspects of the kinship model of Christian community. This is the first study, to my knowledge, however, that has sought to carefully construct a structural and behavioral model of the ancient Mediterranean family and then utilize the model as a grid with which to understand a broad sampling of conceptions about Christian community, from the time of Jesus of Nazareth to the mid-third century c.e. I will adopt a topical, rather than chronological, approach to summarize my findings.

The Mediterranean Family Model

Underlying the differences between various ancient family systems (for example, Roman versus Judean), which I acknowledged in an earlier chapter, there existed in the ancient world a circum-Mediterranean traditional social system whereby a number of societal traits—kinship ideals included—were similar in various Mediterranean regions. I will here refrain from reiterating the extensive list of kinship traits shared among Mediterranean peoples, which I discussed in chapter 2.

I will, however, remind the reader of two foundational aspects of the ancient Mediterranean family that members of the Jesus movement appropriated and reworked as they sought to apply the PKG model to their local communities. These two characteristics are particularly indispensable to a proper understanding of the early church's self-identification as a family. They warrant brief restatement in the present context because they represent kinship values that are, as a rule, quite foreign to the experience of modern Westerners: the emphasis on the group over the individual and the priority of the sibling bond. These qualities of ancient kinship orientation help explain much of what constituted the family value system (and corresponding behavioral components) shared by patrilineal kinship groups throughout the Mediterranean region. They also form the basis for the Christian conception of the church as a surrogate family.

The Highly Corporate Nature of the Ancient Family

The corporate nature of ancient kinship systems is a reflection of broader societal conventions. The ancient Mediterranean world exemplifies what cultural anthropologists call a collectivist society. For most persons, the health and survival of the group(s) to which they belonged took precedence over their own personal advancement and well-being. Since the family constituted the primary focus of group loyalty for persons in Mediterranean antiquity, the high solidarity so characteristic of the ancient family simply represented an intensification of the general cultural conviction that one's personal identity was strongly embedded in the group to which one belonged.

In chapter 2, I discussed contrasts that anthropologists have observed between collectivist cultures and descent group family structures, on the one hand (for example, Mediterranean antiquity), and individualistic societies and kindred family systems, on the other (for example, modern America). In societies that value the group over the individual, one typically finds families organized according to lineage. Individualistic cultures, by contrast, usually evidence some variation of the "ego-focus" nuclear family so familiar to modern Westerners. Ancient Mediterranean peoples lived in a collectivist society reflecting the corresponding descent group model of family structure and relations. An appreciation of the high-group orientation of the collectivist worldview is an indispensable prerequisite to a proper understanding of (a) the Mediterranean family and (b) its appropriation as the preeminent model for early Christian social organization.

The high-group nature of ancient society, with the patrilineal kinship group as its archetypal expression, explains many of the values and behaviors referenced earlier in this work (see chapter 2): (1) concern for family survival, expressed in preoccupation with inheritance issues and ancestor veneration; (2) the obligation to come to the aid of a family member in need of material support or military assistance; (3) abhorrence of the betrayal of one family member at the hands of another; and (4) concern to preserve the family's public reputation even at the expense of truth. To summarize, the highly corporate nature of the family, along with the centrality of family in the world of pagans and Christians, meant that the well-being of one's patrilineal kinship group was the most important value held by persons in Mediterranean antiquity. The result was an incontestable loyalty to one's family. Family membership in antiquity was, of course, determined by consanguinity (blood relation).

The Priority of the Sibling Bond

The primary locus for the intense kinship solidarity and loyalty associated with a collectivist family system is not the marriage relationship. Rather, in Mediterranean antiquity, the behaviors associated with family loyalty and piety find expression predominantly among persons who are related to one another by blood, and who therefore seek to protect the honor of—and provide for the material needs of—their patrilineal kinship groups. My survey of ancient literature revealed that sibling solidarity, tangibly demonstrated in the generous support of one's brothers and sisters in nearly every area of life (for example, material and emotional), constituted the preeminent expression of family solidarity in Mediterranean society (chapter 2). Conversely, sibling betrayal represented the most reprehensible of behaviors for persons socialized into the descent group system of family ideals. Indeed, even today in the rural Mediterranean, sibling strife constitutes "the paradigm of implacable enmity."[1]

These two values—the highly corporate nature of the ancient family and the priority of the sibling bond—are the foundational characteristics of the ancient Mediterranean family, as evidenced by the numerous quotations from the source materials cited in chapter 2. Jesus of Nazareth and his earliest followers adopted and reworked these values to construct their powerful and enduring metaphor of the church as a kinship group (see chapter 3). During the two hundred years that followed, Christians continued to view the family model as central to their social vision for the communities to which they belonged. In this book, I have detailed various permutations that the family model experienced during the first three centuries of the common era. It will help here, in the conclusion of my project, to remind the reader of several general characteristics of the church family model that remained constant throughout the literature surveyed.

The corporate nature of the ancient family meant that Christians who put this metaphor into practice exercised genuine concern to preserve the honor of their local church communities and to meet the material needs of the group's individual members. Christians also demanded (and at times exercised) a high degree of loyalty to the church family. This, too, finds explanation in the collectivist approach to family life. The priority of the sibling bond meant that early Christian writers possessed a powerful linguistic symbol—brother-sister terminology—with which to

socialize community members into conforming to family standards or to marginalize those perceived to be betrayers of the brotherhood. These various characteristics
of the kinship model, as it was used by the early Christians, can be treated under
the rubrics of "rhetoric" and "praxis."

THE CHURCH AS A FAMILY

First, I will offer some final reflections on the rhetorical use of family language by
the authors surveyed in the course of the book. A summary of the practical expressions of family solidarity evidenced among the early Christians will follow.

Family as Rhetoric

My examination of early Christian writings has confirmed Roger Keesing's observations that kinship terminology is often used "in situations when [a] person is violating the norms of kinship," or in situations in which one individual is "trying to
manipulate" another.[2] The appropriation of family language as a rhetorical device
used to engender desired behaviors is a common strategy among Christian authors,
and both of Keesing's categories can be amply illustrated from the writings of the
early Christians.[3] I will now evaluate this strategy in the context of the broader
debate surrounding the rhetorical-manipulative use of religious symbols in general.

Controlling models, such as the family metaphor, offer "organizing power and
integrating vision" to religious communities.[4] It would be naive to deny, however,
that such powerful symbols are also potentially destructive. Earlier scholars working
in the field readily acknowledged both the positive and negative aspects of the persuasiveness of religious language.[5] Recent, postmodern, treatments of ancient Christian texts increasingly emphasize the negative, manipulative applications of religious
metaphor. Indeed, postmodern thinkers, in nearly all areas of literary and social
theory, have consistently transposed issues of truth and argument into questions of
power and rhetoric. As a result, postmodern readings of Christian documents tend
to be highly suspicious in their assessment of the ends to which rhetorical language
is used by ancient writers.

The postmodern deconstructionist approach to reading materials generated by
the Jesus movement has produced several sharply negative evaluations of the ancient
authors' use of religious symbols, in general, and the kinship metaphor, in particular. Scholars such as Graham Shaw, Stephen Moore, and Elizabeth Castelli, for
example, forcefully charge Paul of Tarsus with wholesale manipulation in his
rhetorical strategies—Paul utilizes symbolic language only to reinforce the community's highly stratified hierarchy of power and privilege.

Graham Shaw's monograph *The Cost of Authority: Manipulation and Freedom in the New Testament* contends that both the author of Mark's Gospel and Paul of Tarsus are wholly manipulative in their rhetorical strategies. According to Shaw, Mark's presentation of Jesus is such that the reader must either reject Jesus as an enigma or else share in the church's understanding of Jesus. For Shaw, "God" is the manipulative device of those who wield power.[6] In a later work, Shaw claims regarding the God of theism that "the only function of that God is to deter change; he is the classic ally of the privileged and powerful."[7]

Stephen Moore is another scholar who has recently attempted to read early Christian literature through the lens of postmodernism. Building on the seminal thinking of Michel Foucault, Moore contends that the exercise of discipline in early Christ-confessing communities is inextricably "bound up with power." Discipline has only one purpose, according to Foucault: the production of "docile bodies."[8] Hence, according to Moore, Paul of Tarsus uses the threat of divine judgment (Rom 2:16, 29; 1 Cor 4:5) to extract admissions, acknowledgments, agreements, and confessions. In his own experience as a former monk, Moore recalls that during his time in the monastery, the image of the tortured Jesus on the cross was used to enact what Foucault calls "the quiet game of the well behaved," that is, to reinforce the community's hierarchy.[9]

The wholesale skepticism reflected in such postmodern treatments of early Christian imagery extends to a recent evaluation of Paul's use of an aspect of the kinship metaphor, as well. In my analysis of Paul's first letter to the community at Corinth, I located in his use of the kinship model Paul's charge to the Corinthians to be his "imitators" (1 Cor 4:14-17). Paul, I suggested, reminds his readers that he is their spiritual progenitor. Like a good Mediterranean father, he then challenges his offspring to behave in a manner characteristic of the new family to which they now belong. From information gathered elsewhere in 1 Corinthians, which elucidates Paul's conception of the kinship metaphor, one fairly presumes that such behavior would reflect as its central component the commendable sibling-like solidarity characteristic of a group of persons who relate to one another as members of a Mediterranean family.

Elizabeth Castelli, however, has recently taken a much less positive view of Paul's motivation and strategy.[10] She interprets the imitation *topos* as a manipulative rhetorical scheme that, according to one reviewer, "serves purposes of power and social control in the interests of pre-determined norms which exclude 'deviancy.'"[11] In Castelli's own words, Paul's comments about imitating his behavior (1 Cor 11:1; Phil 3:17; 1 Thess 1:6, 2:14) move "only in one direction . . . the hierarchical view of imitation . . . power relations; an issue of 'group identity' . . . exclusivity . . . sameness."[12] Paul seeks to exclude alternative behaviors in areas relating to the physical dimensions of life, such as sexual behavior and food practices. Paul therefore has little tolerance for diversity in his communities. According to Castelli, "By promoting the value of sameness he [Paul] is also shaping relations of power."[13]

Negative evaluations of the use of religious symbols are thus increasingly common in postmodern interpretations of New Testament writings. Paul of Tarsus has become a particular focus of attention in this regard. As Thiselton has noted, "If Castelli and Moore were correct, Paul's appeal on behalf of unity and well-being of the whole community might be said to have arisen from a combination of self-deception (of the kind diagnosed by Niebuhr) and manipulation (of the kind noted in the claims of Graham Shaw to whom Castelli alludes)."[14] The other early Christian writings examined in my previous chapters are, of course, open to similarly negative readings. The kinship metaphor is then reduced to a rhetorical strategy adopted solely to reinforce the hierarchical social order of early Christian communities.

Such interpretations of Paul, however, simply cannot command acceptance given the abundant evidence to the contrary uncovered in the course of this survey.[15] The source material that I have examined and extensively cited demands a more balanced evaluation of the Christians' use of the family metaphor. Obviously I am unable to enter into an extended dialogue with postmodern philosophy and reading theory in the present context. It should be clear by now, however, that I take a more historical-contextual approach to the source material—specifically, I assume that the meaning that the ancient author intended his writing to communicate to his readers is both (a) discoverable and (b) relevant to the interpretation of the text.[16] This approach to ancient texts, so self-evident to the historian trained in the grammatical-historical method of interpretation, can no longer be taken for granted.[17]

Castelli, for example, attaches the following disclaimer to her postmodern reading of Paul, referred to above: "Whether Paul *meant* or *intended* that his discourse be understood in the way I have argued is not a question that I have answered. . . . My reading is not the only possible or plausible one."[18] This disclaimer, however, renders Castelli's analysis, and the conclusions she reaches, virtually unassailable from a strictly historical perspective. Indeed, it is precisely what Paul "meant or intended" by his utilization of the family metaphor that has occupied my attention in a significant portion of this work (see chapter 4). To dismiss authorial intention, along with the meaning of ancient texts in their original historical and cultural contexts, is wholly to remove literary and historical analysis from the realm of relative objectivity.[19] As is the case with many postmodern readings, one learns more from Castelli's monograph about *her response* to Paul's writings than about Paul's intentions in the historical and cultural context in which he lived.[20]

Those who place a premium on the meaning Paul intended in, for example, 1 Corinthians, and who are optimistic about the possibility of identifying his intentions, have come to interpretations markedly different from those of Castelli and Moore. With respect to Paul's central symbol of a crucified cult figure, several studies have argued along different lines to a similar conclusion: Paul's appeal to "Christ crucified" has nothing to do with "Moore's notion of pointing to an image of a tortured man to promote moral blackmail."[21] Rather, Paul employs the symbol of the rejection and humiliation of Jesus in order to attack the oppression of low-status church members by the privileged in the Corinthian community.[22]

The same applies more specifically to the imitation theme. Paul exhorts the Corinthian community to imitate a pattern of humility and servanthood for the purpose of neither conformity nor control. Instead, as Stephen Pogoloff demonstrates, Paul desires to protect those who might otherwise be marginalized or in some sense considered socially inferior.[23] Castelli's monograph also fails to convincingly refute the findings of Robert Jewett, who demonstrates that Paul was highly concerned for tolerance and for the acceptance of a significant amount of diversity in his communities.[24]

Religious symbols are, indeed, powerful, and it would be naive to deny their abuse throughout human history. A rigorous and sophisticated approach avoids both the extreme skepticism and pessimism evidenced in the postmodern readings mentioned above (for example, "the Nietzschean assumption that *all* controlling models in *all* theology *necessarily* function as disguised power-bids") and the kind of blind optimism that has so often resulted in the employment of religious models to legitimate political self-interest (resulting, to be sure, in the kind of "power-bids" that understandably have generated the very cynicism postmodernism reflects).[25] As Thiselton rightly remarks in his discussion of the usages of religious language, "We need more patiently to *look* at the *variety of particular cases* which together reflect certain patterns of what Wittgenstein calls 'overlapping and criss-crossing.' Some particular cases reflect self-giving service in creative love; others, manipulation in the interests of power."[26]

Examples that fit both of Thiselton's categories have surfaced in the course of this study. Negatively, I observed that Ignatius transferred the father metaphor from the divine to the human realm to legitimate the authority of local church leadership. Similarly, Clement of Rome presented obedience to God on the part of Old Testament patriarchs as a model for his readers to imitate. Clement's intention was that those in the Corinthian community who had rebelled and removed their overseers would instead submit to recognized community leaders. As I now reflect back on my survey, however, I am surprised to discover just how seldom the kinship metaphor is used purely in the service of power by the writers whose works I have examined.

For example, the locus of power in the Mediterranean patrilineal kinship group was in the family's patriarch. Correspondingly, among the various images that make up the church-family model, the father metaphor has the greatest potential for abuse. A local transition from plurality leadership to one-man oversight (circa 110 C.E. in the eastern Mediterranean) opened the door for the use of paternal language as a device to legitimate the concentration of power in the hands of a single individual. Community members could then be encouraged to submit to the fatherly authority of the local church leader, in order to reinforce community hierarchy. Here, of all places, the interpreter would expect to encounter religious language employed for Nietzschean, self-serving, ends. It is striking, therefore, to observe just how rarely the authors whose works I examined exercised this option in their use of the father metaphor. For the most part, the writers surveyed persist in assigning father imagery to the divine realm, appropriating for themselves instead a sibling role in their interactions with persons in the communities to which they write.

Of course, the sibling model itself was not immune to use as a vehicle for social control, as illustrated by Cyprian's use of the betrayal theme to marginalize recalcitrant schismatics. Most often, however, sibling language is employed by these early Christian writers not to delineate the boundaries between orthodox and heterodox Christians but rather to encourage (or describe) family-like behavior among community members. It is here, I suggest, that the PKG model offered the kind of "organizing power and integrating vision" that gave the early Christians their social identity and stability, and that made their communities so attractive to displaced and fragmented urbanites in antiquity.[27] At its best, the realization of PKG sibling solidarity meant that the individual Christian, whether slave or free, Roman or barbarian, could count on her brothers and sisters in the faith to provide the affective and material support necessary for survival in the ancient world. Judging by the amount of evidence gathered in the course of this project, tangible expressions of family solidarity were quite commonplace among Christians who lived in the Roman Empire during the first three centuries of the common era.

The student of the Jesus movement would do well to evaluate the integrity of Christian family rhetoric in precisely this context. Deconstructing ancient writings by removing them from their sociohistorical contexts and reading them with a hermeneutic of suspicion yield very little historical insight. The historian must instead interpret the family metaphor in the culture in which it was used. What he will discover, as I believe my study has amply demonstrated, is that the persons who typically benefited from the employment of the kinship metaphor in ancient Christian circles were not community leaders, who thereby legitimated their own positions of authority and reinforced the social hierarchy.

Rather, those who had the most to gain from the image of the church as a family were the poor, the hungry, the enslaved, the imprisoned, the orphans, and the widows. For brother-sister terminology in antiquity had nothing to do with hierarchy, power, and privilege, but everything to do with equality, solidarity, and generalized reciprocity. Richard Horsley identifies a "pattern of horizontal reciprocal social-economic relations" that characterized the earliest Christian communities.[28] I maintain that the broadly attested and deeply rooted early Christian conception of the church as a family of surrogate siblings best explains the pattern of behavior Horsley describes. As one of the early Christians' contemporaries disparagingly quipped, "Their first lawgiver persuaded them that they are all brothers of one another" (Lucian, *Peregr.* 13).

Family as Praxis

Examples abound of sibling solidarity enjoined by Christian writers and practiced in early Christian communities. Paul constantly uses brother-sister language to challenge his communities to treat one another like Mediterranean siblings. Such behavior includes the following: (1) refraining from avenging a wrong suffered at the hand of another community member (1 Cor 6:1-11); (2) equitable distribution of the community's resources to meet the pressing needs of indigent Christians (2 Corinthians 8–9); (3) honoring (rather than seeking honor from) one's siblings in the faith (Rom 12:10); and (4) manumitting (or, at least, in other ways treating as a "beloved brother") a slave who had become a Christian (Phlm 15b-16).

Paul also draws upon the family loyalty theme to argue that the Christian's primary focus of loyalty should be her faith family of siblings (1 Cor 7:12-16). Moreover, Paul's writings regularly reveal the kind of affective relationship between author and readers that one would expect among siblings in a Mediterranean family (for example, 1 Thess 2:7b-8, 11-12; 2:17—3:8).

Sources from the second century reveal much the same emphasis. *1 Clement* refers to the practice of certain individuals who sold themselves into bondage and slavery to acquire finances to help the community's poor and starving (55.2). Ignatius is aware of churches that are using their resources to manumit slaves upon conversion (*Pol.* 4.3). Justin Martyr describes the administration of a common community fund from which the local Christian leader "takes care of orphans and widows, and those who are in want on account of sickness or any other cause" (1 *Apol.* 67). Clement of Alexandria devotes a whole treatise to the theme of generalized reciprocity. The high-status community member must recognize that he "holds possessions and gold and silver and houses as gifts of God . . . for his brothers' sakes rather than his own" (*Quis Div.* 16). Pagans, too, are aware of the Christians' self-identification and behavior as a family. They also recognize that the kinship metaphor provides the obvious explanation for the Christian practice of generalized reciprocity expressed in the sharing of material resources (Lucian, *Peregr.* 13).

For the third century, I narrowed my geographical focus to the North African metropolis of Carthage. The radical rejection of the secular world so characteristic of Carthaginian Christianity rendered the kinship metaphor especially appropriate as a symbol for community life. Perpetua's exchange of attachment to her earthly father for complete loyalty to her heavenly father set a benchmark for commitment to the Christian family, which was immortalized in Perpetua's first-person account of events leading up to her martyrdom. The commitment of Perpetua and other Carthaginian confessors is not left unrewarded, as their fellow Christians, in accordance with typical Mediterranean family practices, travel to their prison cells to visit with them and to meet their material needs for food and clothing (see Tertullian, *Ad Mart.* 1.1). Tertullian writes of care extended to "the support and burial of the poor . . . children who are without their parents . . . aged men who are confined to the house . . . shipwrecked sailors, and . . . any in the mines, on islands or in prisons" (*Apol.* 39.6-7).

Cyprian reveals an African church whose moral code demands that one church member cease from his profession, but whose family orientation guarantees that the brother's material needs will continue to be met, now through the community's resources. Again and again in Cyprian's writings, the reader encounters the Carthaginian overseer's concern to provide daily necessities for imprisoned confessors and for the poor in the church (*Ep.* 5.1.2; 7.2; 12.2.2; 13.7.1). Most striking is Cyprian's generous response to the appeal of an outlying church that requests financial assistance to redeem members held hostage by bandit raiders (*Ep.* 62).

The evidence of early Christian kinship solidarity during the first three centuries of the common era, moreover, is hardly exhausted in the sources I have cited.[29] As a final indication of the ubiquitous nature of the family metaphor, I offer a quotation from an important third-century source. Around 260 c.e., a devastating plague afflicted the great city of Alexandria. Eusebius records a letter written by Dionysius, the overseer of the Christian community in the city:

> The most, at all events, of our brethren in their exceeding love and affection for the brotherhood were unsparing of themselves and clave to one another, visiting the sick without a thought as to the danger, assiduously ministering to them, tending them in Christ, and so most gladly departed this life along with them; being infected with the disease from others, drawing upon themselves the sickness from their neighbours, and willingly taking over their pains. . . . In this manner the best at any rate of our brethren departed this life, certain presbyters and deacons and some of the laity. . . . So, too, the bodies of the saints they would take up in their open hands to their bosom, closing

their eyes and shutting their mouths, carrying them on their shoulders and laying them out; they would cling to them, embrace them, bathe and adorn them with their burial clothes, and after a little while receive the same services themselves, for those that were left behind were ever following those that went before. But the conduct of the heathen was the exact opposite. Even those who were in the first stages of the disease they thrust away, and fled from their dearest. They would even cast them in the roads half-dead, and treat the unburied corpses as vile refuse. (*Hist. Eccl.* 7.22)

Dionysius begins his description with the use of kinship terminology: "brethren," "the brotherhood." He closes with a pointed contrast, comparing the behavior of his Alexandrian Christians with behavior among blood kin groups in the surrounding community (for example, they "fled from their dearest"). He clearly views his church community as a well-functioning kin group, and he is proud that they are living up to their family ideals.

I argued above that instances of the rhetorical use of the family metaphor need to be carefully evaluated and neither summarily dismissed as abusive nor uncritically accepted as constructive. Care must also be exercised in the reading of descriptive text-segments such as that cited from Eusebius, above. Gerhard Lohfink is correct to assert that such passages are "public relations" texts that paint an ideal picture. "This is how the Christians wish to be seen, how they would like to be."[30] Certainly the marginalization of pagan family behavior, in the above letter, as wholly impious— they "fled from their dearest"—smacks of hyperbole and exaggeration. To some degree, the same is likely the case for the idealized picture of the Jesus movement in Alexandria. As Lohfink notes, "It is impossible to draw conclusions from texts of this sort about the concrete reality of the Christian communities in a direct and unreflected way."[31]

Two considerations, however, prevent us from dismissing as wholesale propaganda the examples of the practical expression of sibling solidarity encountered in the course of this study. The first is the ubiquitous nature of the evidence. Data portraying the early Christians living out their family symbolism in day-to-day community life is simply too extensive to ignore or reinterpret. Moreover, much of this evidence surfaces not in conscious attempts to portray the early Christians as virtuous siblings against the foil of pagan impiety (as is the case with the quotation from Dionysius's letter, above). Rather, many of the most striking examples of early Christian communities putting metaphor into practice arise, one might say, almost in passing, in general correspondence from one Christian to other members of the family of faith. Cyprian's letter to Eucratius, the overseer at Thenae, is representative (see chapter 6). Eucratius had previously written Cyprian to seek his advice concerning the propriety of a Christian teaching the craft of acting. Cyprian disallowed the activity in question but encouraged the Thenan Christians to provide food, clothing, and shelter for the former actor.

Apart from the fortuitous survival of Cyprian's reply to Eucratius, the student of early Christian social practices would remain unaware of the Carthaginian church's policy of undertaking the material support of those whose livelihoods were adversely affected by their commitment to the Christian faith. In similar fashion, the reader learns from Ignatius's epistle to Polycarp—again incidentally—that churches in the East were drawing money from the common fund to manumit slaves who had converted to the Jesus movement. From Paul's correspondence, a scenario can be pieced together that shows Paul's Gentile churches sending alimentary aid to their indigent surrogate siblings in Jerusalem. In none of these texts can the author be reasonably charged with conscious posturing in an effort to portray the Christian family of faith in a positive light. Illustrations of this kind could be multiplied.

A second and final consideration also argues for a positive evaluation of the evidence for sibling solidarity among the early Christians. Lohfink, who cautioned above against uncritical readings of Christian literature, nevertheless maintains that text-segments like those cited in the course of this book "surely reflect a portion of the reality of the communities themselves."[32] Lohfink is writing as an insider (that is, his inclusive language in the following excerpt suggests he understands himself to be a Christian), but his comments nevertheless reflect sound historical judgment:

> It would be a miserable hermeneutic to tone down ancient Christian texts merely because we moderns, in our skeptical resignation, no longer consider it possible for communities to take the gospel seriously. The few important voices of the ancient *opponents* of Christianity should preserve us from a hermeneutic born of a bad conscience, desirous of preparing a historical alibi for our own conditions.[33]

Lohfink's point: even individuals inimical to the Jesus movement nevertheless acknowledged the family-like behavior that characterized local Christian communities. I have already cited and discussed the observations of Lucian of Samosata (chapter 5). Lucian, who can hardly be charged with bias in favor of the Christian movement, explicitly related the surrogate sibling idea to the practice of sharing material resources that he observed among the Christians he had encountered in various locales in the empire. The Roman emperor Julian was an avowed pagan who postdates the time frame covered by my survey. His observations nevertheless form a fitting summary to the present discussion. Julian writes to Arsacius, High-Priest of Galatia, as part of his attempt to encourage renewed interest in paganism:

Why do we not observe that it is their [the Christians'] benevolence to strangers, their care for the graves of the dead and the pretended holiness of their lives that have done the most to increase atheism?. . . When . . . the impious Galilaeans support not only their own poor, but ours as well, all men see that our people lack aid from us. (*Letter to Arsarcius*)

The extensive amount of evidence from Christian writings, along with the confirming voice of pagan detractors such as Lucian and Julian, encourages the student of Christian social formation to take seriously the early Christians' claim that the family metaphor found tangible expression in the day-to-day activities of their local communities throughout the Roman Empire.

CONCLUSION

More consistently uniform than the various theological formulations and convictions championed by the early Christians, the social organization of the pre-Constantinian house churches was perhaps the single most common and identifiable characteristic of the Jesus movement. Arland Jacobson's comments relate specifically to the first century, but his observations could be extended into the middle of the third century:

It is well known that the early Christian church was a house-church movement. It could hardly have been different early on. Indeed the continuity between Q and early Christianity is probably not to be found in its theology so much as in its ecclesiology. The persistence of group formation, that is, may have been a more powerful factor in early Christianity than the persistence of theological conceptions, and that, in turn, may indicate that we need to pay at least as much attention to the specific social context of the early church as to its theology.[34]

It has been the concern of this study to pay attention, as Jacobson has expressed it, "to the specific social context of the early church." That context, as passage after passage has demonstrated, was the patrilineal kinship group. From first-century Palestine to third-century Carthage, the social matrix most central to early Christian conceptions of community was the surrogate kinship group of siblings who understood themselves to be the sons and daughters of God. For the early Christians, the church was a family.

Abbreviations

MODERN SOURCES

ABD	*Anchor Bible Dictionary*
ACW	Ancient Christian Writers
ANF	*The Ante-Nicene Fathers*
ANRW	*Aufstieg und Niedergang der römischen Welt*
BK	*Bibel und Kirche*
BTB	*Biblical Theology Bulletin*
CIL	*Corpus Inscriptionum Latinarum*
ConBNT	Coniectanea biblica, New Testament
CRINT	Compendia rerum iudaicarum ad Novum Testamentum
DJG	*Dictionary of Jesus and the Gospels*
EPRO	Etudes préliminaires aux religions orientales dans l'empire romain
FB	Forschung zur Bibel
FC	Fathers of the Church
HNTC	Harper's New Testament Commentaries
HR	*History of Religions*
HTR	*Harvard Theological Review*
HUT	Hermeneutische Untersuchungen zur Theologie
ICC	International Critical Commentary
ILS	*Inscriptiones latinae selectae*
JBL	*Journal of Biblical Literature*
JETS	*Journal of Evangelical Theological Society*
JJS	*Journal of Jewish Studies*
JRH	*Journal of Religious History*
JRS	*Journal of Roman Studies*

JSNT	*Journal of the Study of the New Testament*
JSNTSup	JSNT Supplement Series
JSOT	*Journal for the Study of the Old Testament*
JTS	*Journal of Theological Studies*
LCL	Loeb Classical Library
LEC	Library of Early Christianity
NICNT	New International Commentary on the New Testament
NIGTC	New International Greek Testament Commentary
NovT	*Novum Testamentum*
NovTSup	Novum Testamentum Supplements
NTS	*New Testament Studies*
OCD	*Oxford Classical Dictionary*
OTP	*Old Testament Pseudepigrapha*
PG	*Patrologia graeca*
PKG	patrilineal kin group
PW	A. F. Pauly, *Real-Encyclopädie der classischen Altertumswissenschaft.* New edition G. Wissowa.
RAC	*Reallexikon für Antike und Christentum*
RHR	*Revue de l'histoire des religions*
RQ	*Römische Quartalschrift für christliche Altertumskunde und Kirchengeschichte*
SBL	Society of Biblical Literature
SBLDS	SBL Dissertation Series
SBLMS	SBL Monograph Series
SBLSP	*SBL Seminar Papers*
SBT	Studies in Biblical Theology
SD	Studies and Documents
Sem	*Semitica*
SJLA	Studies in Judaism in Late Antiquity
SJT	*Scottish Journal of Theology*
SNTSMS	Society for New Testament Studies Monograph Series
TAPA	*Transactions of the American Philological Association*
TDNT	*Theological Dictionary of the New Testament*
TDOT	*Theological Dictionary of the Old Testament*
TF	*Theologische Forschung*
TU	Texte und Untersuchungen
TynOTC	Tyndale Old Testament Commentaries
VC	*Vigiliae christianae*
WBC	Word Biblical Commentary
WMANT	Wissenschaftliche Monographien zum Alten und Neuen Testament
WUNT	Wissenschaftliche Untersuchungen zum Neuen Testament
ZNW	*Zeitschrift für die neutestamentliche Wissenschaft*

ANCIENT SOURCES

Names of biblical book abbreviated according to *JBL* "Instructions for Contributors" (*JBL* 117 [1998] 560). For DSS abbreviations see Geza Vermes, ed. *The Dead Sea Scrolls in English* (4th ed.; London: Penguin, 1995) v-vii. Other abbreviations are as follows:

APOCRYPHA, PSEUDEPIGRAPHA, RABBINIC, AND RELATED WORKS

3 Apoc. Bar.	*3 Apocalypse of Baruch*
Gk. App. Ez.	*Greek Apocalypse of Ezra*
Jos. Asen.	*Joseph and Aseneth*
Josephus	
Ant.	*Antiquities of the Jews*
J. W.	*Jewish War*
Ag. Ap.	*Against Apion*
Life	*Life*
Jub.	*Jubilees*
Mishnah	
B. Bat.	*Baba Batra*
Ber.	*Berakhot*
Pes.	*Pesaḥim*
Zab.	*Zabim*
Philo of Alexandria	
Ab.	*On Abraham*
Mos.	*Life of Moses*
Spec. Leg.	*On the Special Laws*
Ps.-Philo	Pseudo-Philo
Bib. Ant.	*Biblical Antiquities*
Ps.-Phocylides	*Pseudo-Phocylides*
Ps. Sol.	*Psalms of Solomon*
Sib. Or.	*Sibylline Oracles*
Syr. Aḥ.	*Syriac Ahiqar*
T. 12 Patr.	*Testament of the 12 Patriarchs*
T. Dan	*Testament of Dan*
T. Gad	*Testament of Gad*
T. Job	*Testament of Job*
T. Jos.	*Testament of Joseph*
T. Judah	*Testament of Judah*
T. Levi	*Testament of Levi*
T. Reub.	*Testament of Reuben*
T. Sim.	*Testament of Simeon*
T. Zeb.	*Testament of Zebulon*
T. Jac.	*Testament of Jacob*
T. Mos.	*Testament of Moses*

GRECO-ROMAN WRITINGS

Aelius Aristides	
Or.	*Orationes*
C. Theod.	*Codex Theodosianus*
Cicero	
Leg.	*De Legibus*
Leg. Man.	*Pro Lege Manilia*
Off.	*De Officiis*
Corp. Herm.	*Corpus Hermeticum*
Dio Cassius	
Hist.	*Historiae*
Dio Chrysostom	
Or.	*Orationes*
Dionysius of Halicarnassus	
Hist.	*Historiae*
Rhet.	*De Arte Rhetorica*
Epictetus	
Diss.	*Dissertationes*
Euripides	
Supp.	*Supplices*
Isocrates	
Ep.	*Epistulae*
Or.	*Orationes*
Julian the Apostate	
Asar.	*Letter to Arsarcius*
Lucian	
Peregr.	*The Death of Peregrinus*

Marcus Aurelius
   Med.   *Meditationes*

Orosius
   Hist. contra Pag.   *History against the*
                            Pagans

Ovid
   Met.   *Metamorphoses*
   Pet.   *Petronius*

Plato
   Tim.   *Timaeus*
   Resp.   *Respublica*
   Symp.   *Symposium*

Pliny, Elder
   Ep.   *Epistulae*
   HN   *Naturalis Historia*

Plutarch
   Ant.   *Life of Antony*
   Brut.   *Life of Brutus*
   Cat. Mai.   *Life of Cato the Elder*
   Mar.   *Life of Marius*
   Marc.   *Life of Marcellus*
   Non posse   *Non posse suaviter vivi*
                            secundum Epicurum
   Quaest. conv.   *Quaestiones convivales*
   Ti. Gracch.   *Life of Tiberius*
                            Gracchus
   Sull.   *Life of Sulla*

Pseudo-Demosthenes
   Ep.   *Epistulae*

Pseudo-Julian
   Or.   *Orationes*

Pseudo-Plato
   Ep.   *Epistulae*

Pseudo-Sallust
   Ep.   *Epistulae*

Quintillian
   Inst. Orat.   *Institutio Oratoria*

Seneca
   Ep. Mor.   *Epistulae Morales*

   Socratic Epp.   *Socratic Epistles*

Suetonius
   Claud.   *Life of Claudius*

   Syr. Men.   *Syriac Menander*

Tacitus
   Agr.   *Agricola*
   Ann.   *Annales*
   Hist.   *Historiae*
   Tit. Ulp.   *Titulae ex corpore*
                            Ulpiani

Xenophon
   Mem.   *Memorabilia Socratis*

WRITINGS OF THE
EARLY CHURCH

Acta Cyp.   Acts of Cyprian

1 Clem.   1 Clement

Clem. Al.   Clement of
                    Alexandria
   Paed.   *Paedagogus*
   Protr.   *Protrepticus*
   Quis Div.   *Quis Dives Salvetur?*
   Strom.   *Stromateis*

Cyprian of Carthage
   Ad. Donat.   To Donatus
   De Cath. Eccl.   On the Unity of the
                            Church
   De Mort.   On Mortality
   Dom. Or.   The Lord's Prayer
   Ep.   Epistles
   Laps.   The Lapsed

Eusebius
   Hist. Eccl.   *Ecclesiastical History*
   Praep. Evang   *Preparation for the*
                           Gospel

Gos. Thom.   Gospel of Thomas

Hermas   Shepherd of Hermas
   Sim.   *Similitudes*
   Vis.   *Visions*

Ignatius (*Ign.*)   Ignatius of
                Antioch

     Eph.   *Letter to the Ephesians*
     Magn.   *Letter to the*
                Magnesians
     Phild.   *Letter to the*
                Philadelphians
     Pol.   *Letter to Polycarp*
     Rom.   *Letter to the Romans*
     Smyrn.   *Letter to the*
                Smyrnaeans
     Trall.   *Letter to the Trallians*

Irenaeus
     Adv. Haer.   *Against Heresies*

Jerome
     De viris illust.   *De Viris Illustribus*
     Ep.   *Epistles*

Justin Martyr
     1 Apol.   *1 Apology*
     2 Apol.   *2 Apology*
     Dial. Tryph.   *Dialogue with Trypho*

     Mart. Pol.   *Martyrdom of*
                Polycarp

Minucius Felix
     Oct.   *Octavius*

Novatian
     De Spec.   *On Spectacles*

Origin
     C. Cels.   *Against Celsus*

Pass. Perp.   *The Passion of*
                Perpetua

Pontius
     Vit. Cyp.   *Life of Cyprian*

Tatian
     Ad. Gk.   *Address to the Greek*

Tertullian
     Ad Mart.   *To the Martyrs*
     Ad Nat.   *To the Nations*
     Ad Scap.   *To Scapula*
     Apol.   *Apology*
     De Bapt.   *On Baptism*
     De Cor.   *On Military Service*
     De Fuga   *On Flight during*
                Persecution
     De Orat.   *On Prayer*
     De Pat.   *On Patience*
     De Praesc. Haer.   *Prescription against*
                Heretics
     De Spec.   *On Spectacles*
     De Test. Anim.   *On the Testimony*
                of the Soul
     De Virg. Vel.   *On the Veiling of*
                Virgins

Theophilus of Antioch
     Auto.   *Autolycus*

Notes

1. CHRISTIANITY IN ITS SOCIAL ENVIRONMENT

1. Millar, *The Roman Near East*, 21.

2. The issue of proper terminology is a vexing one. Familiar terms such as *Christian* and *Christianity* are somewhat anachronistic, since they communicate to the modern reader the idea of a monolithic, centralized movement, which would not become a reality prior to Constantine, in the fourth century. Consistent employment of more accurate alternatives, however—such as "Jesus' earliest followers" (for those who followed the historical Jesus) or "Christ-confessing communities" (for post-Easter, Pauline congregations)—proves unwieldy at times. Such specification, moreover, leaves us without a fully suitable term ("the Jesus movement" comes close but lacks a corresponding adjective) to describe the phenomenon of early Christianity as a whole, from its origins in first-century Palestine to the establishment of communities throughout the eastern Roman Empire. For these reasons, I will retain the familiar terms *Christian* and *Christianity* at many points in the pages that follow while at the same time attempting to be more specific and sensitive to historical realities where the argument lends itself to such an approach.

3. Robin Lane Fox, *Pagans and Christians*, 271. The tenuous nature of our source material makes it difficult to estimate accurately the numbers of Christians living in the pre-Constantinian Roman Empire. As Stephen G. Wilson observes, "[W]e are better informed about the scatter than the density of early Christian communities" (*Related Strangers*, 25). Fox conservatively surmises that Christians constituted but a small minority of the population (*Pagans and Christians*, 265-71). Wilson agrees, estimating that circa 100 C.E. Christians constituted between .14 and .35 percent (100,000 to 250,000) of the total population; circa 200 C.E. saw the numbers increase to between 1.4 and 2.5 percent (1 to 1.5 million) of the approximately 60 million persons in the empire (*Related Strangers*, 25). Figures given for later decades increase substantially. William H. C. Frend, for example, contends that Diocletian's decision to persecute the Christians represented a reaction to the significant inroads Christians were making on pagan society in both number and influence

(*The Rise of Christianity*, 440–63). Ramsay MacMullen maintains a Christian population of some 5 million circa 300 C.E. (*Christianizing the Roman Empire*, 85).

Assuming that the above estimates are generally accurate, one must explain the significant increase in the number of Christians in the empire between 200 and 300 C.E. Recently, Rodney Stark, assuming a steady growth of 40 percent per decade, estimates approximately 7,000 Christians circa 100 C.E., and 217,000 circa 200 C.E. The exponential curve that results from Stark's model then explains a marked increase to some 6 million Christians in the empire by the year 300 C.E. (*The Rise of Christianity*, 6–7). I would want to qualify Stark's analysis with two observations: (1) I believe his estimate for 100 C.E. is low. Wilson is likely more accurate in this regard. And, (2) the steady growth rate Stark assumes fails to take into account the highly variable effects of disease, famine, and local opposition to the Christian movement. At any rate, Fox's general conclusion, cited in the text above, is shared by others who study early Christianity. Wilson, on his part, concurs that "[w]hile by the end of the second century [the Christian movement] was still not a massive presence, certainly not as significant as Judaism, yet compared with similar cults or sects its growth was remarkably sustained" (*Related Strangers*, 26). So, also, MacMullen: "No other new cult anywhere nearly approached the same success" (*Christianizing the Roman Empire*, 110). It is the comparative success of early Christianity that demands explanation.

4. See Walsh, *The Triumph of the Meek*.

5 . Dodds, *Pagan and Christian*.

6. Dodds, *Pagan and Christian*, 133.

7. "Any account of pagan worship which minimizes the gods' uncertain anger and mortals' fear of it is an empty account" (Fox, *Pagans and Christians*, 38, see also 64–66).

8. Betz, ed. *The Greek Magical Papyri*.

9. Garrett, *The Demise of the Devil*.

10. Burkert, *Ancient Mystery Cults*, 21–29.

11. Dodds, *Pagan and Christian*, 135.

12. Dodds, *Pagan and Christian*, 136–38.

13. Fox, *Pagans and Christians*, 324.

14. Lohfink, *Jesus and Community*.

15. Wilson, "Voluntary Associations: An Overview," in Kloppenborg and Wilson, eds., *Voluntary Associations*, 13. The ensuing discussion is particularly indebted to the fine collection of essays in this book.

16. Wilson, "Voluntary Associations: An Overview," 14.

17. Note the discussion in Wilken, *The Christians*, 31–47.

18. McCready, "*Ekklesia* and Voluntary Associations," in Kloppenborg and Wilson, eds., *Voluntary Associations*, 69–70.

19. Malherbe, *Social Aspects of Early Christianity*, 87–91.

20. Judge, "The Early Christians as a Scholastic Community," 4–15, 125–37; Hans Conzelmann, "Paulus und die Weisheit," 231–44; Wilken, "Collegia, Philosophical Schools, and Theology," 268–91; and, more recently, Mason, "*Philosophiai*."

21. Scholars increasingly refer in the literature not to "Jews"/"Jewish" but, rather, to "Judeans"/"Judean." To ancient hearers the term *Ioudaios* carried connotations of ethnicity, religion, and homeland. Since the word "Jew" lacks these connotations for most English readers, I have generally opted from the more historically accurate alternative.

22. Meeks, *The First Urban Christians*, 80–81.

23. Reitzenstein, *Die hellenistischen Mysterienreligionen.*

24. Kloppenborg, "Collegia and *Thaisoi*," 18. For example, *synagoge* is attested as a self-designation in some pagan associations; *ekklesia* and *episkopos* are used as group and leadership designations, respectively, by members of churches and collegia; *Therapeutae,* Philo's term for a celibate monastic group of Egyptian Judeans, is elsewhere used to describe members of certain Graeco-Roman associations on Delos (Wilson, "Voluntary Associations: An Overview," 4).

25. The voluntary groups to be compared with the Christian *ekklesia* reflect Kloppenborg's threefold taxonomy—domestic, cult, and professional associations—plus two Kloppenborg does not discuss: synagogues and philosophical schools ("Collegia and *Thaisoi*," 22–23). The chart is, of course, a heuristic device intended to serve as a summary analysis of a variety of highly complex and fragmentary pieces of evidence (literary, epigraphic, and so forth). It is inevitably both too specific (we lack the evidence necessary to make confident assertions in several areas) and too general (no allowance made for variation over time, geography, or among different expressions of the same kind of association). Some of the generalizations reflected in the chart will be nuanced in the discussion that follows. For a more thorough treatment, the reader is encouraged to consult Kloppenborg and Wilson, eds., *Voluntary Associations,* and the literature referenced there. Wholly excluded from consideration are the community at Qumran and Philo's Therapeutae. The former will be dealt with in some detail in a later chapter.

26. Wilson, "Voluntary Associations: An Overview," 1.

27. Devotion to a god or a goddess has recently been established as "a ubiquitous feature of ancient associations" (Wilson, "Voluntary Associations: An Overview," 7); "all associations were 'religious' inasmuch as piety was fully embedded in other dimensions of ancient culture" (Kloppenborg, "Collegia and *Thaisoi*," 18).

28. An association on Delos, circa second century B.C.E. (cited by Kloppenborg, "Collegia and *Thiasoi*," 18).

29. See *CIL* 6.642 (97 C.E.) for Silvanus; *CIL* 6.641 (during Hadrian's reign) for the Great Mother.

30. Mason, "*Philosophiai*," 33.

31. On the Stoics and Epicureans, see Culpepper, *The Johannine School,* 101–44. The classic discussion of the distinction between the cults and the schools remains Arthur Darby Nock's *Conversion.* Nock argued that the two groups originally differed markedly in their social functions and the corresponding needs they met, as well as in their various activities. Near the end of the first century, however, the line between school and cult began to blur as the philosophical schools became more religious. Early Christianity was exemplary, in Nock's estimation, in its ability to effectively fuse the two categories.

The quasi-religious orientation of the Epicureans is particularly fascinating in view of their materialistic worldview. Helmut Koester claims that Epicurus redefined the concept of piety in terms of the ideal of the wise man who cultivates true happiness and friendship among persons of like mind. Koester notes, "Thus the school became a kind of mystery club, because it provided the environment of religious fulfillment for its members, and its founder was seen as a divine figure. Friendship, community, and mutual pastoral care were understood as religious duties, while the regular common meals of the members and the memorial festivals on the birthdays of the founder and of other distinguished members were liturgical celebrations" (*Introduction to the New Testament,* vol. 1, 147).

32. The translation is Dennis E. Smith's ("Table Fellowship as a Literary Motif").

33. Dennis E. Smith, "Meal Customs (Greco-Roman)."

34. The Therapeutae in Egypt and the community at Qumran are the exceptions. For each, table fellowship was central to group definition. Meals at Qumran and among the Therapeutae differed, however, from the occasional meals of the typical association. For these Judean groups, eating together constituted a routine part of an ongoing communal lifestyle. Evidence for shared social activities in the Diaspora synagogue is fragmentary. Communal feasting apparently played some part in Judean activities at Delos and Sardis, for Josephus cites decrees protecting the practice of fund gathering for this very purpose (*Ant.* 14.214–16, 260–61).

35. For the Mithraic meal, see Kane, "The Mithraic Cult Meal," 313–51. The structural layout of the cult's meeting place (the mithraeum)—laid out as a dining room with a pair of facing benches for reclining at table in the Roman style—emphasizes the importance of the communal meal. Iconography ties the meal to the cult's central myth. The other key activity was a ritual reenacting the celestial journey of the soul. Archaeological and literary evidence points to the centrality of this ritual for cult gatherings (Beck, "The Mysteries of Mithras," 182–83).

36. Wilson, "Voluntary Associations: An Overview," 3.

37. According to Shmuel Safrai: "To a large degree the restoration of the Diaspora's subordination to the Land of Israel is to be credited to Rabban Simon" (mid-second century C.E.) ("The Era of the Mishnah and the Talmud [70–640]," 337). Similarly, see Smallwood (*The Jews under Roman Rule*, 476). Smallwood and Safrai, however, are probably too optimistic in their approach to the rabbinical source material.

38. Ekkehard Stegemann and Wolfgang Stegemann have recently qualified the above consensus by arguing that membership in the Christian *ekklesia* did not extend to the absolute highest (the Roman *ordines*) or lowest (*ptochoi*) strata of society until the second century. They note, for example, the lack of unambiguous prosopographic evidence of *ordo* membership in Paul's churches and conclude that 1 Corinthians 1:26-31 must be read rhetorically rather than literally (*The Jesus Movement*, 288–316).

39. Gerd Theissen identifies seventeen members of the Corinthian church by name from Paul's letters. He maintains that nine belong to the upper classes. The percentage must not mislead us. It is probable that elites among the community were singled out in the correspondence specifically because of their social status. Moreover, at least two of Theissen's four criteria for ascertaining social status are of questionable value: (1) serving the church or Paul; (2) the ability to travel (see Holmberg, *Sociology and the New Testament*, 45). Nevertheless, Theissen's analysis, combined with Paul's statement from 1 Corinthians 1:26, confirms the presence of at least a few elites among the Christians at Corinth. This, in turn, mirrors the social makeup of the surrounding culture (Theissen, *The Social Setting of Pauline Christianity*, 69–119).

40. The most promising literary database for a prosopographical analysis similar to Theissen's is the corpus of Cyprian of Carthage. My reading of Cyprian's writings suggests the presence of both elites and non-elites in the Christian communities of third-century North Africa. Cyprian is to be situated among the former, while the many indigent persons who rely for their survival upon the community's resources clearly represent the lower classes of Carthaginian society (see chapter 6). As is the case with Paul, it is the former, not the latter, who are referred to by name in Cyprian's correspondence.

41. Most recently, by McCready, who lists this as one of the church's four distinguishing traits ("*Ekklesia* and Voluntary Associations," 63).

42. Wilson cites the Agrippinilla inscription as representative ("Voluntary Associations: An Overview," 11). On the inscription, see McLean, "The Agrippinilla Inscription," 239–70.

Kloppenborg identifies the cult associations as potentially the most inclusive. Belonging to the association of Zeus at Philadelphia are "men and women, freeborn and slaves" (Kloppenborg cites *Sylloge Inscriptionum Graecarum*³ 985 ["Collegia and *Thiasoi*," 25]). The healing cult of Asclepius was also accessible to sufferers regardless of their social status; serious illness in antiquity knew no social boundaries. Harold Remus even talks of "an extended Asclepius family" at Pergamum to which the second-century elite Aristides belonged ("Voluntary Associations and Networks," 164). As Remus's insightful network analysis reveals, however, Aristides and his aristocratic friends were deeply committed to their relationships as social equals while at the same time serving as devotees to the cult of Asclepius. Wilson is surely correct in his suspicion that Aristides and his fellow elites constituted "an upper-class clique" in the Asclepius association at Pergamum ("Voluntary Associations: An Overview," 11). We see the same dynamic at work in the Christian community in Corinth, where upper-status persons tended to group together at mealtime—a tendency that, Paul argued, was wholly at odds with shared group values (1 Cor 11:17-34).

43. For a most insightful comparison of leadership in Paul's churches with leadership as conceived and exercised in the dominant culture of Greco-Roman antiquity, see Clarke, *Serve the Community of the Church*.

44. Waltzing, *Étude historique*, vol. 3, 162–76.

45. For the Mithraic *cursus*, see Beck, "The Mysteries of Mithras," 180–81.

46. See Feldman, "Diaspora Synagogues," 48–66; and, most recently, Andrew D. Clarke, *Serve the Community of the Church*, 126–41.

47. Kloppenborg, "Collegia and *Thiasoi*," 18.

48. Clarke, *Serve the Community of the Church*, 76.

49. The terms are *fratres*, *syndexioi*, and *mystai*, respectively (Beck, "The Mysteries of Mithras," 180).

50. See chapter 5 for the rise of the monepiscopate and the formalization of one-man leadership in the local Christian communities. The title *father*, for example, so central to the cult of Mithras, is not associated with any leadership position among the early Christians until early in the second century. For women in early Christianity, the literature is extensive. Karen Jo Torjeson traces through several centuries the increasing restriction of leadership roles to men in the Christian church (*When Women Were Priests*, 1993).

51. Most helpful on all this is Mason, "*Philosphiai*."

52. See Mason, "*Philosphiai*," 41, for references.

53. Mason, "*Philosphia*," 41–42. Mason notes, however, that, unlike the Greeks, the Romans tended to treat Judaism not as a philosophy but as a cult (see Suetonius, *Tib.* 36; and Tacitus, *Ann.* 2.85, for the expulsion of Judeans from Rome on allegedly religious grounds in 19 C.E.). This should caution us against a reductionistic analysis that attempts to isolate any single characteristic listed in figure 1.1 as exclusively defining for the life and orientation of a given voluntary group.

54. The text cited is from a fragment of Aristobulus's preserved in Eusebius. The translation is by A. Yarbro Collins in *OTP* 2.841.

55. The translation is Mason's. He finds the *philosoph-* root used 212 times by Philo (*"Philosophiai,"* 43).

56. I have in mind here Galen (circa 150 C.E.), and the Christians Justin Martyr (circa 150), Athenagoras (circa 180), and Clement of Alexandria (circa 200).

57. For example, Wilken, "Collegia, Philosophical Schools and Theology," 268–91.

58. Mason here draws upon the work of Abraham Malherbe ("Gentle as a Nurse," 203–17). My chronology is from Hemer, *The Book of Acts.*

59. The Judean rebellions of the first and second centuries in Judea and North Africa, respectively, constitute the key exceptions.

60. Mason, *"Philosophiai,"* 37. The discussion that follows owes much to Mason.

61. Gummere, trans., *The Epistles of Seneca,* 237.

62. Nock, *Conversion,* 177.

63. Mason, *"Philosophiai,"* 35.

64. Church and Brodribb, trans., *Complete Works of Tacitus,* 659.

65. Thus, we increasingly see scholars refer in the literature not to "Jews" but, rather, to "Judeans." Mason, who adopts this practice, gives the reason, wholly consonant with the above discussion, that "to ancient ears [*Ioudaios*] had an ethnic/regional sense, no less than *Babylonios* or *Aigyptios*" (*"Philosophiai,"* 55 n. 1).

66. Nock, *Conversion,* 161, my emphasis.

67. Wilken, *The Christians,* 124–25, emphasis mine.

68. Aphrahat, Sixth Demonstration, cited by Robert Doran (*Birth of a Worldview,* 65).

69. McCready, *"Ekklesia* and Voluntary Associations," 62. See also Gager, *Kingdom and Community,* 140.

70. Only a few exceptions can be found (Wilson, "Voluntary Associations: An Overview," 9–10). McCready draws our attention to the lack of "exclusive epithets such as 'holy,' 'called,' 'beloved of God'" among non-Christian groups (*"Ekklesia* and Voluntary Associations," 63; see also Rom 12:1; Col 3:12; 1 Cor 7:24). See also MacMullen, *Paganism in the Roman Empire,* 92.

71. On conversion, see Nock, *Conversion.* Mason, indebted to Nock, defines the term "conversion" as "a radical break with one's previous way of living and the resolute adoption of a new path." Mason illustrates conversion to philosophy from the lives of several ancient personalities, including Dio of Prusa and Polemo. He also draws attention to the routine use of such terms as *epistrophe, conversio,* and *metanoia,* to characterize the acceptance of philosophy (*"Philosophiai,"* 33).

72. Wilson cites evidence for both Christians and Judeans ("Voluntary Associations: An Overview," 10).

73. For baptism as a "washing" or "cleansing," see Acts 22:16 and Hebrews 10:22. For the death-resurrection connection, see Romans 6:3-11 and Colossians 2:11-12. North African Christians placed a special emphasis on baptism (see Tertullian, *De Bapt.*). The centrality of this rite, whereby a person is born into the family of God, is later evidenced by the great and richly decorated baptismal fonts uncovered in many fourth-century North African churches. See John G. Davies, *The Architectural Setting of Baptism.*

74. Meeks, *The First Urban Christians,* 78.

75. Bartchy, "Community of Goods in Acts," 313.

76. McCready, *"Ekklesia* and Voluntary Associations," 63.

77. Wuthnow, Hunter, Bergesen, and Kurzweil, *Cultural Analysis,* 102–6.

78. Kloppenborg, "Edwin Hatch, Churches and *Collegia*," 237.

79. Waltzing, *Étude historique*, vol. 1, 329 n. 3.

80. Bömer, *Untersuchungen*, vol. 1, 172–78.

81. Kloppenborg, "Edwin Hatch, Churches and *Collegia*," 237.

82. Bömer, *Untersuchungen*, vol. 1, 178.

83. Nock, "The Historical Importance of Cult-Associations," 105. For the use of *adelphos* at Eleusis, see Burkert, *Ancient Mystery Cults*, 45.

Neither can we argue for a family model for the devotees of Mithras based on the fact that the highest of seven successive grades of progress in the cult is titled *pater* (see Jerome, *Ep.* 107.2). Moreover, extant monuments of the Mithraic mysteries—underground chapels, sculptured scenes, and inscriptions—are all dated decades after the earliest Christian congregations well established (Vermaseren, *Mithras*, 29–30; Gordon, "Mithraism and Roman Society," 93).

84. Meeks, *The First Urban Christians*, 225 n. 73.

85. Malina, "Dealing with Biblical (Mediterranean) Characters," 131.

86. Also lacking among the mysteries is the practice of apparent kinship traits (assistance with funerals and lawsuits) across the boundaries of social class. Marvin Meyer's observation that adherents to the mysteries "were frequently close-knit and egalitarian" in their relationships with one another ("Mystery Religions") has received much needed clarification by Scott Bartchy, who remarks, "[D]evotees of the mysteries . . . rarely had to overcome any serious status differential among them to become 'close-knit'; they all had been able to pay the high initiation fees, so this reputed 'egalitarianism' would not have required embracing a new view of the poor in their cities" ("Agnostos Theos," 313 n. 39). As Burkert notes, "[T]he essential feature is the coming together of equals in a common interest" (*Ancient Mystery Cults*, 32).

87. Burkert, *Ancient Mystery Cults*, 44.

88. Burkert, *Ancient Mystery Cults*, 32.

89. Meeks, *The Origins of Early Christian Morality*, 28.

90. Meeks, *The First Urban Christians*, 78.

91. Wright, trans., *The Works of the Emperor Julian*, 69, 71.

2. Mediterranean Family Systems: Structure and Relationships

1. Hanson, "BTB Readers Guide: Kinship," 183.

2. Patrilineal (or "agnatic") descent is one of several expressions of descent group family structure. Others include matrilineal (or "uterine") descent (from an ancestress down through a series of female links—that is, through daughter, daughter's daughter, and so forth), and cognatic descent (from an ancestor or ancestress through a series of links that can be male or female or any combination of the two) (Keesing, *Kin Groups and Social Structure*, 17). See also Hanson, "The Herodians and Mediterranean Kinship. Part I," 75–84.

Patrilineal descent is common to first-century Roman, Greek, and Judean kinship groups. As Hanson has demonstrated from the Herodian genealogies, however, the patrilineal principle is often complemented with cognatic descent in order to serve the ultimate family goal of enhancing the honor of the kinship group. For two of Herod's sons, Aristobolus and Alexander, the honor gained is that of association with Hasmonean royalty through their mother Mariamme's line of descent (Hanson, "The Herodians and Mediterranean Kinship. Part I," 82).

3. Introductory level discussions include Fox, *Kinship and Marriage;* Keesing, *Kin Groups and Social Structure;* Schusky, *Manual for Kinship Analysis;* and Lingenfelter, *Transforming Culture.*

"Kindred systems" and "descent groups" are technical expressions utilized by anthropologists to label the two broad types of family systems under discussion. Kinship studies employ a specialized terminology, and in this regard, the glossaries in Keesing (*Kin Groups and Social Structure,* 147–51) and Schusky (*Manual for Kinship Analysis,* 71–79) are helpful.

For Judean marriage laws and customs, see Stephen D. Moore, *Judaism;* Neufeld, *Ancient Hebrew Marriage Laws;* Issakon, *Marriage and Ministry;* Elon, *The Principles of Jewish Law;* Epstein, *Marriage Laws;* Epstein, *The Jewish Marriage Contract;* Mace, *Hebrew Marriage;* Swidler, *Women in Judaism;* Christopher J. H. Wright, *God's People;* and Cohen, *The Jewish Family.*

Works treating Roman marriage include Corbett, *The Roman Law of Marriage;* Alon Watson, *The Law of Persons;* Gardner, *Women in Roman Law;* Rawson, ed., *The Family in Ancient Rome;* Dixon, *The Roman Family;* and Treggiari, *Roman Marriage.*

For Greek laws and customs, note Lacey, *The Family in Classical Greece;* Verner, *The Household of God;* Lefkowitz and Fant, *Women's Life in Greece and Rome;* and Pomeroy, *Goddesses, Whores, Wives, and Slaves.*

4. Hanson, "BTB Reader's Guide," 184.

5. Pre-scientific views about procreation are closely related to the patrilineal family model. That both father and mother share in procreation (sperm and egg) is not a universal notion. Many peoples with a strong patrilineal bent have favored some version of a procreation myth that is strange to scientific Western sensibilities. The mother is thought of as kind of an incubator in which the father plants the seed. Robin Fox offers as an example the Tikopia peoples, for whom the mother is simply the "shelter-house of the child"—she does not create it. The point is that this inevitably affects the idea of consanguinity. From our perspective, both father and mother are genetically connected to the child and therefore consanguine. But if we took the view that the mother had no part in the creation of the child, then she would not be a "consanguine"; she would simply be the father's wife—like a stepmother in our society (Fox, *Kinship and Marriage,* 119–20). See, especially, Stevens, "Maternity and Paternity," 47–53.

6. I make three assumptions methodologically:

a. One can convincingly postulate a circum-Mediterranean traditional social system whereby a number of societal traits—kinship ideals included—are similar in various Mediterranean regions (Stegemann and Stegemann, *The Jesus Movement,* 2). On this, see Davis, *People of the Mediterranean;* Boissevain, "Uniformity and Diversity in the Mediterranean," 1–11; Malina, "Dealing with Biblical (Mediterranean) Characters," 128; Malina and Neyrey, *Portraits of Paul;* and Horden and Purcell, *The Corrupting Sea.*

b. Since kinship is central to the first-century Mediterranean world, the limited number of surviving texts devote a proportionately generous amount of space to kinship issues.

c. Peasant society in the Mediterranean region has remained relatively static for the two millennia since the early Christian documents were written.

These three factors will inform my construction of a model of Mediterranean family.

7. Osiek and Balch, *Families in the New Testament World,* 42.

8. Thus, we are not totally surprised to find the author of *Pseudo-Phocylides* extolling the affective aspect of marriage (195–97). Moreover, Herod's great love for Mariamme shows that their relationship constitutes more than a strictly contract-oriented marriage (Josephus, *Ant.* 15.210-12, 218, 240). The Herod-Mariamme union, however, precisely illustrates the point at hand. The key reason Herod initially marries Mariamme is to enhance the honor of his family with Hasmonean royalty—a classic illustration of contractual alliance. Later, blood ultimately triumphs over affection again, as Herod's mother and sister convince him to condemn his beloved Mariamme to death (*Ant.* 15.185-240).

Recent discussions of Roman imperial marriages generally confirm the above observations, although the sources reveal more of an affective component in Roman marriages than is the case with their Judean and Greek counterparts.

9. Current studies in Mediterranean kinship reveal much of the same. Ian Whitaker, for example, notes of Gheg values in Albania: "Romantic feelings between men and women played little part in the expected behavior pattern of husbands and wives. In brief, I would categorize the marital tie in Gheg society as one based on economic and social factors . . . and containing little emotional dependence" ("Familial Roles," 198).

10. Examples of alliance-building marriages abound. In their efforts to assure the integrity of the so-called Second Triumvirate, for example, "the soldiers crowded round the three leaders and demanded that Octavius should cement the alliance by marrying Clodia, the daughter of Antony's wife Fulvia by her first husband" (Plutarch, *Ant.* 20). Later, after Fulvia dies, Octavius's half-sister Octavia marries Antony in a further attempt to obviate animosity between the two Roman leaders (*Ant.* 31).

11. Among Roman families, varying practices surrounding the issue of *manus* resulted in greater variety in the kinds of relationships experienced by married women with their natal families. Those wives who had come into *manus* shared the legal and religious position of blood agnates in the husband's family. This was not the case in Judean families. However, the practice of *manus*, typical in early Rome, was relatively uncommon by the time of Cicero and is not widely attested during the imperial period. The result is that, by our period, most wives were not legally considered to share blood ties with their husbands and their children. This is revealed by a series of social and legal shifts that attempt to ameliorate a most practical effect of such an arrangement: the ineligibility of children to inherit from an intestate mother who had not entered into *manus* (see the *Senatusconsultum Orfitianum*, circa 178 C.E., *Tit. Ulp.* 26.7).

12. Malina, *The New Testament World*, 99.

13. It was common for a divorced or widowed woman to return to her own blood family upon the demise of her marriage. Glaphyra, the daughter of Archelaus, king of Cappadocia, marries Herod's son Alexander in a classic PKG alliance. After Herod has Alexander killed, he sends Glaphyra back to Archelaus. The scenario is repeated when Glaphyra's ensuing spouse, King Juba of Libya, also dies. Again, she returns to the residence of her father (Josephus, *Ant.* 17.11; 17.349-50).

14. Cited in *OTP*, 2.501 n. c.

15. Narrative romances like Tobit are particularly enlightening, since they typically reflect cultural ideals, especially in the area of kinship. The real world demanded certain compromises. On the one hand, anthropologists assure us that for patrilineal systems, patrilocal residence is, indeed, the norm (Fox, *Kinship and Marriage*, 115). Nevertheless, access to arable land, along with other

ecological or social factors, often necessitated neolocal or even matrilocal residence. Keesing, for example, notes that among the Chimbu of New Guinea, the patrilocal residence ideal is sacrificed due to land availability. The result is that a percentage of men live and garden in territories unrelated to their patriline (*Kin Groups and Social Structure*, 57). We are not surprised, then, to find Jesus' disciple Peter residing with his mother-in-law in first-century Judean society (Mark 1:29-31).

16. What is surprising, however, is the response of Jesus related in the following verse: "But he said, 'Honorable rather are those who hear the word of God and obey it!'" The role of women was significantly redefined in the family of faith during the early years of the Jesus movement.

17. Malina, "Mother and Son."

18. Fallers and Fallers, "Sex Roles in Edremit," 243–60.

19. Fallers and Fallers, "Sex Roles in Edremit," 253.

20. Fallers and Fallers, "Sex Roles in Edremit," 254.

21. Fallers and Fallers, "Sex Roles in Edremit," 249.

22. Whitaker, "Familial Roles," 198.

23. Syme, *The Roman Revolution*, 225 n. 2.

24. Durham, *Some Tribal Origins*, 148.

25. Matthew's version reads similarly (19:27-30). Luke, however, includes "wife" in the list of relations to be sacrificed to follow Jesus (18:28-30).

26. Peristiany, "Introduction," 9.

27. Peristiany, "Introduction," 8.

28. Rose, "Eteocles," 408.

29. Kirsten Nielsen has put forth the provocative thesis that Satan's activity in the Book of Job and in the temptation story in Matthew may be appropriately read in terms of sibling rivalry (*Satan—The Prodigal Son*).

30. Opposing Archelaus and requesting direct Roman rule are an embassy of fifty Palestinian Judeans supported by some eight thousand Roman Judeans.

31. Malina, *The New Testament World*, 33.

32. Du Boulay, "Lies, Mockery and Family Integrity," 389–406.

33. Du Boulay, "Lies, Mockery and Family Integrity," 405.

34. Du Boulay, "Lies, Mockery and Family Integrity," 405–6.

35. Du Boulay, "Lies, Mockery and Family Integrity," 406.

36. Malina, *Christian Origins*, 103.

37. Malina, *Christian Origins*, 105.

38. Some would substitute the term "exclusively" here. Du Boulay's study of modern Greek village family life is a case in point. The agonistic and adversarial relationship *between* families in the village, which she so graphically describes, has as its corollary a deep sense of loyalty and commitment *among* family members. Indeed, Du Boulay offers the family as "the only group within which unconditional obligations are recognized"—a virtual definition of generalized reciprocity ("Lies, Mockery and Family Integrity," 391).

39. In harmony with Old Testament practice, the term "brother" is used not just to denote one's immediate siblings but in a broader sense, of others in Israel, or, in Tobit's case, presumably of his fellow captives who had been transported to the Assyrian capital of Nineveh. A blood relationship continues to form the context, however, since the patriarch Abraham is the common

ancestor. Still, this broadening of sibling terminology beyond the confines of one's immediate PKG sets the stage for a more comprehensive use of PKG terminology in a wholly metaphorical sense (that is, apart from any consanguinity) among the early Christians (see chapter 3). More to the point here, however, is the simple observation that it is the sibling terminology that explains Tobit's behavior to the reader—he treated his "brethren"—whoever they are defined to be—as a PKG brother should.

40. Among the greater military disasters of Roman history was the massacre of three legions under Varus in 9 C.E. Six years later, the Roman army led by Germanicus comes upon the fatal locale and proceeds to bury the bones of the three legions. Note the proliferation of kinship terminology in Tacitus's account: "And so the Roman army now on the spot, six years after the disaster, in grief and anger, began to bury the bones of the three legions, not a soldier knowing whether he was interring the relics of a relative or a stranger, but looking on all as kinsfolk and of their own blood, while their wrath rose higher than ever against the foe" (*Ann.* 1.62).

41. Lingenfelter, *Transforming Culture*, 113.

42. Hanson, "The Herodians and Mediterranean Kinship. Part I."

43. Keesing, *Kin Groups and Social Structure*, 59, italics added.

44. Rose, "Lares," 578.

45. Wilken, *The Christians*, 56.

46. Koch, "Pietas."

47. Malina, *The New Testament World*, 25–50.

48. The capitalized term in the NRSV text is misleading. I understand Jesus' physical origins to be in view in the comments of his opponents. This is quite apparent in verse 41, and it is only reasonable to read the expression "Where is your father" (v. 19) as a proleptic expression of what is to be more graphically stated later in the dialogue. The *Acts of Pilate* (2.3) has Judean leaders charging Jesus: "You were born of fornication."

49. Hanson, "The Herodians and Mediterranean Kinship. Part III," 15.

50. Goody, *The Oriental, the Ancient and the Primitive*, 17.

51. Hanson, "The Herodians and Mediterranean Kinship. Part III," 16.

52. A word search reveals that the key term translated "inheritance" in the NRSV—the Hebrew substantive *naḥalah* (which is found only three times in the first three books of the Pentateuch)—occurs forty-seven times in Numbers and twenty-five times in Deuteronomy, the two books of the Torah that outline the division of the land in detail.

53. Legal guidelines about inheritance are found throughout Mediterranean society. In addition to the ancient Israelite concerns mentioned above, Hanson provides source references for laws in Old Babylonia, Nuzi, Ugarit, Greece, Rome, and late Judaism ("The Herodians and Mediterranean Kinship. Part III").

54. The phrase "my ancestral inheritance" reflects a genitive construction in both LXX Greek and MT Hebrew that may literally be rendered "the inheritance of my fathers."

55. One might expand the idea of inheritance to include not only the "movable and immovable property" mentioned above by Hanson but also one's spiritual legacy. Judean testamentary literature, for example, typically details the distribution of tangible wealth as a subset of its broader focus, namely, the ethical-spiritual heritage that a dying patriarch passes on to his offspring (see *T. Job; T. 12 Patr.; T. Ab.; T. Mos.;* and so forth). Note, also, the seminal work of Johannes Munck in this regard ("Discours d'adieu," 155–70).

3. ORIGINS OF THE SURROGATE KIN GROUP IDEA

1. Recent expositors understand the expression "one father" in the first clause to refer not to Abraham but to Yahweh, according to the parallelism with "one God" in the following question, and according to the analogy of Deuteronomy 32:6, cited above (Ralph L. Smith, *Micah-Malachi*, 321).

2. The Hebrew term *ah* ("brother") is used, of course, in a variety of senses in Old Testament literature. Excluding for the moment idioms and specialized usages, we find the term referring to (1) one born of the same mother and/or father as another (Gen 4:2, 8); (2) a relative in a wider sense (for example, "nephew," Gen 13:8); (3) a member of the same tribe (Num 18:2, 6); (4) a member of the same people, that is, Israel (Exod 2:11; 4:8; and so forth). It is the last usage that is in view here.

3. Thus we find the expression "sons of Israel" (1272 times), rather than "sons of God," as the normal circumlocution used to denote the Israelites.

4. English translations, again, prove problematic. The NRSV is hopelessly misleading, since "brother" has been consistently rendered "member of your community." The NIV is somewhat better. Verse 2, however, erroneously implies that "fellow Israelite" and "brother" represent two different individuals. They are instead identical—a fellow Israelite is a "brother," as the real contrast between a "foreigner" and a "brother" (see v. 3) indicates.

5. Quotations of apocryphal works are from the RSV (Metzger, ed., *The Oxford Annotated Apocrypha*).

6. Van Der Horst, "Pseudo-Phocylides," 2.574 n. c.

7. See, for example, the various approaches of N. T. Wright (*Jesus and the Victory of God*, 275–78); Lohfink (*Jesus and Community*, 26–50); I. Howard Marshall ("Church," 122–25); and Stegemann and Stegemann (*The Jesus Movement*, 191–213). A generation ago, Joachim Jeremias pointedly asserted, "The sole meaning of the entire activity of Jesus is the gathering of God's eschatological people" (*New Testament Theology*, 167).

8. McVann, "Family-Centeredness," 70–73; Malina and Rohrbaugh, *Social-Science Commentary*, 201–3, see also 100–101; Gundry, *Mark*, 178.

9. The passage cited above prepares the reader, for example, for Mark 6:1-6, in which Jesus and his mission are essentially rejected by his own villagers.

10. Important contributions to the discussion have come from Jeremias, *The Prayers of Jesus;* Vermes, *Jesus the Jew;* Bauckham, "The Sonship," 245–60; and Barr, "Abba Isn't 'Daddy,'" 28–47.

11. See chapter 1 for the distinction between early churches and Greco-Roman social models. See also Meeks, *The First Urban Christians*, esp. 90–91; Dodds, *Pagan and Christian*, 136–38; and N. T. Wright, *The New Testament*, 365.

12. E. P. Sanders, *Jesus and Judaism*, 320. Consonant with such an assertion, Sanders specifically argues against innovation in Jesus' conception of the kingdom (137–38) and later energetically resists the idea that Jesus' miracles were somehow without parallel in the ancient world (161–63).

13. E. P. Sanders, *Jesus and Judaism*, 319.

14. E. P. Sanders, *Jesus and Judaism*, 320.

15. E. P. Sanders, *Jesus and Judaism*, 240.

16. E. P. Sanders, *Jesus and Judaism*, 319.

17. The exception, of course, is the community at Qumran, which will be addressed in the ensuing discussion. Among the early Israelites, David's travels with his brigand band form an apt parallel (1 Sam 21–30). Again, times of crisis demanded exceptions. At one point in the narrative,

David even uses kinship terminology to persuade his men to share their material resources with others in the camp who had not participated firsthand in a particular battle (30:21-25). But this is clearly exceptional for the ancient Israelites.

18. Jacobson, "Divided Families," 362–63.

19. Nolland, *Luke 9:21—18:34,* 763

20. Jacobson, "Divided Families," 362, 364.

21. The term in view is *ʾanš.* See I. Howard Marshall, *Commentary on Luke,* 592.

22. Hengel, *The Charismatic Leader,* 9.

23. N. T. Wright, *Jesus and the Victory of God,* 401.

24. For the various interpretations of the passage, see Klemm, "Das Wort," 60–75; Kingsbury, "On Following Jesus," 45–59; and McCane, "Let the Dead Bury Their Own Dead," 31–43. McCane interprets the request of the would-be follower of Jesus to refer to secondary burial. McCane claims it was a common practice to remove a corpse from its original place of burial after approximately one year (during which the flesh would decompose), in order to move the bones to their permanent burial site. Secondary burial is what is meant when the Bible speaks of someone being "gathered to his people" (see Gen 25:8). On this interpretation, as McCane himself observes, the saying of Jesus remains highly offensive to Judean familial piety. Jacobson appropriately adds, "Indeed, since secondary burial is an expression of kinship with the dead, the demand to sever that kinship would be all the more offensive" ("Divided Families," 362–63).

25. Safrai, "Home and Family," 774.

26. Jacobson, "Divided Families," 362.

27. See Hengel, *The Charismatic Leader,* 8–15. Accordingly, we find no entry under Matthew 8:21-22 in an important compendium of Hellenistic parallels to New Testament literature (Boring, Berger, and Colpe, eds. *Hellenistic Commentary*).

28. E. P. Sanders, *Jesus and Judaism,* 252.

29. E. P. Sanders, *Jesus and Judaism,* 255.

30. N. T. Wright, *Jesus and the Victory of God,* 401.

31. I have offered as evidence primarily those text-segments in which the kinship metaphor is explicit. Recent work in the area of personality and culture has shown, however, that a number of Gospel passages that lack kinship terminology nevertheless remain informative for Jesus' conception of his community of followers as a surrogate kinship group. Note, for example, the following familiar passage: "He called the crowd with his disciples, and said to them, 'If any want to become my followers, let them deny themselves and take up their cross and follow me'" (Mark 8:34). Malina compares self-identity in individualist Western culture with the self-orientation of members of collectivist societies, such as those of Mediterranean antiquity. He rightly identifies as one of the core concerns of the collectivist self "family integrity and all that that primary ingroup provides." Malina then observes, "Given the core value of family integrity in collectivist structures, it is no surprise that self-denial and family-denial are almost parallel." In the Synoptic tradition, then, "self-denial is family-denial" (Malina, "A Social Psychological Model," 114, 118).

32. General consensus holds the community at Qumran to have been an Essene settlement (Schiffmann, *Reclaiming the Dead Sea Scrolls,* 78–81, 103–5). The Essenes are described by several Greek and Latin writers, including Philo (*Every Good Man Is Free,* 75–91; *Hyp.* 11.1–18), Josephus (*J. W.* 2.119-61; *Ant.* 18.1.5, 18-22), and the Roman Pliny (*HN* 5.15.73). The settlers at Qumran, however, were not the only Essenes. Philo and Josephus describe Essenes in Judean villages and cities, and the

Damascus Document (found at Qumran but known earlier from a manuscript uncovered at the turn of the twentieth century in the Cairo Genizah), provides rules for Essenes located in "the towns of Israel" who, unlike those at Qumran, may "take a wife and beget children" (CD 12.19, 7.6-7).

33. Translations of the Dead Sea Scrolls are taken from Vermes, ed. *The Dead Sea Scrolls in English*, 95.

34. Vermes, *An Introduction to the Complete Dead Sea Scrolls*, 110.

35. Vermes, ed. *The Dead Sea Scrolls in English*, 95.

36. Van der Minde, "Thanksgiving Hymns," 6.439.

37. Dupont-Sommer, "Les Livre des Hymnes," 10–12.

38. Lohfink, *Jesus and Community*, 49.

39. The term rendered "students" must instead be rendered "brothers." The translation "students" represents a conjectural reading, *mathētai* apparently adopted to contrast properly with the preceding *didaskalos* ("teacher"). It finds no manuscript support. Rather, *adelphoi* ("brothers") appears in every edition of the Greek text that I consulted. It is also reflected in the translations of all English versions (KJV, NASB, NIV, RSV, ASV, JB, NEB, and so forth) other than the NRSV. Again, the NRSV's attempt at gender-neutral language has served to obfuscate a central point of the passage.

40. With Lohfink (*Jesus and Community*, 47), I trace the sayings in the above citation back to the historical Jesus. Earlier overstatements of the strongly authoritarian nature of the father's role in Mediterranean family systems have been appropriately challenged and nuanced in recent years, particularly with respect to the Roman family. Scholars now increasingly distinguish between the severe picture of patriarchy reflected in the Roman legal tradition, on the one hand, and the reality of daily life, on the other (Garnsey and Saller, *The Roman Empire*, 136–41; Christopher J. H. Wright, "Family," 2.766-68). Much evidence suggests that paternal moderation was a virtue. Moreover, statistical studies reveal an early mortality, which left most sons fatherless by marriage age (Saller, *Patriarchy*). "Thus, in contrast to a popular misconception, there were few old patriarchs dominating large extended households" (Bartchy, "The Lasting Contributions," 3). Jewish practice and life span likely were similar.

It is still fair to maintain, however, that the authority component, at times expressed in what would appear to modern Western sensibilities as harsh patriarchal domination, remained a central feature of the Mediterranean idea of fatherhood (Pilch, "Beat His Ribs," 101–13). And it is precisely this aspect of the PKG father model that Jesus had in mind—and reserved for God alone—in text-segments like those cited above (confirmed by the presence of the contrasting expressions "servant" and "be humbled . . . humble themselves" in Matt 23:11-12).

41. There is some question as to the application of the injunctions in the *Damascus Document* to the Qumran community. Although the document is attested at Qumran, much of the content addresses Essene practices in the villages. It is fair to assume, however, that the community's guardian figure adopted both the authoritative and the providential roles of a Mediterranean father as he presided over the group.

42. Vermes, *An Introduction to the Complete Dead Sea Scrolls*, 96–97. Jesus' community and the earliest Christian congregations were, by contrast, relatively egalitarian in nature. Here is yet another area of contrast, one that, regrettably, I will be unable to address. I was hardly surprised, however, to find a correlation between the strongly hierarchical orientation of the Qumran community and the use of "father" terminology to describe the community's guardian figure. Second-century

Christian leaders will resort to precisely the same linguistic-symbolic strategy in order to reinforce what will become an increasingly hierarchical church organizational model.

43. Discussions of the political, economic, and religious situation (an inseparable triad) during the first century of the common era are too numerous to list. On the general state of political affairs in the Roman Near East, see most recently, Millar, *The Roman Near East.* For Rome and the Jews, Smallwood's contribution remains the standard treatment (*The Jews under Roman Rule*). For an excellent summary of the economic situation and its role in the First Jewish Revolt, see Goodman, *The Ruling Class of Judaea,* chapter 5. Douglas Oakman presents a more extensive treatment (*Jesus and the Economic Questions of His Day*). Convictions held by the sectarians at Qumran, of course, constitute the most extreme response to a temple and priesthood that are perceived to be hopelessly defiled and corrupt (see esp. 1QpHab). Similar feelings, however, are reflected in other literature of the era (*T. Moses* 7:510; *Ps. Sol.* 4:1, 9-11).

44. See Cohen, *From the Maccabees.*

45. Stendahl, "The Apostle Paul"; Dunn, *Jesus, Paul, and the Law.*

46. Douglas, *Purity and Danger;* E. P. Sanders, *Paul and Palestinian Judaism.*

47. The festival of Passover, Israel's most important celebration of divine deliverance from pagan oppression, served, of course, as yet another painful yearly reminder of past enslavement and liberation and, by implication, of biblical promises yet to be fulfilled.

48. Esler, *Community and Gospel,* 76–86.

49. Neusner, "Mr. Sanders's Pharisees," 155.

50. Vermes, *The Dead Sea Scrolls in English,* 7.

51. Vermes, *The Dead Sea Scrolls in English,* 9.

52. Douglas, "Deciphering a Meal"; Goody, *Cooking, Cuisine and Class.*

53. Bartchy, "Table Fellowship," 796.

54. Bartchy, "Table Fellowship," 796.

55. Dennis E. Smith, "Table Fellowship as a Literary Motif."

56. Bartchy, "Table Fellowship," 798.

57. Bartchy, "Table Fellowship," 797.

58. Bartchy, "Table Fellowship," 797.

59. Bartchy, "Table Fellowship," 798.

60. Malina and Rohrbaugh, *Social-Science Commentary,* 209.

61. Guelich, *Mark 1—8:26.*

62. Guelich, *Mark 1—8:26,* 297.

63. Westerholm, "Clean and Unclean," 128.

64. Bartchy, "Table Fellowship," 797. The options were, perhaps, not quite so mutually exclusive. John Nolland, speaking of rabbinic practices, nuances the contrast: "Acts of mercy and keeping of the commandment are the two major categories for rabbinic ethics. Where, for the rabbis, works of mercy supplement the fundamental duty of keeping the commandments, in the new Christian perspective already exemplified by John [the baptizer] love of neighbor occupies the fundamental place and helps to clarify the meaning and application of the commandments" (*Luke 1—9:20,* 149).

65. E. P. Sanders, *Jesus and Judaism,* 326.

66. Bartchy, "Table Fellowship," 796.

67. N. T. Wright, *Jesus and the Victory of God,* 389.

4. THE COMMUNITIES OF PAUL OF TARSUS

1. See, for example, John Dominic Crossan's chronological stratification of early Christian texts (*The Historical Jesus*, 427). My survey of early Christian literature in the present work must be selective, and the letters of Paul prove to be a more useful and datable collection of source material than do the canonical Gospels. Unlike the Gospels, Paul's letters were written to identifiable Christian communities, and they contain information about (and directives to) those congregations. Moreover, nearly all scholars date the completed Gospels later than Paul's epistles. Finally, efforts to situate each Gospel in its sociohistorical context prove highly problematic.

2. Nearly all New Testament scholars maintain Pauline authorship for Romans, 1 and 2 Corinthians, Galatians, Philippians, 1 Thessalonians, and Philemon.

3. Although some argue otherwise (Wanamaker, *1 and 2 Thessalonians*, 37–45), most scholars continue to assume that 1 Thessalonians is Paul's earliest extant letter and, therefore, the earliest New Testament witness to early Christian beliefs and behaviors (Kümmel, *Introduction to the New Testament*, 257; Krentz, "Thessalonians").

4. The Greek terms and their breakdown is as follows: *adelph** ("brother"/"sister") = 118 occurrences (*adelphē* = 5; *adelphos* = 113); *patēr* ("father") = 40; *klēronom** ("inherit"/"inheritance"/"heir") = 14 (*klēronomeo* = 6; *klēronomia* = 1; *klēronomos* = 7).

5. Douglas, *Natural Symbols*, 22.

6. Wuthnow et al., *Cultural Analysis*, 104.

7. Keesing, *Kin Groups and Social Structure*, 126.

8. Banks, *Paul's Idea of Community*, 51.

9. The opponents are variously identified as Gnostics (Schmithals, *Gnosticism of Corinth*), legalistic Judaizers (Barrett, *The First Epistle to the Corinthians*), or (for those Paul responds to in his second extant letter) proponents of a "divine man" theology (Georgi, *The Opponents of Paul*). None of these proposals has found wide acceptance in the scholarly community.

10. Gordon Fee's commentary on 1 Corinthians is representative. For Fee, the most serious problem in the community is the fallout between the Corinthians and their apostle-founder. The letter, then, becomes an apologetic on Paul's part for his apostolic authority (*The First Epistle to the Corinthians*).

11. The new approach emerged from increasing dissatisfaction with traditional methodology. Jerry Sumney, for example, has recently challenged students of Paul's Corinthian letters to exercise restraint in applying the "mirror technique," a methodology by which the scholar seeks to reconstruct the views of the members of the Corinthian community from Paul's corrective remarks. Unfortunately, the mirror technique has served only to produce a myriad of viewpoints concerning the various parties in Corinth, none of which is finally persuasive to the majority of the scholarly community (*Identifying Paul's Opponents*).

12. Dale B. Martin, *The Corinthian Body*, 69.

13. Dale B. Martin, *The Corinthian Body*, 69; see also Theissen, *The Social Setting of Pauline Christianity*, 121. The usage of the terms is not unique to Paul. "Weaker" is often used in political rhetoric to refer to the lower classes (Plato, *Resp.* 569B; Euripides, *Supp.* lines 433-38) (Martin, *The Corinthian Body*, 269 n. 23).

14. The bracketed clause may be a part of Paul's response. I am convinced, however, that it

belongs instead among the Corinthians' own sentiments for, as Martin notes, Paul will later respond by emphasizing the resurrection of the body rather than its destruction (*The Corinthian Body*, 264 n. 3).

15. Martin persuasively argues against assigning the above slogans to a specific first-century philosophical school or orientation. To identify the proponents of these ideas as either Cynics or Stoics, for example, is to force the slogans under a rubric that is too narrow. This is not to deny that phrases such as the above can be found in sources identified as Cynic or Stoic in origin. But as Martin notes, "In the first century, phrases and doctrines that originated among early Cynics and later Stoics had attained a wide currency in the general marketplace of popular, moral philosophy in the Roman Empire" (*The Corinthian Body*, 72).

16. Theissen, *The Social Setting of Pauline Christianity*, 121–74.

17. Martin, *The Corinthian Body*, 87–103.

18. Margaret M. Mitchell, *Paul and the Rhetoric of Reconciliation*.

19. Welborn, "Clement," 1.1058. Extant examples of the concord genre include Thrasymachus, *Peri Politeas*; Antiphon, *Peri Homonoias*; Isocrates, *Or.* 4; *Ep.* 3, 8, 9; Pseudo-Plato, *Ep.* 7; Pseudo-Demosthenes, *Ep.* 1; *Socratic Epp.* 30–32; Pseudo-Sallust, *Ep.* 2; Dio Chrysostom, *Or.* 38–41; Aelius Aristides, *Or.* 23–24; [Herodes Atticus,] *Peri Politeas*; and Pseudo-Julian, *Or.* 35.

20. Margaret M. Mitchell, *Paul and the Rhetoric of Reconciliation*.

21. Martin, *The Corinthian Body*, 68.

22. Cited by Martin, *The Corinthian Body*, 41.

23. Martin, *The Corinthian Body*, 41.

24. Martin, *The Corinthian Body*, 45.

25. Martin, *The Corinthian Body*, 42.

26. Martin, *The Corinthian Body*, 43, italics added.

27. Martin, *The Corinthian Body*, 67–68.

28. Even in works in which the kinship model might seem to offer a persuasive rhetorical device, family terminology is generally missing. For example, several of Dio Chrysostom's *Orations* (38–41) reflect the concord genre. In each case, the author appeals for harmony not between differing social groups in a given city but, rather, between cities that have been at odds with each other (Nicomedia and Nicaea, 38–39; Apameia and Prusa, 40–41). In this case, equals are addressed, and one would think that shared Greek origins would encourage Dio to utilize sibling terminology in his attempts to challenge the factious cities to peace and concord. Although "fraternity" (*hē adelphotēs*) and "concord of brothers" (*adelphōn homomoia*) occasionally surface in one of the orations (38.15), the general appeal throughout the four works is based on the fact that the opposing cities are neighbors, not brothers: "Better not to quarrel with any man at all, but least of all, in my opinion, with those who are so close, yes, real neighbors" (*tous engus outō kai astygeitonas*) (*Or.* 40.16; see also 40.22). Isocrates' Fourth Oration, the *Panegyricus*, similarly lacks sibling terminology in a context in which one would expect such rhetoric to be highly effective. The author's agenda is to praise the city of Athens and to challenge the warring Greek city-states to unite against a common Persian foe. Although Isocrates makes reference to a "kinship which exists among us" (*tēs sungeneias*), the usage of the term is, in its context (43), wholly peripheral to the author's broader challenge to concord. When he discusses the relationship among the Greeks—one that should encourage them to join forces against the Persians—

Isocrates uses not kinship terminology but, rather, military terminology, preferring the term "allies" (*tōn summachōn*) (181).

29. The NRSV helpfully renders the vocative *adelphoi*, as "brothers and sisters," thus preserving the gender-neutral intention of Paul's address. The commendable intentions of the NRSV will, however, prove highly problematic later.

30. The phrase "our brother Sōsthenēs" translates *Sōsthenēs ho adelphos.* The translators rightly assume that the article functions anaphorically, and they translate it with a possessive pronoun. "The article implies that [Sōsthenēs] was well known to some Corinthians" (Robertson and Plummer, *A Critical and Exegetical Commentary*, 2). Also, he was known in the capacity "brother."

31. The terms (*schismata* and *erides*) are from the common linguistic stock of the concord genre.

32. The role of Greco-Roman rhetoric in the Corinthian correspondence has lately received renewed interest in the scholarly community. As the above arguments indicate, I am not convinced, with Duane Litfin, that 1 Corinthians 1–4 portrays Paul as repudiating "the role of persuader" and adopting instead "the role of herald" (Litfin, *St. Paul's Theology of Proclamation*). Rather, as Martin and Mitchell have demonstrated, Paul appropriated a form of persuasive rhetoric—the concord speech—as his vehicle for communicating with the Corinthian community. Litfin is off the mark to assert that it is "the *quintessence* of Greco-Roman rhetoric, the stance of the persuader itself, that Paul disavows in 1 Corinthians 1–4" ("Review," 569). Rather, it is the traditional way in which the concord genre was used—to reinforce the social status hierarchy—that Paul radically inverts. As Stephen Pogoloff elsewhere suggests, "Paul rejects not rhetoric, but the cultural values wedded to it" (*Logos and Sophia*, 121).

33. The exception is 1 Cor 9:5: *hoi adelphoi tou kyrio* ("the brothers of the Lord").

34. On Paul's use of the father metaphor, see, most recently, Clarke, *Serve the Community of the Church*, 218–23.

35. An *inclusio* is a literary device that frames a text-segment by beginning and ending the passage with the same term(s) or thematic focus. Paul here begins and ends 1 Cor 4:14-21 with allusions to his role as the readers' spiritual progenitor.

36. The desire to keep legal disputes within one's "family" in Mediterranean society is illustrated, at another level, by the existence of a Judean court, over which the Judean patriarch (notice the surrogate kinship terminology) presided, alongside civic courts well into the post-Constantinian era. A law of 398 even buttressed decisions made in Judean courts with the promise of enforcement by civil authorities (*C. Theod.* 2.1.10 cited in Doran, *Birth of a Worldview*, 59).

37. Vögtle, *Die Tugend- und Lasterkataloge*; Karris, "The Background and Significance of the Polemic," 549–64.

38. Winter, "Civil Litigation," 561.

39. Cited by Martin, *The Corinthian Body*, 77.

40. Alan C. Mitchell, "Rich and Poor," 570.

41. Alan C. Mitchell, "Rich and Poor," 570.

42. See, for example, the speech of Musonius Rufus, "Will the Philosopher Prosecute Anyone for Personal Injury?" His answer is clearly a negative one. To litigate constitutes an admission of injury and, therefore, a denial of the self-control and self-sufficiency characteristic of the wise man (see Lutz, *Musonius Rufus*, 76–81).

43. The quote is from Alan C. Mitchell, "Rich and Poor," 570.

44. A striking parallel occurs in the Greek original that further supports my contention that the primary force of Paul's argument lies not with the "wise man" topos but, rather, with the kinship metaphor. In verse 6, Paul concludes his initial admonition against taking a "brother" to court (*adelphos meta adelphou krinetai*) with the exclamative *kai touto epi apistōn*. He proceeds, in the next two verses, to argue that lawsuits are wrong to begin with among members of God's family. He concludes this challenge, too, with the same grammatical construction: *adelphos/apistōn* (6:8). The primary contrast in the text, therefore, is not between the wise and the foolish. The philosophical *topos* is present, but as a secondary motif. The main contrast is between "unbelievers" and "brothers," as the contrasting final terms of these parallel constructions so clearly indicate: *apistōn/adelphous* (vv. 6/8). Paul assumes, with his readers, that the Corinthian Christians are brothers in the faith. He expects them to behave themselves in accordance with the PKG value system.

45. I must agree with the recent observations of Martin that both those who find in Paul's words a warm endorsement of human sexuality (Moiser, "A Reassessment," 103–22) and those who understand Paul's view of marriage and sex to be wholly negative (Marr, *Sex in Religion*, 75–77) are incorrect in their respective assessments. No New Testament passage has suffered more from the biases of its culture-bound interpreters over the centuries than has 1 Corinthians 7. Martin's commendable contribution is to distance himself consciously from the influences respectively of medieval asceticism and modern psychology's emphasis upon the goodness of human sexuality, in order to discover the meaning of the passage in the context of views about sex and marriage attestable among Paul's contemporaries. Martin's own suggestion, however— that Paul advocates sexual intercourse in marriage *without the presence of desire*—only indicates that much work is left to be done in this regard. Indeed, Martin himself admits that such a view "remains for us almost incomprehensible" (*The Corinthian Body*, 216).

46. Robertson and Plummer, *A Critical and Exegetical Commentary*, 140; Barrett, *The First Epistle to the Corinthians*, 162.

47. I will return to the issue of divided loyalties in my survey of other Christian writers to follow. The problems that arose when only one spouse in a pagan marriage converted to Christianity made for engaging reading and occasioned whole treatises, some of which are extant today (see *Acts of Thomas*).

48. Scot McKnight remarks, "Little did the Jerusalem leaders know that their suggestion would become Paul's *obsession* for nearly two decades" ("Collection for the Saints," 143, italics added). Ernest-Bernard Allo views the collection as "one of the great enterprises of [Paul's] career" (*Saint Paul*, 204). Dieter Georgi describes Paul's efforts along these lines as an "illustrative model of his theology" (*Die Geschichte der Kollekte*, 79).

49. A number of commentators find additional and more specific evidence in Acts 20:1-6. Verse 4 identifies the geographical provenance of a number of Paul's fellow travelers, including references, direct or implicit, to the towns of Berea and Thessalonica (Macedonia), Derbe and Lystra (Galatia), and the province of Asia Minor. Frederick F. Bruce fairly notes, "Most of these traveling companions were probably delegates from various Gentile churches, bearing their respective churches' contributions for the Jerusalem relief fund" (*The Acts of the Apostles*, 423; see also Ollrog, *Paulus und seine Mitarbeiter*, 52–59). If Bruce is correct, then the collection constituted the key reason for Paul's return to Jerusalem. We can then assume that Paul's interactions, at stops along the way to Jerusalem, with Gentile Christians from Tyre (Acts 21:3-4), Ptolemais (21:7), and Caesarea

(21:16) involved, at least in part, a consideration of their participation in the project. McKnight adds the Roman church to the list of possible contributors and concludes, "It is hard to imagine any campaign more embracing of the northern Mediterranean and any project that occupied Paul's attention more than this collection for the saints" ("Collection for the Saints," 144).

50. Ralph P. Martin, 2 *Corinthians,* 256–57.

51. Among the words Paul employs as designations for the gift are *koinōnia* (Rom 15:26), *diakonia* (Rom 15:25, 2 Cor 8:20), *charis* (2 Cor 8:6), *eulogia* (2 Cor 9:5), *logeia* (1 Cor 16:1), and *leitourgia* (2 Cor 9:12) (Dahl, "Paul and Possessions," 37–38).

Given the pressing straits experienced by the Judaean church, it may appear somewhat surprising to find scholars vigorously debating the purpose for Paul's collection. Paul himself reveals, however, that he intended the gift not only to meet practical needs but also to reflect the unity of the church at large as a community of God embracing both Judeans and Gentiles: "If the Gentiles have come to share in their [the Judeans'] spiritual blessings, they ought also to be of service to them in material things" (Rom 15:27). The validity of Paul's Law-free gospel to the Gentiles had been recognized by the Jerusalem leadership at the same time they had challenged Paul to "remember the poor" (Gal 2:10). Now, the tangible response to that mandate, in the form of Paul's collection from his churches, would serve to authenticate the validity of his Gospel and, by extension, the inclusion of Gentiles along with Judeans among God's eschatological people.

Johannes Munck suggests, alternatively, that the presentation of the collection by Paul and his companions to the Jerusalem church was intended by Paul to provoke the nation of Israel to believe in Jesus their Messiah (*Paul and the Salvation of Mankind*). Munck's reconstruction sheds light on at least one difficult passage (2 Cor 9:10-13). Paul, however, nowhere draws an indisputable connection between his understanding of the role of the believing Gentiles in the conversion of Israel and the collection for Jerusalem. We are probably best served by assuming more than a single purpose for the collection. McKnight suggests that "what began as largely an adventure in charity became, as a result of growing tensions, an act of theological unity and eschatological provocation" ("Collection for the Saints," 146).

52. Martin, 2 *Corinthians,* 267. Martin proceeds, however, to make some rather surprising comments about the phrase "your present abundance" (v. 14). The term *perisseuma,* Martin asserts, is "hardly economic prosperity; rather it is their enrichments-by-grace as in 1 Cor 1:7. . . . It is really beside the point to allude here to the presence of some wealthy church members at Corinth" (2 *Corinthians,* 267).

Martin's desire to find a theological purpose for Paul's collection has here led him beyond the boundaries of straightforward exegesis. Perhaps, in light of Romans 15:27, we may read the second clause of the pair ("so that their abundance may be for your need") in terms of the spiritual benefits that the Gentiles receive(d) from the mother church at Jerusalem. Surely, however, the first phrase ("your present abundance and their need") points to some sort of economic prosperity on the part of the readers, and in this regard the presence of several high-status individuals in the congregation at Corinth becomes an important consideration (Theissen, *The Social Setting of Pauline Christianity,* 99–110). We must not neglect the most immediate and obvious purpose for the collection (that is, to meet practical material needs among the Judaean Christians) in our attempts to discern additional, theological intentions on Paul's part. That the term translated "need" (*hysterēma*) in verse 14 can refer to the idea of material necessity may be demonstrated from an unambiguous occurrence of the word later in the epistle (11:9). There, material necessity is clearly in view:

"And when I was with you and was in need (*hysteretheis*), I did not burden anyone, for my needs (*to hysterema*) were supplied by the friends who came from Macedonia" (11:9).

53. Malina, *The New Testament World*, 33.

54. Translation from Cicero, *De Officiis* (trans. W. Miller), except that I have substituted, for the final term in the citation, the cognate "avarice" for Miller's more generic "self-seeking."

55. Karl Donfried's updated collection of essays (*The Romans Debate*) affords the student a balanced and broad introduction into the vast scholarship on Paul's letter to the Romans. Among the issues surrounding which Donfried, in his introductory essay, finds consensus are the following: (1) The fragmentation of the community: Christians at Rome constituted a divided community meeting in separate churches, which apparently did not come together for common worship. Paul thus never applies the term *ekklesia* to the entire Roman community. It is used only in 16:5, of the house-church gathered around Aquila and Priscilla (Lampe, "The Roman Christians," 216–30). (2) The unity of the epistle: Walter Schmithals and others who contend that Romans 16:1-23 is not an original and integral part of the letter are now clearly in the minority (Donfried, "Introduction," lxix–lxx; Gamble, *The Textual History*).

56. Francis Watson, "The Two Roman Congregations," 211.

57. Given present constraints, no attempt can be made to offer detailed support for what follows. It will be obvious to the informed reader that I view Romans as Paul's response to a specific situation among Christians in Rome. Others see Paul's own personal concerns as central to the letter's argument (see Bornkamm, "The Letter to the Romans," 28; Jervell, "The Letter to Jerusalem," 53–64; and Karris, "Romans 14:1—15:13," 84). As Donfried appropriately observes, "Every other authentic Pauline writing, *without exception*, is addressed to the specific situations of the churches or persons involved" ("False Presuppositions," 103). We may assume that the same is true of Romans.

Key primary sources include (1) inscriptions that reveal a diverse community of individually structured Judean synagogues in Rome; (2) the writings of Christian and secular historians that describe an expulsion of Judeans from Rome, circa 49 C.E. (Dio Cassius, *Hist.* 60.6.6; Suetonius, *Claud.* 25.4; Orosius, *Hist. contra Pag.* 7.6.15; Acts 18:1-4); and (3) the book of Romans itself. For current scholarly efforts that have contributed to the above reconstruction of the evidence, see the essays in Donfried, *The Romans Debate* (esp. Wiefel, "The Jewish Community in Ancient Rome"), as well as the monographs by Harry Leon (*The Jews of Ancient Rome*) and Peter Lampe (*Die stadrömischen Christian*). See also Marxsen, *Introduction to the New Testament*, 92–109; and Dunn, *Romans 1–8*, xliv–liv.

58. Dunn concurs: "The growing self-confidence of the gentile Christians in their sense of increasing independence from the synagogue and over against the returning Jewish Christians makes perfect sense as the background and context for Paul's counsel in 14:1 and in the following paragraphs (14:1—15:6)" (*Romans 1–8*, liii).

59. Watson adequately refutes opponents of this perspective (for example, Karris, "Romans 14:1—15:13"; Kümmel, *Introduction to the New Testament*, 310–11) who argue, on the basis of practices referred to in the text of Romans 14, against identifying "the weak" as Judean Christians (Watson, "The Two Roman Congregations," 203–5). Specifically, the debate is between Roman Christians who observe the Mosaic law ("weak") and others who do not ("strong"). For convenience, one may refer to these parties with the expressions "Jewish Christians" and "Gentile Christians." The former group, however, likely included proselytes from the Gentile world while the latter group might have included Judeans like Paul who no longer observed Judean purity codes.

60. See, again, the essays by Wiefel ("The Jewish Community in Ancient Rome") and Lampe ("The Roman Christians"). It is clear from Romans 16 that Christians in Rome met in homes at the time Paul penned his letter. Most also agree that Roman Christianity began as a synagogue-based movement among the Judeans in the city. It is reasonable to assume that unrest at synagogue meetings between Christian and non-Christian Judeans provoked Claudius's edict of 49 C.E. (Suetonius, *Claud.* 25.4). Wiefel has recently put in place a remaining piece of the historical puzzle in his treatment of Dio Cassius's comments. The information Dio relates appears, initially, to contradict the above reconstruction. Dio does not speak of an expulsion of the Judeans under Claudius. Rather, he claims that Judeans lost their right to assemble (*Hist.* 60.6.6). Wiefel's engaging and most plausible suggestion is to understand the denial of free assembly as a first step in moderating the eviction edict: "After Jews were again permitted to return to Rome, synagogue assemblies were prohibited for some time since they were seen as seedbeds of dispute" ("The Jewish Community in Ancient Rome," 94). The benefit of Wiefel's hypothesis is that it fairly harmonizes into a cogent and persuasive order of events the evidence from (1) Suetonius, (2) Orosius, (3) Dio Cassius, (4) Acts, and (5) Romans (see note 57, above, for references). Dating the denial of assembly after the edict of 49 C.E. also properly allows for the emperor's initially cordial attitude toward the Judeans (Josephus, *Ant.* 19.278-91; *J. W.* 5.214-17).

The result for Roman Christianity is a sharp transition, immediately following the 49 C.E. decree, from a synagogue-based social structure to home meetings. The change was only reinforced by the denial of free assembly attested by Dio. Although it represented a degree of moderation on the part of the emperor vis-à-vis the strict edict of expulsion (that is, Judeans could now reside in the city), the denial of assembly meant that Christianity in Rome had to remain a house-church movement at least until the death of Claudius, in 54 C.E. By that time the returning Judean minority would have found a firmly established home-based Christianity, as evidenced by Romans 16. This in turn provided a social context in which Paul's sibling terminology in Romans 14 would have carried great rhetorical force.

61. See Douglas, *Purity and Danger.*

62. Here again we are reminded that eating together—especially at the weekly celebration of the Lord's Supper—constituted for the early Christians the preeminent social expression of family solidarity. Paul elsewhere uses the sibling metaphor to encourage PKG solidarity in precisely this social context: "So then, my brothers and sisters, when you come together to eat, wait for one another" (1 Cor 11:33).

63. Banks, *Paul's Idea of Community,* 50.

64. The pronouns enclosing each of the questions in verse ten (*Su de ti krineis ton adelphon sou; ē kai su ti exoutheneis ton adelphon sou;*) are grammatically unnecessary and clearly emphatic: "Why are *you* judging *your very own* brother?" reasonably reflects the tenor of the original.

65. A conceptual parallel in 1 Corinthians 8 also reflects a concentration of sibling terminology: "And so by your knowledge this weak man is destroyed, the brother for whom Christ died. Thus, sinning against your brethren and wounding their conscience when it is weak, you sin against Christ. Therefore, if food is a cause of my brother's falling, I will never eat meat, lest I cause my brother to fall" (1 Cor 8:11-13 RSV).

66. The translation is Dunn's. The original reads *tē philadelphia eis allēlous philostorgoi.* While acknowledging that the *phil*-word-group can take on a broader meaning in various contexts in

ancient literature, Dunn rightly contends for a kinship connotation in the present context (*Romans 9–16*, 740). Other commentators concur (see Cranfield, *The Epistle to the Romans*, 631–32; Käsemann, *Commentary on Romans*, 345).

67. The original reads *tē timē allēlous proēgoumenoi*. The noun *timē* clearly has its normal sense of "honor" (Bauer, *A Greek-English Lexicon*, 817). The participle has been variously translated as "showing the way" (Dunn, *Romans 1–9*, 741); "outdo" (NRSV); and "preferring" (Cranfield, *The Epistle to the Romans*, 632–33).

68. Cranfield, *The Epistle to the Romans*, 632–33.

69. I am persuaded by Scott Bartchy's understanding of the letter, according to which Onesimus has fled to Paul not *from* Philemon as a fugitive but, rather, *to* Paul as a recognized patron of his master (Bartchy, "Philemon," 5.305-10).

70. Verse 16 is also climactic from a strictly rhetorical perspective. According to the genre of deliberative rhetoric, which Paul employs for the structure of the letter, verse 16 constitutes the striking conclusion of the main body or proof of the letter (Bartchy, "Philemon," 308).

71. Bartchy, "Philemon," 308. See Sir 33:31: "If you have a servant, treat him as a brother, for as your own soul you will need him. If you ill-treat him, and he leaves and runs away, which way will you go to seek him?"

72. Bartchy, "Philemon," 309.

73. Krentz, "Thessalonians," 6.516.

74. Fitzgerald, "Philippians," 5.319.

75. Scholars have long been troubled by the absence of any explicit expression of gratitude on Paul's part for the Philippians' gift in 4:10-20. Western interpreters particularly struggle with the apparent lack of appropriate social graces on Paul's part. Gerald W. Peterman has recently sought a solution to the puzzle in the social context of Paul's world, specifically, in conventions surrounding gift exchange. Balanced reciprocity prevailed in the ancient world: anyone who received a gift or benefit was expected to respond in kind (Peterman draws heavily on Seneca's *On Benefits*). In such a context, an expression of thanksgiving was typically reserved for the person who was in no position to return the favor—that is, a social inferior. A posture of gratitude would, moreover, be interpreted as solicitation for added benefits. Peterman proceeds to draw upon the *topos* of friendship in the ancient world in order to suggest that Paul and the Philippians had a special bond from their partnership in the Gospel that transcended the quid pro quo norm of gift exchange: among friends an expression of gratitude was not only unnecessary, it was deemed inappropriate (*Paul's Gift from Philippi*).

Peterman's insightful observation that expressions of gratitude typically traveled up the social scale, from inferior to superior, sheds new light on Paul's repeated use of the thanksgiving *topos* in relation to God. But the absence of such language in Philippians 4:10-20 does not necessarily reflect the social context of friendship. Paul viewed his readers as siblings in the surrogate family of God. And as we saw in chapter 2, the primary social matrix in which generalized reciprocity was exercised in Mediterranean antiquity was the family. So if, as Peterman argues, verbal expressions of gratitude were relegated to the quid pro quo world of gift exchange among persons of disparate social class, we are hardly surprised to find Paul avoiding such expressions as he interacts with his siblings in the faith, however offensive such omission of gratitude might be to our Western sensibilities.

5. SECOND-CENTURY CHRISTIAN WRITERS

1. Translations of Lucian are taken from Page, ed., *Lucian*. Lucian, *The Passing of Peregrinus* (ed. Thomas E. Page, trans. Austin M. Harmon, 8 vols., LCL, vol. 5; Cambridge: Harvard Univ. Press, 1936).

2. In addition to his knowledge of the practices of Christians in Palestine and Asia, attested in *Passing of Peregrinus*, Lucian traveled widely and is variously associated with Athens, Gadara, Gaul, and, finally, Egypt, where he accepted a post under the Roman administration (Edwards and Browing, "Lucian," 621).

3. The letter is anonymous, representing itself as a writing of the Roman church but providing no information as to the specific identity of the author. The unity and style of the epistle suggest a single author, and early Christian writers unanimously assign the letter to Clement (see the letter of Dionysius to Soter in Eusebius, *Hist. Eccl.* 4.23.11). Hermas does not mention the epistle but corroborates the traditional association of Clement with the letter when he discusses a certain "Clement" who had responsibility to represent the church at Rome in correspondence with other churches (*Vis.* 2.4.3). Laurence Welborn concludes that the author of our letter "must have been a leading personality in the church at Rome, the official correspondent with other churches" ("Clement," 1.1059-60).

4. The information the author provides in the introduction is no longer read in relation to the reign of Domitian and is, therefore, of little use in dating the letter. Most recently, Welborn places the composition of *1 Clement* between 80 and 140 C.E. ("Clement," 1.1060). Cyril Richardson more confidently dates the work to 96-97 C.E. (*Early Christian Fathers*, 34). Davorin Peterlin concurs ("Clement's Answer," 57). I am not convinced that the evidence allows us to be as specific as the conclusions of Richardson and Peterlin suggest. Welborn's broader estimation is more realistic.

5. Irenaeus and Polycarp knew the letter. Clement of Alexandria cites it as Scripture. *1 Clement* is found alongside canonical literature in Codex Alexandrinus (fifth century), a Coptic papyrus codex (fifth century), and a Syriac New Testament (twelfth century) (Richardson, *Early Christian Fathers*, 33 n. 1; Welborn, "Clement," 1.1056). Eusebius quotes Dionysius, the Bishop of Corinth circa 170-180, who claimed that Clement's letter was still being read publicly in the Corinthian church during Sunday meetings (Eusebius, *Hist. Eccl.* 4.23.11).

6. The reader should note, however, that the term "episcopate," a transliteration of the original *episkopēs*, is potentially misleading. The Greek term is best understood, at this point in the history of its usage, in a functional sense, referring to the oversight exercised by Christian community leaders.

7. Translations of *1 Clement* and the Ignatian Epistles are taken from Goold, ed., *The Apostolic Fathers*.

8. Bartchy, "Slave, Slavery," 1100.

9. Such expressions of self-sacrifice may have been quite common. As Carolyn Osiek notes, "The fact that the letter is written from the Roman church to the Corinthian church further indicates that the examples cannot be localized; they belong to a common tradition of early Christian hagiography" ("The Ransom of Captives," 370).

10. Gerhard Lohfink comments on this passage as follows: "This is not a description of the conditions of the church in Corinth at the time the letter was written. At that time the commu-

nity lived with sedition and schism. But these conditions could not be accepted by the other communities. The idea of the responsibility of the entire 'brotherhood,' that is, the entire community of Corinth, for one another—a point stressed frequently—is not the only noteworthy aspect of the letter. It is also important that the church at *Rome* feels responsible for the church of *Corinth* and, despite the tribulations with which it had to cope itself (cf. *1 Clem.* 1.1), charged it through the letter to return to its former state" (*Jesus and Community,* 154). Lohfink's observations are important, since attempts to explain Rome's uninvited intervention in affairs in Corinth seem to consume the efforts of scholars who study *1 Clement.* Welborn, for example, too easily dismisses the suggestion of A. Stuiber ("Clemens Romanus I," cols. 188–97) that the epistle represents a "fraternal correction" of the Corinthian sedition ("Clement," 1.1059).

11. "The deposition of the local Corinthian rulers leads [Clement] to set forth a hierarchical view of ministry and to stress the need for submission to the duly elected clergy" (Richardson, *Early Christian Fathers,* 38). "Clement's overall intention" is, as Peterlin observes, "to stress order" ("Clement's Answer," 62). Walter Wagner elaborates:

> The letter described Jesus and the apostles establishing a procedure in which Jesus called the apostles, and the apostles appointed bishops and deacons to lead congregations. The first bishops and deacons were to be succeeded by other worthies as needed. . . . *1 Clement* stated that opposition to these officials was "exceedingly disgraceful, and unworthy of your Christian upbringing. . . . The Lord's name is being blasphemed because of your stupidity, and you are exposing yourself to danger." To stand against the bishops was to stand against the apostles, Christ, and God. During the argument for proper discipline and order in the church, *1 Clement* uses laikos, the term associated with average or "lay" members, for the first time in the sense that such persons were the lowest rank in the *ekklesia* and were to take orders from the officials (*After the Apostles,* 126).

This represents patent innovation vis-à-vis the conception of Paul of Tarsus.

12. MacDonald, *The Pauline Churches.*

13. Weber, *Economy and Society;* von Campenhausen, *Ecclesiastical Authority;* Holmberg, *Paul and Power.*

14. Malina, *Christian Origins,* 107.

15. Wagner, *After the Apostles,* 127. L. Michael White has recently challenged these "straight-line models of development toward hierarchical institutional order." The sociological model, for example, usually associated with Max Weber and Ernst Troeltsch, assumes a process of development from the fluid charismatic leadership of the earliest Christian congregations toward the routinized leadership of ecclesiastical office that increasingly characterizes the second-century churches. White finds such models too simplistic. He argues instead for a variety of authority structures that "came into play in diverse combinations depending upon the local circumstances of Christian communities." The result, however, is much the same, since the four kinds of authority structures that White postulates are ultimately amalgamated into the notions of ordained office and church order found in mid-second- and third-century Christianity (White, "Christianity," 1.933-34). The process may have been more complex and variegated than previous models allowed, but the outcome—institutionalization and authoritative hierarchy—is the same.

16. As Welborn notes, for example, "Clement's use of the metaphor of the body (chap. 37) has more in common with Menennius Agrippa (in Livy) than with the purposes of the apostle Paul" ("Clement," 1.1057; see Louis Sanders, *L'hellénisme de saint Clement*, 85–91). Herbert Mayer finds an even earlier hierarchical archetype: "Paul's idea of the church as the body of Christ is filled by Clement with wisdom of Greek political experience and speculation" ("Clement of Rome," 539).

17. In 63.2, Clement describes his letter as "an appeal to peace and concord," and the formulaic description "peace and concord" (*eirēnē kai homonoia*), or parts thereof, occur a number of times in the epistle (9.4; 11.2; 49.5; 20.1, 9, 10; 65.1). Moreover, the identification of the problem at Corinth as a stasis ("sedition") appears again and again in *1 Clement* (1.1; 2.6; 3.2; 14.1 [cognate: *akatastasia*]; passim).

18. I recognize that I must be careful not to overdraw the parallel between the Strong and Weak in Corinth, at the time Paul writes, on the one hand, and the deposed presbyters versus the opposition reflected in *1 Clement*, on the other. It is, however, not unreasonable to assume that the recognized presbyters in Corinth also constituted, for the most part, the elite among the community's members. Higher-status Christians typically adopted the common role of patron to the communities to which they belonged and were, therefore, the most likely candidates for church office. Correspondingly, we find skilled household management listed among the qualifications for community leadership found in 1 Timothy 3. Only persons of some means—specifically, higher-status individuals—were heads of households in antiquity. The deposed presbyters in Corinth, therefore, were likely high-status community members. This reinforces my contention that Clement's prescription for the perceived rebellion in Corinth and the rhetorical devices he employs to apply it contrast markedly with Paul's strategies.

19. Welborn, "Clement," 1059.

20. Dale B. Martin, *The Corinthian Body*, 43, italics added.

21. Welborn attributes this to "the rules of the genre" ("Clement," 1059).

22. Welborn, "Clement," 1059.

23. Annie Jaubert has argued that Clement's illustration combines ranks from both Roman and Judean armies, and that the glorification of the Roman army is, therefore, not Clement's intention. Rather, it is (a) the ordered hierarchy and (b) the submission to authority that characterize any effective military organization that Clement has in view (Jaubert, "Les Sources de las Conception Militaire," 74–84).

24. The textual history of the works ascribed to Ignatius is complex. Current consensus confirms the earlier conclusions of Theodor Zahn and Joseph B. Lightfoot, which identify as authentic the seven letters mentioned above (Zahn, *Ignatius von Antiochien*; Lightfoot, *The Apostolic Fathers*; see Brown, *The Authentic Writings of Ignatius of Antioch*). William Schoedel discusses in some detail the various recensions of Ignatius's writings and the authenticity of the above letters (*Ignatius of Antioch*, 1–10).

25. Wagner, *After the Apostles*, 142.

26. Wolf-Dietrich Köhler (*Die Rezeption des Matthäusevangeliums*, 73–96) is more optimistic than Helmut Koester (*Synoptische Überlieferung*, 24–61) in this regard.

27. Schoedel, "Ignatius," 3.386.

28. Wagner, *After the Apostles*, 145.

29. Wagner, *After the Apostles*, 145.

30. See Craig S. Wasink (*Chained in Christ*) for a recent treatment of the role prisons played in the social fabric of Roman society. Wasink discusses the financial aid and moral support so cru-

cial to the welfare and survival of prisoners in antiquity, as he engages in an exhaustive study of primary sources that address the issue.

31. The obligation to free a family member from slavery was a widely held value in the Mediterranean world. The church-family model, then, provides the most plausible explanation for the expectation on the part of certain slaves that "the price of their manumission would be paid from the churches' common funds" (Bartchy, "Slave, Slavery," 1100). David Daube, in another context, comments upon the Exodus account of Israel's deliverance from bondage: "Here God comes to the nation's rescue on the strength of social laws and customs widely recognized in the ancient world and of extraordinary practical and symbolic importance. One of them is that if you become enslaved, your nearest powerful relative is entitled and obliged to secure your freedom" ("Typology in Josephus," 23). For Israel, that "nearest powerful relative" is God. Thus, God instructs Moses, "Then you shall say to Pharoah, 'Thus says the Lord: Israel is my firstborn son. I said to you, "Let my son go that he may worship me"'" (Exod 4:22-23).

32. The motivation for Ignatius's position on the issue is unclear. Perhaps, as Bartchy surmises, the common fund was limited, and resources designated for widows would have been depleted, if every slave who became a Christian had the right to manumission at the community's expense ("Slave, Slavery," 1100). At any rate, as J. Albert Harrill observes, Ignatius here discusses only perceived abuses accompanying corporate manumission. Private manumission is left unaddressed. The text-segment cannot be cited, then, to demonstrate that Ignatius generally opposed the liberation of Christians in slavery (*Manumission of Slaves*, 194).

33. Malina, *The New Testament World*, 33.

34. Several centuries later, the efforts of Christians to meet the practical needs of those outside their ranks would be recognized by pagan leadership as a key reason for the expansion of Christianity: "Why do we not observe that it is [the Christians'] benevolence to strangers, their care for the graves of the dead and the pretended holiness of their lives that have done the most to increase atheism? When the impious Galileans support not only their own poor but ours as well, all men see that our people lack aid from us (that is, the Roman govt.)" (Roman Emperor Julian "the Apostate," *Letter to Arsacius, High-priest of Galatia*).

35. It is clear from his comments at the beginning of the above citation that Ignatius has in mind not the universal brotherhood of humanity—as if his readers were in some sense already brothers to their pagan neighbors—but, rather, the idea that pagans are potential converts and, therefore, potential brothers.

36. Ignatius's opponents appear to represent two streams of early Christian orientation: a docetic orientation (*Trall.* 10; *Smyrn.* 4.2) and a Judaizing approach (*Magn.* 8–10; *Phild.* 5–9). Some conclude that Ignatius responds to two distinct groups of opponents (Schoedel, "Ignatius," 3.385). Others see a single group of Judaizing Christians who had adopted a docetic Christology (Wagner, *After the Apostles*, 147).

37. Richardson, *Early Christian Fathers*, 76.

38. Schoedel, "Ignatius," *ABD* 3.386.

39. For Justin's Apology, I cite Cyril Richardson, ed., *Early Christian Fathers*. English translations of the rest of Justin's works are taken from Ludwig Schopp, ed. *Saint Justin Martyr*. Robert Grant offers 156 C.E. as the date for the *Apology* (the two *Apologies* were originally a single work). Justin was likely martyred in Rome about 165 C.E. (Grant, "Justin Martyr" in *ABD* 3.1133).

40. There is no record, however, that any of the writings of the early Christian apologists were

heard or read by Roman authorities. As a result, most scholars now assume that such works were written primarily to encourage members of the Christian community. A recent treatment of Justin Martyr, for example, concludes that his extant works were "in-school models prepared by the master teacher for use by his [Christian] students" (Wagner, *After the Apostles*, 159).

41. So, for example, in the *Passion of Perpetua*, the Carthaginian martyr tells a graphic story of her own resistance to her pagan father's pleas. "He fell before me weeping and I pitied him as he called me no longer his daughter, but mistress and lady" (8.3). A century later (circa 303 C.E.) seven girls from Thessalonica admitted to studying their Scriptures in secrecy, "considering their own family worse than enemies" (M. Agape, Chione et al., 1, 5; cited in Robin Lane Fox, *Pagans and Christians*, 424). Similarly, it is said of Polycarp that "the very ones who betrayed him were of his own household" (*Mart. Pol.* 6.2).

42. It became increasingly important for Christian apologists to defend the rationality of martyrdom. One of Antoninus Pius's adopted sons, who would one day become emperor, later commented on the foolishness and lack of reflection that, in his view, characterized Christian martyrdoms: "How admirable is the soul which is ready and resolved, if it must this moment be released from the body, to be either extinguished or scattered or to persist. This resolve, too, must arise from a specific decision, not out of sheer opposition like the Christians, but after reflection and with dignity, and so as to convince others, without histrionic display" (Marcus Aurelius, *Med.* 11.3, trans. Arthur S. L. Farquharson). It is to sentiments like these that Justin responds in the excerpt above on page 148.

43. Translations of Plutarch are taken from Page, ed., *Moralia*.

44. The emperor Domitian had his cousin and heir presumptive Flavius Clemens (along with Clemens's wife Domitilla and the current consul Acilius Glabrio) arrested and charged with "atheism"—"they had slipped into Jewish customs." The men were condemned to death. Domitilla was exiled on the island of Pantellaria. The true motives for Domitian's actions are open to speculation. The pretext, however, that was chosen to justify the emperor's behavior—his cousin's religious apostasy—constituted one of the few socially acceptable explanations for disowning a family member (Dio Cassius, *Hist.* 67.14). See the case of Perpetua and her father in chapter 6.

45. The literature on Judean-Christian relations is immense. Important contributions include Reuther, *Faith and Fratricide*; Dunn, *The Partings of the Ways*; Evans and Hagner, *Anti-Semitism and Early Christianity*; and Setzer, *Jewish Responses to Early Christians*. For a useful compendium of sources dealing with the issue, along with a helpful analysis of these materials, see Wilson, *Related Strangers*.

46. Clement of Alexandria expresses similar sentiments: "Now we, I say, we are they whom God has adopted, and of us alone He is willing to be called Father, not of the disobedient" (*Protr.* 12.94).

47. There are some exceptions. Paul hints at an extension of the metaphor beyond the boundaries of the Christian brotherhood when he refers to God as "the Father, from whom are all things" (1 Cor 8:6; see Eph 3:14-15, 4:6). The context demonstrates, however, that Paul still conceives of the fatherhood of God in terms of the narrow confines of the Christian community: "Indeed, even though there may be so-called gods in heaven or on earth—as in fact there are many gods and many lords—yet for us there is one God, the Father, from whom are all things and for whom we exist, and one Lord, Jesus Christ, through whom are all things and through whom we exist" (1 Cor. 8:5-6). The only clear example comes from Acts 17, where the author quotes Paul as he is speaking to the Athenian philosophers: "For 'In him we live and move and have our being'; as even some of your own poets have said, 'For we too are his offspring.' Since we are God's

offspring, we ought not to think that the deity is like gold, or silver, or stone, an image formed by the art and imagination of mortals" (17:28-29). Note that, similarly to Justin, it is the apologetic context in which Paul is speaking that occasions the expansion of the metaphor.

48. The reader is referred to Birger A. Pearson's helpful overview of the history of early Egyptian Christianity ("Christianity in Egypt," 1.954-60). Prior to Clement, the evidence, as Pearson appropriately recognizes, is "scanty and ambiguous, and has been subject to diametrically opposed interpretations" (959). Scholarly consensus rejects as historically unreliable the information that Eusebius provides about Alexandrian Christianity as it existed before the late second century. Most of the other source material typically appealed to in reconstructions of the earlier period is of questionable date or provenance, or both (*Secret Gospel of Mark, Epistle of Barnabas, 2 Clement, Apocalypse of Peter, Protevangel of James*) (Pearson, "Christianity in Egypt," 1.956-57). The alleged association of Mark with the region remains a topic of debate (Pearson, "Christianity in Egypt," 1.956-57; see Morton Smith, *Clement of Alexandria*). History begins to emerge from the mist of legend and speculation with Demetrius (189–232 C.E.), who is the first Alexandrian bishop of whom anything concrete is known (Pearson, "Christianity in Egypt," 1.955). Clement's works, then, written near the end of the second century, provide us with our earliest reliable witness to beliefs and social practices of what had perhaps only recently become the orthodox expression of Christianity in Alexandria.

49. It has been common for scholars to argue that definitive borderlines between "orthodoxy" and "heresy" were established in Egypt rather late (Koester, *Introduction to the New Testament*, 2.239), and there is some debate concerning the degree to which beliefs later identified as orthodox prevailed at the time Clement wrote. Some assume a highly variegated picture in Egypt as late as the end of the second century (Wagner, *After the Apostles*, 179). Colin H. Roberts contends, however, that Pantaenus (circa 180s) played a central role in purging the catechetical school of Alexandria of gnostic influence and establishing its focus as orthodox (*Manuscript, Society and Belief*). Recent studies of material remains from Egyptian Christianity disprove older scholarly claims that Coptic Christianity originated in a primarily gnostic milieu. From earliest times, one finds concurrent literary production of codices containing both gnostic and orthodox material. Tito Orlandi has demonstrated that the orthodox codices display a more accurate and precise orthography and linguistic consistency, and that they are more carefully constructed. The logical conclusion, which Orlandi and others draw, is that the gnostic writings did not enjoy the same status as sacred books (Orlandi, "Coptic Literature," 55–56). As Pheme Perkins concludes, "The translators and copyists of the surviving gnostic materials were probably attempting to emulate a tradition that was established in the larger Christian community" (*Gnosticism and the New Testament*, 181). Finally, as Pearson rightly observes, "there must presumably have been sufficient 'orthodoxy' in Alexandria before Demetrius for Irenaeus, writing about 180, to include the church in Egypt among the churches scattered throughout the world that preserve the catholic faith with 'one heart and one soul'" (*Adv. Haer.* 1.10.2, cited in "Christianity in Egypt," 1.959). A comparison of the theologies of Irenaeus and Clement might lead us to question the accuracy of Irenaeus's claim. Differences obtain with respect to what is emphasized as orthodox doctrine by these two Christian theologians. Perhaps we should be cautious, however, in overemphasizing these differences. For as we move from theology to sociology, we find that the orientation that characterized Clement's Christianity consistently reflects the social model with which we have now become eminently familiar— for Clement, the church is a family.

50. Clement's works are fascinating with respect to both the extent to which and the creativity with which he makes use of the PKG model. Like Ignatius, Clement challenges his readers to submit to church authorities "just as to fathers" (*To the Newly Baptized*). Unlike the previous authors surveyed, Clement's God has a maternal, as well as a paternal, nature: "And while the unspeakable part of Him is Father, the part that has sympathy with us is Mother" (*Quis Div.* 37). The metaphor is fluid, however, for elsewhere it is the church that is identified as "mother" of the faithful (*Paed.* 1.5; 1.6). The *Instructor* represents an expansion of the kinship model to include in the church family the Greek *paidagogos*, whose role is to train the Christian to emulate God his father. Clement's *paidagogos* is identified at the outset of the work as Jesus (*Paed.* 1.7). The limitations of the present project necessarily exclude discussion of these various innovations. I must limit my treatment of both Clement and Irenaeus to providing evidence for (a) the broad employment of kinship terms in their writings and (b) the practical expression of family-like solidarity in the communities that they represent.

51. Wagner, *After the Apostles*, 173.

52. Translations of Clement are from Page, ed., *The Rich Man's Salvation*.

53. See, for example, William L. Lane's commentary on the text: "The specific form of sacrifice Jesus demanded of this man is not to be regarded as a general prescription to be applied to all men, nor yet as a demand for an expression of piety that goes beyond the requirements of the Law. The command to sell his property and to distribute the proceeds to the poor was appropriate to this particular situation" (*The Gospel According to Mark*, 367).

54. The information is provided by the account of Eusebius (*Hist. Eccl.* 5.1-3).

55. See the discussions in Keresztes, "Marcus Aurelius a Persecutor?" 321–41; Frend, *The Rise of Christianity*, 183–84; and Wagner, *After the Apostles*, 205–6.

56. Frend calls *Against Heresies* "the classic statement of orthodoxy in the primitive Greek-speaking church" (*The Rise of Christianity*, 244). Irenaeus almost certainly wrote in Greek, and fragments of his works survive in that language. The manuscripts containing *Against Heresies* are, however, in Latin and Armenian (Wagner, *After the Apostles*, 268 n. 1.). I will limit my references in the section on Irenaeus to evidence from *Against Heresies*.

57. Henry Chadwick notes, to Irenaeus's credit, that "even after the numerous recent discoveries of Gnostic documents, [the five books of *Against Heresies*] remain an essential and remarkably fair-minded source for the history of the second-century sects" (*The Early Church*, 80).

58. A most valuable recent overview of gnostic beliefs and origins can be found in Rudolph, *Gnosis*. For the doctrine of the ascent of the soul through the planetary spheres, see pages 173–86.

59. English translations taken from Coxe, ed., *Against Heresies*.

60. This is hardly to imply that we can fully trust Irenaeus's descriptions of his opponents' behavior. Firsthand knowledge of gnostic ideology and behavioral practices, reflected in the documents uncovered at Nag Hammadi, serves as an important corrective to Irenaeus's polemic, regardless of the general reliability of his account (see n. 57, above). This is particularly the case with respect to gnostic social practice, for it is here that the statements of the heresiologists are "woefully inadequate" (Rudolph, *Gnosis*, 207). Irenaeus himself hints at the fact that among certain gnostic sects, the kinship metaphor apparently did find some kind of application in community life, for there is evidence of salutations exchanged between "brother" and "sister," and of a self-awareness of the gnostic community as "a great family which shares the same origin" (Rudolph, *Gnosis*, 206); (see *Adv. Haer.* 1.6.3). What we lack, however, is evidence of any tangible

expression of these sibling relationships in terms of the PKG values surveyed in the course of this book. Specific examples of sibling solidarity in the form of generalized reciprocity or familial loyalty—even rhetorical challenges to such activity—are simply absent from gnostic literature. Correspondingly, Rudolph observes that "very little is known about the form and composition of the 'earthly' [gnostic] society," and later concludes that there was "no gnostic 'church,'" as "church" was understood to function socially among the early Christians (*Gnosis*, 207, 213). At any rate, we are concerned in the above analysis not with gnostic but with Christian social practices in Gaul, for which Irenaeus does provide some background, information that is later confirmed by the account of Lyons's pogrom from the pen of Eusebius.

61. Patrilocal residence is reflected elsewhere in the text, where Irenaeus cites John 14:2: "For there are many mansions in the Father's house" (3.19.3).

62. The Latin term is *fraternitate*. A fragment from Irenaeus's Greek original has survived for this passage. The portion quoted above is cited by Eusebius. The kinship framework is present in the original: *adelphotēti* (*Hist. Eccl.* 5.7.2).

6. North African Christianity

1. Timothy Barnes reflects the general consensus of the scholarly community when he identifies the Scillitan martyrs as "the first African Christians of whom any precise knowledge is preserved" (*Tertullian*, 60). The text consists of a transcript of the trial of several Christians before the governor Vigellius Saturninus, proconsul in 180–81. The Christians on trial come from a small and obscure town near the great metropolis of Carthage.

2. "Africa, The Church in Roman," *Oxford Dictionary of the Christian Church*, 22.

3. Barnes, *Tertullian*, 69–70.

4. The quotation is from Musurillo, ed., *Acts of the Christian Martyrs*, xxv. I cite Musurillo's translation throughout.

5. Barnes believes Perpetua may have been a representative of the senatorial class. She is described as being of high birth, of good education, and nobly married (*Pass. Perp.* 2.1; echoed in *CIL* 8.870). The language points toward senatorial rank. Her *nomen* (the middle name of a Roman freeperson), Vibia, also suggests a high-status background. Three Vibii served as African proconsuls in the first century, none after the reign of Vespasian (Barnes, *Tertullian*, 70).

6. Barnes, *Tertullian*, 263. See also Barnes, "Pre-Decian *Acta Martyrum*," 509–31.

7. Fox, *Pagans and Christians*, 401. The work as a whole provides "invaluable testimony for the Christian community of Carthage in the early third century" (Barnes, *Tertullian*, 263). The document's claim to be regarded as authentic and contemporary has been vindicated (see n. 8 in this chapter). The varying style of the document also confirms its claim to consist of a narrative that quotes two key sources: a first-person account of Perpetua's trial and prison experiences (3–10), and Saturus's description of his vision (11–13). Still unresolved are debates concerning the original language in which the work was composed, and the degree (if any) of Montanist influence (Barnes, *Tertullian*, 265–66; Musurillo, *Acts of the Christian Martyrs*; Fox, *Pagans and Christians*, 439, 746 n. 97).

8. The historicity of the narrative's broad outline has been generally acknowledged. Various details, however, are obviously fabricated. Barnes traces a number of these fabrications to a Montanist theological agenda, including Perpetua's visions concerning her brother Deinocrates. The

visions clearly imply that "a martyr (but perhaps not anyone else) can effect the release of a soul from hell and secure its admittance to heaven" (Barnes, *Tertullian*, 77–79).

9. Of the interaction between father and daughter at the public trial scene, Frend observes, "It was precisely the situation that had worried Celsus, and the father's evident inability to control his daughter brought on him the procurator's anger" (*The Rise of Christianity*, 291).

10. Frend, *The Rise of Christianity*, 291.

11. Jerome relates that Tertullian was the son of a centurion in the proconsul's guard, but the historical value of this information is suspect (Jerome, *De viris illust.* 53). Barnes rejects Jerome's assertions that Tertullian was a priest and that his father was a Roman soldier, arguing instead that Jerome's deductions arise from a misreading of Tertullian (*Tertullian*, 2–12). Frend places more confidence in the account (*The Rise of Christianity*, 348).

12. Barnes has counted at least thirty literary sources upon which Tertullian draws in his *Apology*. Included are the works of Herodotus, Varro, Pliny the Younger, King Juba of Mauretania, Hermippus, and Josephus (*Tertullian*, 196). Barnes sees in Tertullian a thinker who was attempting to build a bridge between paganism and Christianity. The thesis has not been universally received, and it stumbles over Tertullian's own claim to the contrary (Frend, *The Rise of Christianity*, 349, 358): "What have the philosopher and Christian in common, the disciple of Greece and the disciple of heaven?" (*Apol.* 44.18). Indeed, as I shall demonstrate below, the theme of sibling loyalty finds especially profuse application in the writings of Tertullian and Cyprian precisely because of its ability to vividly symbolize a community highly polarized vis-à-vis the surrounding pagan world.

13. Frend detects Montanist influence in Tertullian's writings as early as his treatise against Marcion (circa 207) (*The Rise of Christianity*, 364 n. 73). He also finds strong Montanist influence in Carthage among the martyrs Perpetua and Felicitas and their circle (*The Donatist Church*, 117–18). See also an inscription opposing second marriages, a Montanist doctrine: *CIL* 8.25045.

14. Quotations from the works of Tertullian are taken from Deferrari, ed., *The Fathers of the Church*.

15. Barnes finds further evidence to this effect in the *Passion of Perpetua*. The document, whose character is "Montanist through and through," nevertheless demonstrates that North African theological dissensions had not yet divided the church irreparably. The Montanist party was still recognized as a part of the catholic church, as evidenced by the fact that Perpetua was rapidly accepted as a catholic, not a Montanist, martyr (Barnes, *Tertullian*, 77–79). Tertullian's use of sibling terminology to address catholic Christians during his Montanist period (discussed above) confirms Barnes's observations.

16. Blood relatives are clearly addressed in the above citation. Tertullian sets "*father*, mother, and all our relatives" (italics added) over against "God," near the end of the passage. The former cannot represent relations in the church community, since Tertullian typically reserves the metaphorical use of paternal language for God alone. Blood-family relatives must, therefore, be in view.

17. The narrator instructs the reader, at the beginning of the *Passion*, that Perpetua had two brothers, only one of which was a Christian (2.6). Both brothers later visit her and eat with her in prison (16.4).

18. Lohfink, *Jesus and Community*, 155.

19. Extant literary sources for mid-third-century history are scarce and often unreliable. The account of Cassius Dio, the consular Greek historian, ends circa 229 C.E., during his second consulate. Herodian, another Greek historian, penned a chronicle that began with the accession of Commodus (180 C.E.) and ended during the chaotic year of 238. Even the *Historia Augusta*, itself of

questionable reliability (though at times based on sound material), breaks down entirely after detailing the beginning of the reign of Philip the Arab (244 C.E.). The *Historia* only picks up again with the closing passages of the *vita* of Valerian. (For a possible explanation of the gap in the *Historia*, see Mattingly, "The Religious Background," 213–15.) The lacuna leaves the period from 244 to 259 unattested, and the student must resort, for literary accounts of the political history of the period, to those shreds of evidence provided by later compilers, epitomators, and chronographers (Aurelius Victor, Zonarus, et al.). The Cyprianic corpus—consisting of a dozen treatises and eighty-two letters, all written between 249 and 258—therefore constitutes a collection of "precious historical documents" (Graeme W. Clarke, *The Letters of Cyprian*, 1.5).

20. The property that Cyprian possessed in Carthage suggests that he was from a local established family of significant resources. The land, which included urban *horti* (*Ep.* 81.1.1; *Acta Cyp.* 2.1), is most likely to have come to him by inheritance. Confirming Cyprian's social location are references to a good education and to secular acquaintances who held posts in local government (Pontius, *Vit. Cyp.* 2, 14; see Jerome, *De viris illust.* 67). Note also Cyprian's reputation as a *rhetor* (Jerome, *De viris illust.* 67) (see Graeme W. Clarke, "The Secular Profession," 633–38). His trial and manner of execution indicate that Cyprian was treated—and acted— as an *honestior*, a man of the upper classes (*Acta Cyp.* 5.4; see Garnsey, *Social Status and Legal Privilege*, 103). The evidence is insufficient, however, to support Ekkart Sauser's contention that Cyprian belonged to the senatorial class (*Bekenner seiner Herrlichkeit*, 87). Clarke is more on target to limit the assignment of Cyprian's social status more generally to curial rank (*The Letters of Cyprian*, 1.125 n. 64).

21. Cyprian remarks, in *Ep.* 59.6.1, that he has been held in esteem by his people "for four years now as bishop." The letter was written in the summer of 252 and suggests that Cyprian became bishop sometime between summer 248 and the first half of 249 (Graeme W. Clark, *The Letters of Cyprian*, 1.127 n. 78). Cyprian's rapid accession to the episcopate, as a very recent convert to Christianity, is best explained on the assumption that he was a man of authority and stature in a highly class-conscious society. Across the Mediterranean, in contemporary Pontic Comana, the search for a local bishop focused predominantly upon "those who appeared to be outstanding in eloquence, birth and other distinguished qualities" (reported by Gregory of Nyssa in his *Vita Gregorii Thaumaturgi* [*PG* 46.933]). Ambrose, Basil, and Augustine represent other examples of "irregular" episcopal advancement (Hess, *The Canons of the Council of Sardica*, 105 n. 3).

Cyprian's rapid advancement, however, finds additional explanation elsewhere. It was not only Cyprian's social location at the upper echelon of society that made him an attractive candidate for the episcopate. Evidence suggests that popular (if not clerical) enthusiasm for Cyprian's advancement to the office of bishop may be partially attributed to Cyprian's behavior upon conversion to Christianity. His willingness to sell all of his worldly goods in order to care for the poor was both an act of charity and one of total commitment to the Christian cause (Pontius, *Vit. Cyp.* 2, 14; see Jerome, *De viris illust.* 67). For, as Graeme W. Clarke appropriately notes, "Cyprian would be selling his secular social status along with his patrimony" (*The Letters of Cyprian*, 1.17).

22. Graeme W. Clarke, *The Letters of Cyprian*, 1.19-20.

23. The evidence Cyprian provides is actually much broader in scope. The letters reflect communications with Christian communities in Spain (*Ep.* 67), in Gaul (referred to in *Ep.* 68), in Cappadocia (referred to in *Ep.* 75), and in Rome (*Epp.* 9, 20, 27, and so forth).

24. The fact that Cyprian was not a particularly creative thinker renders his insights especially helpful for the present argument, for we may surmise that Cyprian was hardly alone in his

conception of Christian community. As Graeme W. Clarke notes, "That precious insight into the world of the mid-third century—what people in the society in which he moved were saying and thinking, what issues they considered uncontroversial, what topics they regarded as worth-while to argue about—would have been obscured by a mind more creative, more original or more adventurous than Cyprian's. All the evidence converges to suggest that the reactions regis-tered by Cyprian he inherited from predecessors or shared with peers" (*The Letters of Cyprian*, 1.5). The same surely obtains for Cyprian's view of the church as a family.

25. The letters are not all from Cyprian's hand. Among the collection that has survived are six-teen letters which occasioned Cyprian's response. Another six epistles represent synodal or collective letters of the African church but, nevertheless, clearly bear the marks of Cyprian, the presiding bishop. The sixty remaining epistles are Cyprian's own (Graeme W. Clarke, *The Letters of Cyprian*, 1.7).

26. See Graeme W. Clarke (*The Letters of Cyprian*, 1.122 n. 48) for a history of scholarship.

27. Graeme W. Clarke isolates the first four letters as nonpersecution documents and then sug-gests that the following order for the next twenty-three letters "will carry the reader through a rea-sonably intelligent sequence from very early 250 until high summer of that year": *Epp.* 7, 5, 6, 13, 14, 11, 10, 12, 15, 16, 17, 18, 19, 8, 9, and 20–27 (*The Letters of Cyprian*, 1.12).

28. Graeme W. Clarke's translation of the *Epistles* will be cited throughout.

29. Cyprian addresses *Epistle* 2 to his "brother Eucratius" but refers to him in closing as "my dearest son" (2.2.3). Because Eucratius is clearly a fellow bishop, the inconsistency has occasioned some discussion in the literature. Adolph von Harnack attributed the filial form of address at the end of the epistle to a simple difference in age between the two bishops (*Über vorlorene Brief*, 27). Antonius A. R. Bastiaensen offers the possibility that Eucratius first served under Cyprian in Carthage (*Le cérémonial épistolaire*, 154). The departure from the far more common sibling term of address is unimportant to the present survey, however, since it is evidenced on only a single occa-sion elsewhere in Cyprian's writings (*Ep.* 69).

30. See Graeme W. Clarke's comment: "In Cyprian we have practical evidence of the Church constituting a society within a society, a regular *tertium genus*, with an elaborate alimentary system (under the bishop's control) for supporting widows and those in need (orphans, sick, prisoners, visitors, etc.)" (*The Letters of Cyprian*, 1.163 n. 12). Clarke, however, fails to locate the practice of gen-eralized reciprocity in the context of the family model. Indeed, he almost totally ignores Cypri-an's abundant kinship terminology in his otherwise outstanding and detailed four-volume com-mentary on the *Epistles*. The North African Christian community is not simply "a society within a society." It is an alternative family, as the juxtaposition of kinship terminology with references to PKG behavior throughout Cyprian's letters clearly demonstrates.

31. Cyprian's willingness to take on the actor's support has sparked discussion about the gener-ous financial resources apparently available to the leader of the Christian church at Carthage. It is, of course, rather speculative to extrapolate from examples of individual alimentary assistance, such as that represented in the letter to Eucratius, an estimation of the economic well-being of the church at Carthage. References to alimentary aid among North African Christians occur again and again, however, in the Cyprianic corpus. For Graeme W. Clarke, the Carthaginian church's resources are significant enough to suggest that the city had suffered little from the economic woes experi-enced elsewhere in the mid-third-century Roman Empire (*The Letters of Cyprian*, 1.13).

32. Perhaps the family model itself gave rise to such a practice. Some century and a half ear-lier, a Christian visionary beheld a number of maidens with whom he was finally convinced to

stay the night. The maidens reasoned with the reluctant shepherd as follows: "You shall sleep with us as a brother and not as a husband, for you are our brother and for the future we are going to live with you, for we love you greatly." One can imagine the North Africans, chastized in connection with the above events, responding to the challenges of Cyprian and their local leader Pomponius in much the same way as the shepherd does when he assures his readers of the probity of his behavior: "[The maidens] did nothing else but pray, and I also prayed with them unceasingly and not less than they" (Hermas, *Sim. 9.11.1*). Irenaeus's polemic against the Gnostics draws upon the same *topos*. In some circles, apparently, more than praying was going on: "Others of them, again, who pretend at first to live in all modesty with them as sisters, have in course of time been revealed in their true colours, when the sister has been found with child by her [pretended] brother" (*Adv. Haer.* 1.6.3).

33. Information provided by the letter—that those who have vowed to remain chaste can later change their minds and marry, if "they are unwilling or unable to persevere" in their virginity (4.2.3)—suggests that such vows made at this time in North African Christianity were of a private and uncomplicated nature and could be rescinded without much formality. Neither Tertullian nor Cyprian mentions any public, official ceremony of consecration to perpetual virginity (Graeme W. Clarke, *The Letters of Cyprian*, 1.176 n. 22).

34. For a recent discussion of the right of a Roman husband who confronted his wife's adulterous lover, see Treggiari, *Roman Marriage*, 271–75. See also Corbett, *The Roman Law of Marriage*, 127.

35. Graeme W. Clarke, *The Letters of Cyprian*, 1.19.

36. *Epistle 7* is the earliest of the surviving Decian letters. Cyprian is already safe in hiding, but there are as yet no imprisoned confessors. Apparently, the details of Decius's orders and their implications for the faithful are not yet widely appreciated. By the time *Epistles 5–6* are penned (the two letters were written about the same time, early 250 C.E.), a number of confessors have been imprisoned. The persecution is still in its initial stages, however, since the confessors are freely visited in prison without threat to those who minister to their needs. In *Epistle 13*, written to the confessors, Cyprian makes reference to an interval that has passed since his previous correspondence (13.1), and it is now clear that the losses to the flock as a whole are significant. In the parallel *Epistle 14*, to the Carthaginian clergy, Cyprian expresses his regrets concerning many who have succumbed to pagan pressure: "This hostile tempest have [*sic*] overwhelmed not only the majority of our people—what has caused us the greatest distress of all is that it has involved in its devastating wake even a portion of the clergy" (14.1.1) (on all this, see Graeme W. Clarke, *The Letters of Cyprian*, 1.198, 181, 189, 254, 261; and Duquenne, *Chronologie des letters*, 62).

37. For the background to the Decian persecution, consult Frend, *Martyrdom and Persecution*, 389. More specific discussions of Decius's motivation include Alföldi, "Zu den Christenverfolgungen," 323–48; and Molthagen, *Die römische Staat und die Christen*, 70.

38. Cyprian's flight suggests that imperial orders first sought the compliance of bishops. Bishop Fabian is the first known victim in Rome, and Dionysius of Alexandria is sought out immediately upon the receipt of the imperial orders (Eusebius, *Hist. Eccl.* 6.40.2). Cyprian was one of several bishops to flee, and he was subject to some criticism for his decision. Cyprian claims his hiding is necessary for "the general peace of the community." He fears that his "presence may provoke an outburst of violence and resentment among the pagans" (7.1). *Epistle 20* (20.1.2) expands on the circumstances of Cyprian's departure and confirms his contention that he was, to cite Graeme W. Clarke, "a well-known figure, and a marked man" (*The Letters of Cyprian*, 1.199 n. 3). The reference

to *desiderium*, above (7.1), may imply a previous letter written to Cyprian from Carthage, an epistle that criticized his flight and expressed a corresponding "longing" for Cyprian's return to his post. According to Clarke, though, Cyprian simply assumes here that "the *desiderium* which he feels himself is shared by his clergy and his flock." Cyprian is not on the defensive in this early block of correspondence. If he were, his reference to mutual *desiderium* would certainly be "a bold front to assume" (*The Letters of Cyprian*, 1.199 n. 2).

39. Graeme W. Clarke draws attention to evidence for a widespread refugee movement among Christians trying to escape the consequences of Decius's orders (see Dionysius of Alexandria, according to Eusebius, *Hist. Eccl.* 6.42.2; Gregory of Nyssa, MG 46.945). Perhaps the initiation of the persecution in Rome resulted in the presence of fugitives in Carthage. The early date of the letter, however (see n. 38 in this chapter), suggests that the *peregrini* ("foreigners to the *polis*") are in Carthage for other reasons (*The Letters of Cyprian*, 1.201 n. 10).

40. Sullivan, *The Life of the North African*, 70–71; Graeme W. Clarke, *The Letters of Cyprian*, 1.201 n. 11.

41. Bobertz, "Cyprian as Patron." The sale and disposal of Cyprian's patrimony at the time of his conversion is shrouded in obscurity (see Pontius, *Vit. Cyp.* 2.7, 15.1; Jerome, *De viris illust.* 67; Cyprian, *Ep.* 81). Deferrari seems to accept the information provided by Pontius, that Cyprian's friends restored his property to him by buying it back, and that Cyprian would have sold the gardens again had not the outbreak of persecution necessitated a change in his plans (Deferrari, ed., FC, 36, vi). At any rate, it is clear from the above excerpt that at the time *Epistle* 7 was written, Cyprian had significant personal resources at his disposal. Later, at another stage in the persecution, Cyprian's *bona* were officially forfeited (66.4.1), as were those of all bishops (66.7.2).

42. The presence of imprisoned confessors moves the Letter beyond the date of *Epistle* 7, but still before April 250 C.E., when torture began to be introduced for recalcitrant confessors (see *Ep.* 10, 11, 12) (Graeme W. Clarke, *The Letters of Cyprian*, 1.190).

43. As noted in the case of Perpetua, earlier in this chapter, responsibility for meeting an imprisoned person's need for daily sustenance fell to the prisoner's family. The family model adopted by the Carthaginian Christians thus provides the background to Cyprian's challenge to the church to provide for the imprisoned confessors. See Wasink, *Chained in Christ*.

44. Graeme W. Clarke, *The Letters of Cyprian*, 1.185 n. 8.

45. This would also apply to Graeme W. Clarke's suggestion that the individuals concerned may have been more than victims of incidental poverty—that they suffered *because* they had remained steadfast in their faith (1.185 n. 8). Later in the Decian period, certain Carthaginian Christians are driven from their homes (either as refugees or, officially, as exiles), and forfeit their property (see *Ep.* 8.3.1, 24.1.1). The present letters (5–6) contain no indication, however, that such was the case at this time. Indeed, the freedom the church had to visit the imprisoned in great numbers clearly argues the contrary.

46. Graeme W. Clarke, *The Letters of Cyprian*, 1.254.

47. As is typically the case with monetary figures in ancient literature, it is difficult to ascertain a clear idea of the purchasing power of the donations involved here. More than a century previous, Pliny's (generous) pensions for his freedmen seem to have been between 70 and 85 sesterces per person per month. In the late 170s in North Africa, at Sicca Veneria, all the necessities of life for a child apparently required approximately 10 and 8 sesterces for a boy and girl, respectively (*ILS* 6818). On all this, see Duncan-Jones, *The Economy of the Roman Empire*.

48. Graeme W. Clarke, however, probably makes too much of a change in the *incipit.* The expression *fratribus carissimis* ("dearest brothers"), which appeared in *Epistles* 7 and 5 (see above), is noticeably absent from the *incipit* here in *Epistle* 14. According to Clarke, the defection of "a portion" of the church leaders in the face of the persecution likely explains the omission. By the time Cyprian pens *Epistle* 14, there are apparently some "troublesome characters" among the ranks of the Carthaginian clergy (*The Letters of Cyprian,* 1.182 n. 1). What Clarke fails to relate, however, is the fact that Cyprian opens the body of his letter with the phrase "dearly beloved brothers" (14.1.1), and that he closes the letter with similarly endearing terms of affection ("my most dear and cherished brothers") (14.4.1).

49. For Cyprian's nonepistolary works, I cite Deferrari, ed., FC, 36.

50. The only exceptions occur in *Epistle* 10, in which Cyprian claims that "our Mother the Church takes great pride" in the faith and fortitude of the confessors (10.1.1); and in *De habitu virginum,* in which "Mother Church rejoices" because of the presence of the holy virgins among her children (3). The image otherwise occurs only in contexts that are polemical in nature.

51. On this, see Plumpe, *Mater ecclesia.*

52. For Cyprian's use of the biblical text, see Fahey, *Cyprian and the Bible.*

53. The change is clearly intentional, for in a previous letter, written before the outbreak of the controversy, Cyprian had addressed the same imprisoned Roman confessor, Maximus, as one of "his dearly beloved brothers" (*Ep.* 28.1.1). Later, upon his return to the orthodox fold, Maximus is again addressed in sibling terms (see *Ep.* 51.1.1, discussed below).

54. Elsewhere, Cyprian denounces Novatian as one who has "failed to maintain charity with his brethren" (*Ep.* 55.24.1). Those who follow Novatian "must realize that it is an act of impiety to abandon their mother" (*Ep.* 44.3.2). To one wavering member of the surrogate family (Antonianus), who is attracted to the teachings of Novatian, Cyprian exhorts: "Your duty is clear. As a loyal brother and as a fellow bishop who is at one with us, you should not lend a ready ear to the words of apostates and slanderers" (*Ep.* 55.7.3).

55. Cyprian's handling of the parable of the good Samaritan is revealing. No sibling terminology occurs in the Gospel text (Luke 10:25-37). Rather, the issue in the original narrative is the proper treatment of a "neighbor" (*plēsion*). So pervasive is the family model in Cyprian's thinking about Christian community, however, that he must interject into the parable the sibling idea: "Do we simply walk past our *brother* lying there half-dead, like the priest and levite . . . Do we imitate Christ's teaching and example, snatch our wounded *brother* from the jaws of our foe?" (*Ep.* 55.19.2).

56. The dating is Graeme W. Clarke's (*The Letters of Cyprian,* 3.29). Numidian towns were always subject to raids from hill-tribesmen and nomadic bandits. The disbanding, in 238 C.E., of the African legion III Augusta, stationed at Lambaesis, likely exacerbated barbarian problems in Numidia. Inscriptions reveal a tumultuous period for Numidia and its western neighbor Mauritania Caesariensis during the 240s and 250s. The latter decade, in particular, saw authorities suppress (1) a formidable uprising of the tribesmen of the Bavares and of the Quinquengentanei, and (2) the lawless activities of a group led by a bandit leader named Faraxen (*ILS* 1194, 2767, 3000), on which see Graeme W. Clarke, "Barbarian Disturbances," 78–85.

57. Frend, *The Rise of Christianity,* 350. The importance of baptism and the baptismal controversies for North African Christians is best understood in this light. Baptism symbolized the complete renunciation of the pagan world and its values.

7. Summary and Evaluation

1. Peristiany, "Introduction," 9.

2. Keesing, *Kin Groups and Social Structure*, 126.

3. In some cases, the person addressed is "violating the norms of kinship." Paul, for example, draws upon the sibling metaphor to censure community members who take their fellow Christians to court (1 Cor 6:1-10). The Roman presbyters who write to Cyprian of Carthage while he is in hiding during the Decian persecution use sibling language and the theme of family loyalty to encourage Cyprian to return to his post (*Ep.* 8.2.1-2). Cyprian's pointed reply, again framed in sibling terminology, informs his detractors that his flight is in the best interests of the "brethren" (*Ep.* 20.1.2). In each case, a perceived violation of kinship norms has elicited the sibling metaphor. More potentially manipulative usages of the family metaphor include Clement of Rome's dissonant juxtaposition of concord rhetoric with brother terminology to reinforce the established ecclesiastical hierarchy in Corinth (*1 Clement*). Cyprian's use of the *topos* of sibling betrayal, in his attempts to marginalize heterodox teachers and their followers, also demonstrates the inherent emotive power of family language as a tool to demarcate the boundaries of the social group.

4. Thiselton, *Interpreting God*, 29.

5. Note, for example, the work of Ian Ramsey (*Religious Language*). Ramsey refused to reject models as necessarily deceptive. He recognized the positive potential of religious models but offered safeguards to prevent their abuse; more on Ramsey's suggestions below. A number of recent writers on the subject are not as generous.

6. Shaw, *The Cost of Authority*, 283.

7. Shaw, *God in Our Hands*, x.

8. Stephen D. Moore, *Poststructuralism*, 109.

9. Stephen D. Moore, *Poststructuralism*, 114.

10. Castelli, *Imitating Paul*.

11. Thiselton, *Interpreting God*, 141.

12. Castelli, *Imitating Paul*, 113–14.

13. Castelli, *Imitating Paul*, 119–20.

14. Thiselton, *Interpreting God*, 141.

15. I must limit my observations to the writings of Paul. Paul is the only writer of those surveyed here whose leadership strategy and motivation have been the subject of both extensive postmodern analyses and historically and culturally nuanced rebuttals.

16. For a general critique of postmodern theory, see, for example, O'Neill, *The Poverty of Postmodernism*. For a negative assessment of the philosophical underpinnings of the postmodern enterprise, see Norris, *The Contest of Faculties;* and Bernstein, *The New Constellation*.

17. See Hirsch, *Validity in Interpretation*.

18. Castelli, *Imitating Paul*, 118.

19. Castelli's anachronistic observation about the lack of tolerance for diversity in Paul's communities is a case in point. The Pauline churches appear radically innovative, and highly tolerant of social diversity, when appropriately examined against the backdrop of their own historical and cultural milieu.

20. I am not, of course, claiming absolute objectivity for the present enterprise. My presuppositional fingerprints are, I readily acknowledge, discernible throughout the book, and the reader thereby learns a great deal about my *response* to the writings surveyed in the process. Nor am I suggesting a return to the naive modernist assumption that total objectivity is an obtainable goal in the historical enterprise. We will, of course, never approach total clarity and consensus in our reading of ancient texts, due to both the limitations of the source material and the socialization of the historian in her own cultural matrix. However, the acknowledgment of our sociocultural biases (in my opinion, the single most valuable contribution of postmodernism), along with a proper appreciation of the nature and extent of our source materials, should serve the inquirer as a reliable point of departure for historical analysis. Extreme postmodernism's conviction that cross-cultural historical analysis and critique are impossible because the interpreter is thoroughly imprisoned within her own cultural narrative is, itself, a metanarrative that renders the postmodern enterprise highly vulnerable to epistemological criticism. As Wright pointedly queries, "By what right does the postmodernist claim to be standing still, observing the rest of the world going round and round in its biased circles?" (Borg and Wright, *The Meaning of Jesus*, 213; see Fischer, *Historians' Fallacies*, 42–43 n. 4).

21. Thiselton, *Interpreting God*, 142.

22. Peter Marshall, *Enmity at Corinth*; Andrew D. Clarke, *Secular and Christian Leadership in Corinth*.

23. Pogoloff, *Logos and Sophia*.

24. Jewett, *Christian Tolerance*.

25. The description of Nietzsche's approach is from Thiselton, *Interpreting God*, 28; italics added.

26. Thiselton, *Interpreting God*, 32, italics added. Ramsey has proposed a helpful methodology for the use of religious models. He acknowledges both the constructive and the destructive potential of religious images. Among the safeguards he suggests to obviate the abuse of such symbols is the use of models or pictures in plurality, in multiform clusters. It is the use of isolated or single controlling models that tends toward distortion and manipulative abuse (see Ramsey, *Religious Language*).

27. The quotation is from Thiselton, *Interpreting God*, 29.

28. Horsley, "General Introduction," 5.

29. Other writings containing much evidence in support of my thesis include *The Didache, Martyrdom of Polycarp, Epistle to Diognetus*, Minucius Felix's *Octavian*, the works of Theophilus of Antioch, and the Shepherd of Hermas, along with the apocryphal Acts and the bulk of Eusebius's *Ecclesiastical History*.

30. Lohfink, *Jesus and Community*, 161.

31. Lohfink, *Jesus and Community*, 162.

32. Lohfink, *Jesus and Community*, 162.

33. Lohfink, *Jesus and Community*, 162.

34. Jacobson, "Divided Families and Christian Origins," 379.

Bibliography

"Africa, the Church in Roman." In Cross and Livingstone, eds. *The Oxford Dictionary of the Christian Church.* Oxford Univ. Press, 22–23.

Alföldi, Andreas. "Zu den Christenverfolgungen in der Mitte des 3. Jahrhunderts." *Klio* 31 (1938): 323–48.

Allo, Ernest-Bernard. *Saint Paul: Seconde épître aux Corinthiens.* 2nd ed. Paris: Gabalda, 1956.

Andersen, Francis I. *Job: An Introduction and Commentary,* TynOTC 13. London: InterVarsity, 1976.

Arnold, Clinton E. *Ephesians: Power and Magic.* Grand Rapids: Baker, 1992.

Banks, Robert. *Paul's Idea of Community: The Early House Churches in Their Historical Setting.* Grand Rapids: Eerdmans, 1980.

Barnes, Timothy D. "Pre-Decian *Acta Martyrum.*" *JTS* 19 (1968) 509–31.

———. *Tertullian: A Historical and Literary Study.* New York: Oxford Univ. Press, 1971.

Barr, James. "Abba Isn't 'Daddy.'" *JTS* 39 (1988): 28–47.

Barrett, Charles K. *The First Epistle to the Corinthians.* Peabody, Mass.: Hendrikson, 1968.

Bartchy, S. Scott. "Community of Goods in Acts: Idealization or Social Reality?" In *The Future of Early Christianity: Essays in Honor of Helmut Koester,* ed. B. Pearson et al., 309–18. Minneapolis: Fortress Press, 1991.

———. "Philemon, Epistle To." In *ABD,* ed. D. N. Freedman, 5.305–10. New York: Doubleday, 1992.

———. "Table Fellowship." In *DJG,* ed. J. B. Green and S. McKnight, 796–800. Downers Grove, Ill.: InterVarsity, 1992.

———. "*Agnostos Theos:* Luke's Message to the 'Nations' about Israel's God." In *SBLSP* 1995, ed. Eugene H. Lovering Jr., 304–20. Atlanta: Scholars, 1995.

———. "Slave, Slavery." In Martin and Davids, eds. *Dictionary of the Later New Testament and Its Developments,* 1098–1102. Downers Grove, Ill.: InterVarsity, 1997.

———. "The Lasting Contributions of Greece and Rome to Our Thinking about Families." In *Religion and Family: A Practical Theology Handbook.* Louisville: Westminster John Knox, forthcoming.

Bastiaensen, Antonius A. R. *Le cérémonial épistolaire des chrétiens latins.* Nijmegen: Dekker and Van de Vegt, 1964.

Bauckham, Richard J. "The Sonship of the Historical Jesus in Christology." *SJT* 31 (1978): 245–60.

Bauer, Walter. *Orthodoxy and Heresy in Earliest Christianity.* Trans. R. A. Kraft and G. Krodel. Philadelphia: Fortress Press, 1971.

———. *A Greek-English Lexicon of the New Testament and Other Early Christian Literature.* Ed. W. F. Arndt, F. W. Gingrich, and F. W. Danker, 2nd ed. Chicago: Univ. of Chicago Press, 1979.

Beck, Roger. "The Mysteries of Mithras." In Kloppenborg and Wilson, eds., *Voluntary Associations,* 176–85.

Bernstein, Richard J. *The New Constellation: The Ethical-Political Horizons of Modernity/Postmodernity.* Cambridge: Polity, 1991.

Betz, Hans Dieter, ed. *The Greek Magical Papyri in Translation including the Demotic Spells.* Vol. 1. Chicago: Univ. of Chicago Press, 1986.

Bihlmeyer, Karl. *Die Apostolischen Väter.* Tübingen: Mohr, 1956.

Bobertz, Charles A. "Cyprian of Carthage as Patron: A Social Historical Study of the Role of Bishop in the Ancient Christian Community of North Africa." Ph.D. diss., Yale Univ., 1988.

Boissevain, Jeremy. "Uniformity and Diversity in the Mediterranean: An Essay in Interpretation." In *Kinship and Modernization in Mediterranean Society,* ed. J. G. Peristiany, 1–11. Rome: Center for Mediterranean Studies, 1976.

Bömer, Franz. *Untersuchungen über die Religion der Sklaven in Griechenland und Rom.* 2 vols. Mainz: Akademie der Wissenschaften und der Literatur, 1958–63.

Borg, Marcus J., and N. T. Wright. *The Meaning of Jesus: Two Visions.* San Francisco: HarperSanFrancisco, 1999.

Boring, M. Eugene. "Prophecy (Early Christian)." In *ABD,* ed. D. N. Freedman, 5.495–502. New York: Doubleday, 1992.

Boring, M. Eugene, Klaus Berger, and Carsten Colpe, eds. *Hellenistic Commentary to the New Testament.* Nashville: Abingdon, 1995.

Bornkamm, Günther. "The Letter to the Romans as Paul's Last Will and Testament." In Karl P. Donfried, ed., *The Romans Debate,* 16–28.

Boyd, Gregory A. *Cynic Sage or Son of God?* Wheaton, Ill.: Victor, 1995.

Brown, Milton. *The Authentic Writings of Ignatius of Antioch.* Durham, N.C.: Duke Univ. Press, 1963.

Bruce, F. F. *The Acts of the Apostles.* 3rd ed. Grand Rapids: Eerdmans, 1990.

Burkert, Walter. *Ancient Mystery Cults.* Cambridge: Harvard Univ. Press, 1987.

Campenhausen, Hans von. *Ecclesiastical Authority and Spiritual Power in the Early Church.* Trans. J. A. Baker. London: Black, 1969.

Carcopino, Jérôme. "Survivances par substitution des sacrifices d'enfants." *RHR* 106 (1932): 592–99.

Castelli, Elizabeth A. *Imitating Paul: A Discourse of Power.* Louisville: Westminster John Knox, 1991.

Chadwick, Henry. *The Early Church.* The Penguin History of the Church. Ed. Owen Chadwick. London: Penguin, 1967.

Church, Alfred John, and William Jackson Brodribb, trans. *The Complete Works of Tacitus.* Ed. M. Hadas. New York: Random House, 1942.

Clarke, Andrew D. *Secular and Christian Leadership in Corinth: A Socio-Historical and Exegetical Study of 1 Corinthians 1–6.* Leiden: Brill, 1993.

————. *Serve the Community of the Church: Christians as Leaders and Ministers.* Grand Rapids: Eerdmans, 2000.

Clarke, Graeme W. "The Secular Profession of St. Cyprian of Carthage." *Latomus* 24 (1965): 633–38.

————. "Barbarian Disturbances in North Africa in the Mid-Third Century." *Antichthon* 4 (1970): 78–85.

————. *The Letters of Cyprian of Carthage.* 4 vols, ACW, ed. J. Quasten, W. J. Burghardt, and T. C. Lawler; trans. G. W. Clarke. New York: Newman, 1984–86.

Cohen, Shaye J. D. *From the Maccabees to the Mishnah.* LEC. Philadelphia: Westminster, 1987.

————, ed. *The Jewish Family in Antiquity.* BJS 289. Atlanta: Scholars, 1993.

Collins, John J. "Essenes." In *ABD*, ed. D. N. Freedman, 2.619–26. New York: Doubleday, 1992.

Conzelmann, Hans. "Paulus und die Weisheit." *NTS* 12 (1965): 231–44.

Corbett, Percy E. *The Roman Law of Marriage.* Oxford: Clarendon, 1930.

Coxe, A. Cleveland, ed. "Against Heresies." In *The Apostolic Fathers with Justin Martyr and Irenaeus.* ANF 1. Grand Rapids: Eerdmans, 1979 [1884].

Cranfield, Charles E. B. *The Epistle to the Romans.* ICC. Edinburgh: T. & T. Clark, 1979.

Cross, Frank L., and Elizabeth A. Livingstone, eds. *The Oxford Dictionary of the Christian Church.* New York: Oxford Univ. Press, 1974.

Crossan, John Dominic. *The Historical Jesus: The Life of a Mediterranean Jewish Peasant.* New York: HarperCollins, 1991.

Culpepper, R. Alan. *The Johannine School: An Evaluation of the Johannine School Hypothesis.* SBLDS 26. Missoula, Mont.: Scholars, 1975.

Dahl, Nils A. "Paul and Possessions." In *Studies in Paul: Theology for the Early Christian Mission,* ed. N. A. Dahl and P. Donahue. Minneapolis: Augsburg, 1977.

Daube, David. "Typology in Josephus." *JJS* 31 (1980): 18–36.

Davies, John G. *The Architectural Setting of Baptism.* London: Barrie and Rockliff, 1962.

Davies, W. D., and Dale C. Allison. *A Critical and Exegetical Commentary on the Gospel according to Saint Matthew.* Vol. 2. ICC. Edinburgh: T. & T. Clark, 1991.

Davis, John H. *People of the Mediterranean: An Essay in Comparative Social Anthropology.* Library of Man. London: Routledge and Kegan Paul, 1977.

Deferrari, Joseph, ed. *The Fathers of the Church.* Vols. 10, 36, and 40. New York: Fathers of the Church, 1950, 1958, 1959.

Dixon, Suzanne. *The Roman Family.* Baltimore: Johns Hopkins Univ. Press, 1992.

Dodds, E. R. *Pagan and Christian in an Age of Anxiety.* The Wiles Lectures. Cambridge: Cambridge Univ. Press, 1965.

Donfried, Karl P. "False Presuppositions in the Study of Romans." In Karl P. Donfried, ed., *The Romans Debate,* 102–25.

————. "Introduction," in Karl P. Donfried, ed., *The Romans Debate,* lxix–lxx.

————. "A Short Note on Romans 16." In Karl P. Donfried, ed., *The Romans Debate,* 44–52.

Donfried, Karl P., ed. *The Romans Debate.* 2nd ed. Peabody, Mass.: Hendrikson, 1991.

Doran, Robert. *Birth of a Worldview: Early Christianity in Its Jewish and Pagan Context.* Explorations. Boulder, Colo.: Westview, 1995.

Douglas, Mary. *Purity and Danger.* London: Routledge and Kegan Paul, 1966.

————. *Natural Symbols: Explorations in Cosmology.* New York: Pantheon, 1970.

————. "Deciphering a Meal." *Daedalus* 101 (1972): 61–81.

Downing, Gerald F. *Cynics and Christian Origins.* Edinburgh: T. & T. Clark, 1992.

Du Boulay, Juliet. "Lies, Mockery and Family Integrity." In *Mediterranean Family Structures,* ed. J. G. Peristiany, 389–406. Cambridge: Cambridge Univ. Press, 1976.

Duncan-Jones, Richard P. *The Economy of the Roman Empire: Quantitative Studies.* Cambridge: Cambridge Univ. Press, 1974.

Dunn, James D. G. *Romans 1–8.* WBC 38a. Waco, Tex.: Word, 1988.

———. *Romans 9–16.* WBC 38b. Waco, Tex.: Word, 1988.

———. *Jesus, Paul, and the Law.* Louisville: Westminster John Knox, 1990.

———. *The Partings of the Ways: Between Christianity and Judaism and Their Significance for the Character of Christianity.* Philadelpha: Trinity Press International, 1991.

Dupont-Sommer, A. "Les Livre des Hymnes découvert près de la mer Morte (1QH)." *Sem* 7 (1957): 1–120.

Duquenne, Luc. *Chronologie des letters de s. Cyprien.* Subsidia hagiographia 54. Bruxelles: Soc. des Bollandistes, bd Saint-Michel, 1972.

Durham, Mary Edith. *Some Tribal Origins: Laws and Customs of the Balkans.* London: Allen and Unwin, 1928.

Edwards, Walter Manoel, and Robert Browing. "Lucian." In *OCD,* ed. N. G. L. Hammond and H. H. Scullard, 621. Oxford: Oxford Univ. Press, 1970.

Elon, Menachem. *The Principles of Jewish Law.* Jerusalem: Hebrew Univ. Press, 1975.

Epstein, Louis M. *Marriage Laws in the Bible and the Talmud.* Cambridge: Harvard Univ. Press, 1942.

———. *The Jewish Marriage Contract.* New York: Arno, 1973.

Esler, Philip Francis. *Community and Gospel in Luke-Acts.* SNTSMS 57. Cambridge: Cambridge Univ. Press, 1987.

Evans, Craig, and Donald Hagner. *Anti-Semitism and Early Christianity.* Minneapolis: Fortress Press, 1993.

Fahey, Michael A. *Cyprian and the Bible: A Study in Third-Century Exegesis.* Beiträge zur Geschichte der biblischen Hermeneutik 9. Tübingen: Mohr, 1971.

Fallers, Lloyd A., and Margaret C. Fallers. "Sex Roles in Edremit." In *Mediterranean Family Structures,* ed. J. G. Peristiany, 243–60. Cambridge: Cambridge Univ. Press, 1976.

Farquharson, Arthur S., trans. *Marcus Aurelius, Emperor of Rome, 121–180.* Oxford: Oxford Univ. Press, 1989.

Fee, Gordon D. *The First Epistle to the Corinthians.* NICNT. Grand Rapids: Eerdmans, 1987.

Feldman, Louis H. *Jew and Gentile in the Ancient World: Attitudes and Interactions from Alexander to Justinian.* Princeton: Princeton Univ. Press, 1993.

———. "Diaspora Synagogues: New Light from Inscriptions and Papyri." In *Sacred Realm: The Emergence of the Synagogue in the Ancient World,* ed. S. Fine, 48–66. Oxford: Oxford Univ. Press, 1996.

Fischer, David. *Historians' Fallacies.* New York: Harper and Row, 1970.

Fitzgerald, John T. "Philippians, Epistle to the." In *ABD,* ed. D. N. Freedman, 5.318–26. New York: Doubleday, 1992.

Fox, Robin. *Kinship and Marriage: An Anthropological Perspective.* Baltimore: Penguin, 1967.

Fox, Robin Lane. *Pagans and Christians.* New York: Knopf, 1986.

Frend, William H. C. *Martyrdom and Persecution in the Early Church.* Oxford: Oxford Univ. Press, 1965.

———. *The Donatist Church: A Movement of Protest in Roman North Africa.* Oxford: Clarendon, 1971.

———. *The Rise of Christianity.* Philadelphia: Fortress Press, 1984.

Gager, John G. *Kingdom and Community: The Social World of Early Christianity.* Englewood Cliffs, N.J.: Prentice-Hall, 1975.

Gamble, Harry. *The Textual History of the Letter to the Romans.* SD. Grand Rapids, Mich.: Eerdmans, 1977.

Gardner, Jane F. *Women in Roman Law and Society.* Bloomington: Indiana Univ. Press, 1986.

Garnsey, Peter. *Social Status and Legal Privilege in the Roman Empire.* Oxford: Oxford Univ. Press, 1970.

Garnsey, Peter, and Richard Saller. *The Roman Empire: Economy, Society, and Culture.* Berkeley: Univ. of California Press, 1987.

Garrett, Susan R. *The Demise of the Devil: Magic and the Demonic in Luke's Writings.* Minneapolis: Fortress Press, 1989.

Georgi, Dieter. *Die Geschichte der Kollekte des Paulus für Jerusalem.* TF 38. Hamburg-Bergstedt: H. Reich. Evangelischer Verlag, 1965.

———. *The Opponents of Paul in Second Corinthians.* Philadelphia: Fortress Press, 1986.

Goodman, Martin. *The Ruling Class of Judaea.* Cambridge: Cambridge Univ. Press, 1987.

Goody, Jack. *Cooking, Cuisine and Class: A Study in Comparative Sociology.* Themes in the Social Sciences. Cambridge: Cambridge Univ. Press, 1982.

———. *The Oriental, the Ancient and the Primitive: Systems of Marriage and the Family in the Pre-Industrial Societies of Eurasia.* Studies in Literacy, Family, Culture, and the State. Cambridge: Cambridge Univ. Press, 1990.

Goold, G. P., ed. *The Apostolic Fathers.* 2 vols, LCL, trans. Kirsopp Lake, vol. 1. Cambridge: Harvard Univ. Press, 1912, 1985.

Gordon, Richard L. "Mithraism and Roman Society." *Religion* 2 (1972): 92–121.

Grant, Robert M. "Justin Martyr." In *ABD,* ed. D. N. Freedman, 3.1133–34. New York: Doubleday, 1992.

Guelich, Robert A. *Mark 1—8:26.* WBC 34a. Dallas: Word, 1989.

Gundry, Robert H. *Mark: A Commentary on His Apology for the Cross.* Grand Rapids, Mich.: Eerdmans, 1993.

Hagner, Donald A. *Matthew 14–28.* WBC 33b. Dallas: Word, 1995.

Hanson, K. C. "The Herodians and Mediterranean Kinship. Part I: Genealogy and Descent." *BTB* 19 (1989): 75–84.

———. "The Herodians and Mediterranean Kinship. Part II: Marriage and Divorce." *BTB* 19 (1989): 142–51.

———. "The Herodians and Mediterranean Kinship. Part III: Economics." *BTB* 20 (1990): 10–21.

———. "BTB Readers Guide: Kinship." *BTB* 24 (1994): 183–94.

Harnack, Adolf von. *Über vorlorene Brief und Actenstucke die sich aus der Cyprianischen Briefsammlung ermitten lassen.* Texte und Untersuchungen zur Geschichte der altchristlichen Literatur 23.2. Leipzig: Hinrichs, 1902.

Harrill, J. Albert. *Manumission of Slaves in Early Christianity.* HUT 32. Tübingen: Mohr-Siebeck, 1995.

Hemer, Colin J. *The Book of Acts in the Setting of Hellenistic History.* Winona Lake, Ind.: Eisenbrauns, 1990.

Hengel, Martin. *The Charismatic Leader and His Followers,* trans. J. Greig. New York: Crossroad, 1981.

Hess, Hamilton. *The Canons of the Council of Sardica, A.D. 343: A Landmark in the Early Development of Canon Law.* Oxford: Oxford Univ. Press, 1958.

Hirsch, Eric D. *Validity in Interpretation.* New Haven: Yale Univ. Press, 1967.

Holmberg, Bengt. *Paul and Power: The Structure of Authority in the Primitive Church as Reflected in the Pauline Epistles.* Philadelphia: Fortress Press, 1980.

————. *Sociology and the New Testament: An Appraisal.* Minneapolis: Fortress Press, 1990.

Hommel, Hildebrecht. "Herrenworte im Lichte sokratischer Überlieferung." *ZNW* 57 (1966): 1–23.

Horden, Peregrine, and Nicholas Purcell. *The Corrupting Sea: A Study of Mediterranean History.* Malden, Mass.: Blackwell, 2000.

Horsley, Richard A. "General Introduction." In *Paul and Empire: Religion and Power in Roman Imperial Society,* ed. R. A. Horsley, 1–8. Harrisburg, Pa.: Trinity Press International, 1997.

Issakon, Abel. *Marriage and Ministry in the New Temple.* Lund: Gleerup, 1965.

Jacobson, Arland D. "Divided Families and Christian Origins." In *The Gospel Behind the Gospels: Current Studies on 'Q,'* ed. Ronald A. Piper, 361–80. NovTSup 75, Leiden: Brill, 1995.

Jaubert, Annie. "Les Sources de las Conception Militaire de l'Eglise en 1 Clement 37." *VC* 18 (1964): 74–84.

Jeremias, Joachim. *The Prayers of Jesus,* trans. J. Bowden et al. Philadelphia: Fortress Press, 1978.

————. *New Testament Theology.* New York: Charles Scribner's Sons, 1971.

Jervell, Jacob. "The Letter to Jerusalem." In Karl P. Donfried, ed., *The Romans Debate,* 53–64.

Jewett, Robert. *Christian Tolerance. Paul: Message to the Modern Church.* Philadelphia: Westminster, 1982.

Judge, Edwin A. "The Early Christians as a Scholastic Community." *JRH* 1 (1960): 4–15, 125–37.

Kane, J. P. "The Mithraic Cult Meal in Its Greek and Roman Environment." In *Mithraic Studies,* ed. J. R. Hinnells, 313–51. Manchester, England: Manchester Univ. Press, 1975.

Karris, Robert J. "The Background and Significance of the Polemic of the Pastoral Epistles." *JBL* 92 (1973): 549–64.

————. "Romans 14:1—15:13 and the Occasion of Romans." In Karl P. Donfried, ed., *The Romans Debate,* 65–84.

Käsemann, Ernst. *Commentary on Romans.* Trans. G. W. Bromiley. 4th ed. Grand Rapids: Eerdmans, 1980.

Keesing, Roger M. *Kin Groups and Social Structure.* New York: Holt, Rinehart and Winston, 1975.

Keresztes, Paul. "Marcus Aurelius a Persecutor?" *HTR* 61 (1968): 321–41.

Kingsbury, Jack D. "On Following Jesus." *NTS* 34 (1988): 45–59.

Klemm, Hans G. "Das Wort von der Selbstbestattung der Toten." *NTS* 16 (1969–70): 60–75.

Kloppenborg, John S. *The Formation of Q: Trajectories in Ancient Wisdom Collections.* Studies in Antiquity and Christianity. Philadelphia: Fortress Press, 1987.

————. "Edwin Hatch, Churches and *Collegia.*" In *Origins and Method: Towards a New Understanding of Judaism and Christianity,* ed. Bradley H. McLean, 213–38. JSNTSup 86, Sheffield, England: Sheffield Academic Press, 1993.

————. "Collegia and *Thaisoi.*" In Kloppenborg and Wilson, eds., *Voluntary Associations,* 16–30.

Kloppenborg, John S., and Stephen G. Wilson, eds. *Voluntary Associations in the Graeco-Roman World.* London: Routledge, 1996.

Koch, Carl. "Pietas." In *PW.* Stuttgart: Metzler, 1951.

Koester, Helmut. *Synoptische Überlieferung bei den Apostolischen Vätern.* Texte und Untersuchungen zur Geschichte der alchristlichen Literatur 65. Berlin: Akademie, 1957.

————. *Introduction to the New Testament.* 2 vols. Philadelphia: Fortress Press, 1982.

Köhler, Wolf-Dietrich. *Die Rezeption des Matthäusevangeliums in der Zeit vor Irenäus.* WUNT 2/24. Tübingen: Mohr, 1987.

Krentz, Edgar M. "Thessalonians, First and Second Epistles to the." In *ABD*, ed. D. N. Freedman, 6.515–23. New York: Doubleday, 1992.

Kümmel, Werner Georg. *Introduction to the New Testament*. Trans. H. C. Kee, 17th ed. Nashville: Abingdon, 1975.

Lacey, W. K. *The Family in Classical Greece*. Aspects of Greek and Roman Life. Ithaca, N.Y.: Cornell Univ. Press, 1968.

Lampe, Peter. *Die stadrömischen Christian in den ersten beiden Jahrhunderten: Untersuchungen zur Sozialgeschichte*. 2nd ed. WUNT 2/18. Tübingen: Mohr, 1989.

———. "The Roman Christians of Romans 16." In Karl P. Donfried, ed., *The Romans Debate*, 216–30.

Lane, William L. *The Gospel According to Mark*. NICNT 2. Grand Rapids, Mich.: Eerdmans, 1974.

Lefkowitz, Mary R., and Maureen B. Fant. *Women's Life in Greece and Rome: A Sourcebook in Translation*. Baltimore: Johns Hopkins Univ. Press, 1982.

Leon, Harry J. *The Jews of Ancient Rome*. Rev. ed. Peabody, Mass.: Hendrikson, 1960.

Lightfoot, Joseph B. *The Apostolic Fathers*. 3 vols. 2nd ed. London: Macmillan, 1926.

Lingenfelter, Sherwood. *Transforming Culture: A Challenge for Christian Mission*. Grand Rapids: Baker, 1992.

Litfin, Duane. *St. Paul's Theology of Proclamation: 1 Corinthians 1–4 and Greco-Roman Rhetoric*. SNTSMS 79. Cambridge: Cambridge Univ. Press, 1994.

———. "Review of M. Bullmore's *St. Paul's Theology of Rhetorical Style*." *JBL* 116 (1997): 568–70.

Lohfink, Gerhard. *Jesus and Community: The Social Dimension of Christian Faith*. Trans. J. P. Galvin. Philadelphia: Fortress Press, 1982.

Lutz, Cora. *Musonius Rufus: The Roman Socrates*. New Haven: Yale Univ. Press, 1947.

Lütgert, Wilhelm. *Amt und geist im Kampf*. Gütersloh: Bertelsmann, 1911.

Luz, Ulrich. "Das Primatwort Matthäus 16.17–19 aus wirkungsgeschichtlicher Sicht." *NTS* 37 (1991): 415–33.

MacDonald, Margaret Y. *The Pauline Churches: A Socio-historical Study of Institutionalization in the Pauline and Deutero-Pauline Writings*. SNTSMS 60. Cambridge: Cambridge Univ. Press, 1988.

Mace, David R. *Hebrew Marriage*. London: Epworth, 1953.

Mack, Burton. *The Lost Gospel: The Book of Q and Christian Origins*. San Francisco: HarperSanFrancisco, 1993.

MacMullen, Ramsay. *Paganism in the Roman Empire*. New Haven: Yale Univ. Press, 1981.

———. *Christianizing the Roman Empire*. New Haven: Yale Univ. Press, 1984.

Malherbe, Abraham J. "Gentle as a Nurse: The Cynic Background to 1 Thess 2." *NovT* 12 (1970): 203–17.

———. *Social Aspects of Early Christianity*. Rockwell Lectures of 1975. Baton Rouge: Louisiana State Univ. Press, 1977.

Malina, Bruce J. *The New Testament World: Insights from Cultural Anthropology*. Atlanta: John Knox, 1981.

———. *Christian Origins and Cultural Anthropology: Models for Interpreters*. Atlanta: John Knox, 1986.

———. "Dealing with Biblical (Mediterranean) Characters: A Guide for U. S. Consumers." *BTB* 19 (1989): 127–41.

———. "Mother and Son." *BTB* 20 (1990): 54–64.

———. "A Social Psychological Model of Self-Denial." *BTB* 24 (1994): 106–21.

Malina, Bruce J., and Richard L. Rohrbaugh. *Social-Science Commentary on the Synoptic Gospels*. Minneapolis: Fortress Press, 1992.

Malina, Bruce J., and Jerome H. Neyrey. *Portraits of Paul: An Archaeology of Ancient Personality*. Louisville: Westminster John Knox, 1996.

Marr, G. Simpson. *Sex in Religion: An Historical Survey*. London: Allen and Unwin, 1936.

Marshall, I. Howard. *Commentary on Luke*. NIGTC. Grand Rapids: Eerdmans, 1978.

————. "Church." In *DJG*, ed. J. B. Green and S. McKnight, 122–25. Downers Grove, Ill.: InterVarsity, 1992.

Marshall, Peter. *Enmity at Corinth: Social Conventions in Paul's Relations with the Corinthians*. WUNT 2/23. Tübingen: Mohr, 1987.

Martin, Dale B. *The Corinthian Body*. New Haven.: Yale Univ. Press, 1995.

Martin, Ralph P. *2 Corinthians*. WBC 40. Waco, Tex.: Word, 1986.

Marxsen, Willi. *Introduction to the New Testament*. Philadelphia: Fortress Press, 1968.

Mason, Steve. "*Philosophiai*: Graeco-Roman, Judean and Christian." In Kloppenborg and Wilson, eds., *Voluntary Associations*, 31–58.

Mattingly, Harold. "The Religious Background of the *Historia Augusta*." *HTR* 39 (1946): 213–15.

Mayer, Herbert T. "Clement of Rome and His Use of Scripture." *CTM* 42 (1971): 536–40.

McCane, Byron. "Let the Dead Bury Their Own Dead." *HTR* 83 (1990): 31–43.

McCready, Wayne O. "*Ekklesia* and Voluntary Associations." In Kloppenborg and Wilson, eds., *Voluntary Associations*, 59–73.

McKnight, Scot. "Collection for the Saints." In *Dictionary of Paul and His Letters*, ed. G. F. Hawthorne, R. P. Martin, and D. G. Reid, 143–47. Downers Grove, Ill.: InterVarsity, 1993.

McLean, Bradley H. "The Agrippinilla Inscription: Religious Associations and Early Christian Formation." In *Origins and Method: Towards a New Understanding of Judaism and Christianity. Essays in Honor of John C. Hurd*, ed. Bradley H. McLean, 239–70. JSNTSup 86, Sheffield: JSOT, 1993.

McVann, Mark. "Family-Centeredness." In *Biblical Social Values and Their Meaning*, ed. J. J. Pilch and B. J. Malina, 70–73. Peabody, Mass.: Hendrickson, 1993.

Meeks, Wayne A. *The First Urban Christians: The Social World of the Apostle Paul*. New Haven: Yale Univ. Press, 1983.

————. *The Origins of Early Christian Morality: The First Two Centuries*. New Haven: Yale Univ. Press, 1993.

Meier, John P. *A Marginal Jew: Rethinking the Historical Jesus*. 2 vols. New York: Doubleday, 1991–94.

Metzger, Bruce, ed. *The Oxford Annotated Apocrypha*. New York: Oxford Univ. Press, 1977.

Meyer, Marvin W. "Mystery Religions." In *ABD*, ed. D. N. Freedman, 4.941–45. New York: Doubleday, 1992.

Migne, Jacques-Paul, ed. *Patrilogiae Cursus Completus*. 138 vols. Turnholt: Brepols, 1960.

Millar, Fergus. *The Roman Near East, 31 BC–AD 337*. Cambridge: Harvard Univ. Press, 1993.

Minde, Hans-Jürgen van der. "Thanksgiving Hymns." In *ABD*, ed. D. N. Freedman, 6.438–41. New York: Doubleday, 1992.

Mitchell, Alan C. "Rich and Poor in the Courts of Corinth: Litigiousness and Status in 1 Corinthians 6:1-1." *NTS* 39 (1993): 562–86.

Mitchell, Margaret M. *Paul and the Rhetoric of Reconciliation: An Exegetical Investigation of the Language and Composition of 1 Corinthians*. HUT 28. Tübingen: Mohr, 1991.

Moiser, Jeremy. "A Reassessment of Paul's View of Marriage with Reference to 1 Cor 7." *JSNT* 18 (1983): 103–22.

Molthagen, Joachim. *Die römische Staat und die Christen im zweiten und dritten Jahrhundert*. Göttingen: Vandenhoeck & Ruprecht, 1970.

Moore, George F. *Judaism*. Cambridge: Harvard Univ. Press, 1946.

Moore, Stephen D. *Poststructuralism and the New Testament: Derrida and Foucault at the Foot of the Cross*. Minneapolis: Fortress Press, 1994.

Munck, Johannes. "Discours d'adieu dans le Nouveau Testament et dans la littérature biblique." In *Aux sources de la tradition chrétienne (M. Goguel Festschrift)*, ed. O. Cullmann and P. Menoud, 155–70. Paris: Neuchatel, 1950.

———. *Paul and the Salvation of Mankind*. Trans. F. Clarke. Atlanta: John Knox, 1959.

Musurillo, Herbert, ed. *Acts of the Christian Martyrs*. Oxford Early Christian Texts. Oxford: Oxford Univ. Press, 1972.

Neufeld, Ephraim. *Ancient Hebrew Marriage Laws*. London: Longmans, Greene, 1944.

Neusner, Jacob. "Mr. Sanders's Pharisees and Mine." *Bulletin for Biblical Research* 2 (1992): 143–69.

Nielsen, Kirsten. *Satan—The Prodigal Son: A Family Problem in the Bible*. Biblical Seminar 50. Sheffield: Sheffield Academic, 1997.

Nock, Arthur Darby. "The Historical Importance of Cult-Associations." *Classical Review* 38 (1924): 105–9.

———. *Conversion: The Old and the New in Religion from Alexander the Great to Augustine*. London: Oxford Univ. Press, 1933.

Nolland, John. *Luke 1—9:20*. WBC 35a. Dallas: Word, 1989.

———. *Luke 9:21—18:34*. WBC 35b. Dallas: Word, 1993.

Norris, Christopher. *The Contest of Faculties: Philosophy and Theory after Deconstruction*. New York: Methuen, 1985.

Oakman, Douglas E. *Jesus and the Economic Questions of His Day*. Studies in the Bible and Early Christianity 8. Lewiston, N.Y.: Edwin Mellen, 1986.

Ollrog, Wolf-Henning. *Paulus und seine Mitarbeiter*. WMANT 50. Neukirchen-Vluyn: Neukirchener, 1979.

O'Neill, John. *The Poverty of Postmodernism*. London: Routledge, 1994.

Orlandi, Tito. "Coptic Literature." In *Roots of Egyptian Christianity*, ed. B. A. Pearson and J. E. Goehring, 55–56. Philadelphia: Fortress Press, 1986.

Osiek, Carolyn. "The Ransom of Captives: Evolution of a Tradition." *HTR* 74 (1981): 365–86.

Osiek, Carolyn, and David L. Balch. *Families in the New Testament World*. The Family, Religion, and Culture. Louisville: Westminster John Knox, 1997.

Page, Thomas E., ed. *The Rich Man's Solution*. Trans. G. W. Butterworth. LCL, Cambridge: Harvard Univ. Press, 1919.

———. *Seneca*. 10 vols. Trans. R. M. Gummere, vol. 3. LCL. Cambridge: Harvard Univ. Press, 1920.

———. *Plutarch's Moralia*. 15 vols. Trans. F. C. Babbitt, vol. 2. LCL. Cambridge: Harvard Univ. Press, 1928.

Pearson, Birger A. "Christianity in Egypt." In *ABD*, ed. D. N. Freedman, 1.954–60. New York: Doubleday, 1992.

Peristiany, John G. "Introduction." In *Mediterranean Family Structures*, ed. J. G. Peristiany, 1–26. Cambridge: Cambridge Univ. Press, 1976.

Perkins, Pheme. *Gnosticism and the New Testament.* Minneapolis: Fortress Press, 1993.

Peterlin, Davorin. "Clement's Answer to the Corinthian Conflict in AD 96." *JETS* 39 (1996): 57–69.

Peterman, Gerald W. *Paul's Gift from Philippi: Conventions of Gift Exchange and Christian Giving.* SNTSMS 92. Cambridge: Cambridge Univ. Press, 1997.

Pilch, John J. "'Beat His Ribs While He Is Young' (Sir 30:12): A Window on the Mediterranean World." *BTB* 23 (1993): 101–13.

Pitt-Rivers, Julian. "Pseudo-Kinship." In *International Encyclopedia of the Social Sciences*, ed. D. L. Sills, 408–13. New York: Macmillan, 1968.

Plumpe, Joseph C. *Mater ecclesia: An Inquiry into the Concept of the Church as Mother in Early Christianity.* Washington, D.C.: Catholic Univ. of America Press, 1943.

Pogoloff, Stephen. *Logos and Sophia.* SBLDS 134. Atlanta: Scholars, 1992.

Pomeroy, Sarah B. *Goddesses, Whores, Wives, and Slaves.* New York: Schocken, 1975.

Ramsey, Ian T. *Religious Language: An Empirical Placing of Theological Phrases.* London: SCM, 1957.

Rawson, Beryl, ed. *The Family in Ancient Rome: New Perspectives.* Ithaca, N.Y.: Cornell Univ. Press, 1986.

Reitzenstein, Richard. *Die hellenistischen Mysterienreligionen nach ihren Grundgedanken und Wirkungen.* 3rd ed. Stuttgart: Teubner, 1927, 1956.

Remus, Harold. "Voluntary Associations and Networks: Aelius Aristides at the Asclepieion in Pergamum." In Kloppenborg and Wilson, eds., *Voluntary Associations*, 146–75.

Reuther, Rosemary. *Faith and Fratricide: The Theological Roots of Anti-Semitism.* New York: Seabury, 1974.

Richardson, Cyril C., ed. *Early Christian Fathers.* New York: Macmillan, 1970.

Riesner, Rainer. "Essener und Urkirche in Jerusalem." *BK* 40 (1985): 64–76.

Roberts, Colin H. *Manuscript, Society and Belief in Early Christian Egypt.* London: Oxford Univ. Press, 1979.

Robertson, Archibald, and Alfred Plummer. *A Critical and Exegetical Commentary on the First Epistle of St. Paul to the Corinthians.* ICC. 2nd ed. Edinburgh: T. & T. Clark, 1978.

Rohde, Joachim. "Häresie und Schisma im ersten Clemensbrief und in den Ignatius-Briefen." *NovT* 10 (1968): 217–33.

Rose, Herbert Jennings. "Eteocles." In *OCD*, ed. N. G. L. Hammond and H. H. Scullard, 408. Oxford: Clarendon, 1970.

———. "Lares." In *OCD*, ed. N. G. L. Hammond and H. H. Scullard, 578–79. Oxford: Clarendon, 1970.

Rudolph, Kurt. *Gnosis: The Nature and History of Gnosticism.* Trans. R. L. Wilson. 2nd ed. San Francisco: HarperSanFrancisco, 1987.

Safrai, Shmuel. "The Era of the Mishnah and the Talmud (70–640)." In *A History of the Jewish People*, ed. H. H. Ben-Sasson, 307–82. Cambridge: Harvard Univ. Press, 1976.

———. "Home and Family." In *The Jewish People in the First Century: Historical Geography, Political History, Social, Cultural and Religious Life and Institutions*, ed. S. Safrai and M. Stern. CRINT. Philadelphia: Fortress Press, 1976.

Saldarini, Anthony J. "Rabbinic Literature and the NT." In *ABD*, ed. D. N. Freedman, 5.602–4. New York: Doubleday, 1992.

Saller, Richard P. *"Familia, domus* and the Roman Conception of Family." *Phoenix* 38 (1984): 336–55.

———. *Patriarchy, Property and Death in the Roman Family.* Cambridge: Cambridge Univ. Press, 1994.

Saller, Richard P., and B. D. Shaw. "Tombstones and Roman Family Relations in the Principate: Civilians, Soldiers and Slaves." *JRS* 74 (1984): 124–56.

Sanders, Ed P. *Paul and Palestinian Judaism: A Comparison of Patterns of Religion.* Minneapolis: Fortress Press, 1977.

———. *Jesus and Judaism.* Philadelphia: Fortress Press, 1985.

———. *Judaism: Practice and Belief 63 B.C.E.–66 C.E.* Philadelphia: Trinity Press International, 1992.

Sanders, Louis. *L'hellénisme de saint Clement de Rome et le Paulinisme.* Louvain: Studia Hellenistica in Bibliotheca Universitatis, 1943.

Sauser, Ekkart. *Bekenner seiner Herrlichkeit: Das Zeugnis frühchristlicher Martyrer.* Innsbruck, Austria: Rauch, 1964.

Schiffmann, Lawrence H. *Reclaiming the Dead Sea Scrolls.* Philadelphia: Jewish Publication Society, 1994.

Schmithals, Walter. *Gnosticism of Corinth.* Trans. J. E. Steely. Nashville: Abingdon, 1971.

Schoedel, William R. *Ignatius of Antioch: A Commentary on the Letters of Ignatius of Antioch.* Hermeneia. Philadelphia: Fortress Press, 1985.

———. "Ignatius, Epistles of." In *ABD,* ed. D. N. Freedman, 3.384–87. New York: Doubleday, 1992.

Schopp, Ludwig, ed. *Saint Justin Martyr: Father of the Church.* Vol. 6. Trans. T. B. Falls. New York: Christian Heritage, 1948.

Schusky, Ernest L. *Manual for Kinship Analysis.* Studies in Anthropological Method. New York: Holt, Rinehart and Winston, 1964.

Setzer, Claudia J. *Jewish Responses to Early Christians.* Minneapolis: Fortress Press, 1994.

Shaw, Graham. *The Cost of Authority: Manipulation and Freedom in the New Testament.* London: SCM, 1983.

———. *God in Our Hands.* London: SCM, 1987.

Smallwood, E. Mary. *The Jews under Roman Rule: A Study in Political Relations.* SJLA 20. 2nd ed. Leiden: E. J. Brill, 1981.

Smith, Dennis E. "Table Fellowship as a Literary Motif in the Gospel of Luke." *JBL* 106 (1987): 613–38.

———. "Meal Customs (Greco-Roman)." In *ABD,* ed. D. N. Freedman, 4.650–53. New York: Doubleday, 1992.

———. "Table Fellowship." In *ABD,* ed. D. N. Freedman, 6.302–4. New York: Doubleday, 1992.

Smith, Morton. *Clement of Alexandria and a Secret Gospel of Mark.* Cambridge: Harvard Univ. Press, 1973.

Smith, Ralph L. *Micah-Malachi.* WBC 32. Waco, Tex.: Word, 1984.

Stark, Rodney. *The Rise of Christianity: A Sociologist Reconsiders History.* Princeton, N.J.: Princeton Univ. Press, 1996.

Stegemann, Ekkehard W., and Wolfgang Stegemann. *The Jesus Movement: A Social History of Its First Century.* Trans. O. C. Dean Jr. Minneapolis: Fortress Press, 1999.

Stendahl, Krister. "The Apostle Paul and the Introspective Conscience of the West." *HTR* 56 (1963): 199–215.

Stevens, Maryanne. "Maternity and Paternity: Foundations for Patriarchy." *BTB* 20 (1990): 47–53.

Stuiber, A. "Clemens Romanus I." In *RAC,* ed. T. Klauser, cols. 188–97. Stuttgart: Hierscmann, 1957.

Sullivan, Daniel D. *The Life of the North Africans as Revealed in the Works of St. Cyprian.* Washington, D.C.: Catholic Univ. of America, 1933.

Sumney, Jerry L. *Identifying Paul's Opponents: The Question of Method in 2 Corinthians.* JSNTSup 40. Sheffield: Sheffield Academic Press, 1990.

Swidler, Leonard. *Women in Judaism.* Metuchen, N.J.: Scarecrow, 1976.

Syme, Ronald. *The Roman Revolution.* Oxford: Oxford Univ. Press, 1939.

Theissen, Gerd. *The Social Setting of Pauline Christianity: Essays on Corinth.* Ed. and trans. J. H. Schütz. Philadelphia: Fortress Press, 1982.

———. *The Gospels in Context: Social and Political History in the Synoptic Tradition.* Trans. L. M. Maloney. Minneapolis: Fortress Press, 1991.

Thiselton, Anthony C. *Interpreting God and the Postmodern Self: On Meaning, Manipulation and Promise.* Grand Rapids: Eerdmans, 1995.

Torjesen, Karen Jo. *When Women Were Priests: Women's Leadership in the Early Church and the Scandal of Their Subordination in the Rise of Christianity.* San Francisco: HarperSanFrancisco, 1993.

Treggiari, Susan. *Roman Marriage: Iusti Coniuges from the Time of Cicero to the Time of Ulpian.* Oxford: Clarendon, 1991.

Van Der Horst, P. W. "Pseudo-Phocylides." In *OTP,* ed. J. H. Charlesworth. New York: Doubleday, 1985.

Vermaseren, Maarten J. *Mithras: The Secret God.* New York: Barnes and Noble, 1963.

Vermes, Geza. *Jesus the Jew: A Historian's Reading of the Gospels.* Philadelphia: Fortress Press, 1973.

———. *An Introduction to the Complete Dead Sea Scrolls.* Minneapolis: Fortress Press, 2000.

———, ed. *The Dead Sea Scrolls in English.* 4th ed. London: Penguin, 1995.

Verner, David C. *The Household of God: The Social World of the Pastoral Epistles.* Chico, Calif.: Scholars, 1983.

Vögtle, Anton. *Die Tugend- und Lasterkataloge im Neuen Testament: Exegetisch, religions- und formgeschichtlich Untersucht.* Neutestamentliche Abhandlungen 16. Munster: Aschendorff, 1936.

Wagner, Walter H. *After the Apostles: Christianity in the Second Century.* Minneapolis: Fortress Press, 1994.

Walsh, Michael. *The Triumph of the Meek: Why Early Christianity Succeeded.* San Francisco: Harper and Row, 1986.

Waltzing, Jean. *Étude historique sur les corporations professionelles chez les Romains.* 4 vols. Louvain: Peeters, 1895–1900.

Wanamaker, Charles A. *1 and 2 Thessalonians.* NIGTC. Grand Rapids: Eerdmans, 1990.

Wasink, Craig S. *Chained in Christ: The Experience and Rhetoric of Paul's Imprisonments.* JSNTSup 130. Sheffield: Sheffield Academic, 1996.

Watson, Alon. *The Law of Persons in the Later Roman Republic.* Oxford: Clarendon, 1967.

Watson, Francis. "The Two Roman Congregations: Romans 14:1—15:13." In Karl P. Donfried, ed., *The Romans Debate,* 203–15.

Webb, Robert L. *John the Baptizer and Prophet: A Socio-Historical Study.* JSNTSup 62. Sheffield: Sheffield Academic, 1991.

Weber, Max. *Economy and Society: An Outline of Interpretive Sociology.* 2 vols., ed. G. Roth and C. Wittich. Berkeley: Univ. of California Press, 1978.

Welborn, Laurence L. "Clement, First Epistle of." In *ABD,* ed. D. N. Freedman, 1.1055–1060. New York: Doubleday, 1992.

Westerholm, Stephen. "Clean and Unclean." In *DJG*, ed. J. B. Green and S. McKnight, 125–32. Downers Grove, Ill.: InterVarsity, 1992.

Whitaker, Ian. "Familial Roles in the Extended Patrilineal Kingroup in Northern Albania." In *Mediterranean Family Structures*, ed. J. G. Peristiany, 195–203. Cambridge: Cambridge Univ. Press, 1976.

White, L. Michael. "Christianity: Early Social Life and Organization." In *ABD*, ed. D. N. Freedman, 1.927–35. New York: Doubleday, 1992.

Wiefel, Wolfgang. "The Jewish Community in Ancient Rome and the Origins of Roman Christianity." In Karl P. Donfried, ed., *The Romans Debate*, 85–101.

Wilken, Robert L. "Collegia, Philosophical Schools, and Theology." In *The Catacombs and the Colosseum*, ed. S. Benko and J. J. O'Rourke, 268–91. Valley Forge, Pa.: Judson, 1971.

———. *The Christians As the Romans Saw Them*. New Haven: Yale Univ. Press, 1984.

Wilson, Stephen G. *Related Strangers: Jews and Christians 70–135 C.E.* Minneapolis: Fortress Press, 1995.

———. "Voluntary Associations: An Overview." In Kloppenborg and Wilson, eds., *Voluntary Associations*, 1–15.

Winter, Bruce W. "Civil Litigation in Secular Corinth and the Church: The Forensic Background to 1 Corinthians 6.1-8." *NTS* 37 (1991): 559–72.

Wright, Christopher J. H. *God's People in God's Land: Family, Land, and Property in the Old Testament.* Grand Rapids: Eerdmans, 1991.

———. "Family." In *ABD*, ed. D. N. Freedman, 2.761–69. New York: Doubleday, 1992.

Wright, N. T. *The New Testament and the People of God*. Christian Origins and the Question of God, vol. 1. Minneapolis: Fortress Press, 1992.

———. *Jesus and the Victory of God*. Christian Origins and the Question of God, vol. 2. Minneapolis: Fortress Press, 1996.

Wright, Wilmer C., trans. *The Works of the Emperor Julian.* 3 vols. LCL. Cambridge: Harvard Univ. Press, 1923.

Wuthnow, Robert, James Davidson Hunter, Albert Bergesen, and Edith Kurzweil. *Cultural Analysis: The Work of Peter L. Berger, Mary Douglas, Michel Foucault and Jürgen Habermas.* London: Routledge, 1984.

Zahn, Theodor. *Ignatius von Antiochien.* Gotha: Perthes, 1873.

Index of Ancient Sources

New Testament